Palgrave Studies in Maritime Politics and Security

Series Editor
Geoffrey F. Gresh, Springfield, VA, USA

The world's oceans cover over 70% of the planet's surface area. Global shipping carries at least 80% of the world's traded goods. Offshore oil and gas account for more than one-third of world energy production. With the maritime domain so important and influential to the world's history, politics, security, and the global political economy, this series endeavors to examine this essential and distinct saltwater perspective through an interdisciplinary lens, with a focus on understanding the ocean historically, politically, and from a security lens. Through a spectrum of engaging and unique topics, it will contribute to our understanding of the ocean, both historically and in a contemporary light, as source, avenue, and arena: a source of food and energy; an avenue for the flow of goods, people, and ideas; and an arena for struggle and warfare. The series will use an interdisciplinary approach—integrating diplomatic, environmental, geographic, and strategic perspectives—to explore the challenges presented by history and the contemporary maritime issues around the world.

More information about this series at
http://www.palgrave.com/gp/series/16675

Leszek Buszynski · Do Thanh Hai
Editors

Maritime Issues and Regional Order in the Indo-Pacific

Editors
Leszek Buszynski
Strategic and Defense Studies Centre
Australian National University
Hughes, ACT, Australia

Do Thanh Hai
East Sea Institute
Diplomatic Academy of Vietnam
Hanoi, Vietnam

ISSN 2730-7972 ISSN 2730-7980 (electronic)
Palgrave Studies in Maritime Politics and Security
ISBN 978-3-030-68037-4 ISBN 978-3-030-68038-1 (eBook)
https://doi.org/10.1007/978-3-030-68038-1

© The Editor(s) (if applicable) and The Author(s), under exclusive license to Springer Nature Switzerland AG 2021
This work is subject to copyright. All rights are solely and exclusively licensed by the Publisher, whether the whole or part of the material is concerned, specifically the rights of translation, reprinting, reuse of illustrations, recitation, broadcasting, reproduction on microfilms or in any other physical way, and transmission or information storage and retrieval, electronic adaptation, computer software, or by similar or dissimilar methodology now known or hereafter developed.
The use of general descriptive names, registered names, trademarks, service marks, etc. in this publication does not imply, even in the absence of a specific statement, that such names are exempt from the relevant protective laws and regulations and therefore free for general use.
The publisher, the authors and the editors are safe to assume that the advice and information in this book are believed to be true and accurate at the date of publication. Neither the publisher nor the authors or the editors give a warranty, expressed or implied, with respect to the material contained herein or for any errors or omissions that may have been made. The publisher remains neutral with regard to jurisdictional claims in published maps and institutional affiliations.

Cover illustration: Nino Marcutti/Alamy Stock Photo

This Palgrave Macmillan imprint is published by the registered company Springer Nature Switzerland AG
The registered company address is: Gewerbestrasse 11, 6330 Cham, Switzerland

Acknowledgments

The editors would like to express their gratitude to the Diplomatic Academy of Vietnam, which arranged and funded the conference held in November 2019, upon which this volume is based. Our appreciation is extended to Nguyen Thuy Anh who cleared much necessary paperwork to prepare for the volume; her services are much appreciated. The patience and perseverance of the authors deserves commendation as they turned conference presentations into publishable chapters, not always an easy task for those with a busy schedule. Our thanks go to them.

The Indo-Pacific Between Strategy and Regional Order

The Indo-Pacific is a developing idea, one that can be understood as a cooperative venture connecting the Western Pacific with the Indian Ocean area. It can be viewed as an emerging strategic concept prompting the development of security relationships including military exercises and giving direction to force deployments. It could also be understood as a proposal for expanded region building as the institutional structures of the Western Pacific are extended to the Indian Ocean area to create a wider regionalism. Its very nascence has stimulated skepticism and even derision from some commentators who regard it as an idea whose time will never come. Skeptics point out that strategic interests are too diverse and institutional structures cannot be developed over so wide an area to include countries with dissimilar views and interests. However, new ideas are normally met with some form of skepticism, criticism, and even mockery as the natural tendency of many observers in international affairs is to think in terms of the current status quo and the interests and ideas that support it. Too often, deeply held convictions about international affairs are constructed on the basis of past experience and familiarity with the status quo forming the underlying assumption of many articles, one line publications, and blogs. Slow incremental changes to the status quo can be ignored or rationalized as unimportant and inconsequential until their effects accumulate and reach a tipping point that brings sudden and unexpected shifts. Notions of regions and the institutional structures that support them do not stand still and change over time according to the purpose that brought them into being. Some notions may not develop further as their need declines. Others, however, open the horizons for an expansion into wider areas as they serve an urgent need and are vigorously supported and adopted by governments. It is this process of change and development of the Indo-Pacific idea that the contributors to this volume have attempted to identify, one which in future years will have far-reaching effects

One way or another, the Indo-Pacific idea was stimulated by the rise of China. There was a time in 2003–2004 when Chinese leaders Hu Jintao and Premier Wen Jiabao talked of China's "peaceful rise" in an attempt to assuage concerns among Asian neighbors and the international community about China's intentions. Under Hu Jintao, China strove to work with regional institutions such as the ASEAN Regional Forum and the East Asian Summit. In 2002 China joined with ASEAN to conclude the Declaration of the Conduct of the Parties to the South China Sea (DOC) and in 2003 signed onto ASEAN's Treaty of Amity and Cooperation (TAC) which was a reassurance to Southeast Asia that China would abide by a good neighbor policy. Under Hu Jintao, China hosted the Six Party Talks beginning in 2003 to bring about a resolution to North Korea's nuclear program which seemed promising. Commentators wrote of China's "charm offensive" and wrote of the skill of its diplomats in mitigating regional concerns about its intentions. Had China continued along this path, it could have devised a resolution of the South China Sea and the North Korean nuclear issues thereby contributing to regional stability. It would have elevated its reputation and acquired the respect that it craves as a responsible stakeholder and global leader. However, it was not to be. When in 2013 Xi Jinping took over as leader of China, he followed another and more assertive path for complex reasons related to domestic politics. Xi's main priority was to hold the Chinese Communist Party together and to ensure its survival in a time of wrenching change, to this end he invoked national aspirations in the "China Dream." The turn toward an aggressive form of nationalism accompanied the increasingly tight political and social controls imposed by the Chinese Communist Party to protect its position in a society and economy that has less need for it. When a country the size of China resorts to a bellicose form of nationalism in maritime territorial disputes with its neighbors; develops an ocean-going naval capability to challenge the US; asserts its position in the South China Sea against the ASEAN claimant; also moves against Japan in the East China Sea; and places pressure on India by arming and equipping

Pakistan and sending naval units into the Indian Ocean, an identifiable and disturbing pattern emerges. Previously it seemed that China would be integrated into a regional and global order which gave rise to hopes that an era of peace and prosperity was near. Under Xi Jinping, however, it seemed that China was bent on challenging and dismantling that regional and global order upon which the prosperity of the regional countries had been founded.

The contributors to this volume have examined the two responses to China's behavior and the formulation of the notion of the Indo-Pacific, one is strategic and the other is region building. The strategic response involves the development of security relationships that would ensure the maintenance of equilibrium in the face of China's rise and assertiveness. The lessons of history show that in a system of competing states the balance of power will be maintained, and as one power rises the others will adjust their relationships to balance its power. Enemies become partners, new alliances are formed and new combinations are negotiated. Similar shifts and adjustments to security relationships, whether bilateral, trilateral, and quadrilateral, have taken place in response to China's assertiveness not only in the Western Pacific but involving India as well in a wider Indo-Pacific theatre. The US, Japan, and to some extent India have formulated notions of the Indo-Pacific as a strategic response to China's assertiveness and a deterrent. The second response can be called region building and involves an effort to accommodate China within institutional arrangements that would span the wider Indo-Pacific. This response has been pursued by ASEAN, and also by Japan and India as complementary to the strategic approach. Its logic is that an overtly strategic response to China's rise would simply trigger polarization and conflict, which could destroy the peace of the region and China's size as second economic power and its role as a major trading partner of everyone is necessary for the economic health of the region. Subjecting China to a balance of power is well-nigh impossible when economic and trading ties have reached a high level of connectedness. Building upon the idea of the Indo-Pacific as a region gives expression to the aspiration that China's leaders could be accommodated and induced to accept the rules of a wider maritime order and that they would adjust their behavior accordingly.

Maritime Issues That Drive the Indo-Pacific Idea

The South China Sea is central to the notion of the Indo-Pacific as it involves the geopolitical interests of all players. As the chapters in this volume explain, the South China Sea is a strategic waterway for Japan, the US, and India that depend on the sea-lanes that run through it for their trade. Indeed, China's behavior in this area, more than anything else, has brought the various players together in support of the Indo-Pacific notion. In relying on power to secure control of the South China Sea, China's behavior has become a critical indicator of its intentions and ambitions. Central to the idea of order is respect for international law and the avoidance of force or coercion in the resolution of territorial or maritime disputes and claims. Ultimately, law is the only available means to regulate and manage international maritime and territorial disputes on an equitable basis and to ensure compliance with norms and cooperative relations. In this respect, the concern is that China does not play by the rules that the major powers and regional actors recognize as underlying order in the Indo-Pacific and that its ambitions allied with a developing military capability will tempt it to rely increasingly on force and coercion in the settlement of disputes. China's rejection of the Arbitral Tribunal's ruling on its claim to the South China Sea in July 2016 and the pressure it brings to bear on the ASEAN claimants there, Vietnam, the Philippines, and Malaysia, undermine confidence in the expectation that it can be peacefully integrated into the prevailing regional order. China's rejection of international law in the South China Sea and its resort to power brings with it trepidation and resentment stimulating the search for a countervailing response.

Beginning in December 2013, China began dredging sand from the sea floor and constructing military facilities on seven features it has occupied in the Spratly Islands of the South China Sea. In September 2015, when President Obama expressed concern to Xi Jinping over Chinese militarization of the South China Sea, Xi retorted that "relevant construction activity that China is undertaking in the Nansha Islands does not target or impact any country and there is no intention to militarize" (Reuters 26 September 2015). Nonetheless, China went ahead and constructed those military facilities regardless. In his chapter in this volume, **Gregory Poling** notes China's resort to gray zone coercion in the South China Sea purposely avoiding overt military force which would trigger responses from others while relying on deniability. This, he explains, has caught everyone "flat-footed." Accordingly, China continues with its effort to control all water, airspace and seabed within the nine-dash line and to prevent the ASEAN states from engaging in any activities within their EEZs without Chinese permission. **Poling** stresses the significance of the South China issue not just for the region but for the international community in that if China was to succeed in its campaign of coercion, a dangerous precedent would be set for how a powerful China would approach other problems and territorial disputes. It would also undermine the role of international law "which would be a deeply destabilizing turn." Poling surmises that it would represent a "return to pre-World War Two international politics, in which laws, norms, and institutions no longer moderate the exercise of power by larger states."

Yoji Koda has noted that China's militarization of those artificial islands in the Spratly and Paracel Islands poses a serious military threat. In line with the development of its unconventional and asymmetric Anti-Access and Area Denial (A2AD) operations, China would create situations which would erode the US position in the region. **Koda** stresses the importance of the US naval presence in the Western Pacific for Japan's security and calls for an aligned strategy between the Japanese and American navies and a mutual capability that would deter China. **Koda** notes that Japan, indeed, has pursued this approach on the basis that it cannot manage China alone and is vulnerable to Chinese pressure in the East China and South China Seas. **Martin Sebastian** examines China's gray zone operations against the ASEAN claimants, Vietnam, Malaysia, and the Philippines, to intimidate them and push them out of their territorial claims. He notes that the maritime militia is coordinated by the Chinese coast guard (white hulls) which work with the navy (gray hulls) and comes under the People's Armed Police reporting to the Central Military Commission (CMC). This means the Coast Guard is actually a paramilitary force headed by a Rear Admiral who previously took part in the Chinese navy's mission in the Gulf of Aden. **Sebastian** concludes that these gray zone operations cannot be met by the ASEAN claimants alone and may require the intervention of international support. **Marites Vitug** explains that the Philippines was frustrated by Chinese action around Scarborough Shoal in 2012 and appealed to arbitration by the Law of the Sea Tribunal in January 2013. The Tribunal endorsed its rights to its declared EEZ in its ruling of July 2016 and validated fourteen of the fifteen points raised by the Philippines. However, the new president of the Philippines, Rodrigo Duterte, slid into a dependent relationship with

China for reasons related to his expectation of economic support and his personal resentments against the Americans. Duterte disregarded the Arbitral Tribunal's ruling, and as **Vitug** clarifies Duterte's pivot toward China has threatened Philippine sovereign rights over the West Philippine Sea (WPS). Under Duterte, the Philippines defected from a potential ASEAN alignment over the South China Sea and weakened ASEAN's negotiating position with China.

Indeed, the South China Sea issue goes well beyond the capacity of ASEAN to manage on its own. The ten-member group is divided between the claimants and countries such as Cambodia, Laos, and Thailand which value their relationship with China and are not concerned by this issue. What are the options available for ASEAN? There have been many calls for cooperation and dialogue to resolve the maritime disputes in the South China or to bring about a stable or non-threatening situation. However, efforts in this direction so far have been fruitless. **Carl Thayer** examines whether multilateral dialogue with China conducted in various forums between 2016 and 2018 has had any discernible impact on the situation in the South China Sea and whether it has contributed to restraint and provided a means for the resolution of disputes. He concludes pessimistically that China's behavior was unmoderated and neither did these multilateral forums mitigate major power rivalry. However, **Nguyen Chu Hoi** examines environmental issues in the South China Sea and suggests that the parties to the dispute could work on "blue solutions" which would bring them together in cooperation. The hope is that cooperation over environmental issues may stimulate cooperation over other issues to reduce tensions.

The maritime disputes of the East China Sea have had a major impact upon Japan and contributed to the expression and development of Japan's Indo-Pacific strategy. In this volume, **Tomotaka Shoji** explains the connection between the East and South China Seas as Japan's trade and oil imports from the Middle East are vulnerable to interdiction as they run through these areas. **Shoji** notes that China's maritime expansion in both the South China and East China Seas challenges freedom of navigation as one of the pillars of Japan's Indo-Pacific strategy, which is critical for Japan's island economy. China has adopted similar gray zone operations in both the South China and East China Seas prompting Japan to link both together in its Indo-Pacific strategy. China's maritime militia with fishing vessels coordinated by the coast guard was sent into the Japanese-claimed EEZ around the Senkaku/Diaoyu islands to press China's claims.

Chinese pressure was intensified after the Japanese government in 2012 purchased three of the five islands which were in private hands, and subsequently intrusions by the Chinese maritime militia increased. Japan was disturbed by China's declaration of an Air Defense Identification Zone (ADIZ) around the Senkaku/Diaoyu islands on 23 November 2013 regarding it as an attempt to force international compliance with its territorial claims. **Cao Qun** argues that China's ADIZ does not cover all the Senkaku/Diaoyu islands and cannot be regarded as a means to strengthen its claim to the islands and will not legitimize China's claims. He argues it was not a reaction to the Japanese government's purchase of three of the five islands from private Japanese citizens in late 2012 as was surmised by the Japanese press of the time. **Cao Qun** claims that from the perspective of international law an ADIZ has no implications for sovereignty. **Yannhuei Song** examines the complex legal positions of the Japan–China maritime dispute and notes some positive developments since Japanese Prime Minister Abe visited Beijing in 2018, but remains skeptical that a resolution would be possible.

THE INDO-PACIFIC AS STRATEGY

These maritime issues cannot be managed within the context of existing institutions in the Western Pacific and draw in external powers. The problem is that a yawning imbalance has arisen as China is too big and its ambitions too extensive to be limited or balanced within the Western Pacific. The Indo-Pacific idea is a product of this imbalance which brings in other players such as India and also Australia similarly concerned about China's actions. Japan's Indo-Pacific Strategy was outlined by Shinzo Abe's address to Indian Parliament on 22 August 2007, and his speech in Nairobi on 28 August 2016 when he raised the idea of the "free and open Pacific and Indian Oceans." As **Yoji Koda** points out, Japan shares with the US a view of the Indo-Pacific as a means to orchestrate a common strategy and an alignment of likeminded states to create a counterweight against China. **Tomotaka Shoji** explains the importance of security cooperation between Japan and ASEAN in relation to the South China Sea as based on the Vientiane Vision of November 2016. This vision was unveiled by Defence Minister Tomomi Inada at the second ASEAN–Japan Defence Ministers' Informal Meeting and covered both bilateral and multilateral defense cooperation with ASEAN members to strengthen maritime security and regional order. Japan moved quickly to engage India on the basis of common democratic values as a response to China's growing presence in the Western Pacific. Japan has conducted bilateral naval exercises with India called JIMEX (Japan–India Maritime Exercise); they were conducted in Indian waters in December 2013, and again in October 2018. Japan has been negotiating a military logistics pact or an Acquisition and Cross-Servicing Agreement (ACSA) with India which would allow Japanese naval vessels access to fuel and services at major Indian naval bases in the Andaman and Nicobar Islands. Japan is a low-profile and non-controversial promoter of security relationships in the Indo-Pacific area and can tread where the US cannot. It has actively promoted two forms of trilateralism, with the US and India, and also the US and Australia; it has also supported quadrilateral dialogue which brings the US together with Australia and India in response to China's inroads into the Western Pacific. The Japanese hope that quadrilateralism will develop workable strategic cooperation before China further expands its power into the region. In this volume there are many references to quadrilateralism which could be viewed as simply a meeting of the leaders of the four countries, or as an incipient alliance with consequences for the security of the Indo-Pacific.

The Indo-Pacific makes no sense without India. As **Udai Bhanu Singh** explains in this volume, India has a strategic interest in the Indo-Pacific idea which has drawn it into security cooperation with both Japan and the US. He stresses India's interest in the cooperative dynamics of the Indo-Pacific and the upgrading of its Look East Policy to its Act East Policy in November 2014. This policy extended India's vision beyond ASEAN to embrace the wider Indo-Pacific. Concerns about Chinese naval activities in the Indian Ocean and China's expanding relationship with Pakistan have troubled India, and **Singh** claims that for this reason the significance of the Quadrilateral Security Dialogue would grow for India. He views Vietnam is a key pillar of India's Act East Policy as it is strategically placed and close to the South China Sea, and he views Indonesia as a partner. Nonetheless, Prime Minister Narendra Modi responded to conflicting pressures as he promoted India's Indo-Pacific policy. While stressing the US role in Indian policy and affirming freedom of navigation, he was careful to avoid being cast as part of an anti-China coalition. This balancing act was seen in Modi's speech at the Shangri-La Dialogue in Singapore in June 2018 when he stressed the importance of the strategic partnership with the US; while declaring that China was important for global peace and progress, India struggled to balance the deterrent role of the Indo-Pacific idea while avoiding a deterioration of the relationship with China, an increasingly difficult task as events developed.

The US followed Japan into the Indo-Pacific when President Trump called for a "Free and Open Indo-Pacific" before the Asia-Pacific Economic Cooperation (APEC) CEO Summit in Da Nang in November 2017. On 30 May 2018, the US Pacific Command became INDOPACOM to reflect the growing importance of India, and the "connectivity" between the Indian and Pacific oceans. The area west of India has been designated part of the US Central Command (CENTCOM) and Africa command (AFRCACOM), and is excluded. President Trump mentioned in his address at Da Nang the key principles as respect for the rule of law, individual rights, freedom of navigation and overflight and open shipping lanes. However, Trump has disappointed many in the region because of his surprising contrariness and inattention to regional affairs. **Derek Grossman** laments that the implementation of the US Indo-Pacific strategy has fallen victim to conflicting approaches between President Trump and his strategists at the Department of Defense and Department of State. He claims that despite these "self-inflicted wounds" this strategy has been successful because US allies and partners can only rely on the US to balance China's military and economic power. The US offers an attractive vision for the region in terms of a rules-based order whereas it is uncertain what China can offer. Indeed, **Grossman** detects the self-defeating nature of China's behavior in these maritime disputes with neighbors since it uplifts America's importance to the region and instead of undermining the US role it has made it even more necessary. **Grossman** expresses the hope that the US role and the development of quadrilateralism and the notion of the Indo-Pacific would induce China to willingly integrate into the rules-based order to avoid conflict.

THE INDO-PACIFIC AS REGION BUILDING

Initially espousing the Indo-Pacific as a strategy, Japan has revised it to embrace the idea of region building as well. After Shinzo Abe visited Beijing in October 2018 to remove tensions with China, Japan played down the deterrent role of the Indo-Pacific idea. Japan dropped the term Indo-Pacific strategy and introduced the idea of an Indo-Pacific Vision while emphasizing its region building and accommodative intentions. **Toshiya Takahashi** notes that the Japan's region building theme has roots in past Japanese policies toward the region. The "Fukuda Doctrine" which was promulgated by Prime Minister Takeo Fukuda in 1977 laid the basis for Japan's relationship with Southeast Asia and Japanese investment in regional manufacturing industries. In this spirit, Japan's Ministry of Foreign Affairs (MOFA) in November 2019 published its own vision of the Indo-Pacific that embedded maritime security in a multidimensional framework including development, human security, and quality infrastructure projects. **Takahashi**, stresses what he calls Japan's "value diplomacy" which is intended to create a network of cooperative norms to integrate China and bind it to cooperative rather than confrontational activities. As part of the region-building project, Japan is obliged to keep the door open to China which cannot be done if security cooperation in the Indo-Pacific is directed against it. Nonetheless, the MOFA declaration on the Indo-Pacific Vision disguises Japan's strategic purpose and its concern with strengthening maritime security around the South China Sea. In effect, Japan moves on two tracks in relation to the Indo-Pacific, and though they be in an uneasy relationship, region building and development continue alongside the promotion of strategic objectives in quadrilateralism, and naval deployments.

Senia Febrica explains Indonesia's critical role in forging the ASEAN Indo-Pacific Outlook. She examines Indonesia's maritime geography between the Indian and Pacific Oceans, which motivated President Jokowi to declare the Global Maritime Fulcrum vision in 2014. This vision was extended to and became the basis of Indonesia's negotiating position over the Indo-Pacific idea. Indonesian Foreign Minister Marty Natalegawa in 2013 paved the way for ASEAN's entry into the Indo-Pacific by proposing regional cooperative architecture based on the ASEAN Regional Forum (ARF) and the East Asian Summit (EAS), which could be expanded to the wider region. His successor as Foreign Minister was Retno Marsudi who drew on Marty's broad sweep in drafting Indonesia's Indo-Pacific cooperation idea and brought it into the ASEAN consultative process. The Indonesian draft of the Indo-Pacific idea contained three main principles which were intended to avoid any overt association with security or strategy. The first was the centrality of ASEAN as the driver of cooperation; the second was inclusivity to avoid alienating China; and the third was the focus on non-traditional maritime security concerns such as maritime crimes, connectivity for economic growth and sustainable development. **Febrica** notes that that there is an expectation that cooperation over non-traditional security issues could spill over to other more sensitive issues and evolve into effective regional cooperation. These principles were carried over into the ASEAN Outlook.

ASEAN's approach to the Indo-Pacific was expressed in its Indo-Pacific Outlook, which was proclaimed on 23 June 2019 as an essentially region building exercise intended to deflect attention away from the strategic approach. Both Japan and India have declared that they would work with ASEAN in developing the Indo-Pacific idea which made them receptive to ASEAN's region building agenda. However, ASEAN was challenged to ensure its relevance to an unfamiliar Indian Ocean area which went well beyond its core area of Southeast Asia. That would mean connecting with Indian Ocean regional bodies such as the Bay of Bengal Initiative for Multi-Sectoral Technical and Economic Cooperation (BIMSTEC) and the Indian Ocean Rim Association (IORA) which could undermine ASEAN as a grouping. In this connection, **To Anh Tuan** with **Do Thanh Hai** point to the rationale of ASEAN's Indo-Pacific Outlook which is the preservation and strengthening of ASEAN's centrality. This means ensuring that it would not be sidelined or displaced by any cooperative institutions that may be created under the Indo-Pacific idea, and that any so created should be based on ASEAN-led institutions. **To** and **Do** also explain that ASEAN sought to avoid entanglement in great power rivalry which could tear the grouping apart, and for that reason ASEAN was at pains to distance itself from US strategy in particular. They affirm that it was important for ASEAN's Indo-Pacific Outlook to be distinguished from the US idea of FOIPS and to disavow any strategic intention. ASEAN had to balance inclusiveness, which meant engaging and not alienating China, while stressing international law and a rules-based order, as the foundation stone of the regional association.

The contributors to this volume have outlined two themes or approaches toward the notion of the Indo-Pacific. Those by Japanese and US contributors stress the notion of a strategic area that can deal with the rise of China and its deployment of military power, the extension of its influence in the Belt and Road Initiative, and above all its challenge to the rules of the prevailing regional order. ASEAN contributors emphasize region building and the importance of developing accommodative structures in the Indo-Pacific that can engage China. Yet others, Japanese and Indian contributors, explain the complexity of their government's responses and their evolution as they move on both tracks in varying degrees but these tracks may conflict and how they relate to each other may create difficulty. The strategic approach may provoke Chinese counteraction and hostility resulting in instability and possible conflict which could destroy any effort at region building. However, an excessive focus on region building would offer little resistance to Chinese pressure in both maritime disputes, the South China and East China Seas and no incentive to join the accommodative regional structures that have been proposed, which may even encourage further assertiveness. The lack of one unified or integrated approach which brings all players together does not discredit the notion of the Indo-Pacific but points down the road to its future possibilities as it could go one way or another. China may realize that its assertiveness is creating more enemies that it can cope with, and it could move to reduce tensions with neighbors in these maritime disputes. In order to undermine emerging coalitions or security relationships against it, China could engage its neighbors in meaningful dialogue paving the way for its accommodation in a wider region. The pressure for a strategic response would drop and quadrilateralism would simply become a routine meeting held on the side of larger meetings. If China ignores these signals and continues on its current path of pressing against its neighbors, the strategic approach would become the dominant response and would shape the future of the Indo-Pacific as a strategic theatre.

Leszek Buszynski

Contents

1. **A Brittle Status Quo in the South China Sea** 1
   Gregory B. Poling
2. **China's Military Strategy in the South China** 17
   Yoji Koda
3. **China's Gray Zone Operations in the South China Sea; Manipulating Weaknesses** 39
   Martin A. Sebastian
4. **The Philippine Pivot to China: Threat to Stability in the West Philippine Sea** 51
   Marites Dañguilan Vitug
5. **The South China Sea in Multilateral Forums: Five Case Studies** 71
   Carlyle A. Thayer
6. **Blue Solutions to South China Sea Environmental Problems** 87
   Nguyen Chu Hoi
7. **Assessing Europe's Perspectives on the South China Sea** 103
   Nicola Casarini

8	Nexus of the East and South China Seas: A Japanese Perspective Tomotaka Shoji	119
9	Misperceptions of China's East China Sea ADIZ: Technical Flaws and Legal Facts Cao Qun	135
10	The Legal Contest in the East China Sea Yann-huei Song	149
11	Historical Continuities, Geopolitical Interests, and Norms in Japan's Free and Open Indo-Pacific Toshiya Takahashi	165
12	Toward an Improved Understanding of the US Indo-Pacific Strategy Derek Grossman	187
13	India and the Indo-Pacific Udai Bhanu Singh	211
14	Indonesia and the Indo-Pacific: Cooperation, Interests, and Strategies Senia Febrica	233
15	ASEAN and Its Indo-Pacific Outlook To Anh Tuan and Do Thanh Hai	257

Conclusion: Geographical Connectedness and Conceptual Discrepancy — 275

Index — 285

Editors and Contributors

About the Editors

Leszek Buszynski is an Honorary Professor with the Strategic and Defence Studies Centre at the Australian National University, Canberra, Australia. He was Professor of International Relations in the Graduate School of International Relations at the International University of Japan from 1994 to 2010. He has published widely on Asia-Pacific security issues and the South China Sea since it emerged as a major issue. He is a Co-editor of *The South China Sea: From Regional Maritime Dispute to Geostrategic Competition* (Routledge 2020) and the Author of *The Geopolitics of the Western Pacific, China, Japan and the United States* (Routledge 2019) and "ASEAN, Grand Strategy and the South China Sea" in Anders Corr (editor) Great Powers, Grand Strategies: The New Game in the South China Sea (US Naval Institute Press, 2018). He is also the Author of *Negotiating with North Korea: The Six Party Talks and the Nuclear Issue* (Routledge, 2013) and a Co-editor of The South China Sea Maritime Dispute: Political, legal and Regional Perspectives (Routledge 2014).

Do Thanh Hai is a Senior Fellow at the Diplomatic Academy of Vietnam (DAV). His previous positions include Vacation Scholar at the University of New South Wales at the Australian Defence Force Academy in Canberra and Deputy Director of the Centre for Political and Security

Studies of the DAV's Institute for Foreign Policy and Strategic Studies in Hanoi. He obtained his doctorate from the Australian National University and his Master's Degree from Erasmus Mundus Global Studies Program. He has also published in *The Pacific Review*, *The ASAN Forum*, CSIS *PacNet*, *Journal of International Review* (DAV), and a number of news outlets. He is the Author of *Vietnam and the South China Sea: Politics, Security and Legality* (Routledge 2017). He is a co-editor of *The South China Sea: From Regional Maritime Dispute to Geostrategic Competition* (Routledge 2020).

Contributors

Nicola Casarini is a Senior Fellow Asia at the Institute of International Affairs (IAI) in Rome. Prior to this, he was Visiting Professor at the Graduate Institute in Geneva; Public Policy Scholar at the Wilson Center, Washington, D.C.; Senior Analyst at the EU Institute for Security Studies in Paris; and Marie Curie Research Fellow at the European University Institute in Florence. He holds a Ph.D. in international relations from the London School of Economics and Political Science. He has published various books, numerous articles, and papers on Asia–Europe relations, Asia's security and transatlantic relations. Nicola is the Author of the monograph: *Remaking Global Order. The Evolution of Europe-China Relations and its Implications for East Asia and the United States* (Oxford University Press).

Senia Febrica holds a Ph.D. from the University of Glasgow and is a Knowledge Exchange Associate with the One Ocean Hub at the University of Strathclyde, Scotland. Prior to this, she was a Researcher for the American Studies Center at the Universitas Indonesia, a Gerda Henkel Stiftung postdoctoral fellow (2015–2017), and a United Nations-Nippon Foundation Fellow (2012–2013). She is the Author of *Maritime Security and Indonesia: Cooperation, Interests, and Strategies* (Routledge 2017). Her research sits at the intersection between International Relations, Security Studies, and the study of international organizations. Specifically, it focuses on maritime security cooperation and the particular challenges it poses in the Southeast Asia region with special attention to Indonesia, Malaysia, Singapore, and the Philippines.

Derek Grossman is a Senior Defense Analyst at RAND and focuses on a range of national security policy and Indo-Pacific security issues. He holds an M.A. from Georgetown University in US national security policy and a B.A. from the University of Michigan in political science and Asian studies. He is particularly interested in China's relationships with Taiwan, Vietnam, Japan, India, Pakistan, the Pacific Islands, and the Koreas. Grossman served over a decade in the Intelligence Community (IC), as an Intelligence Briefer to the Director of the Defense Intelligence Agency (DIA), and to the Assistant Secretary of Defense for Asian & Pacific Security Affairs. Grossman served at the National Security Agency (NSA). He also worked at the CIA on the President's Daily Brief staff.

Nguyen Chu Hoi is a retired professor from the Vietnam National University (VNU). His positions included standing Vice-Chairman of Vietnam Fisheries Society (VINAFIS); Director of Haiphong Institute of Oceanology; Director of Vietnam Institute of Fisheries Economics and Planning; and Deputy Administrator of Vietnam Administration of Seas and Islands (2008–2012). He received a B.Sc. from VNU (1974), and a Ph.D. in natural science from the University of Warsaw, Poland (1984). He has been a task-leader of over 50 projects and has published some 46 books and 230 papers in overseas and Vietnamese journals and proceedings. His main area of research is coastal and marine science and governance policy, including marine pollution management, integrated coastal management, and marine spatial planning.

Yoji Koda is a retired Vice Admiral and a Graduate of the Japan Defense Academy (1972), the JMSDF Naval Staff College, and the US Naval War College. He commanded the JS Sawayuki Destroyer, the Flotilla Three and the Fleet Escort Force at sea. He was also the Director General (DG) for Plans and Operations, Maritime Staff and the Director of Staff at Joint Staff as well as the Commandant of the JMSDF Sasebo District. He retired from JMSDF as the Commander-in-Chief of the Self-Defense Fleet in 2008. He was a Research Fellow at the Asia Center at Harvard University (2009–2011). His articles include "The Russo-Japanese War: Primary Causes of Japanese Success," *U.S. Naval War College*; "A New Carrier Race: Strategy, Force Planning and JS Hyuga," *U.S. Naval War College; and* "The U.S.-Japan Alliance: Responding to China's A2/AD Threat," *Center for New American Security*.

Gregory B. Poling is a Senior Fellow for Southeast Asia and the Director of the Asia Maritime Transparency Initiative at the Center for Strategic and International Studies (CSIS), Washington, D.C. He oversees research on US foreign policy in the Asia-Pacific, with a particular focus on the maritime domain and the countries of Southeast Asia. He holds an M.A. in international affairs from American University and a B.A. from St. Mary's College of Maryland. He has published in *Foreign Affairs*, the *Wall Street Journal*, *Nikkei Asian Review*, and *Foreign Policy*, among others. He is the Author or Co-author of multiple works, including *The Thickening Web of Asian Security Cooperation: Deepening Defense Ties Among U.S. Allies and Partners in the Indo-Pacific* (RAND Corporation, 2019); *Building a More Robust U.S.-Philippines Alliance* (CSIS, August 2015); and *A New Era in U.S.-Vietnam Relations: Deepening Ties Two Decades after Normalization* (CSIS, June 2014).

Cao Qun is the Associate Senior Editor of *China International Studies*, and a Researcher specializing on the South China Sea and Sino-Japanese dispute over the Diaoyu Dao/Senkaku Islands, and ADIZ rules. His most recent books published in Chinese are *The U.S. Air Defense Identification Zones: A Historical and Legal Study* (Beijing: China Ocean Press, 2020) and *A Study of the Russian Government's Decision-making before the Russo-Japanese War: 1894-1904* (Beijing: China Society Press, 2015). His English language articles include "No Need to Worry About a Potential South China Sea ADIZ" (*South China Sea Strategic Situation Probing Initiative*, 6 July 2020), "A Chinese Perspective on the RAND ADIZ Report: Technical Flaws Lead to Strategic Misunderstanding" (*Asia Maritime Transparency Initiative*, 12 March 2018).

Martin A. Sebastian is a retired Captain of Royal Malaysian Navy. He joined the Maritime Institute of Malaysia (MIMA) in 2001. Prior to that he completed three years of secondment with the Department of Peacekeeping Operations (DPKO), United Nations Headquarters, New York. He served in the Office of Military Affairs (OMA) as a Strategic Planner in the Military Planning Service (MPS). In OMA, he was the Team Leader for the Africa Planning Team II covering West African peacekeeping missions. In the Royal Malaysian Navy, he held various Command and Staff appointments. He holds an M.B.A. from Charles Sturt University, Australia and is a Member of the Chartered Institute of Logistics and Transport, United Kingdom. He is an alumnus of the International Ocean

Institute after undergoing a course on Ocean Governance at Dalhousie University, Canada.

Tomotaka Shoji is the Head of the Asia and Africa Division at the National Institute for Defense Studies (NIDS), Japan. He holds B.A., M.A., and Ph.D. degrees from the University of Tokyo as well as an M.Sc. in Strategic Studies from S. Rajaratnam School of International Studies (RSIS, Singapore). His recent publications include "Japan's Security Cooperation with ASEAN: Pursuit of a Status as a 'Relevant Partner'" (*NIDS Journal of Defense and Security*, No. 16, December 2015); "Vietnam's Omnidirectional Military Diplomacy: Focusing on the South China Sea" (*NIDS Journal of Defense and Security*, No. 17, December 2016); "Vietnam's Security Cooperation with the United States: Historical Background, Present and Future Outlook" (*NIDS Journal of Defense and Security*, No. 19, December 2018); and a chapter on Southeast Asia in the *NIDS East Asian Strategic Review 2017*. He also contributed to the *NIDS China Security Report 2019*.

Udai Bhanu Singh is a Senior Research Associate and the Head of the Southeast Asia and Oceania Centre, Manohar Parrikar Institute for Defence Studies and Analyses (MP-IDSA), New Delhi. He obtained a B.A. Honours and Masters in History, and an M.Phil. and Ph.D. from Jawaharlal Nehru University, New Delhi. He specialises in Southeast Asia with a special focus on Myanmar. His co-edited works include: with Lalit Mansingh and Anup K. Mudgal entitled PURBASA: *East Meets East: Synergising the North-East and Eastern India with the Indo-Pacific*, Pentagon Press, New Delhi, 2019, and with Rumel Dahiya, *ASEAN-India Relations: A New Paradigm*, Pentagon Press, New Delhi, 2018. He has participated in Track 2 and 1.5 dialogues with Myanmar, New Zealand, and Australia.

Yann-huei Song is a Research Fellow in the Institute of European and American Studies, Academia Sinica, Taipei, Taiwan. He holds an M.S. from Indiana State University, Indiana; a Ph.D. from Kent State University, Ohio; and an L.L.M. and J.S.D. from the School of Law (Boalt Hall), University of California. He is a Member of the editorial boards of *Ocean Development and International Law*, *Chinese (Taiwan) Yearbook of International Law and Affairs*, and *Taiwan Journal of International Law*. He has published over 100 articles in Chinese and English journals or books including a contribution to *Cooperation and Engagement in the Asia-Pacific Region* (Brill, Boston, 2020), and *Evolving Concept of the Rule of Law and Development of the Cross-Strait Legal Systems during the Last Four Decades: Festschrift in Honor of Professor Jerome A. Cohen on His 90th Birthday* (Angle, Taipei, 2020).

Toshiya Takahashi is an Associate Professor of International Relations at Shoin University, Japan, and a part-time Lecturer in Niigata University, Japan. He received his Ph.D. from the Australian National University in 2017. His research interest is in Japan's security and foreign policy, its approach to regionalism, and Japanese politics. He is a Member of the APEC Study Center of Japan and the APEC round table conference with the Ministry of Foreign Affairs of Japan and the Ministry of Economy, Trade and Industry of Japan. He has published in the *East Asia Forum*, an academic and is the Author of *China in Japan's National Security: Domestic Credibility* (Abingdon, Routledge, 2020).

Carlyle A. Thayer is an Emeritus Professor at the University of New South Wales (UNSW) at the Australian Defence Force Academy in Canberra. He holds a B.A. from Brown University and an M.A. from Yale University, and a Ph.D. from the Australian National University. He was the C. V. Starr Distinguished Visiting Professor at the School of Advanced International Studies, Johns Hopkins University in Washington, D.C., in 2005 and the Inaugural Frances M. and Stephen H. Fuller the Distinguished Visiting Professor of Southeast Asian Studies, Center for International Studies, Ohio University, Athens, Ohio, in 2008. He is also the Director of Thayer Consultancy, a small business registered in Australia in 2002 that provides political analysis of current regional security issues and other research support to selected clients.

To Anh Tuan is a Deputy Director General at the East Sea (South China Sea) Institute, Diplomatic Academy of Vietnam (DAV). Earlier he was a Deputy Director General from 2011 to 2016 of the Department for International Organizations in the Ministry of Foreign Affairs and a Member of the Task Force for Vietnam's Chairmanship of ASEAN in 2010. In 2008–2009, he was a Member of the Task Force for Vietnam's non-permanent membership at the United Nations Security Council. In 2005–2006, he was a diplomat at the Permanent Mission of Vietnam to the United Nations in New York. He holds an M.A. and Ph.D. from St. John's University (New York). He was the Editor of *Impacts of Domestic*

Factors to the American Foreign Policies under the Trump Administration (National Political Publishing House, Vietnam).

Marites Danguilan Vitug is one of the Philippines' most accomplished Journalists and bestselling Author. Currently, she is the Editor at large of www.rappler.com and is the former Editor of Newsbreak, a pioneering political magazine. She has written eight books on Philippine current affairs including *Rock Solid: How the Philippines won its maritime dispute against China,* which won the National Book Award for the best book in journalism in 2019. Marites's works have been published in foreign periodicals, including the *Nikkei Asia Review, Nieman Reports, Newsweek, International Herald Tribune*; and books and journals, including *The Politics of Environment in Southeast Asia* (Routledge: London and New York), The Journal of Environment and Development (University of California in San Diego), and "Open Justice Philippine Case Study: Transparency and Civic Participation in the Selection of Supreme Court Justices," in *Open Justice: An Innovation-Driven Agenda for Inclusive Societies,* Ministry of Justice and Human Rights of Argentina, 2019.

Acronyms

A2AD	Anti-Access and Area Denial
ACSA	Acquisition and Cross-Servicing Agreement
ADIZ	Air Defense Identification Zone
ADMM	ASEAN Defence Ministers Meeting (plus)
AEP	Act East Policy
AFRACOM	African Command
AI	Artificial intelligence
AIS	Automatic Identification System
AMM	Annual Ministerial Meeting
AMTI	Asia Maritime Transparency Initiative
AOIP	ASEAN Outlook on the Indo-Pacific
APC	Armoured Personnel Carrier
APEC CEO	Asia-Pacific Economic Cooperation Chief Executive Officer
APEC	Asia-Pacific Economic Cooperation
ARF	ASEAN Regional Forum
ASBM	Anti-Ship Ballistic Missiles
ASEAN	Association of Southeast Asian Nations
ASW	Anti-Submarine Warfare
BIMSTEC	Bay of Bengal Initiative for Multi-Sectoral Technical and Economic Cooperation
BMD	Ballistic Missile Defence
BRI	Belt and Road Initiative
C4ISR	Command, Control, Communications, Computers, Intelligence, Surveillance, and Reconnaissance
CBD	Convention on Biological Diversity
CCG	China Coast Guard

CENTCOM	Central Command
COC	Code of Conduct
COLREGS	Convention on International Regulations for Preventing Collisions at Sea
CPTPP	Comprehensive Progressive Trans-Pacific Partnership
CSI	Crime Scene Investigation
CSIS	Center for Strategic and International Studies (Washington, D.C.)
CSIS	Centre for Strategic and International Studies (Jakarta)
CSO	Community Service Organization
CUES	Code for Unplanned Encounters at Sea
CVN	Nuclear-powered Aircraft Carrier
DFA	Department of Foreign Affairs
DOC	Declaration on the Conduct of Parties in the South China Sea
EAS	East Asian Summit
EBSA	Ecologically and Biologically Significant Area
EEZ	Exclusive Economic Zone
ESS	European Security Strategy
EU	European Union
F-BMD	Fleet Ballistic Missile Defence
FOIP	Free and Open Indo-Pacific
FONOP	Freedom of Navigation Operation
FSA	Fish Stock Assessment
FTA	Free Trade Agreement
GEP	Green Economy Progress
GMF	Global Maritime Fulcrum
GMP	Global Marine Product
HA/DR	Humanitarian Assistance and Disaster Relief (HA/DR)
ICJ	International Court of Justice
IDR	Indonesian Rupiah
INDOPACOM	Indo-Pacific Command
IOC	Indian Ocean Commission
IOCWESTPAC	Intergovernmental Oceanographic Commission for the Western Pacific
IORA	Indian Ocean Rim Association
ISP	Information Sharing Posture
ITLOS	International Tribunal for the Law of the Sea
IUU	Illegal Unreported and Unregulated Fishing
JASDF	Japan Air Self-Defense Force
JCG	Japan Coast Guard
JGSDF	Japan Ground Self-Defense Force
JIMEX	Japan–India Maritime Exercise
JMSDF	Japan Maritime Self-Defense Force

JSDF		Japan Self-Defense Force
LAOC		Law of Armed Conflict
LDP		Liberal Democratic Party
LME		Large Marine Ecosystem
LRIT		Long-Range Identification and Tracking
MARPOL		International Convention for the Prevention of Pollution from Ships
MMDA		Maritime/Multi-Domain Awareness network
MMEA		Malaysia Maritime Enforcement Agency
MOD		Ministry of Defence
MOFA		Ministry of Foreign Affairs
MOU		Memorandum of Understanding
MPA		Marine Protected Area
MSY		Maximum Sustainable Yield
NAM		Non-Aligned Movement
NDPG		National Defense Program Guidelines
NGO		Non-Governmental Organization
ODA		Official Development Assistance
OSV		Offshore Support Vessels
PACOM		Pacific Command
PLA		People's Liberation Army
PLA-AF		People's Liberation Army Air Force
PLA-N		People's Liberation Army-Navy
PRC		People's Republic of China
PSC		Production Sharing Contracts
PSO		Public Service Organization
RCEP		Regional Comprehensive Economic Partnership
ROE		Rules of Engagement
RUF		Rules for the Use of Force
SAGAR		Security and Growth for All in the Region
SAR		Synthetic Aperture Radar
SCS		South China Sea
SIPRI		Stockholm International Peace Research Institute
SLOC		Sea Lines of Communication
TAC		Treaty of Amity and Cooperation
TPP		Trans-Pacific Partnership
TSD		Trilateral Security Dialogue
UAV		Unmanned Air Vehicle
UN		United Nations
UNCLOS		United Nations Convention on the Law of the Sea
UNEP		United Nations Environment Programme
USV		Unmanned Surface Vehicle
UUV		Unmanned Underwater Vehicle
VFA		Visiting Forces Agreement
WPS		West Philippine Sea

List of Maps

Map 2.1	Navigation routes in the Western Pacific	30
Map 6.1	The large coral systems or offshore islands groups in the SCS (East Sea in Vietnamese)	89
Map 6.2	Increases in sea level of the SCS (according to satellite data) *Source* The Ministry of Natural Resources and Environment of Vietnam	92
Map 9.1	South Korea's ADIZ	138
Map. 14.1	Map of Indonesia (*Source* This map was produced by Dr. I Made Andi Arsana, Department of Geodetic Engineering, Faculty of Engineering Universitas Gadjah Mada)	234

CHAPTER 1

A Brittle Status Quo in the South China Sea

Gregory B. Poling

The South China Sea disputes have entered an important new phase defined by several mutually reinforcing trends. First, China's completion of most major infrastructure at its artificial island bases in the Spratly Islands has since the end of 2017 allowed it to project power short of military force in a continuous manner throughout the entirety of the South China Sea. For its neighbors, this mostly means a persistent and overwhelming presence by the China Coast Guard (CCG) and maritime militia which have engaged in increasingly brazen acts of intimidation. Second, Beijing has managed to defang any threat of multilateral diplomatic pressure. This has as much to do with the inauguration of Rodrigo Duterte as president of the Philippines, and that country's subsequent meek South China Sea policy, as it does Beijing's canniness in seizing the opportunities presented to it. In either case, China has successfully blunted international pressure while using the renewed talks on a China–ASEAN Code of Conduct (COC) and offers of limited bilateral negotiations to forestall other, potentially more effective, diplomacy by

G. B. Poling (✉)
Center for Strategic and International Studies, Washington, DC, USA
e-mail: GPoling@csis.org

© The Author(s), under exclusive license to Springer Nature Switzerland AG 2021
L. Buszynski and D. T. Hai (eds.), *Maritime Issues and Regional Order in the Indo-Pacific*, Palgrave Studies in Maritime Politics and Security, https://doi.org/10.1007/978-3-030-68038-1_1

the Southeast Asian claimants. And third, those parties still interested in pushing back on Chinese assertiveness—primarily Vietnam and external actors like Australia, Japan, the United States, and some European countries—have been unable to regain the initiative they held briefly in 2015–2016 when international opinion swung decidedly against Beijing due to its island-building campaign and the Philippines' arbitration case.

Chinese gray zone coercion led by the CCG and militia have caught these states flat-footed, with no clear ideas how to push back on a power projection strategy that purposely avoids military force and relies on deniability. These interested parties have also failed to coordinate effectively among themselves or rally a broader coalition in support of their efforts. On its current trajectory, the South China Sea seems headed for a future as a Chinese lake. This would have serious implications for the national interests of the like-minded outside parties still concerned about the disputes. It would seriously undermine the United Nations Convention on the Law of the Sea, set a dangerous precedent that international laws and norms do not necessarily apply in Asia amid China's rise, and seriously undermine the credibility of the United States as a regional security provider—after all, why should Southeast Asian states support a US forward-deployed presence that only seems to protect the US navy's interests but not their own?

But the current status quo is not stable. This chapter will focus on the coercive aspects of China's strategy, but it is important to recognize how it interacts with the diplomatic processes. The coercive forces Beijing has unleashed seem very likely to lead to violence at some point. And its diplomatic game will eventually run out of steam, largely because it plays on Southeast Asian expectations while deferring substantive negotiations in order to keep talks going without admitting China's unwillingness to make compromises. These two factors will likely feed on each other—a clash may lead to a diplomatic breakdown, which in turn could prompt greater adventurism at sea, and so on. This dynamic might already be emerging in Sino-Vietnamese relations. The major question is not whether the currently brittle status quo will shatter; it is whether those parties still interested in the South China Sea will be positioned to seize the initiative when it does.

Moving into a New Phase of Coercion

China finished most of the dredging and island-building to expand its South China Sea bases in 2016, with the last documented new landfill taking place in the Paracel Islands in mid-2017 (AMTI 2017b). By late 2017, it had largely completed the installation of hard infrastructure on the islands. This included airstrips, helipads, hangars, harbor facilities, fuel and ammunition storage, and radar and sensor arrays across both the Paracel and Spratlys Islands (AMTI 2017a, b). For the last two years, there has been little new construction worth noting. The one exception to this was the installation of an "Ocean E-Station"—an unmanned surveillance and communications platform built by China Electronics Technology Group Corporation—at remote Bombay Reef in the Paracels in mid-2018 (AMTI 2018a). Similar platforms have been installed in waters off Hainan. These E-Stations could point to future Chinese plans to extend its surveillance capabilities to other areas of the South China Sea, like Scarborough Shoal off the coast of the Philippines, without incurring the monetary and diplomatic costs of more large-scale island-building.

With island-building and infrastructure construction largely finished, China moved quickly to deploy both military and law enforcement platforms to its new bases in the Spratly Islands. The period from 2017 to 2018 saw the first landings of military patrol and transport aircraft on Subi and Mischief Reefs in the Spratlys, jamming platforms deployed to Mischief and Fiery Cross Reefs, and surface-to-air and anti-ship cruise missiles emplaced at all three of those facilities. It also saw more frequent rotations by J-11 fighter jets, the first landing of an H-6 K bomber, and an increase in the number of anti-ship and anti-air missile systems deployed to Woody Island in the Paracels. And throughout the South China Sea the port facilities at China's outposts allowed an ever-greater presence by the People's Liberation Army-Navy (PLA-N) and the CCG, with virtually every modern class of ship in both services calling regularly at the major outposts in the Spratlys (Mangosing 2018; Gordon and Page 2018; Macias 2018; AMTI 2018b, 2018c, 2018d).

Beijing's island-building spree has increased its ability to project naval force, as well as air power once it chooses to deploy fighter jets to the Spratlys. But the most important change in the dynamics of the South China Sea has been the significant increase in Chinese law enforcement and paramilitary presence throughout the nine-dash line. Thanks to their ability to rest and replenish at Fiery Cross, Mischief, and Subi rather than needing to return to Hainan and Guangzhou, CCG vessels have recently been able to conduct long-term operations in ways they never could before. This presence has been most visible during tense stand-offs with competing claimants as well as through regular operations at a handful of submerged features over which China claims sovereignty but does not have any permanent presence.

THE GROWING REACH OF THE CHINESE COAST GUARD

It is well-known that CCG ships have remained permanently on-station at Scarborough Shoal since China seized the feature from Filipino control in 2012. Less often remarked upon is the persistent CCG presence at Luconia Shoals off the coast of Malaysia and around Second Thomas Shoal where the Philippines maintains a small garrison aboard the grounded BRP *Sierra Madre*. The CCG began regularly patrolling Luconia Shoals in late 2013. It left briefly in late 2015 as a political olive branch during Malaysia's ASEAN chairmanship, but returned a few months later. In recent years, both the length and frequency of those deployments has increased, as shown by the Automatic Identification System (AIS) transmissions which the CCG vessels seem to purposely broadcast in order to signal their sovereignty over the submerged feature. Data collected by the Asia Maritime Transparency Initiative (AMTI) shows that at least one CCG ship was on-station at Luconia Shoals on 258 out of 365 days between September 2018 and September 2019. At Second Thomas Shoal, a similar story has played out though with higher stakes given the permanent Philippine garrison at the feature. CCG ships have been patrolling near Second Thomas since mid-2013, facilitated by the Chinese facilities at Mischief Reef just 20 nautical miles away. But they have become noticeably more persistent of late, with CCG ships broadcasting AIS from Second Thomas on at least 215 of the 365 days between September 2018 and September 2019 (AMTI 2019a, 2019e). These same vessels also occasionally extend their patrols closer to Philippine shores, covering other submerged features like Half Moon Shoal.

The increased CCG presence does not just passively signal Chinese sovereignty over disputed features. These vessels are increasingly being used to interfere with the lawful activities of other claimants and put pressure on their forces occupying disputed real estate in the Spratlys. In May 2018, a CCG vessel harassed a civilian boat ferrying supplies to the *Sierra Madre*, by launching a helicopter which flew dangerously close over the Filipino boat (Esmaquel 2018). The CCG ship was accompanied by a PLA-N vessel which reportedly hung back during the operation, highlighting how Beijing uses the CCG as the vanguard of such actions while maintaining the implicit threat of military intervention should other claimants respond too forcefully. In May 2019, another CCG ship blocked the route of three resupply vessels headed to the *Sierra Madre* (Viray 2019). These operations surely raise memories in Manila of March 2014 when the CCG blockaded the garrison at Second Thomas for weeks, forcing the Armed Forces of the Philippines to airlift in supplies and eventually run the blockade with civilian vessels while a US surveillance plane hovered overhead (Douglas 2017). The CCG also appears to have increased its interference with Malaysian oil and gas operations near Luconia Shoals. In May 2019, CCG ship Haijing 35111 spent two weeks harassing the Sapura Esperanza, a drilling rig commissioned by a Royal Dutch Shell subsidiary to drill new natural gas wells in block SK 308. AIS signals and photos posted to social media showed that the vessel repeatedly maneuvered in an unsafe manner near offshore supply vessels operating between the rig and the coast of Sarawak State, and came threateningly close to the Sapura Esperanza itself (AMTI 2019b; East Pendulum 2019).

Malaysian authorities are aware of these activities, as evidenced by irregular deployments of Royal Malaysian Navy ships to monitor the CCG at Luconia Shoals. For instance, two Malaysian warships, the 3502 and 176, patrolled near the Haijing 3306 in September and October 2018, while the naval auxiliary vessel *Ka Bunga Mas* 5 operated just 2 nautical miles from the Haijing 5401 in September 2019. But these naval vessels have limited options. The CCG vessels regularly maneuver in an unsafe manner in violation of the Convention on the International Regulations for Preventing Collisions at Sea, or COLREGS, in order to intimidate civilian vessels, but they refrain from direct military force. And even if the Malaysian authorities did want to escalate matters, their naval vessels are smaller and in most cases outgunned by their CCG counterparts (the Haijing 3306, for example, displaces 4000 tons while the 35111 sports a 76 mm cannon). And when it comes to Vietnam, CCG harassment has been taken to a whole new level. After leaving Malaysian waters in late May 2019, the Haijing 35111 made a brief return to Hainan before heading to Vietnamese waters to start what became a months-long standoff involving dozens of ships on both sides. In mid-June, the 35111 started by harassing the Hakuryu-5, a rig contracted by Russia's Rosneft to drill a new natural gas well in Block 06-01 northwest of Vanguard Bank. AIS signals showed the exact same methods it had employed off the Malaysian coast—approaching threateningly close to the rig and, more worryingly, maneuvering unsafely around offshore supply vessels traveling between Vung Tau and the Hakuryu-5 (AMTI 2019b).

Unlike with the harassment off Malaysia, the 35111 did not give up after two weeks. Instead it operated around the Hakuryu-5 for nearly a month, briefly traveled to Fiery Cross Reef in mid-July to rest and replenish, and then took up its station again. While it was at Fiery Cross, other CCG ships took up its patrol around the rig and multiple CCG ships continued to patrol close to the Hakuryu-5 through mid-October. At the same time, China escalated horizontally by deploying the Haiyang Dizhi 8, a state-owned survey vessel, along with a large escort force of CCG ships to conduct surveys of Vietnam's continental shelf to the northeast of Block 06-01. The vessel spent more than two months surveying this area before moving farther north, where it continued its activities until October 23. It left only when the Hakuryu-5 finally completed its drilling operations. At least four CCG ships escorted the survey ship at all times according to AIS, though reports suggest the number is much higher. At one point, this included the 12,000-ton Haijing 3901, the largest coast guard vessel in the world (AMTI 2019b). Nor does this horizontal harassment apply only to Vietnam. AIS transmissions show that another Chinese survey ship, the Shi Yan 2, spent at least a week in early August surveying Malaysian waters near the earlier standoff over the Sapura Esperanza. And from at least mid to late August survey vessel Haiyang 4 undertook a survey of a portion of the extended continental shelf jointly claimed by Malaysia and Vietnam (Poling and Hiebert 2019). But unlike Hanoi, Kuala Lumpur chose not to speak out about either of these incidents nor did it seem to have responded by deploying naval or law enforcement vessels. Vietnam sent its own law enforcement vessels to attempt to block the path of the Haiyang Dizhi 8 and to protect the Hakuryu-5. But like Malaysia's navy near Luconia Shoals, they were outmatched in both size and armaments. Hanoi nonetheless put up a spirited resistance, refusing to cancel the drilling operations or to concede to the Chinese survey. In mid-October, Nguyen Minh Hoang, a major general in the People's Army of Vietnam and member of the National Assembly, claimed that there were more than 40 Chinese and 50 Vietnamese vessels in the area, though it is unclear how many of these were CCG and how many were militia (Zhou 2019).

Barely a month and a half after the standoff over the Hakuryu-5 drilling operation and the Haiyang Dizhi 8's survey, a new cycle of escalation began off the Malaysian coast. In early December, two CCG vessels began harassing the West Capella, a drilling ship contracted by Malaysia's state-owned Petronas to conduct exploration off Sabah. On December 21, the West Capella moved to waters off Sarawak. It began a months-long operation to drill exploratory wells in two blocks—ND1 and ND2—just outside the limits of Malaysia's 200-nautical-mile EEZ. These wells were drilled on an area of the seabed claimed by both Kuala Lumpur and Hanoi as part of their extended continental shelves. Unsurprisingly, by early January, Vietnam had deployed a couple of militia boats to monitor and try to warn the West Capella to leave the area. But the bigger problem were the CCG and Chinese militia vessels that soon began harassing the ship. For nearly six months, multiple CCG and militia boats engaged in the same kind of high-stakes game of chicken with Malaysian offshore supply vessels that they earlier employed in Blocks SK308 and off the Vietnamese coast. This often occurred right under the noses of Malaysian navy and coastguard patrols sent out to protect the West Capella's operations (AMTI 2020a). And when Petronas didn't back down, Beijing again deployed the Haiyang Dizhi 8. The survey ship along with a large CCG and militia escort arrived on April 15 and began a weeks-long survey through Malaysian waters (AMTI 2020b). As had occurred months early off Vietnam, the ship departed only after the West Capella completed its operations and went home in mid-May.

THE THIRD FORCE: THE MARITIME MILITIA

This brings up the other major change in the South China Sea status quo—the growing reach of China's maritime militia. This label is not rhetorical—the People's Armed Forces Maritime Militia as it is increasingly known in English is mandated by Chinese law. Article 36 of the China Military Service Law of 1984 requires citizens to serve in the militia, without distinguishing land from maritime service. In 2013, the country's defense white paper specifically strengthened the maritime militia's role in defending claims of sovereignty (Nguyen and Ton 2019). That same year, Chinese President Xi Jinping visited the Tanmen township maritime militia in Hainan and called them a model for others to follow (Kennedy and Erickson 2016). Andrew Erickson and Conor Kennedy at the US Naval War College have spent years compiling public documentation of the militia's activities in the South China Sea, which are far from secret in Chinese-language media and online sources (Erickson 2019). The maritime militia have been involved in operations around the South China Sea for years. Some of their number harassed the USS Impeccable in 2009. They were reportedly involved in sparking the 2012 standoff at Scarborough Shoal. And most spectacularly, dozens of Chinese fishing vessels engaged Vietnamese law enforcement and civilian ships in 2014 during a months-long campaign to defend the drilling operations of China's Haiyang Shiyou 981 deepwater drilling rig. But like the CCG, their presence in the nine-dash line has grown considerably since the completion of China's port facilities in the Spratly Islands. Today it is increasingly difficult for Southeast Asian actors to operate anywhere in the South China Sea without risking a confrontation with these paramilitary actors.

The militia are difficult to track for obvious reasons. Much of their value to Beijing is in their deniability; they serve as eyes and ears for the PLA-N and CCG and can directly harass ships from other states without being definitively proven to be working for the state. They also tend to carry weak Class-B AIS transceivers that often cannot be picked up by satellite—the only means of detecting AIS far from shore—and even those with stronger AIS broadcasts disable them most of the time. To grapple with this, CSIS teamed up with Vulcan's Skylight Maritime Initiative for a six-month study in 2018 that used other remote sensing tools to get a sense of the scale and distribution of the militia. Using a combination of low light imaging, synthetic aperture radar, and high-resolution satellite imagery, correlated with the limited AIS available, this effort determined that the maritime militia constitutes the largest fleet of ships currently operating in the Spratlys. These vessels congregate primarily at Mischief and Subi Reefs, but often gather in smaller clusters around Philippine-, Vietnamese-, and Taiwanese-held features. They average over 50 meters and about 550 tons—considerably larger than the fishing vessels of any of their neighbors. And their numbers have been growing considerably—from no more than 100 at any given time in 2017 to about 300 in August 2018 (Poling 2019).

China's large fleet of fishing vessels has no commercial rationale. Remote sensing data shows that they loiter in large clusters for weeks at a time. In almost every case, when captured in satellite imagery they are riding at anchor without nets in the water. If they were full-time fishers, most would have gone bankrupt long ago. And if they all took up fishing tomorrow, their estimated catch rates would overwhelm the Spratly Islands fishery in short order (Poling 2019). The truth of this investigation was soon confirmed by China's massive deployment of militia vessels, backed by a couple of PLA-N and CCG ships, around Thitu Island starting in December 2018. At that time, Manila began long-overdue work to build a beaching ramp and repair its runway on the island. In response, dozens of Chinese militia vessels poured out of Subi Reef and dropped anchor between 2 and 5.5 nautical miles from Thitu. Around December 20, the initial deployment peaked at 95 ships, none of which appeared to be fishing and only one of which was broadcasting AIS (AMTI 2019c).

The Armed Forces of the Philippines confirmed that it monitored 275 individual Chinese vessels around Thitu between January and March 2019 (Gomez 2019). In June, the ships briefly pulled back, prompting the Philippines' special envoy to China Ramon Tulfo to crow that Beijing was sending a goodwill message to President Duterte (Mangosing 2019). But by the next month they were back and, while the numbers have fluctuated, they continue to congregate around Thitu. China's display of force around Thitu has been the largest militia deployment of late, but not the only one. Chinese fishing vessels now regularly cluster around the outposts of other claimants in the Spratlys for days or weeks at a time, without engaging in much if any actual fishing. In March and April, AMTI collected imagery around Philippines-occupied Loaita Island (*Kota*) and Loaita Cay (*Panata*). Every image revealed Chinese vessels—at one point 15—riding at anchor near the facilities. On March 29, four Chinese vessels had dropped anchor less than half a nautical mile from the garrison at Loaita Cay, which is the smallest and most vulnerable Philippine outpost in the Spratlys. It is easy to imagine how provocative such a deployment must be to an isolated garrison with no independent means of resupply or evacuation in case of an emergency. Like its counterparts in Malaysia and Vietnam, the Armed Forces of the Philippines is aware of these deployments, which are frequently backed by CCG and PLA-N vessels, but its options to respond are limited. The Philippine Navy deployed one of its World War Two-era tank landing ships to Loaita Cay in response to the deployment there (AMTI 2019d). But it is unclear what, if anything, the vessel would have been prepared, or able, to do in response to violence from the militia. In December 2019, the Philippine Navy deployed one of its flagships, a former US Coast Guard cutter recommissioned as the BRP Ramon Alcaraz, to Thitu Island in response to the militia deployment there (AMTI 2019c). But again, it is unclear how a navy ship could or should respond to violence initiative by a militia vessel. And even if it had responded in the case of violence, it would have been outmatched by the CCG and PLA-N ships on-station to back up the militia.

Vietnam has also been targeted by militia deployments. AMTI's research with Vulcan showed that Chinese militia vessels frequently cluster around Vietnamese outposts, including in Union Banks. One group of these, the nine vessels of the Yue Mao Bin Yu fleet, broadcast AIS frequently enough to show that when operating near Hughes and Johnson Reefs, they often approach provocatively close to the nearby Vietnamese facilities at Collins, Lansdowne, and Grierson Reefs, and Sin Cowe Island (Poling 2019). Subsequent satellite imagery collections have confirmed that they never appear to fish during these visits and often anchor less than 1 nautical mile from the isolated Vietnamese bases. The maritime militia also joined the CCG in the 2019 operation to escort the Haiyang Dizhi 8 survey vessel near the Vietnamese coast. It is unclear how many ships were involved as the vast majority do not broadcast AIS, but at least one, the Qiong Sansha Yu 00114, did (CSIS 2019b).

And then there is the well-known case of the Yuemaobinyu 42212, which collided with and sunk a Filipino fishing boat, the F/B Gem-Ver, at Reed Bank in June 2019. A great deal about the incident was suspicious—the 42212 had struck an anchored vessel at night, reportedly turned off its lights after doing so, and fled the scene leaving the Filipino fishers to drown had a passing Vietnamese boat not rescued them. These details led to immediate speculation in the Philippine press that the vessel might have been part of the maritime militia and had intentionally struck the Gem-Ver. That is impossible to know given the publicly available data. But an investigation by AMTI and the Center for Advanced Defense Studies has shown that the ship is not just a commercial fishing boat. On several occasions it was commissioned for Chinese government-backed research, it sailed out of the Bohe Port in Dianbai which hosts a publicly acknowledged maritime militia unit, and its patchy AIS history is highly suspicious (AMTI 2019e). All of this suggests that there is a fair chance the Yuemaobinyu 42212 does operate as part of the militia at least some of the time. But the difficulty of finding a smoking gun to prove that is exactly the point—the militia is valuable to China in large part because it maintains a level of deniability that the PLA-N and CCG do not enjoy. Militia vessels that take things too far and cause a collision by their reckless behavior can always claim to have been civilians involved in an unfortunate accident.

What Lies Ahead

China's recent actions show that it remains committed to the goal of controlling all water, airspace, and seabed within the nine-dash line, at least to the point of preventing neighboring states from undertaking any unilateral actions within their EEZs without prior Chinese permission. The harassment of Philippine construction at Thitu shows that while Beijing is not prepared to use military force at this time to dislodge other claimants from the features they occupy, it will increasingly seek to prevent them from upgrading those facilities. China is willing to accept occupation by other claimants but wants their facilities to remain as vulnerable as possible, especially to future blockade as was attempted at the Sierra Madre in 2014. The recent operations to interfere with energy development off the coasts of Malaysia and Vietnam confirm that China is not only unwilling to accept new oil and gas concessions in the South China Sea—it now believes its position is strong enough to block new drilling within *existing* concessions. Vietnam and Malaysia are so far resisting this pressure, at least when projects are deemed critical enough. But they cannot be expected to do so forever. If the recent operations near Vanguard Bank and off Sarawak are a blueprint for things to come, then direct resistance will become increasingly futile. Vietnam directly contested the harassment of the Hakuryu-5 and the survey of the Haiyang Dizhi 8 as much as possible, and probably more strongly than China expected. The same was true for Malaysia's patrols around the West Capella. But they cannot keep up this tempo of operations forever.

And while these efforts by Vietnam and Malaysia were successful, just as Hanoi's resistance to the deployment of the Haiyang Shiyou 981 was in 2014, they cannot possibly muster the same response to every future attempt at oil and gas drilling. Even if they wanted to, how many foreign companies will show the same willingness as Rosneft to accept this level of risk and undertake drilling in the face of overt Chinese threats? What happens if an offshore supply ship is sunk due to miscalculation or intent? If that level of risk must be accepted for all future drilling in the South

China Sea, Malaysia and Vietnam will find few willing to invest in their offshore sectors. And the same will be true for the other claimants if this pattern of behavior spreads. These operations by the CCG and maritime militia are not necessarily meant to convince the neighbors to back down in every episode; they are meant to steadily raise the risks of operating within the South China Sea to unacceptable levels. If that continues, Southeast Asian claimants will eventually have only two options: partner with China in all activities within their EEZs and continental shelves, or forego their maritime rights altogether.

This strategy will inevitably lead to violence. Beijing has empowered hundreds of poorly trained, nonuniformed militia ships to purposely maneuver in a reckless and illegal manner near other vessels. Another Gem-Ver-like incident is just over the horizon; and the next time it might result in loss of life for the Southeast Asian parties involved. That will likely derail the current diplomatic façade (both the COC talks and bilateral negotiations) unless those efforts fall apart first due to frequent oil and gas standoffs. So, what happens then? The collapse of the current status quo will present opportunities for both the Southeast Asian claimants and outside partners to embark on a more realistic effort to manage the disputes. Part of this effort should involve negotiations among the claimants, with China invited to participate, outside the ASEAN context on concrete issues like fisheries management and seabed resources. There is no reason for the non-claimant members of ASEAN to be involved in such discussions (they do not want to be, and any effort to do this at the ASEAN level would be doomed to fail just as it has since the 1990s). Such a multilateral effort outside of ASEAN would allow the claimants for the first time to develop a realistic plan to manage the proximate triggers for violence—fishing disputes, oil and gas development, and law enforcement interactions. If they could come up with their own shared negotiating points, they could present those to Beijing.

And why would China agree to take up such a diplomatic effort, which would require real concessions from it for the first time? That would require a change in Beijing's cost–benefit analysis. China correctly calculates that it has been steadily gaining ground since 2016 with little cost. But if it begins to pay concrete diplomatic and economic costs for its bad behavior, it may decide that seeking face-saving compromises to manage the disputes would be more beneficial than its current coercive approach. Public naming and shaming at the same levels seen in 2015 and 2016 would be part of this approach. But in addition, regional states and outside parties like the United States should cooperate to unmask and better publicize the actions of Chinese forces, especially the maritime militia. If they cannot operate under a cloak of deniability, they will lose much of their value to Beijing. And if they can be publicly identified and their beneficial ownership traced, they can be targeted by direct economic sanctions just as has happened to Russian entities engaged in paramilitary actions in the Ukraine or Chinese companies known to smuggle to North Korea. These efforts, combined with growing maritime domain awareness capabilities for regional states and a continued, robust security presence by the United States and outside parties, could shift China's calculus in favor of compromise. That will not happen overnight, and it will not be a smooth process or one without risk. But the only alternatives appear to be conflict sparked by China's current strategy or Southeast Asian acquiescence to Chinese control over their EEZs and continental shelves.

If the United States and like-minded partners such as Australia, Japan, and European states fail to help Southeast Asian claimants bend Beijing toward a more equitable compromise, they will find the entire Indo-Pacific a far less open and stable region. If the South China Sea disputes were resolved in Beijing's favor through a unilateral campaign of coercion, and without it paying significant cost for those actions, it would set a dangerous precedent for how an increasingly powerful China approaches other problems in the region. It would also suggest that international law need not apply in China's backyard, which would be a deeply destabilizing turn. It would amount to a return to pre-World War Two international politics, in which laws, norms, and institutions no longer moderate the exercise of power by larger states. And it would cement the retreat of US power from the region. It is hard to see how the US–Philippines alliance could survive such an abject failure of the United States to help preserve an ally's lawful rights. And more broadly, it is unlikely that partners in Southeast Asia would continue to support a forward-deployed American military presence when it had so clearly been unable to secure their interests against Chinese coercion.

References

Asia Maritime Transparency Initiative (AMTI), "A Constructive Year for Chinese Base Building," AMTI, December 14, 2017a, https://amti.csis.org/constructive-year-chinese-building/.

Asia Maritime Transparency Initiative (AMTI), "China's Continuing Reclamation in the Paracels," AMTI, updated August 9, 2017b, https://amti.csis.org/paracels-beijings-other-buildup/.

Asia Maritime Transparency Initiative (AMTI), "An Accounting of China's Deployments to the Spratly Islands," AMTI, May 9, 2018a, https://amti.csis.org/accounting-chinas-deployments-spratly-islands/.

Asia Maritime Transparency Initiative (AMTI), "China Quietly Upgrades a Remote Reef," AMTI, November 20, 2018b, https://amti.csis.org/china-quietly-upgrades-bombay-reef/.

Asia Maritime Transparency Initiative (AMTI), "Exercises Bring New Weapons to the Paracels," AMTI, May 24, 2018c, https://amti.csis.org/exercises-bring-new-weapons-paracels/.

Asia Maritime Transparency Initiative (AMTI), "China Lands First Bomber on South China Sea Island," AMTI, May 18, 2018d, https://amti.csis.org/china-lands-first-bomber-south-china-sea-island/.

Asia Maritime Transparency Initiative (AMTI), "Signaling Sovereignty: Chinese Patrols at Contested Reefs," AMTI, September 26, 2019a, https://amti.csis.org/signaling-sovereignty-chinese-patrols-at-contested-reefs.

Asia Maritime Transparency Initiative (AMTI), "Under Pressure: Philippine Construction Provokes a Paramilitary Response," AMTI, February 6, 2019b, https://amti.csis.org/under-pressure-philippine-construction-paramilitary-response/.

Asia Maritime Transparency Initiative (AMTI), "Updated: China Risks Flare-Up over Malaysian, Vietnamese Gas Resources," AMTI, updated December 13, 2019c, https://amti.csis.org/china-risks-flare-up-over-malaysian-vietnamese-gas-resources/.

Asia Maritime Transparency Initiative (AMTI), "Still Under Pressure: Manila Versus the Militia," AMTI, updated April 16, 2019d, https://amti.csis.org/still-under-pressure-manila-versus-the-militia/.

Asia Maritime Transparency Initiative (AMTI), "Seeking Clues in the Case of the Yuemaobinyu 42212," AMTI, October 15, 2019e, https://amti.csis.org/seeking-clues-in-the-case-of-the-yuemaobinyu-42212/.

Asia Maritime Transparency Initiative (AMTI), "Malaysia Picks a Three-Way Fight in the South China Sea," AMTI, February 21, 2020a, https://amti.csis.org/malaysia-picks-a-three-way-fight-in-the-south-china-sea/.

Asia Maritime Transparency Initiative (AMTI), "Update: Chinese Survey Ship Escalates Three-Way Standoff," AMTI, updated May 18, 2020b, https://amti.csis.org/china-risks-flare-up-over-malaysian-vietnamese-gas-resources/.

Douglas, Jake, "Counter-Coercion Series: Second Thomas Shoal Incident," AMTI, excerpted from Michael Green et. al, *Countering Coercion in Maritime Asia: The Theory and Practice of Gray Zone* (Washington, DC: CSIS/Rowman & Littlefield, 2017), https://amti.csis.org/counter-co-2nd-thomas-shoal/.

East Pendulum (@HenriKenhmann) Twitter account, June 30, 2019, https://twitter.com/HenriKenhmann/status/1145338072818544641.

Erickson, Andrew, "The China Maritime Militia Bookshelf," AndrewErickson.com, updated May 21, 2019, http://www.andrewerickson.com/2019/05/the-china-maritime-militia-bookshelf-complete-with-latest-recommendations-fact-sheet-4/.

Esmaquel II, Paterno, "China Chopper Harasses PH Rubber Boat in Ayungin Shoal—Lawmaker," Rappler, updated May 31, 2018, https://www.rappler.com/nation/203720-chinese-helicopter-harass-rubber-boat-ayungin-shoal-spratly-islands.

Gomez, Jim, "Manila Protests 'Swarming' Chinese Boats Near Island," Associated Press, April 1, 2019, https://www.navytimes.com/news/your-navy/2019/04/01/manila-protests-swarming-chinese-boats-near-island/.

Gordon, Michael R., and Page, Jeremy, "China Installed Military Jamming Equipment on Spratly Islands, U.S. Says," *Wall Street Journal*, April 9, 2018, https://www.wsj.com/articles/china-installed-military-jamming-equipment-on-spratly-islands-u-s-says-1523266320.

Kennedy, Conor M., and Erickson, Andrew S., "From Frontier to Frontline: Tanmen Maritime Militia's Leading Role Part 2," Center for International Maritime Security, May 17, 2016, http://cimsec.org/frontier-frontline-tanmen-maritime-militias-leading-role-pt-2/25260.

Macias, Amanda, "China Quietly Installed Missile Systems on Strategic Spratly Islands in Hotly Contested South China Sea," CNBC, May 2, 2018, https://www.cnbc.com/2018/05/02/china-added-missile-systems-on-spratly-islands-in-south-china-sea.html.

Mangosing, Frances G., "China Military Planes Land on PH Reef," *Philippine Daily Inquirer*, April 18, 2018, https://globalnation.inquirer.net/165824/china-military-planes-land-ph-reef.

Mangosing, Frances G., "Chinese Militia Vessels Start Pull Out Near Pag-asa Island—Mon Tulfo," *Philippine Daily Inquirer*, June 6, 2019, https://globalnation.inquirer.net/176005/chinese-militia-vessels-start-pull-out-near-pag-asa-island-mon-tulfo.

Nguyen, Hong Thao, and Ton, Nu Thanh Binh, "Maritime Militias in the South China Sea," Maritime Awareness Project, June 13, 2019, http://maritimeawarenessproject.org/2019/06/13/maritime-militias-in-the-south-china-sea/.

Poling, Gregory B., "Illuminating the South China Sea's Dark Fishing Fleets," CSIS Stephenson Ocean Security Project, January 9, 2019, https://ocean.csis.org/spotlights/illuminating-the-south-china-seas-dark-fishing-fleets/.

Poling, Gregory B., and Hiebert, Murray, "Stop the Bully in the South China Sea," *Wall Street Journal*, August 28, 2019, https://www.wsj.com/articles/stop-the-bully-in-the-south-china-sea-11567033378.

Viray, Patricia Lourdes, "China Coast Guard Blocked Resupply Mission to Ayungin Shoal—DND," *Philippine Star*, September 19, 2019.

Zhou, Laura, "As Coastguard Boats Circle, Vietnam Prepares for Bigger Challenge in South China Sea," *South China Morning Post*, October 12, 2019, https://www.scmp.com/news/china/diplomacy/article/3032536/coastguard-boats-circle-vietnam-prepares-bigger-challenge.

CHAPTER 2

China's Military Strategy in the South China

Yoji Koda

INTRODUCTION

In 2012, President of People's Republic of China, General Secretary of the Communist Party of China, and Chairman of the Central Military Commission, Xi Jinping, declared "The great rejuvenation of the Chinese nation"—a clear national goal of China (*China Daily* 2014). The national goal is to build a Great Modern Socialist Country by communist China's centennial year of 2049 with socialistic core values. As a paramount leader of rising China, it is not unusual, but rather a natural and appropriate action for President Xi to proclaim such a national objective over 1.4 billion Chinese people. At the same time, however, from the eyes of most international community members, under the new national objective of its Great Rejuvenation, China seems to have initiated a serious challenge against today's long-familiarized and firmly established international norms and customs—and also against the overwhelming global dominance of the United States (US).

Y. Koda (✉)
Japan Maritime Self-Defense Force (Vice Admiral, retired), Tokyo, Japan

China's Military Strategy: Anti-Access and Area Denial (A2AD)

A2AD is a term used by Western security thinkers to best describe and explain China's current military strategy (McDevitt and Saunders 2011). Needless to say, A2AD is widely interpreted as a Chinese military strategy aimed against the US. This strategy depends on sea denial which is a concept not just specific to China. It is, in general, a strategic concept used by an inferior power against a superior power. A typical example of this concept was the "Sea Denial" strategy of Admiral Sergey G. Gorshkov of the Soviet Navy which was clearly inferior to the US Navy (USN). Sea denial was intended to deter and counter the USN and other allied European navies in the Atlantic theater as well as Japan Maritime Self-Defense Force (JMSDF) in the Pacific Ocean (Ushirogata 2017). The key objective of China's A2AD strategy, described as Anti Access, means keeping US military forces out of proximate areas in the Indo-Pacific regions during peacetime and crisis periods. Area Denial means preventing US forces from conducting free and unimpeded military operations against China in war time. However, China is surrounded by external powers and faces an unfavorable geography in all directions. It faces a landmass to the north and west, and sea toward south and east. In addition to these geopolitical features, US military forces have the capability to surround and attack China from seawards, from western, southern, and eastern directions. For China to defend itself it has to keep US military forces out of critical parts of the Indo-Pacific, this is the objective of the A2AD strategy (McDevitt and Saunders 2011). However, China needs time to accomplish this objective and it also needs extremely large and capable military capabilities comparable to US forces. China's immediate objective is therefore to build a security posture to keep US forces away from the nearby areas such as the South China Sea and its adjoining land features as well as the East China Sea, the Western Pacific, and the Eastern Indian Ocean,

However, it is extremely difficult, practically almost impossible for China and the People's Liberation Army (PLA), to reach these goals by winning an all-out and head-on war against superior US forces in this region. Taking advantage of the proximity of the SCS to China, inferior PLA forces could challenge superior US forces only in familiar neighboring areas and regions, but not in distant outer areas. A key tenet of China's A2AD is to build sufficient capabilities to attack and neutralize US forces at key weak-points, that would mean entrapping them in places where their war-fighting capabilities would be substantially reduced. Thus, in theory, the PLA will gain victory over constrained US forces by conducting concentrated strike operations against "sitting-duck"-type targets. In such a scenario, it would be unmistakable that the hunter is PLA and the sitting ducks are weakened US forces whose Achilles's Heels would be identified, attacked, and disabled. For the PLA, building-up a force to fully meet the requirements of this strategy has been a matter of highest priority. For this reason, it has been developing the necessary military capabilities as conventional and high-end equipment and systems to implement its A2AD strategy. These include anti-ship ballistic missiles (ASBMs), hypersonic anti-ship/land-attack missiles, submarine forces, and offensive sea-bed mine capabilities. Along with this, there are unconventional and asymmetric A2AD operations. The PLA has been building anti-satellite capabilities (including satellite-killer satellites), cyber-attack capabilities employed to destroy networks of ocean-floor fiber-optical cables for internet connections, electro-magnetic pulse capabilities, and others that will focus on neutralizing the US forces' Command, Control, Communications, Computers, Intelligence, Surveillance, and Reconnaissance (C4ISR) capabilities. These specialized Chinese capabilities would disable the nerve networks which connect the "brain" (national command authority and military headquarters) and the "muscles" (front-line fighting forces), as well as all the sensors, which function for US forces like the eyes, ears, nose, mouth/tongue, fingertips, and body skin of a human body.

The ultimate objective of China's A2AD is to weaken the will and determination of the US and eventually convince the American people to abandon the long-maintained policy of engagement in the Western Pacific region. When China successfully develops the above military capabilities to support its strategy, it will then demonstrate them to the US leadership and the American people to weaken American resolve and to achieve its objective without fighting. In this above-mentioned context, one key aim of A2AD is to keep US forces out of peripheral areas, such as the Western Pacific, the South China Sea and chokepoints around the archipelagic states of the Philippines, Indonesia, and Malaysia, such as the Malacca/Sunda straits, and the eastern Indian Ocean. In the case of crises or wars, China would demonstrate these military capabilities to the American public to deter US military intervention in these areas. In this way, China would weaken US determination to keep its military presence in the Indo-Pacific by signaling that a fight against PLA would entail an extremely high cost.

A2AD AND THE PLA

Now it is necessary to examine each component of China's PLA from the viewpoint of its capability to support China's foreign policies, such as the Belt and Road Initiative (BRI). The PLA has been rapidly growing as a result of more than two decades of special budget allocations. The one million-strong PLA Army (PLA-A) still lacks US Army style expeditionary capabilities that would fully support China's foreign policy. The PLA-A is a homeland defense force that can deliver a crushing blow to any invader, including US forces. The PLA-A, together with its recently developed marine force, has the capability to attack and occupy Taiwan, in the case of non-intervention by US forces. Additionally, the PLA-A with its marines is capable of invading and seizing the western tip of Japan's Southwest (Ryukyu) Islands to say nothing of disputed maritime features in the South China Sea, which China thinks is its historical backyard. But, taken as a whole, the PLA-A is not structured to support China's foreign policy objectives. In recent years, the PLA Navy (PLA-N) has become a top service, accorded the highest national priority. The PLA-N has been pursuing an aggressive force build-up program for almost two-decades. Assessments may differ of the exact size of PLA-N with its three fleets, but it is generally ranked as the second-largest blue-water navy in the world today. The inventory of major PLA-N equipment includes two aircraft carriers (CV), large surface combatants, both diesel-electric and nuclear-powered submarines, and various types of amphibious ships/craft, as well as a fair number of fixed-wing and rotary-wing naval aircraft. One noteworthy event in recent years was the rapid construction of large multi-purpose fleet supply/replenishment ships in bulk. This could be a PLA-N's effort to strengthen China's poor logistic support capabilities in distant areas in the absence of oversea naval bases.

However, despite its growing size and the improved qualities of the above-mentioned naval assets, the PLA-N's ability to support China's foreign policies is limited and will continue to be so into the near future. The reasons behind this are: first, its poor logistic support capabilities in distant waters though the PLA-N is actively trying to correct this problem; second, there is a serious lack of full-sized overseas naval bases to support the PLA-N's distant water operations; and third, China's unfavorable maritime geography as its bases on the mainland are confined by the South China Sea and the East China Sea, as well as by the circumferential Pacific island chains stretching in an arc from Japan to Taiwan, then from the archipelagos of the Philippines and Indonesia/Malaysia to the Malay peninsula, the gulf of Thailand, and finally to Vietnam. The PLA-N is also not capable of effectively protecting China's vast and globally spread Sea Lines of Communications (SLOCs) for national survival. However, the PLA-N is capable of strongly supporting army and marines amphibious operations in the East China and South China Seas as well as against Taiwan, or Japan's Southwest Islands.

The PLA Air Force (PLA-AF) is, in general, a subordinate homeland defense force to the PLA-A. So, like the Army, it has poor out-of-area operations capabilities. The lack of overseas military airbases is an obstacle preventing the PLA-AF to conduct air-operations abroad in the way the US air force has been able to do. Because of this restriction, the PLA-AF faces the same constraints as the PLA-N and it will be extremely difficult to improve its expeditionary capabilities in a short time. In this regard, PLA-AF's ability to support China's foreign policy in air spaces distant from the mainland is and will continue to be extremely limited. With regard to the PLA's rocket force, there is one thing that should be mentioned. China has developed a unique long-range anti-ship ballistic missile (ASBM) force that is designed to shoot and kill/damage capital ships of the US navy, such as aircraft carriers, large amphibious ships, fleet supply ships, and strategic prepositioning ships which approach China and its surrounding waters in Indo-Pacific region. China's ASBMs, such as the DF-21 and DF-26, have been called "carrier killers" and they can target the US navy's capital ships rushing to conflict areas in the Indo-Pacific distant from the US mainland.

Impact of China's A2AD Strategy on the South China Sea

As previously mentioned, the PLA-N and PLA-AF do not have sufficient capabilities to support China's foreign policies and to protect China's national interests abroad, especially in distant areas from the mainland. However, the PLA has an overwhelming military advantage in China's adjoining waters, the East China and South China Seas, in comparison with most of China's neighbors. No single country in this region, including Japan, can match China's military capabilities at the present time. In recent years, China's robust military capabilities and its illegally militarized artificial islands in the South China Sea have been casting dark clouds over the coastal countries of the South China Sea—The Philippines, Indonesia, and Malaysia, Brunei, Singapore, Thailand, Cambodia, and Vietnam as well as Taiwan. In addition to this military imbalance, each country has its specific trade and economic ties with China, although they may differ. In this context, China has been increasing its ability to influence these countries through its strong economy and robust military capabilities. At the same time, however, almost all of these countries want a clear American policy toward China, and a visible American military presence in the region. They also want to maintain good economic and trading relationships with the US. In recent years, these countries have avoided taking a clear position, either to support the US or China, when multinational and international efforts were made to resolve many China-related and China-generated regional problems. These countries are torn between the mutually exclusive rivalry between the US and China, and have no other option but to adopt politically ambiguous positions. In the current security situation in the South China Sea, China seems to be in advantageous position over the US from the military and security point of view. The present stalemated situation there complicates America's ability to handle China's A2AD and its supporting military/diplomatic actions. At the same time, this situation also hinders China's free political and military maneuver in the region as the ambiguous positions adopted by the regional countries, as well as America's military presence, combine to make China's position more complicated. In this regard, there will be much room for the US, Japan, and other regional actors to deal with China in the South China Sea.

Neutralizing China's Militarized Artificial Islands in the South China Sea

China's militarization of seven artificial islands in Spratly Islands will pose a serious threat to all the military forces operating in the South China Sea, and to the coastal countries as well, especially Vietnam and the Philippines. Since 2015, on several occasions the public media and major western think tanks reported that the PLA had deployed capable military forces and equipment on its man-made artificial islands. It is also public knowledge that China had completed building airfields: one was enlarged on Woody Island in the Paracels and three were constructed on newly reclaimed artificial islands in the Spratly Islands, namely, Fiery Cross, Subi, and Mischief reefs. China also had built and improved modern port facilities on all the artificial/expanded islands (Brunnstrom 2016a). The Chinese Government strongly rebutted the frequent criticisms made by the international community, especially the US, that it has militarized the South China Sea. Instead, Beijing clearly made counter arguments saying that any actions to protect the nation's territory and waters are matters of China's national sovereignty (Nakazawa 2019). In addition to this, China occasionally makes seemingly benign but disingenuous announcements on its establishment of non-military meteorological and navigation-aid stations with civilian personnel on these artificial islands (Wee and Blanchard 2016b). The PLA has deployed the latest model H-6 bomber and J-11 fighters to Woody Island (Long 2018; Panda 2015). Military transport aircraft have landed on these three air-capable artificial islands in the Spratlys and it is just a matter of time for the PLA to deploy combat aircraft such as fighters and bombers there. The Chinese Government does not confirm public and media reports about its military assets but it has also become a well-known fact that the PLA has deployed and fielded a wide range of modern military equipment. That includes various types of radars, anti-air/surface missiles, and guns, electronic warfare systems together with supporting facilities such as barracks, sports fields, supply and maintenance depots, and ammunition-magazines (Stashwick 2016). In this regard, China's militarization of the South China Sea seems to have been progressing substantially along its planned and envisioned track. Also, the PLA, which is supported by a robust militarized operational environment in the South China Sea, has been regarded as the most potent challenge against US and regional military forces alike. However, China's fortified features in the Spratlys with their military capabilities are not impregnable, and the PLA is no "superman" as it operates in the South China Sea.

Japan's experience of defending distant islands in the Pacific during World War Two clearly shows the extreme difficulty of such operations. For China, maintaining sea and air control/superiority against invading adversary forces will be an absolute necessity but it will be an extremely difficult task for the PLA, even in the nearby South China Sea. In addition to this, another key condition to defend the islands will be to maintain logistic supply lines from the Chinese mainland; and especially from Hainan Island which is a main forward base for staging forces and for combat operations to protect China's remote artificial islands in the South China Sea. However, without any logistic support China's fortified remote islands would be nothing but "deadwood." That was the most serious and bitter lesson that Imperial Japan, as well as its army and navy, learned through its island defense operations in the second half of World War Two. Imperial Japan failed to defend any single island against amphibious assault operations conducted by combined US navy and US Marine Corps teams.

US forces have been, and still are, the major counter to the PLA's challenges in the South China Sea and they will remain so in the foreseeable future. At the same time, however, there are many measures that the regional militaries may adopt. Especially, the roles of Vietnam and the Philippines would become critical, and one advantage they have is geographic location in relation to the Paracel and Spratly Islands. Vietnam's coastline is an ideal location to check and control Hainan Island and Woody Island in the Paracels. Similarly, Palawan Island of the Philippines is an optimum location to cover all of China's artificial islands in the Spratlys. Many strategic thinkers simply draw arcs representing missile-launching ranges from China's artificial islands, and explain how dangerous they would be for the US and regional militaries. But this could be reversed If Vietnam and the Philippines properly deploy surface to surface land-attack missiles that have sufficient firing ranges (roughly 500 km) to reach these artificial islands. If this would be realized, China's artificial and militarized Islands, which have been called "illegal game-changers" in the South China Sea, could be described as a "group of helpless frogs in front of small but brave snakes." Vietnam could also conduct a blockade or isolation operations against Woody Island which is China's "capital island" in the South China Sea and connects Hainan Island and these artificial islands in the Spratlys. Vietnam should develop a plan to deploy its six Kilo-class submarines for this purpose. If this would occur, China's military capabilities in the southern part of the South China Sea, especially those in the Spratlys would be substantially countered.

One thing that is seriously lacking among the coastal states of the South China Sea is an Information Sharing Posture (ISP) and Maritime/Multi Domain Awareness Network (MMDA) that would provide common situational understanding and operational pictures to military commanders and national decision makers. Each country should first develop and improve its own maritime surveillance capabilities. Then, the regional countries facing the South China Sea should jointly develop information sharing and domain awareness networks. To realize this capability, both Japan and US should play a larger role to assist the unilateral and multinational efforts of the regional nations in this direction. If completed, such networks would enable the South China Sea countries to detect China's assertive marine activities at a much earlier stage and enable effective deterrent actions to be taken promptly. Last but not least, these regional countries should develop and improve their own air defense and coastal defense capabilities that are an important prerequisite for the success of the afore-mentioned military posture to deter and counter the PLA in the South China Sea. The new posture would force the PLA to seek increased budget allocations and military units and to allocate more military resources to suppress the regional state's operational capabilities.

Impact of A2AD on Japan's Maritime Strategy

Japan has a unique constraint that has been a core element of the nation's security policy and strategy since the promulgation of the present constitution in May 1947. Due to an interpretation of the constitution, Japan's post-war military, the Japan Self-Defense Force (JSDF), is prohibited from having strategic strike capabilities that could be used against the territory of an aggressor to weaken its war waging/fighting capabilities. Because of this strict constraint imposed on national security, the constitution has been widely referred as the "Pacifist Constitution" in Japan. In strict and full compliance with the Pacifist Constitution, the JSDF was limited "exclusively" to defensive operations to protect Japan's territory and its sea/air spaces as well as the nation's SLOCs. These fundamental missions have been comprehensively designated as Japan's Homeland Defense. At the same time, however, given this posture under the Pacifist Constitution, the JSDF alone cannot repel enemy aggression, and cannot hold back an enemy's military pressure for a prolonged period of time. It is also clear that this posture will not bring enemy aggression to an end in a short time while the aggressor's capabilities will be untouched and will continue to be operating in waves of strikes over Japan until the collapse of the JSDF. In this context, the fundamental value of the Japan–US security alliance can be understood as a "Shield and Spear" relationship that defines strategic mission sharing between the JSDF and US forces. In this alliance posture, US forces are the spear and are tasked to conduct strategic strike operations against an aggressor to weaken its national war-fighting capabilities, to bring the war to an end at the earliest opportunity. In return, JSDF's Homeland Defense Operations would act as a shield, they would relieve US forces from laborious and complicated defensive operations around Japan, to enable them to conduct strike operations against an aggressor's strategic targets. In order for Japan to realize this deterrent posture, the safe arrival of US reinforcements from Hawaii and/or mainland US is indispensable. Another important mission of the JSDF is to support and ensure the safe arrival of US reinforcements to their operational areas in and around Japan by reducing an adversary's threats. So, the JSDF, especially the Japan Maritime Self-Defense Force (JMSDF) is tasked to conduct maritime operations, mainly anti-submarine warfare (ASW) operations around the Western Pacific in full support of the US 7th Fleet.

A regional contingency that has a serious impact on Japan's security and national survival would call in US military involvement, and it is an important task for the JSDF, especially the JMSDF, to support US forces deployed to meet the regional contingency. In such a case, the JMSDF would conduct various support operations that are similar to those mentioned above in the Indo-Pacific. At present, a key focus of JMSDF strategy is to maintain a sufficient capability to meet the various challenges of the PLA-N. This will protect Japan's vital SLOCs and support operations by US naval forces in the region, as well as contributing to Japan's island defense operations. At the same time, however, there should be additional measures to cope with the PLA-N's new maneuvers under the A2AD strategy. The JMSDF should develop countermeasures to deal with future maritime security challenges and to counter China's deployment of anti-ship ballistic missiles (ASBMs) which will be the PLA's key weapons systems to prevent US naval forces and reinforcements from arriving on the scene. If China succeeds in the use of ASBMs, a core tenet of Japan's defense policy and military strategy, which depends on "Shield and Spear" mission sharing between the JSDF and US forces will collapse. Then, Japan will have to fight against an aggressor by itself without US forces. This is the ultimate scenario for Japan, and it should develop the best possible strategy to prevent this from happening.

In any case, the JMSDF should take into account China's substantial naval build-up including the construction of new aircraft carriers and naval air-arms, major surface combatant, submarine forces as well as its growing amphibious forces. In addition to the PLA-N's fighting capabilities for traditional all-out/high-end combat, the JMSDF, and more importantly the JSDF as a whole should concentrate their best efforts to develop countermeasures to cope with the PLA's unconventional and non-kinetic capabilities such as anti-satellite, cyber-attack, destruction of sea-bed network of fiber-optical cables, and electro-magnetic pulse capabilities. Finally, the JMSDF also has to take into consideration the PLA-N's new base construction in the South China Sea. This includes the new naval base complex in Sanya/Yulin ("Sanya" hereafter) in Hainan Island and the recently completed artificial islands, especially three with long airstrips and port facilities in the South China Sea. They could have a serious impact on the JMSDF's operations and without appropriate planning, the JMSDF may fail to adopt countermeasures through cooperation with other regional naval powers.

Bilateral JMSDF and USN Efforts to Counter China's Challenge

In order for the JMSDF to fully respond to China's A2AD strategy, the most important requirement is to develop and maintain sufficient operational capabilities against the PLA-N. In this process, the JMSDF should closely cooperate with the US navy because China's strategy is directed against US naval forces in the region. China strongly intends to create situations favorable to itself which would erode the US determination to intervene in Indo-Pacific issues by deploying naval forces. The JMSDF and the US navy could jointly develop functioning ASBM defense systems to neutralize China's ASBMs. If any of these American capital ships, such as nuclear-powered aircraft carriers (CVNs) and/or large amphibious ships, are heavily damaged or lost to Chinese ASBM strikes while operating in the Western Pacific, there could be enormous casualties that the American people would not accept. China's ASBMs could close doors for alternative approaches by the US navy from the south through several adjacent seas north of Australia, and from the west via the Indian Ocean. If this were the case, the US navy would have few practical options to counter China's new challenge as driven by A2AD. In this situation, it is more than likely that both the US leadership and the American public could lose interest in maintaining American forces in the conflict area at such a high cost. Weakening the US resolve to stay forward-deployed in the Indo-Pacific region without actually fighting is a primary objective of China's A2AD strategy and will continue to be so in the future. Therefore, if this situation really comes to pass at some point in the future, China will achieve its strategic objectives with relative ease, and this would be the worst scenario for Japan and the US. In this regard, Japan and the US should prevent that scenario from happening, and at any cost.

China's development of increasingly potent weapons systems that support A2AD is the primary reason for Japan and the US to jointly develop new defense capabilities. Japan and the US are already fully and jointly involved in development and deployment of Ballistic Missile Defense (BMD) systems for national defense. If Japan and the US continue in this way, it would be much easier to develop countermeasures against China's ASBMs in their terminal-homing-phase at sea, that would be a new add-on to the existing BMD capability. In order for the JMSDF and the US navy to realize the capacity for terminal interception, a new initiative will be required such as the development of Fleet Ballistic Missile Defense (F-BMD) systems to kill and neutralize incoming ASBMs from China.

CHINA'S ACHILLES' HEEL

All PLA-N forces are contained in two semi-enclosed water areas, the South China and East China Seas. For the PLA-N forces to operate outside of China's immediate littoral areas, they would have to pass through straits and channels—"chokepoints"—in order to enter the open oceans. This complicates the PLA's strategy and operations as deployments in contingency and wartime scenarios could become extremely difficult and troublesome. In this regard, the existence of several chokepoints in the First Island Chain, which surrounds the PLA-N's bases and areas of operations in South China and East China Seas, is a godsend for Japan and the US. The chokepoints will become real obstacles for China's naval strategy accentuated by the fact they are controlled by other countries, and China has no control over them. In this regard, the PLA-N cannot count on free transit by its operational units through these chokepoints in contingencies and war time. Furthermore, from the naval operations point of view, there are very few "real" channels with sufficient depth that connect the South China Sea with the outer oceans and seas along the First Island Chain. In particular, submarine deployments are much more complicated than surface forces as the minimum depth for safe submerged passage through the channels/chokepoints is about 100 m to 150 m. There are only four chokepoints in the First Island Chain surrounding the South China Sea that meet this criterion

These four chokepoints are the Bashi Channel between Taiwan and the Philippines with a depth of 1500 m, the Mindoro Strait between Luzon and Palawan Islands of the Philippines with a depth of 400 m, the Sibutu Passage at the western tip of the Sulu Islands of the Philippines with a depth of 300 m, and the Lombok Strait between the Bari and Lombok Islands of Indonesia with a depth of 250 m. There are many other straits such as the Malacca and Sunda Straits which are known as core and indispensable maritime corridors, but they are too shallow for submerged submarines transit. In addition to this, both the Malacca and Sunda Straits are not under China's control, so China would have many fundamental problems in a time of crisis and war. PLA-N forces, including aircraft-carrier task units, cannot pass through the straits freely, let alone submarines. For PLA-N submarines that sortie from Sanya Base in Hainan Island to the outer sea and oceans, or in a reversed track, they would have to take one of the three routes through chokepoints (see Chart-1):

Route A: Sanya base–South China Sea–Bashi Strait–Pacific Ocean
Route B: Sanya base–South China Sea–Mindoro Strait–Sulu Sea–Sibutu Passage–Celebes Sea–South of Mindanao Island–Pacific Ocean
Route C: Sanya base–South China Sea–Mindoro Strait–Sulu Sea–Sibutu Passage–Celebes Sea–Makassar Strait–Lombok Strait–Indian Ocean.

The situation in the East China Sea is much worse than the South China Sea and unfavorable to China. Japan's Southwestern Islands, stretching from Kyushu to Taiwan, practically become a "1000 km-long dam" that places huge corks in several key drainage gates/chokepoints there. Further, the PLA-N has to take into account the JMSDF's robust fighting capabilities that are the most capable in Asia. In this context, if China tries to deploy PLA-N and PLA-AF forces and units through Japan's Southwestern Island chain against the US, it would have to remove and annihilate JSDF forces that are tasked with conducting island defense and chokepoint control operations. In this case, PLA operations against the JMSDF will be complicated. As the most capable and reliable allied country of the US, Japan's defense operations can counter the PLA-N and prevent China from controlling these key chokepoints in the island chain. In both the South China and East China Sea, the god-created geography does not support China's A2AD strategy, China can self-righteously construct illegal artificial islands in the South China Sea, but it cannot change this geography and the unfavorable location of these islands (Map 2.1).

Chokepoint control operations by US allies and friendly countries around the two seas could impose substantial barriers to PLA-N out of the area operations. For example, Japan can physically block the chokepoints in its southwestern islands chain, thereby preventing PLA-N units from transiting out to the open oceans to fight US naval forces. Additionally, the JMSDF is capable of controlling the Bashi Strait in the outer high seas; and Australian forces may block and control the high-sea areas south of the Mindanao Island in the Philippines and the Lombok Strait in the Indonesian archipelago, if Australia accepts this role. Similarly, the Indian navy could control the waters outside the key chokepoints, such as the Malacca and Sunda Straits that connect the South China Sea

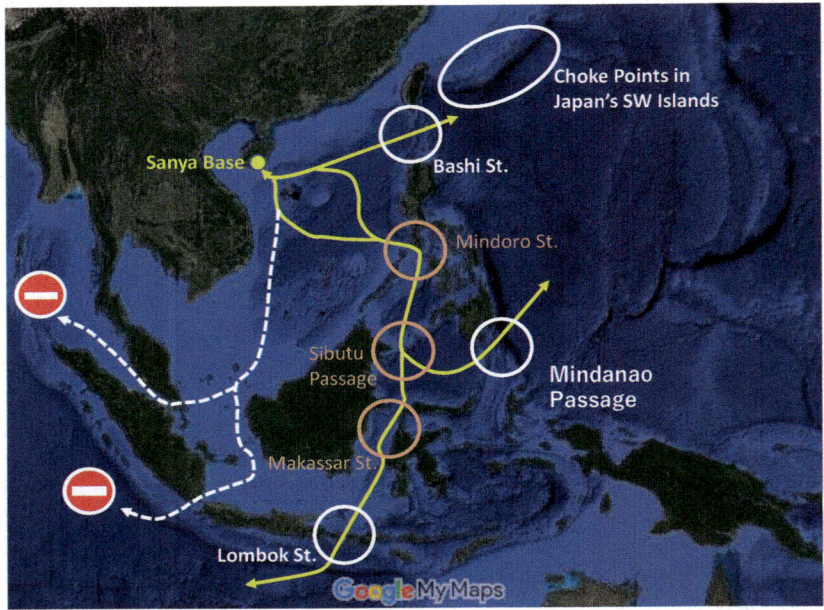

Map 2.1 Navigation routes in the Western Pacific

and the Indian Ocean. The constrictive geographic nature of its homewaters would be the most difficult obstacle preventing China's navy from becoming a real blue-water navy to support its A2AD strategy and the nation's foreign policy objectives. For China, a functioning USN–style blue-water navy with global-reach is the means to establish China's ultimate ambition of becoming a global power to replace the US. However, until China solves this difficult geographic problem it will remain a regional power in a military sense. China may have many options to overcome this problem, but it will have to pay a huge price for any solution. For Japan and the US, and perhaps Australia and India as well, these chokepoints surrounding China have been, and will be, "God given treasures" to deter China and the PLA-N. Japan carries a huge responsibility to control several chokepoints in the 1000 km-long southwestern islands chain that surrounds the East China Sea. The JSDF's new Island Defense Initiative, which envisages joint JSDF operations, would strengthen the defense posture of key islands located at the chokepoints (Defense of Japan 2019). This hardened island defense posture will substantially improve the JMSDF's chokepoint control operations. In this context, this new initiative for southwestern islands defense is Japan's strategy to counter China's A2AD.

Indispensable Strategic Elements: New Technologies

In order for Japan to deter the PLA-N from conducting aggressive operations against it, new and innovative technologies will be the key. In this way Japan can meet China's A2AD challenge. In addition to fleet anti-ship ballistic missile defenses, new and innovative technologies for anti-submarine warfare (ASW) operations will be vital for the JMSDF. There are several existing programs for the JMSDF to improve its ASW capabilities for SLOC protection, such as Bi/Multistatic sonar operations and new non-acoustic sensors. Additionally, below are some examples of new technologies, which pose a challenge for the JMSDF and the regional navies as well, including (1) Command, Control, Communications & Computers, and Intelligence, Surveillance & Reconnaissance (C4ISR), and Artificial Intelligence (AI). In all military operations, C4ISR capabilities are key factors for successful operations. In any C4ISR theater or domain, new technologies, such as surveillance from space, intelligence collection by extremely long-endurance un-manned aircraft, sea-bed acoustic devices, and deployable/expandable sensors, which are supported by artificial intelligence (AI) and advanced data-processing systems, will be game-changers for the JMSDF's future maritime operations. ASW will be most important for SLOC protection and chokepoint operations. (2) Un-manned Vehicles; both large and small long-endurance un-manned air (UAV), un-manned surface (USV), and un-manned underwater (UUV) vehicles have a huge potential to complement, but not to replace, conventional manned systems and platforms. In this regard, it is clear that the relationship between manned vehicles and un-manned vehicles must not be mutually exclusive but should be mutually complementary in nature. The deployment of low-cost, medium/high-performance un-manned vehicles in large numbers will extensively make-up for the inherent personnel risks involved in using existing manned systems. At the same time, the use of artificial intelligence (AI) will substantially improve the latest un-manned vehicles' autonomous capabilities, independent from controlling (mother) units at sea or on land. There are several key supporting technologies for un-manned vehicles. The first are extremely high-performance onboard energy-sources with longer endurance at right power-output with minimum size and weight. The second are ultra-low energy consuming onboard devices of all types, including AI, digital devices, and electrical/mechanical/hydraulic systems. The third are onboard external communication systems for command/control and data exchange between other un-manned and/or manned systems as well as shore stations. The keys for the success of un-manned systems include AI supported autonomy and real-time precise and real-time communications with friendly systems. (3) Naval Mines; one almost forgotten combat system after the end of the Cold War was the naval mine. AI and new sensors, supported by the latest acoustic and data-processing technologies, have the potential to transform not only mine laying and sweeping, but also overall naval operations. Those operations conducted at chokepoints can fully meet future maritime high-end war requirements. New types of advanced mines will enable any navy to deploy a much smaller number of mines to meet its operational objectives, and much more efficiently than in the past. These AI mines will be most suitable for offensive mining at the mouth of enemy ports/bases, and defensive mine-operations at strategic chokepoints and at key islands preventing landing by enemies. These AI mines will be able to attack the right target, at the right place, at the right time in full compliance with the national strategy.

Why Indo-Pacific Region, Not Pacific Ocean or South China Sea?

Before making any conclusive comment, it is necessary to reiterate the strategic significance and value of the Indo-Pacific region in constructing a functioning security posture to counter China's A2AD. It is crystal clear that China more than ever has been conducting more assertive and self-righteous maneuvers in the South China Sea since the turn of the century. The situation in the South China Sea has become a matter of urgent concern not only for coastal states but also for external powers the US, Japan, Australia, India, and France as well as the UK. From a geopolitical point of view, it is natural and necessary to expand our strategic vision from the South China Sea into the wider Indo-Pacific region. China's national interest is to support its rapidly growing economy for which it needs to secure its SLOCs that connect its trade with the mainland. For this purpose, China has to build blue-water naval forces capable of conducting far distant operations. In this context, China's security and strategic vision goes beyond the South China Sea and extends to the globe. A2AD is the PLA's tailored strategy to fully meet and realize China's national objectives and to secure national interests globally. If China's A2AD objective is successfully achieved, it is clear that it would be able to deploy its capable naval power through the South China Sea, except toward China's mainland in the north. From the maritime strategy and operations point of view, China's security objectives embrace an easterly direction toward the Western Pacific and a western direction toward the Indian Ocean, as well as southerly directions toward the Indonesian–Malaysian archipelago and Australian waters. This is the main value of the Indo-Pacific region for China. Without understanding this vast picture, stretching from the Pacific to the Indian Oceans, and from the Arctic to Antarctic Oceans, Japan, and US would fail to deal with China's strategy properly. A simple focus on the troublesome South China Sea is the most dangerous and mistaken policy for both Japan and US.

In order for Japan and US to counter China's A2AD, US forces should retain their global deployments and maintain operational flexibility to conduct any type of counter A2AD operations from all sectors around China. This is most important for US military planning and force build-up. In a crisis and war situation with China, it is possible that the US would deploy its forces not only through the Pacific Ocean, but also from Australis toward conflict areas around China. There are two other deployment areas for the US, one is from the east coast of the US across the Atlantic Ocean, through the Mediterranean Sea and the Suez Canal, then the Red Sea to the Indian Ocean. Another would be followed by US forces in Europe which is almost the same route but starting from the Mediterranean Sea. In some situations, these forces may take the southern course, all the way from the Atlantic Ocean around the Cape of Good Hope to the Indian Ocean. It should not be forgotten that a little less than a half of US naval forces are stationed along the east coast of the US, and some in Europe. The US could deploy all possible forces globally from anywhere in the world to attack China from any direction. This global deployment posture of US forces really makes China's planning against US counter A2AD maneuvers difficult and complicated. However, if China seizes the Pratas atolls from Taiwan and fortifies them as it has some of the features in the Spratlys, it would be extremely difficult for the USN and JMSDF to pass though the Bashi Strait between Taiwan and the Philippines to enter the South China Sea. The Bashi Strait is the most familiar and natural route to pass into the South China Sea and Taiwan can control passage through it as Pratas atolls sit just west of the Bashi Strait and south of Hong Kong. They are important to maintain sea-control over the Northeastern part of the South China Sea. The Pratas atolls could be an easy target for China to seize for sea-control purposes and to create an unfavorable operational environment for both JMSDF and USN. The Pratas atolls are an ideal litmus test of Japanese and US determination to protect Taiwan if China resorts to an invasion and both countries should be fully prepared for this scenario.

Conclusion

The PLA-N has the potential to become a real "blue-water" navy and a strong competitor for the US and Japanese navies. In order for the JMSDF and USN to cope with China's new challenges, new strategic and tactical initiatives will be required such as Fleet Ballistic Missile Defense (F-BMD) systems to fully protect US reinforcements, crossing the Pacific Ocean or the Indian Ocean as well as from Australia. Without this capability, their efforts to protect their capital naval assets by countering Chinese ASBMs will be in vain and would simply accelerate China's aggressive maneuvers under A2AD. This initiative is a matter of urgency for both Japan and the US as leading naval powers. Also, for Vietnam and the Philippines, the effective use of geographic proximity to China's strategic spots, such as Hainan and Woody islands as well as Chinese militarized features in the Spratlys, will be very important. Building and maintaining deterrence against China's assertive maneuvers will be an indispensable requirement for the stability of the South China Sea and beyond. The long-range surface to surface land attack missile capability deployed by both the US and Japan will certainly be a game-changer when realized. It should also be noted that the construction of domain awareness networks in the South China Sea among like–minded countries is necessary and should be realized. At the same time, China faces a fatal obstacle in pursuing its A2AD strategy as the chokepoints would, in a worst-case scenario, be fully blocked by adversary forces. They may prevent PLA-N vessels from breaking out from the semi-closed South and East China Seas and reaching the outer oceans. However, Japan and US alone cannot take full control of these chokepoints, so close cooperation with like-minded countries that share a common concern would be vital in countering China's A2AD. This is the reason why Japan has been trying to take the lead in promoting the Quadrilateral Security Dialogue (Quad) since 2007 (Chellaney 2007). For this reason, India will be important to realize the Quad as its navy controls the Bay of Bengal, and the Andaman Sea at the northern mouth of the Malacca Strait. In addition to India, for Japan and the US, close cooperation between Vietnam, the Philippine, and Indonesia is indispensable. It is also important for them to maintain best possible relations with other maritime powers in the region, especially, Singapore and Malaysia, as two key nations. These two countries have strategic value because they hold the Malacca Strait, together with Indonesia and Thailand. They are important for chokepoint control in contingencies or war time. Of course, a close relationship with Thailand as well as Cambodia would be indispensable.

It is no secret that Japan and the US would develop chokepoint control capabilities and postures to counter China's A2AD. If these countries could come together in security cooperation, a network would be created with the intent and capability to exercise direct control over the chokepoints around the South China Sea to deter China. In the best scenario, Quad member navies would be engaged in chokepoint control operations in the high seas. Chokepoint control in the East China Sea is the sole responsibility of Japan, and was mentioned previously, the JSDF has launched a new initiative called Southwestern Islands Defense to improve its capability to control the chokepoints there. In spite of its quickly growing national capabilities propelled by its strong economy, China will face many problems in trying to build-up the PLA-N into a force which can operate powerfully on the open seas. Therefore, Japan and US will need to counter China's strategy by precise coordination and focusing on its Achilles Heel, which is the semi-enclosed nature of the South China and East China Seas. The first key question for Japan and the US is how to be assured of wartime control of these strategic chokepoints. To maintain an advantageous position over the PLA, Japan and the US will have to retain the capability to keep the big "wild birds" (the PLA-N and the PLA Air Force) in their naturally formed "god given" cages of the First Island Chain surrounding the South China and East China Seas. In addition to this, the US forces supported by Japan/JSDF will keep a permanent presence, mainly in the South China Sea, and some in the East China Sea to deter and fight China's assertive actions. This also prevents China from using its military power as a support measure to influence the nation's policies both in the SCS and outer international theater. The second key question is how Japan and the US can help the regional states construct a relatively small but effective strategic deterrent posture against China, and to promote Multi-Domain Awareness Networks in the South China Sea. In order for Japan and US to realize these key initiatives, they will need to develop an aligned strategy and mutual capability at the earliest opportunity to deter China's adventurism.

References

This article represents the personal opinions of the author and not any official position of the JMJSDF or the Government of Japan.

Asia Maritime Transparency CSIS "China Island Tracker" https://search.yahoo.co.jp/search?p=China%27s+Artificial+Islands+AMTI&fr=top_yam19h1_ext_sa&ei=UTF-8&ts=25835&aq=-1&oq=&at=&ai=e.nsjdj6QzibI0Gp2vhJZA.

China Daily 2014, Potential of the Chinese Dream 26 March 2014.

Defense of Japan 2019, Ministry of Defense, Japan, Part-III: Three Pillars of Japan's Defense, https://www.mod.go.jp/e/publ/w_paper/2019.html.

Long Drake 2018, "Chinese Air Force Lands First Bomber on Disputed Woody Island in South China Sea" Defense Post, May 18, https://www.thedefensepost.com/2018/05/18/china-bomber-lands-woody-island/.

Chellaney Brahma 2007, "'Quad Initiative': An Inharmonious Concert of Democracies" *Japan Times*, 19 July, https://www.japantimes.co.jp/opinion/2007/07/19/commentary/quad-initiative-an-inharmonious-concert-of-democracies/#.Xr0qRDh7k2w.

McDevitt Michael and Saunders Phillip 2011, "The PLA Navy's Anti Access Role in Taiwan Contingency" 191 National Defense University Press, 2011.

Nakazawa Katsuji 2019, "Xi Makes Waves in South China Sea Ahead of Summer Conclave—'Missile Test' Around Time of G-20 Shows Posturing to Elders Going to Beidaihe" Nikkei, July 11, https://search.yahoo.co.jp/search?p=Obama-Xi+agreement+on+non-militarization+of+the+South+China+Sea&fr=top_yam19h1_ext_sa&ei=UTF-8&ts=32482&aq=-1&oq=&at=&ai=o.HUCi8PTYOrovhuj_0qcA.

Brunnstrom David 2016a, "China Installs Weapons Systems on Artificial Islands: U.S. Think Tank" Reuters, December 14, https://www.reuters.com/article/us-southchinasea-china-arms/exclusive-china-installs-weapons-systems-on-artificial-islands-u-s-think-tank-idUSKBN1431OK.

Wee Sui-Lee and Blanchard Ben 2016b, "China Mounts Detailed Defense of South China Sea Reclamation" Reuters, December 14, https://www.reuters.com/article/us-china-southchinasea-reef/china-mounts-detailed-defense-of-south-china-sea-reclamation-iduskbn0n001n20150409.

Panda Ankit 2015, "Chinese J-11 Fighters Exercise in the South China Sea After US Navy Patrols" *The Diplomat*, November 2, https://thediplomat.com/2015/11/chinese-j-11-fighters-exercise-in-the-south-china-sea-after-us-navy-patrols/.

Stashwick Steven 2016, "New Weapons on China's Artificial Islands Don't Violate 'Non-Militarization' of South China Sea—Installation May Raise Tensions, But China Has Long Excluded 'Necessary Defense' from Its Pledge" *The Diplomat*, December 30, https://thediplomat.com/2016/12/new-weapons-on-chinas-artificial-islands-dont-violate-non-militarization-of-south-china-sea/.

Ushirogata Keitaro 2017, "Comparative Research on Changes of Military Strategy in Maritime Domain, from 1980 to 2017—From Viewpoint of Area Denial, SLOCs Defense, SLOCs Interruption, and Power Projection" November 2017 (In Japanese translation by author).

CHAPTER 3

China's Gray Zone Operations in the South China Sea; Manipulating Weaknesses

Martin A. Sebastian

INTRODUCTION

China's maritime sovereignty claims in the South China Sea are sending shock waves to the ASEAN claimant states, Malaysia, Vietnam, the Philippines, and Brunei. While China continues to exert its influence in the South China Sea, the continued use of large coast guard vessels called white hulls, maritime militia, and military-trained fishermen to harass claimant states has drawn much attention. Research vessels double up as information gatherers to better understand the landscape. The pursuit of strategic supremacy and marine resources has made China more aggressive, operating in a dubious conceptual space between peace and war, called gray zone operations. These tactics involve coercive actions below a threshold that could typically prompt a conventional military response. Gray zone operations are cost-effective and easy to deploy for China. Normally in pursuit of foreign policy, the military is often used as an instrument of foreign policy because it can be deployed far from the

M. A. Sebastian (✉)
Maritime Institute of Malaysia, Kuala Lumpur, Malaysia

© The Author(s), under exclusive license to Springer Nature Switzerland AG 2021
L. Buszynski and D. T. Hai (eds.), *Maritime Issues and Regional Order in the Indo-Pacific*, Palgrave Studies in Maritime Politics and Security, https://doi.org/10.1007/978-3-030-68038-1_3

state. However, in the case of China, its dubious claims in the South China Sea are enforced through a cunning tactic. This is where China's use of white hulls or law enforcement vessels mask their true intentions since they are directed by military commanders under the Central Military Commission. They show a civilian front with military backing and leadership. This way, law enforcement vessels are best used as instruments of foreign policy instead of military vessels which serves a number of purposes. Firstly, China knows well that by putting on a law enforcement front, other countries will avoid confrontation with China's seemingly harmless white hulls. They will not resort to a response by naval vessels or gray hulls and they will be forced to deploy law enforcement vessels. This is because, regardless of their size, the very firepower of gray hulls will be viewed as excessive and provocative. Secondly, China uses large white hulls which can stay longer at sea while being replenished by offshore stations and operating in the far reaches of China's claim under the nine-dash line. Thirdly, the seemingly harmless white hull vessel with minimal ordnance can actually be packed with extensive communication and intelligence gathering equipment which can connect is to China's gray hulls, the air force, maritime militia, and other auxiliaries as and when required. Fourthly, the ASEAN claimant states are no match for China's large white hulls as their own white hulls are relatively small and intended for coastal policing duties. They do not have the endurance or the ability to "shadow" the presence of China's white hulls for long periods. Finally, a collision between China's white hulls and the gray hulls of the ASEAN claimant states could result in irreparable damage for the gray hulls, like a collision between a truck and a Ferrari. As gray hulls are expensive purchases and limited in number, if they are put out of service by a collision, the combat readiness of the affected ASEAN claimant state will be reduced. This is why they rarely try to engage with China's white hulls.

WHITE AND GRAY HULLS—COASTGUARDS AND NAVIES

White hulls are essentially policemen at sea. They are to exercise national jurisdiction and safeguard sovereign rights over maritime zones and to deter and suppress unlawful activities. They are rarely reported to leave national waters to enforce national laws and engage non-state actors. White hulls are cheap to operate as they do not have sophisticated weapons and expensive systems. They are just the "boats on the beat."

The exercise of national jurisdiction is conducted by law enforcement officers on these white hulls through the powers granted to them by the national authority. In so doing, white hulls are also prepared for maritime safety issues like search and rescue, disaster relief, navigation safety checks, and other non-military duties. As part of an agency of service to the maritime community, these vessels are much like a police patrol car showing its presence at sea and working in concert with coastal communities, Community Service Organizations (CSOs), Public Service Organizations (PSOs), relevant Non-Governmental Organizations (NGOs) as well as Inter-Governmental Organizations (IGOs). In this way they become integrated into a system of good governance at sea and this may be why they were called coast guards in the first place. While collaborating with stakeholders on ocean governance, while hulls engage in information collection, crime scene investigation (CSI) and forensics to ensure that the laws are applied justly. The Rules for the Use of Force (RUF) by white hulls, are generally based on the small caliber and non-lethal weapons which reduce the risk of fatalities and permanent injury in a variety of scenarios. Positive visual criteria are paramount and lethal force is generally applied in self-defense. Force is applied mainly to disable and not to neutralize. Cases are to be thoroughly investigated and are to be submitted to the long arm of the law which will decide whether an offence has been committed and whether conviction is necessary.

Navies, or gray hulls, are instruments of foreign policy. They are trained for combat at sea. The competency of the crew and the combat systems form a symbiotic relationship through man–machine interfaces to maintain an operational tempo to sustain combat operations and deliver payloads at sea and from the sea. They generally participate in maneuvers among themselves or with other friendly nations when within national waters. They often leave these waters for flag-showing visits, participate in collective security, coalition/allied operations or simply conduct capability enhancement or capacity building exercises. The weapons of today's navies are designed for full-spectrum operations, multi-mission tasks and include long-range weapons of mass destruction. Navies are designed to act against formed military units, like their sister services, the air force, and army. The Rules of Engagements (RoE) are governed by the principles of proportionality in accordance with the Laws of Armed Conflict (LOAC) and other instruments of International Humanitarian Laws. Since these vessels are costly, armed, and ready for combat, their readiness and operations are carefully planned. They are not usually used for routine law enforcement patrols when there are coast guard vessels available. That would be like taking an Armored Personnel Carrier (APC) for a street patrol instead of a police patrol car. However, military forces do have the capability to support law enforcement operations through high-technology location detection like communication and signal intercepts. Many military vessels carry helicopters that carry sophisticated equipment for surveillance, intelligence, and even firepower. These can identify, track, and intercept target vessels individually or in concert with other assets. They can also operate faster and far beyond the range of surface vessels. Many countries use their navies as assets for law enforcement; however, this task is carried out by law enforcement detachment (LEDets) onboard. These incidents are then handed over to Investigation Officers (IO) when these ships come ashore. There are many limitations and constraints should they go to the courts.

China has an ambiguous maritime security apparatus which manipulates the common understanding of maritime security. Firstly, in 2018, the Chinese Coast Guard was placed under the People's Armed Police which is governed by the Central Military Commission (CMC). This integration means that the Coast Guard is actually a paramilitary force and not a law enforcement agency. There have been reports that the Chinese Coast Guard is now headed by a Rear Admiral who previously took part in the navy's mission in the Gulf of Aden, and was deputy chief of staff of the East Sea Fleet that was responsible for Taiwan and the East China Sea (Ng and Zhou 2019). In addition, China has also developed a maritime militia with ambiguous powers at sea (Erickson 2016). This third force, trained to fulfill coercive roles, has been involved in many incidents in the South China Sea. The use of large white hulls, navies, and maritime militia in combination with so-called gray zone operations is meant to intimidate and disrupt smaller and weaker countries and, at the same time, to avoid provoking the better equipped and competent navies of external powers. The idea is to make these forces look like bullies as they respond to Chinese actions while China is bullying the smaller ASEAN claimants with impunity.

White Hulls as Law Enforcement Entities

Accurate information is required when exercising the rule of law, and when making decisions on the management and jurisdiction in the maritime zones. As jurisdiction issues come into play, white hulls specialize in law enforcement issues, especially in establishing the facts of the case for investigations. Information collection is necessary before cases can be referred through Investigation Papers (IP) to the Public Prosecutor's office for possible conviction and thereafter to the courts. Investigations are conducted through a number of sources either from a shared awareness network or collaborative partners. White hulls can obtain this information in a number of ways by resort to systems that are openly available like Automatic Identification Systems (AIS) and Long-Range Identification and Tracking (LRIT) systems, Synthetic Aperture Radar (SAR), Visible Infrared Imaging Radiometer Suite (VIIRS), human, communications, and signal intelligence. There are many other Open Source Intelligence (OSINT) means that can track ships and offer pattern analysis. There are also coastal community organizations such as Greenpeace, Global Fishing Watch, and SecureFisheries that are available to provide information and can be used by Governments to address, illegal fishing activities. Asia Maritime Transparency Initiative (AMTI) provides tracking information on Chinese activities in the South China Sea so that claimant states could address these in a collective manner. Illegal Unreported and Unregulated (IUU) fishing, including destructive fishing with cyanides and explosives, is being addressed by IUU ombudsmen in various organizations. As a counter to Chinese white hulls, ASEAN claimant states can deploy leased hulls from Offshore Support Vessels (OSV) which can carry high-speed interceptors with rigid inflatable boats and Unmanned Aerial Vehicles (UAVs). These vessels can be spread out to show their presence and collect information while collaborating with national fishing vessels and offshore gas/oil installations. Law Enforcement Detachments (LEDets) can be on any vessel and can act according to the authority granted to them. They also can be placed onboard naval vessels to monitor maritime territory and provide coordination with white hulls that are deployed. White hulls can collaborate with a number of stakeholders in managing maritime zones, allowing them to detect nodes, disrupt networks, destroy syndicates, and to deter and suppress maritime crimes. White hulls must also bridge the land-sea nexus to better provide information for the political leaders to make the necessary decisions. Executive decision-making must be paramount in safeguarding maritime zones and resources. In taking a collective and innovative approach, the ASEAN claimant states can use white hulls to counter China's aggressive moves in the South China Sea.

China, ASEAN, and the South China Sea

ASEAN has always been a fragmented grouping as member states are divided over maritime boundary issues. This has been a weakness that has been easily manipulated by China in advancing its claims in the South China Sea. China exploits the weak political systems within ASEAN member states as weak governments and corrupt politicians facilitate China's moves at sea. ASEAN made its first strategic mistake by making the South China Sea a claimant state issue and not a collective issue. This decision tragically divides the 10 ASEAN members into just four claimant states and six non-claimants. With only four claimant states to counter China's bold moves in the South China Sea, ASEAN is left weak and those that face China's ambitions are threatened. Vietnam and Philippines both testify to this strategic mistake. As a regional grouping, ASEAN should have resisted China as an aggressor in the South China Sea. Weak political systems in ASEAN also vulnerable to China's charm offensives when comes to delivering interesting projects under the Belt and Road Initiative (BRI). Many ASEAN politicians saw this as a gold mine which added to China's soft power on land and created favorable conditions for its hard power at sea to resist any intervention from other external powers.

Unfortunately, ASEAN's collective weakness and the weaknesses of member states' political systems strengthened China's determination to plough through the South China Sea with its ambitions. The 2002 Declaration of Conduct of Parties on the South China Sea (2002 DOC), the numerous China-ASEAN Group meetings on the DOC, in addition to other meetings on the future Code of Conduct (CoC) were manipulative tactics to convince the global community that China was engaging its regional neighbors diplomatically. At the same time, China would cast external powers trying to make sense of this manipulation as the bad guys on the block. Without an openly forceful stance, China took the opportunity to build structures on atolls in the South China Sea, fortifying the features it occupied into militarized offshore stations and staging areas to support its onward military operations. ASEAN's weaknesses became its own nemesis in allowing China to extend white hull operations where any military intervention would be seen as an act of war. The many incidents that have taken place involving China's white hulls, maritime militia, and other support vessels in the South China Sea were ASEAN's own undoing as a regional grouping and is proof that as a fragmented regional grouping ASEAN unable to address the issues of the South China Sea.

Sovereign Rights—The Battle for Marine Resources

China's excessive sovereignty claims in the South China Sea have impacted upon the ASEAN claimant states in many ways. Firstly, more foreign powers have sent naval vessels into the area and the respective Exclusive Economic Zones (EEZs) of the claimants. China's white and gray hulls are not bed fellows with American gray hulls and there have been many incidents between them. Any error could lead to friction and may develop into a skirmish or worst, a conflict. Secondly, ASEAN must recognize that China's aggressive behavior in the South China Sea will continue as it seeks to exercise its authority over the marine resources of the area. Those resources are both living and non-living. As for living resources, the South China Sea is rich with biodiversity and fisheries which provide a staple diet for coastal countries like Vietnam, Philippines, Indonesia, and Thailand. We are yet to determine the damage caused by the extensive militarization in the South China Sea that has taken place over the past few years. Scientific data including Fish Stock Assessment (FSA) and Maximum Sustainable Yield (MSY) has not been thoroughly collected which makes it difficult to ascertain the situation. Many coral reefs, which are necessary to maintain the biodiversity of the sea, have been reportedly destroyed. No measures for fishery management have been put in place, let alone to safeguard the fragile marine biodiversity in the face of a possible natural or man-made disaster which involves oil/gas platforms. There have been many instances where fishermen from the claimant states have been harassed and intimidated. In one incident in June 2019, a 22-man Filipino fishing boat was reportedly rammed by a Chinese vessel in disputed waters at Reed Bank (Dancel 2019). Though the crew was saved, the fact that the Chinese vessel left the scene after the ramming became national headlines and received international condemnation. However, the incident did not sour the relationship between the two countries. This is not the first ramming incident. In the Paracels, Chinese fishing vessels rammed a Vietnamese fishing vessel at Discovery Reef in March 2019 (Viet Tuan 2019). Reportedly, Vietnamese fishing vessels were regularly attacked and robbed in April and May 2019. In 2016, over 100 Chinese fishing vessels were spotted off Sarawak, Malaysia. A maritime militia vessel rammed a Malaysian Maritime Enforcement Agency (MMEA) vessel in the same year resulting in a gaping hole. Indonesia has reported that Chinese Coast Guard vessels continue to forcibly prevent the apprehension of Chinese fishing vessels poaching in the waters around the Natuna Islands in Indonesia's EEZ. Indonesia has been protecting its marine living resources and has destroyed fishing vessels caught poaching in this area. Although Indonesia is not a claimant state, two high-profile incidents near the Natuna Islands in 2016 intensified its concern over the South China Sea. Violations of Indonesia's EEZ by Chinese fishermen and interference by the Chinese Coast Guard resulted in the establishment of a Fishing Zone and Integrated Marine and Fisheries Center in the islands (Asmara and Syamsudin 2019). In 2018, the Indonesian military inaugurated an integrated unit in the Natunas which will become part of the Regional Defense Joint Command, including the Army, Air Force, and Navy.

As for non-living resources, proved oil and gas reserves in the South China Sea are very modest on a global scale, and only about 20% of those reserves are located in disputed areas. Proved and probable gas reserves in the South China Sea (190 trillion cubic feet, 2.9% of global reserves) are more significant than those of oil (11 billion barrels, 0.6% of global reserves) (U.S. Energy Information Administration 2013). The South China Sea is home to a number of offshore oil and gas platforms which provide claimant states with necessary revenue. Malaysia has a number of offshore platforms in the disputed area, and so do Vietnam and Brunei. Revenue from this non-renewable energy is arranged through Production Sharing Contracts (PSC) and hence the confidence of international partners is necessary in ensuring the continuation of these projects. Malaysia's offshore oil and gas platforms are all situated in the South China Sea and while exploiting this resource Malaysia has encountered a number of issues with its neighbors. These issues have been resolved either through the negotiation of Joint Development such as those with Thailand, or Joint Commercial Areas as with Vietnam, or cooperative agreements over the CA1 and CA2 Deepwater Offshore Blocks with Brunei (The Star 13 December 2010).

However, to engage China in joint development will demand that Malaysia recognize China's sovereignty claims and accept China as a neighbor. China has not relinquished its sovereignty claims under the nine-dash line and the risks are apparent for Malaysia. China is free to bid for production sharing contracts (PSCs) in the various designated blocks but not as a stakeholder in the resource. In so far as Malaysia is concerned, there have been numerous reports on the aggressive maneuvers by China's white hulls. Reports vary from high-speed maneuvers by Chinese vessels to disrupt offshore exploration and send warnings to Malaysians that the area is under Chinese jurisdiction. Chinese Coast Guard vessels and seismic survey vessels continue to ply areas claimed by Malaysia with impunity. Nonetheless, these activities have not endangered lives or hindered the production of oil and gas in the Malaysian EEZ. These actions have been dealt through quiet diplomacy through the exchange of diplomatic notes.

Due to its proximity to China, Vietnam is not as lucky. Vietnam views the importance of marine non-living resources very seriously and is at pains to protect them. The China Vietnam Hai Yang Shi You 981 oil rig crisis reminds us of the importance of fossil fuel/gas and the implications for the Vietnamese economy. In 2018, Vietnam ordered the Spanish energy firm Repsol to suspend its Red Emperor Project off the country's southeastern coast (Reuters 2018). This was the second time in less than a year that Vietnam had cancelled a major oil development in the South China Sea under pressure from China. Vietnam's largest gas project, the Blue Whale Project, reportedly contains large gas reserves, and production is expected to begin in late 2023. Of late, there have been rumors that Exxon Mobil, which has a 64% stake in the project may withdraw due to harassment by China (Clark 2019).

In one incident. In July 2019, China's survey ship Haiyang Dizhi 8, along with Coast Guard, Navy, and Maritime Militia escort ships, entered into Vietnam's EEZ near Vanguard Bank. Over 20 Chinese ships were deployed while Vietnam tried to protect the Hakuyru-5, the Japanese supplied research platform deployed by Vietnam and Russia for joint exploration. Besides engaging the United States, Russia, and Spain, Vietnam has also engaged India in offshore exploration through ONGC Videsh Ltd. The company is seeking the 6th extension for a two-year contract to explore Block 128 where China's nine-dash line crosses the Vietnamese claim (Press Trust of India 2019). The Philippines, on the other hand, is well underway to conduct joint exploration with China. Exploration in Recto Bank (or Reed Bank as it is known internationally) is close to the current Malampaya Fields near Palawan Island. It was reported that China has agreed that Philippines had sovereign rights over the area and wants to share the resources so the joint exploration agreement with China may give Philippines a 60-40 advantage (Tordesillas 2019). In 2013, Brunei and China discussed joint exploration between their oil companies. It was reported later that they entered into an agreement to jointly exploit oil and gas resources. However, the report also added that further progress on joint development will depend on the progress of the Code of Conduct (Zhen 2018). While being aggressive toward Vietnam, China has manipulated the other claimant states by showing a cooperative face in the exploration of the marine non-living resource. This manipulation gives China the advantage and leaves Vietnam alone in addressing these issues.

Conclusion

China's ability to manipulate weakness in a way is a warning to the countries of the Indo-Pacific region to examine the fractures within their political systems, be it in diplomacy, politics, finance, or security. China's uncanny ability to identify these weakness gives it an edge and allows it to continue being aggressive and to escape international condemnation with impunity. The fact that since 2002, China has been able to build so many structures at sea, escape illegal exploitation of marine resources, and aggressively act against the littoral states is testimony to these weaknesses. The South China Sea has exposed fractures in the international and regional orders and also within the national systems. It is time for the international community to stand fast against China's actions as in a matter of time, they will spread into the Indian and Pacific Oceans. Already, we are seeing creeping ventures with smaller states on both sides of the oceans which are connected to the South China Sea. The operational expansion of China's white hulls and their link with China's gray hulls and air force and maritime militia is a forewarning of what is to come. China's offshore stations in the South China Sea coupled with its ability to produce more assets at sea could overwhelm the presence of any competing powers. In addressing China's aggressiveness, the claimant states should not be pushed into an arms race and should be careful to balance cost against the value of maritime security to deploy a number of approaches to safeguard their interests. China has proven that there are cheaper alternatives to expensive military vessels. This is truly a case where might may be seen to be right. In response, collective regional and global effort is required that will encourage China to be a more responsible power. Safeguarding peace in the region should be a shared responsibility to ensure that the South China Sea will be a sea of prosperity and not a sea of adversity. When countries can come together to stop devastation on land and to address depleting jungles, endangered indigenous communities and wildlife, as well as polluted rivers, they should be able to do the same at sea. Only when the international community is serious about the South China Sea can the security of the Indo-Pacific region can be assured.

REFERENCES

Asmara, T. and Syamsudin, A. (2019), "Indonesia to Build an Integrated Marine and Fisheries Centre," BenarNews, 26 Feb.

Dancel, R. (2019). "Chinese Vessel sinks Filipino Fishing Boat in Contested Waters," *The Straits Times*, 12 June.

Clark, H. (2019), "Rumours Exxon Mobil to Quit Vietnam Gas Field," Energy News Bulletin, 11 Sept.

Erickson, A. S. (2016), "Countering China's Third Sea Force: Unmask Maritime Militia before they are Used Again," *The National Interest*, 6 June.

Ng, T. and Zhou, L. (2019) "China Coast Guard Heads to Front Line to Enforce Beijing South China Sea Claims," *South China Morning Post*, 9 Feb.

Press Trust of India (2019). "ONGC Videsh Seeks 2 Year Extension for Exploring Vietnamese Oil Block," Bloomberg, 2 Sept.

Reuters (2018), "Vietnam Scraps South China Sea Oil Drilling Project Under Pressure from Beijing," 23 Mar.

Then, S. (2010). "Malaysia and Brunei Ink Historic Pact for Oil Exploration," *The Star Online*, 13 Dec.

Tordesillas, E. S. (2019). "What China, Philippines Will Get from Joint Exploration," ABC-CBN News, 2 Sept.

U.S. Energy Information Administration. (2013), "South China Sea," 7 Feb. www.eia.gov/beta/international/analysis_includes/regions_of_interest/South_China_Sea/south_china_sea.pdf/.

Viet Tuan (2019), "Chinese Ship Sinks Vietnamese Fishing Vessel Boast off Paracel Islands," *VnExpress*, 7 March.

Zhen, L. (2018), "China and Brunei to Step Up Oil and Gas Development in Disputed South China Sea," *South China Morning Post*, 19 November.

CHAPTER 4

The Philippine Pivot to China: Threat to Stability in the West Philippine Sea

Marites Dañguilan Vitug

INTRODUCTION

Two momentous events happened in the Philippines in 2016, both with far-reaching impact on the country and its foreign policy. On June 30, a new president, Rodrigo Duterte, assumed office. Weeks later, on July 12, 2016, the Philippines won a historic and overwhelming victory in its maritime dispute against China. However, President Rodrigo Duterte's pivot toward China has threatened Philippine sovereign rights over the West Philippine Sea (WPS). By disregarding the 2016 ruling of the international Arbitral Tribunal that invalidated China's nine-dash line, by not seeking the support of the international community in putting pressure on China to uphold the ruling, by not standing up to China's incursions in Philippine waters, and by framing false policy choices—either we talk to China or go to war—the President has weakened the position of the country as well as those of other claimants in ASEAN. As a result, the

---

M. D. Vitug (✉)
Rappler, Manila, Philippines
e-mail: marites.vitug@rappler.com

© The Author(s), under exclusive license to Springer Nature Switzerland AG 2021
L. Buszynski and D. T. Hai (eds.), *Maritime Issues and Regional Order in the Indo-Pacific*, Palgrave Studies in Maritime Politics and Security, https://doi.org/10.1007/978-3-030-68038-1_4

Chinese presence in the WPS has escalated and the Philippines is missing opportunities to use a number of diplomatic options to partly enforce the arbitral ruling, including working with ASEAN claimant countries.

The Arbitral Tribunal's Ruling

What happened on the day the international arbitration panel in The Hague released its ruling in the Philippine maritime case against China already indicated how the new government of Duterte would deal with China. On the evening of July 12, 2016, journalists gathered in the press room of the Department of Foreign Affairs (DFA), waiting for Foreign Secretary Perfecto Yasay to give the first official reaction of the Philippines to its sweeping victory in The Hague. A couple of hours earlier, the Permanent Court of Arbitration had announced the tribunal's decision, releasing the 500-page award on its website. The air was heavy with anticipation—and a hushed silence descended on the room as Yasay stood before the podium to read a prepared statement which was to be carried live on national TV. He appeared morose with no trace of a smile on his face.

> The Philippines welcomes the issuance today of the Award by the Arbitral Tribunal. Our experts are studying the Award with care and thoroughness that this significant arbitral outcome deserves. In the meantime, we call on all those concerned to exercise restraint and sobriety. The Philippines strongly affirms its respect for this milestone decision as an important contribution to ongoing efforts in addressing disputes in the South China Sea. The decision upholds international law, particularly the 1982 UNCLOS. The Philippines reiterates its abiding commitment to efforts to pursue the peaceful resolution and management of disputes with a view to promoting and enhancing peace and stability in the region. (Esmaquel 2016)

With his deliberate manner, Yasay took up three minutes to read the four-paragraph statement after which he hurriedly left. It was a surprising response to a landmark decision that garnered accolades from international legal circles and allies of the Philippines. "Without any other context, you might have thought he was delivering a eulogy," a columnist for CNBC observed (Soong 2016). Yet this was the culmination of the first ever international arbitration case on the South China Sea and gave the Philippines its shining moment. Questions arose: Why was the

Philippines so glum about a historic ruling that was on its side? Why did it choose to bury a euphoric moment instead of using the victory to galvanize a nation?

In the DFA under Foreign Secretary Jose Rene Almendras, who was foreign secretary in the last months of the Aquino administration in 2016, the victory scenario was to begin with a statement that would reflect the significant gains of the Philippines, celebrate the rule of law as a means to settle disputes and achieve peace. It would then call for international support for compliance with the ruling because there was no global policeman to enforce it. His predecessor, Albert del Rosario, under whose watch the arbitration case was filed, had already talked with representatives of various governments for statements of support if the Philippines won. They were expected to follow after the Philippines released its own statement. These countries were going to take the cue from the Philippines. But none of this ever came to be as the Award was issued soon after Aquino stepped down. Near Manila Bay, hundreds gathered to celebrate, released balloons and tossed flowers in the air hours before the ruling was released. When news on the victory spread, #Chexit, short for "China exit," rippled on Twitter. Demonstrators outside the Chinese embassy in Manila waved colorful streamers: China, respect the rights of our fishermen! #Chexit, China out of Ph waters! Some carried a makeshift fishing boat with a Philippine flag planted on it. Emblazoned on the boat was China, out of Philippine territory! As expected, China, in the most vehement terms, rejected the Arbitral Tribunal's ruling. *The People's Daily*, the mouthpiece of the Communist Party, slammed it as "biased" and called it a "political provocation…to violate China's territorial sovereignty, maritime rights over the South China Sea" (Sheng 2016).

However, underneath this apparent exterior that was completely dismissive of the arbitration and its results, which were humiliating for China, was a concern over how the outside world viewed the process. China reached out to the global community, actively put out its position in advertisements in international publications, opinion pieces as well as in video clips. Less than two weeks after the tribunal issued its award, a three-minute video featuring China's side was broadcast repeatedly on the giant screens of New York's Times Square, usually a domain of commercials and pop celebrities. "The video asserted that China's indisputable sovereignty over [the South China Sea islands] has sufficient historic and legal basis" and that the tribunal "vainly attempted to deny

China's territorial sovereignty and maritime rights and interests in the South China Sea," wrote Kate Parlett, an international arbitration lawyer (Parlett 2016). The video also made the point that "China did not participate in the illegal South China Sea arbitration, nor accepts the Award so as to defend the solemnity of international law."

Julian Ku, a Hofstra University law professor who followed the case closely, observed that "China's blizzard of editorials, op-eds by Chinese ambassadors...drew the attention of the global media like nothing else could." He wrote: "Such media gave foreign governments and NGOs a platform to opine on the importance of the award. When China reacted with clearly hostile and nearly frantic language, the global media had found its story. China, the newly risen power, was risking its global reputation in a now landmark international law ruling." In Ku's analysis, "China tried to denigrate through a global publicity campaign the entire legitimacy of a widely accepted international treaty regime. China was an UNCLOS signatory. By refusing to comply, it has reneged on its international obligation, damaged its image among its neighbors and partners around the world. China's global image has suffered a serious blow" (Ku 2016). China was one of the signatories to UNCLOS but it chose to stay outside it and continued to live with the fiction that it has "indisputable sovereignty" over the South China Sea, rejecting the judgment and a tenet countries should abide by, the rule of law. This made the Philippine victory both sweet and bitter. In reality, it was China that forced the Philippine government to seek a third-party arbitration. About two decades of diplomatic dialogues, consultations, back-and-forth cables led to a dead end. Another path had to be taken, another door had to be opened.

What the Philippines Won

It was a stunning victory on both jurisdiction and merits. The international Arbitral Tribunal of the Law of the Sea, formed under the auspices of the Permanent Court of Arbitration, accepted the case because, at its core, the Philippines sought an interpretation of the definitions of islands and rocks by the United Nations Convention on the Law of the Seas or UNCLOS—and the surrounding waters these were entitled to. After all, the seminal UNCLOS provided ways for countries to come together, present their cases to clear up misunderstandings and resolve conflicts over what certain provisions really meant. One of these venues was arbitration. Under the watch of President Benigno Aquino III, the Philippines decided to take China to an international court, triggered by its aggressive actions in Reed Bank and Scarborough Shoal. The tribunal agreed with most of the Philippines' arguments (13 out of 15), which essentially covered five key issues. The five judges ruled this way:

- On historic rights and the nine-dash line: China's claim of historic rights to resources in the waters of the South China Sea is illegal and not compatible with the exclusive economic zones (EEZ) provided by UNCLOS. There is no evidence that China had historically exercised exclusive control over the waters or their resources. Essentially, the tribunal junked China's sweeping nine-dash line claim which covered 80% of the Philippines' EEZ. The tribunal said that China's "nine-dash line" "exceeds the limits of China's maritime zones as provided for by the Convention." Moreover, "upon China's accession to the Convention…any historic rights that China may have had to the living and non-living resources within the 'nine-dash line' were superseded, as a matter of law and as between the Philippines and China, by the limits of the maritime zones provided for by the Convention." The Tribunal continued "…as between the Philippines and China, China's claims to historic rights, or other sovereign rights or jurisdiction, with respect to the maritime areas of the South China Sea encompassed by the relevant part of the 'nine-dash line' are contrary to the Convention and without lawful effect to the extent that they exceed the geographic and substantive limits of China's maritime entitlements under the Convention. The Tribunal concluded that the Convention superseded any historic rights or other sovereign rights or jurisdiction in excess of the limits imposed therein."
- On entitlements to maritime areas and the status of the features, the Tribunal said that none of the Spratly islands is capable of generating extended maritime zones and none of the features claimed by China is capable of generating an EEZ. In other words, none of the Philippines' entitlements overlap with China's, giving the Philippines the exclusive enjoyment of the resources in these areas.
- On the lawfulness of Chinese actions: China had violated the Philippines' sovereign rights in its EEZ by interfering with Philippine fishing and petroleum exploration, constructing artificial islands and

failing to prevent Chinese fishermen from fishing in the zone. Fishermen from the Philippines, like those from China, had traditional fishing rights at Scarborough Shoal and China had interfered with these rights in restricting access. Chinese law enforcement vessels had unlawfully created a serious risk of collision when they physically obstructed Philippine vessels.
- On harm to the marine environment: China had caused severe harm to the coral reef environment and violated its obligation to preserve and protect fragile ecosystems and the habitat of depleted, threatened, or endangered species by building artificial islands. Chinese authorities were aware that Chinese fishermen had harvested endangered sea turtles, coral, and giant clams on a substantial scale in the South China Sea and had not fulfilled their obligations to stop such activities.
- On the aggravation of the dispute: China's recent large-scale land reclamation, dredging, and construction of artificial islands were incompatible with the obligations of a state during dispute resolution proceedings. It permanently destroyed evidence of the natural condition of features in the South China Sea and, by doing so, it extended the dispute (The South China Sea Arbitration Award 2016).

Overall, the ruling removed cobwebs of doubt on the nature of the features in the South China Sea and what belonged to the EEZ of the Philippines. It shrunk the disputed area to a miniscule size, comprising "not more than 1.5 percent of the 3.5 million square kilometers of maritime space in the South China Sea," Supreme Court Justice Antonio Carpio said in his lectures. The Philippines reaped huge rewards. A small country with feeble military muscle won in an international court, notching gains for a case it built based on history and the law of the sea forged by 167 states for years.

Duterte's Pivot to China

The election of Duterte, a city mayor for two decades, came as a surprise to many. He was not part of the Manila elite and has not held any national position. But he launched a hugely successful campaign anchored on his war against drugs. This plus his projection of being a decisive and strong leader, his personality and way of speaking—more the language of the streets—resonated with many Filipinos. At the beginning of his presidency, he announced a major foreign policy shift. As the architect of foreign policy, Duterte turned to China for deliverance via investments, aid, and trade. It was during his state visit to Beijing in October 2016 where he announced, in the Great Hall of the People and before Chinese officials led by Vice Premier Zhang Gaoli, his dramatic shift away from the United States, a long-time ally:

> In this venue, your honors, I announce my separation from the United States. Both in military, not maybe social, but economics also…so I will be dependent on you for a long time I've realigned myself in your ideological flow. (Blanchard 2016)

While he backtracked when he returned to Manila, explaining that he meant "separation of foreign policy" and "not a severance of ties," Duterte had already set the tone for relations with China and marked the beginning of his embrace of the giant neighbor. This showed in the joint statement with President Xi Jinping, issued after their meeting, which called for the handling of disputes in the South China Sea in an "appropriate manner," meaning through talks between the countries directly concerned. It was silent on the arbitral ruling. Even before this visit, Duterte had already showed his preference for China, a rising global power. He said China was going to help the Philippines grow its economy through investments and loans. He had no love lost for the United States. Duterte was angered by President Barack Obama, who said in September 2016 that the war on drugs must be done "the right way. Because the consequences when you do it the wrong way, innocent people get hurt. And you have a whole bunch of unintended consequences that don't solve the problem," he said at a press conference in Laos at the sidelines of the ASEAN summit (Inquirer.net, September 9, 2016). At the time, over a thousand killings of suspected drug users, by the police and vigilante groups, had been reported. Duterte continued

> for a President, Obama, to criticize me in a press conference about the record on human rights, was insulting," Duterte recalled. "I am a Filipino, why do you criticize me in a press briefing? I said, shut up, you're an idiot. He was angry, I was also angry, we go our separate ways, that's okay. (Maitem 2018)

While that appeared to the public to be a defining moment for Duterte and the country's foreign policy, his personal bias for China showed even before the international tribunal issued its ruling against China. In his first cabinet meeting on June 30, 2016, about two weeks before the ruling was released, Duterte telegraphed his sentiment. He said he would not "flaunt" a possible victory. While it was going to be a "moral victory," it would put the country in an "awkward position" because "we need many things, hardware and all [from China]." Rather, it should be a "soft landing" for everybody. These comments were unintentionally aired by state TV which was carrying the meeting live. In the same meeting, then Foreign Affairs Secretary Perfecto Yasay recounted briefings with representatives of various governments, those concerned about freedom of navigation and maritime security. "They seem to project the impression that if the decision will come out and it would be in our favor, they would like for us to make stronger statements. I am averse to that idea and I told them in no unmistakable terms that the first thing that we will do when we get that decision is to study its implications and its ramifications" (Esmaquel 2016). The presidential broadcast staff, Radio-TV Malacañang, abruptly cut the broadcast as Yasay was speaking. On the day the ruling was released, Duterte was in a cabinet meeting. Part of what transpired in the meeting, as the Wall Street Journal reported, showed the seeping influence of China. One cabinet member spoke up saying he had dinner the previous night with the Chinese Ambassador and detailed a long list of demands from the envoy about what the Philippine government should say and not say when the ruling came out. Duterte was apparently irked because, earlier that day, he had already met with the Chinese Ambassador to "offer reassurances" in case of a victory. He was referring to Zhao Jianhua, Beijing's man in Manila, who was said to have easy access to the President (Browne 2016).

When President Rodrigo Duterte decided to visit China in late August 2019, some in the Department of Foreign Affairs were taken by surprise. He had just met with Chinese President Xi Jinping in April, barely four months before, during the Belt and Road Forum in Beijing. In the first half of his six-year term, Duterte has visited China five times and met with Xi eight times, more often than most of his predecessors. What merited another trip this time? The Office of the President announced that Duterte was going to raise the arbitral ruling with Xi—the legal victory of the Philippines that invalidated China's nine-dash line claim over most of the South China Sea—and take up economic and business deals. China has repeatedly refused to recognize the international tribunal's decision handed down in 2016. With public pressure in the Philippines, where popular sentiment is against China, the President—who had decided to set the ruling aside to appease China—was forced to include this in his agenda. A June 2019 survey by the Social Weather Stations (SWS) showed that most Filipinos do not trust China which scored a -24 rating, considered poor (Social Weather Stations 2019). Negative trust ratings for China have been consistent through the years. Moreover, the SWS poll found that nearly nine out of ten Filipinos want Duterte to assert the country's sovereign rights over the West Philippine Sea. It turned out that Duterte's talk with Xi about the tribunal's decision was a public relations spectacle to please the domestic audience in the Philippines. As expected, Xi rejected the ruling. "He (President Duterte) said that the arbitral award is final, binding and not subject to appeal. In response, President Xi reiterated his government's position of not recognizing the arbitral ruling as well as not budging from its position," Presidential Spokesman Salvador Panelo said in a statement (Ranada 2019). The President used the arbitral ruling as a magic wand. By raising it, he hoped to erase negative perceptions that he is subservient to China. Beyond that, though, he had closed the door to other diplomatic options to partly enforce the ruling.

Despite Duterte's setting aside of the tribunal ruling, the DFA, under Secretary Teodoro Locsin, has acted independently. In March 2020, the DFA filed two diplomatic notes with the United Nations, asserting the country's claims in the West Philippine Sea (WPS). These were in opposition to Malaysia's application in December 2019 to define the limits of its extended continental shelf beyond its 200-mile EEZ and to China's response against Malaysia. The Philippines said Malaysia's petition covered Philippine islets in the WPS. The diplomatic notes said that "The area of the Malaysian submission…covers features within the Kalayaan Island Group over which the Republic of the Philippines has sovereignty…" (Tomacruz and Gotinga 2020). China also opposed Malaysia's application in a note in December 2019. China urged the UN Commission on the Limits of the Continental Shelf to disregard Malaysia's submission which "seriously infringed China's sovereign rights and jurisdiction in the South China Sea." China's position was consistent with its claim over large parts of the South China Sea. The Philippines, in response to China, opposed its reassertion of its "historic rights" to the

WPS by reiterating the landmark 2016 arbitral ruling. China's position, the Philippines said in its statement, was "inconsistent with international law, including the United Nations Convention on the Law of the Sea" (Tomacruz and Gotinga 2020). Moreover, in April 2020, the DFA lodged a diplomatic protest with China after it named two districts, "Nansha" and "Xisha," in the South China Sea and declared them under the administrative control of Sansha City. This was a reiteration of the position of the Philippines which, in 2012, protested China's establishment of Sansha City.

Chinese Incursions

Duterte's pivot toward China has become a threat to Philippine sovereign rights over the West Philippine Sea (WPS). His policy has emboldened China as Duterte has not shown strong political will in standing up to China's incursions in Philippine waters. As a result, China has escalated its presence in Philippine waters—through an increase in the number of warships, maritime militia vessels, Coast Guard ships in the WPS. This has been most notable in Pag-asa (Thitu) where as many as 600 maritime militia vessels circled the island from January to March 2019 (Tomacruz and Gotinga 2019). The Chinese Coast Guard (CCG) vessels, for their part, guard the Scarborough Shoal, accompanied by huge blue trawlers, warships, and militia vessels. Harvesting of giant clams has continued. In the area around Ayungin Shoal, a CCG ship that has been lingering was reported. Chinese survey vessels have also operated in Philippine waters, as seen in August 2019. China did not ask permission from the Philippines. What had the most impact, though, was the ramming in June of a Philippine fishing boat—anchored in waters within the country's EEZ—by a Chinese trawler which abandoned 22 fishermen to the elements (Esmaquel and Talabong 2019). Heartbreaking stories of fishermen swimming in the inky waters searching for help as their boat started to sink filled Philippine media. But Duterte dismissed this as a "maritime incident," sparing China of blame.

The following skirmishes have been reported by Philippine authorities (Tomacruz and Gotinga 2019).

Sept. 27, 2016: Chinese Coast Guard harasses Filipino fishermen in Scarborough Shoal.

Nov. 2, 2016: Asia Maritime Transparency Initiative releases images taken at Scarborough Shoal that shows that Chinese blockades continue to restrict access to Scarborough Shoal, with a China Coast Guard craft "anchored just inside the mouth of the lagoon." Philippine Navy reports that three other CCG vessels patrol around Scarborough shoal.

April 2017: A group of Bataan fishermen claim that they were chased off by a CCG vessel while they were fishing in the Union Bank in the Spratly group.

Feb. 5, 2018: *Philippine Daily Inquirer* publishes photos showing China has continued reclamation activities in the WPS.

May 11, 2018: A Chinese navy chopper harasses a Philippine Navy rubber boat resupplying troops in Ayungin Shoal.

June 8, 2018: TV footage of a Philippine news program shows the CCG taking the catch of Filipino fishermen.

Nov. 22, 2018: A Philippine TV journalist and his crew are barred from taking videos near the Scarborough Shoal by CCG.

Feb. 7, 2019: Asian Maritime Transparency Initiative releases satellite images showing a "high of 95" Chinese vessels swarming Thitu Island in the West Philippine Sea.

April 10, 2019: Four China Coast Guard vessels surround Scarborough Shoal, blocking entry to the lagoon thus preventing Filipino fishermen from fishing.

April 16, 2019: Two Chinese vessels harvest giant clams in Scarborough Shoal despite a ban

June 7 to 10, 2019: A Chinese naval vessel patrols Scarborough Shoal.

June 9, 2019: A Chinese vessel sinks a Philippine fishing boat in the West Philippine Sea.

August 3–7, 2019: Chinese survey vessels operate in Philippine waters.

August 20, 2019: China Coast Guard ship lingers in Second Thomas Shoal, goes around it as if in patrol.

Feb. 17, 2020: A Chinese warship aims its gun control director at a Philippine Navy ship after the latter sends a radio message that it is in Philippine waters.

RELATIONS FAVOR BEIJING

July 2019 marked the third anniversary of the Philippines' overwhelming victory in its maritime dispute against China. But during this time, the official narrative in the Philippines has been one of strong defeatist tones. From July 12, 2016, when the international Arbitral Tribunal issued its decision invalidating China's nine-dash line and clarifying the status of certain features in the South China Sea, this ruling has never been given the national attention it deserved. It has not been used as leverage in the country's dealings with China. It has not been part of the country's diplomatic arsenal. In the light of this status quo, it is timely to review the economic benefits from Duterte's 3-year embrace of China. In the beginning of his term, seeking economic deliverance from China was the reason the President said he was "separating" from the United States and "depending" on China. While China has free rein in the West Philippine Sea, the Philippines has yet to see the pledges of foreign direct investment (FDI) and official development assistance which have been slow in coming. While Chinese FDI has grown since Duterte came into office, it has not surpassed those of other countries. Xi and Duterte have become friends but it is clear that the giant neighbor gets most of the benefits. China's FDI in the Philippines has risen dramatically from US$28.79 million in 2017 to $198.68 million in 2018, but China has still not outpaced our traditional sources of FDI like the United States, Singapore, and Japan. In the first quarter of 2019, China ranked second in terms of FDI next to Japan (Vitug 2019). Giving a big picture of FDIs in the country, Bangko Sentral Governor Benjamin Diokno said in a speech in June that the top five investors over the past decade have been Japan, the United States, Hong Kong, ASEAN, and the European Union. He did not cite China as a new entrant with its growing investments (Diokno 2019).

In terms of top sources of Official Development Assistance (ODA), China was a poor performer, not even part of the top 10, in 2017. Japan has been the consistent leader here, followed by the World Bank, the Asian Development Bank, the United States, South Korea, Australia, the United Nations, the Asian Infrastructure and Investment Bank, France, EU, and China. As of March 19, 2019, the National Economic Development Authority reported the top ODA sources, which basically remained the same for the top 5. China climbed to the 8th place. This, despite the much touted "Build Build Build" infrastructure program of the government for which China has pledged loans for roads, bridges, and dams. In trade, China became our biggest source of imports in June 2019, making it our top trading partner. But imports from China overtook Philippine exports, resulting in a wide trade gap. In sum China has not surpassed our country's traditional sources of investments and ODA, the trade picture is uneven in favor of China. But it is in tourism where China has started to lead as China tourist arrivals overtook Korean in April 2019. These economic measures show that the friendship between Xi and Duterte is one-sided. Xi gets to enjoy continued domination in the West Philippine Sea and escalates the presence of warships, Coast Guard, and maritime militia vessels in our waters. This state of relations is expected to continue until 2022 when Duterte ends his six-year term.

Overall, Philippine military-to-military relations with the United States did not deteriorate. In fact, the number of joint exercises increased from the time Duterte assumed office in 2016 until 2019. However, Duterte's unilateral cancelation of the Visiting Forces Agreement (VFA) in February 2020, despite objections from the defense and foreign affairs departments, dealt a huge blow to the armed forces. This meant that joint exercises could no longer take place since it was the VFA that governed such activities. But Duterte changed his mind. In June 2020, the DFA announced the continuation of the VFA. The Mutual Defense Treaty still held and remained the anchor of security relations between the Philippines and the United States. The VFA can be renegotiated under a new administration if it is friendly to the United States. The presidential elections that will take place in May 2022 are crucial for Philippine foreign policy: will the next leader continue to embrace China at the expense of the United States and other allies? That is a big question that remains up in the air.

The Way Forward

How should the Philippines move forward? In his public speeches and press conferences, Duterte has openly asked for options to partly enforce the arbitral ruling. Unfortunately, he has not paid heed to any of them. Supreme Court Justice Antonio Carpio, a leading expert on the WPS, proposed the following in a speech on July 14, 2019:

> The Philippines and Vietnam enter into a sea boundary agreement which Vietnam recently proposed.
> Philippines enters into similar sea boundary agreement with Malaysia on the adjoining EEZs. Malaysia has been proposing this.
> Claimant countries such as the Philippines, Vietnam, Malaysia, Indonesia and Brunei enter into a Convention declaring that, as ruled by the Arbitral Tribunal, no geologic feature in the Spratlys generates an EEZ. This Convention will leave China isolated.

Philippines sends on patrol its 10 new 44-meter multi-role response vessels donated by Japan to the Philippine Coast Guard. This will drive away poachers and assert its sovereign rights over the area.

Philippines welcomes and encourages the freedom of navigation and overflight operations of the US, UK, Canada, France, Japan, India, Australia in the South China Sea, including the West Philippine Sea. The naval and aerial operations of these naval powers have increased in frequency since the 2016 arbitral award.

The Philippines sends its own Navy to join the Freedom of Navigation and Overflight Operations of the foreign naval powers to assert that there is an EEZ in the WPS belonging to the Philippines.

The Philippines invites Vietnam, Brunei, Malaysia and Indonesia to conduct joint freedom of navigation operations in their respective EEZs facing the South China Sea. This will be a common assertion that each of them has their own respective EEZs in the South China Sea (Carpio 2019).

For his part, Ambassador Albert del Rosario said in a statement on September 16, 2019 that the Philippines should "bring the arbitral ruling to the UN General Assembly to seek resolutions to compel Beijing to abide by the ruling." He said the Philippines can present its case to the UN General Assembly which, in turn, can adopt resolutions calling for compliance with the judgment of the international arbitral ruling (Tomacruz 2019). Del Rosario, former foreign secretary, cited the case of *Nicaragua v. USA* when Nicaragua went to the General Assembly after the United States ignored the ruling of the International Court of Justice (ICJ) ordering the it to compensate Nicaragua. The UN General Assembly adopted a number of resolutions calling on the United States to comply with the ICJ judgment. "Nicaragua's resort to the UN had the effect of securing international publicity and of gaining favorable global opinion," Del Rosario said. "The United States...ultimately provided a substantial aid package to Nicaragua." There are lessons to learn from other international cases wherein one of the states did not participate. Primarily, offending states, those that ignored the cases brought against them, eventually partly comply with the international court's ruling in various forms. The case of *Nicaragua v. USA* (1986) cited by Del Rosario is one of them. In the Arctic Sunrise case (2017), Russia refused to participate in a suit filed by the Netherlands. In 2013, Russia seized the Arctic Sunrise, the ship which was flying the Dutch flag, and its crew of Greenpeace activists. The International Tribunal on the Law of the Sea (ITLOS) asked Russia to immediately release the ship and allow the non-Russian crew members to leave the country. At first, Russia stalled but eventually implemented most of the measures required by ITLOS, "saying they did this because they were following domestic legislation, not the ITLOS ruling." Russia, in the end, partially fulfilled the ruling by the ITLOS. The Arctic Sunrise and the crew were released but Russia, as of 2018, had not yet paid compensation to the Netherlands. Making the tribunal ruling work and seeing it come to fruition, partly or fully, will take a long time, way beyond a single president's term. It will require strategic thinking anchored on a strong sense of justice, equity, and sovereign rights.

IMPACT ON ASEAN

The arbitral ruling not only benefited the Philippines but also other claimant countries in Southeast Asia. A number of scholars and public international lawyers have attested to this. Paul Reichler, lead counsel for the Philippines, said, "If China's nine-dash line is invalid as to the Philippines, it is equally invalid to other states bordering the South China Sea like Indonesia, Malaysia, Vietnam and Brunei, and indeed the rest of the international community" (Vitug 2018). Indonesia is not a claimant country but it has maritime conflicts with China which escorts fishing vessels to waters within Indonesia's EEZ near the Natuna Islands in the South China Sea. China has insisted that the area falls within its nine-dash line. Similarly, Robert Beckman, associate professor at the National University of Singapore Faculty of Law, wrote: "Given that the tribunal has ruled that China has no historic rights to resources in the EEZs of other states within the nine-dash line, and that none of the disputed islands is entitled to an EEZ of its own. This means that China has no legal basis under UNCLOS to claim that it has a right to share the fishing or hydrocarbon resources in the EEZs of the ASEAN claimants bordering the South China Sea" (Beckman 2016).

In the past, however, there had been some sensitivities in ASEAN about the move of the Philippines to go to an international tribunal. The Philippines did not consult ASEAN about its plan to file a case against China because it wanted to keep it under wraps. ASEAN did not take this kindly. ASEAN saw it as a "wrong tactical step that undermined its efforts towards engaging China multilaterally..." wrote Tang Siew Mun, head of the ASEAN Studies Centre at the Institute of Southeast Asian Studies (ISEAS) in Singapore (Tang 2016). It is also a fact that ASEAN was not united on the maritime disputes with China over the South China Sea. This was evident in the ASEAN's timid response to the victory of the Philippines. In ASEAN meetings such as the foreign ministers' meeting in Vientiane in 2016 and in Manila in 2017 as well as in the summits in 2017, the communiqués made no mention of the arbitral ruling. Among the ASEAN members, Vietnam was the closest ally of the Philippines. In December 2014, Vietnam submitted its position on the Philippines' arbitration case to the international tribunal, "to protect its legal rights and interests in the East Sea" (Macaraig 2014). It was the first time another claimant country used legal proceedings to challenge China's claims.

Moving forward, the Philippines could use the arbitral ruling to enter into sea boundary agreements with claimant countries in ASEAN. A model would be the Philippines–Indonesia maritime boundary treaty which went into force in 2019. The treaty drew a boundary between the overlapping EEZs of the Philippines and Indonesia. It was first taken up in 1994 (during President Fidel Ramos's time) and was signed by both countries in 2014 (President Benigno Aquino III's term). Duterte and the Indonesian parliament ratified it in 2017 but it was only in 2019 when the Philippine Senate concurred with the ratification. However, no similar agreements between the Philippines and Vietnam and Malaysia were started under Duterte. These cases concern demarcating their overlapping EEZs and the extended continental shelves in the Spratlys. Environmental and marine scientists have proposed setting up a marine protected area in the Spratlys which are the rich spawning grounds of fish in the South China Sea. John McManus, a marine biology professor, has advocated crafting a separate treaty through which claimants declare the Spratlys an international marine protected area and freeze their claims for a fixed period of time. He said that Vietnam and Malaysia have already set up national marine protected areas in the Spratly area (Ward 2019). The Philippines, after its victory in the international Arbitral Tribunal, could have used this momentum to lay the groundwork with ASEAN to achieve this goal. Duterte has missed these twin opportunities to use the arbitral ruling to settle conflicting claims with the Philippines' neighbors and counter Chinese intimidation in the South China Sea.

Conclusion

Overall, under Duterte, the Philippines gravitated toward the ranks of ASEAN countries like Cambodia and Laos, both under China's influence, weakening ASEAN's voice on China's aggressive intrusion in the South China Sea. This was in large contrast to the previous president, Benigno Aquino III, who openly criticized China's expansive claims and assertive actions which brought instability to the region. Duterte's claim that his foreign policy was "independent" was meant to justify his embrace of China and the diminution of relations with the United States, a longtime ally and defense treaty partner. This was seen as early as 2017 when the Philippines chaired the ASEAN. During a summit held in Manila, the Southeast Asian countries took a softer stance toward China, as reflected in the ASEAN chairman's statement which dropped references to "land reclamation and militarization" by China in the South China Sea (Mogato 2017). Nowhere was there a mention of the Philippines' 2016 landmark arbitration victory. It had become clear that Duterte used the cover of an "independent" foreign policy to achieve other goals: to shift from a multilateral to bilateral approach when it came to South China Sea issues; and to advocate a similar stance for ASEAN countries. Duterte departed from ASEAN's multilateral approach when he said during the ASEAN summit in 2017 that the arbitral ruling was "not an issue in ASEAN" but one that was between Manila and Beijing (Salaverria 2017). Duterte disregarded the fact that, in 1992, when the ASEAN foreign ministers met in Manila, they issued their first statement of concern on the South China Sea, marking the beginning of a multilateral concern over the problem. In 1995, it was the Philippines that ran to ASEAN to seek support when China occupied Mischief Reef. While he urged ASEAN members not to take sides between China and the United States because it would be a "strategic mistake" (Aguilar 2019). Duterte himself chose China over the United States. Essentially, he practiced a two-faced diplomacy. Duterte's double game was equally driven by domestic concerns. At the time the Philippines chaired the ASEAN in 2017, when Duterte called on the members to respect each other's independence (Cayabyab 2017), he was being criticized for his brutal war on drugs—which has claimed close to 7000 lives, according to official figures (Rappler 2020)—by the United States and European Union. Thus, he was using his supposed "independent" foreign policy to defend human rights violations on his watch. In sum, the Philippine pivot to China allowed Duterte to play a double game and, ultimately, to enfeeble the voice of ASEAN.

References

Aguilar, K. (2019), "Duterte to ASEAN: Don't Choose Sides Between China and US," Inquirer.net, 30 November, https://globalnation.inquirer.net/181764/duterte-to-asean-dont-choose-sides-between-china-and-us.

Beckman, R. (2016), "The Tribunal Award: What It Mean," *Perspective*, Institute of Southeast Asian Studies, Singapore, 28 July: p 5, https://www.iseas.edu.sg/images/pdf/ASEANFocusSChinaSeaArbitration.pdf.

Blanchard, B. (2016), "Duterte Aligns Philippines with China, Said US Has Lost," Reuters.com, 20 October, https://www.reuters.com/article/us-china-philippines/duterte-aligns-philippines-with-china-says-u-s-has-lost-idUSKCN12K0AS.

Browne, A. (2016), "Rodrigo Duterte Gets a Taste of China's Heavy Hand," *The Wall Street Journal*, 19 July.https://www.wsj.com/articles/man-in-the-middle-rodrigo-duterte-gets-a-taste-of-china-1468909553.

Carpio, A. (2019), "Follow Rule of Law But Aspire for Justice", Rappler, 14 July. https://www.rappler.com/thought-leaders/235405-full-text-carpio-speech-ateneo-rule-law-justice-july-14-2019.

Cayabyab, M. (2017), "Duterte Calls for Respect for Independence in Debut as ASEAN Host," *Inquirer.net*, 29 April, https://globalnation.inquirer.net/155684/duterte-calls-respect-independence-debut-asean-host.

Diokno, B. (2019), "Fueling Growth of FDIs in the Philippines; the BSP as an Enabler,"-The Bank for International Settlements, BIS.org, 19 June, https://www.bis.org/review/r190815d.htm.

Esmaquel II, P. (2016), "PH Calls for 'Restraint, Sobriety' Amid Favorable Ruling on Sea Row Rappler.com, 12 July, https://www.rappler.com/nation/139499-ph-restraint-sobriety-ruling-south-china-sea.

Esmaquel II, P. and Talabong, R. (2019), "TIMELINE: Sinking of Filipino Boat in West PH Sea by Chinese Ship," Rappler, 19 June, https://www.rappler.com/newsbreak/iq/233394-timeline-chinese-sinking-filipino-boat-gem-ver-west-philippine-sea.

Ku, J. (2016), "It Is Beijing's Fault That China Lost Big in the South China Sea Ruling," Quartz, 17 July, https://qz.com/733012/it-is-beijings-fault-that-china-lost-big-in-the-south-china-sea-ruling/.

Macaraig, A. (2014), "Vietnam Joins Philippines in Case vs China," Rappler, 12 December, https://www.rappler.com/nation/77868-vietnam-position-arbitration-china.

Maitem, J. (2018)," Duterte Recalls Obama Criticizing PH Drug War: Insulted But No Hurt Feelings," *Philippine Daily Inquirer*, 3 August, https://globalnation.inquirer.net/168856/duterte-recalls-obama-criticizing-ph-drug-war-insulted-no-hurt-feelings-duterte-obama-us-america-hurt-feelings.

Mogato, M. (2017), "ASEAN Gives Beijing a Pass on South China Sea Dispute, Cites 'Improving Cooperation'" Reuters, 30 April, https://www.reuters.

com/article/us-asean-summit/asean-gives-beijing-a-pass-on-south-china-sea-dispute-cites-improving-cooperation-idUSKBN17W02E.

Parlett, K. (2016), "Jurisdiction of the Arbitral Tribunal in Philippines v. China Under UNCLOS and in the Absence of China," *American Journal of International Law (AJIL Unbound)*, 12 December, pp. 266–272, https://twenty esimp.wpengine.com/wp-content/uploads/attachments/Parlett%2C%20Juri sdiction%20of%20the%20Arbitral%20Tribunal%20in%20Philippines%20v%20C hina%20under%20UNCLOS%20and%20in%20the%20Absence%20of%20C hina.pdf.

Philippine Daily Inquirer. (2016). "Obama to Duterte: Do it the right way," *Inquirer.net*, September 9. https://globalnation.inquirer.net/144411/obama-to-duterte-do-it-the-right-way.

Ranada, P. (2019), "Xi Refuses to Recognize Hague Ruling After Duterte Brings It Up," Rappler, 30 August, https://www.rappler.com/nation/238890-xi-ref uses-recognize-hague-ruling-after-duterte-brings-it-up.

Rappler. (2020), "In Numbers: The Philippines' 'War on Drugs,'" 18 February, https://www.rappler.com/newsbreak/iq/145814-numbers-sta tistics-philippines-war-drugs.

Salaverria, L. (2017), "Duterte: Arbitral ruling not an issue for ASEAN," *Philippine Daily Inquirer*, 28 April, https://globalnation.inquirer.net/155544/dut erte-arbitral-ruling-not-issue-asean.

Sheng, Z. (2016), "People's Daily Slams South China Sea Arbitration Tribunal for Being Political Tool," *People's Daily Online*, 14 July, http://en.people. cn/n3/2016/0714/c90000-9085753.html.

Social Weather Stations (2019), "Second Quarter 2019 Social Weather Survey: Trust in China falls to net 24 (Poor)," Social Weather Stations, 19 July, https://www.sws.org.ph/swsmain/artcldisppage/?artcsyscode=ART-20190719100415.

Soong, M. (2016), "China's Down But Not Out, and the Philippines' Duterte Knows It." CNBC.com, 13 July, https://www.cnbc.com/2016/07/13/che xit-cheer-in-philippines-over-south-china-sea-but-duterte-knows-china-is-still-a-force.html.

Tang, S. (2016), "What Is at Stake for ASEAN?" Perspective, Institute of Southeast Asian Studies," Singapore 28 July: p 16, https://www.iseas.edu.sg/ima ges/pdf/ASEANFocusSChinaSeaArbitration.pdf.

The South China Sea Arbitration Award of 12 July 2016—19 Permanent Court of Arbitration Registry PCA Case N° 2013.

Tomacruz, S. (2019), "Del Rosario urges PH to Bring Hague Ruling to U.N.," Rappler, 16 September, https://www.rappler.com/nation/240277-del-rosario-urges-philippines-bring-up-hague-ruling-eve-un-general-assembly.

Tomacruz, S. and Gotinga, JC (2019), "LIST: China's Incursions in Philippine Waters," Rappler, 22 August, https://www.rappler.com/newsbreak/iq/238236-list-china-incursions-philippine-waters.

Tomacruz, S. and Gotinga, JC. (2020), "PH hits China, Malaysia claims in West Philippine Sea," Rappler, 12 March, https://www.rappler.com/nation/254162-philippines-hits-china-malaysia-claims-west-philippine-sea.

Vitug, M. (2018,) "Rock Solid: How the Philippines Won Its Maritime Case Against China," Ateneo de Manila University Press, Quezon City.

Vitug, M. (2019), "Analysis: Duterte's Pivot Mainly Benefits China," *Positively Filipino*, 17 September, http://www.positivelyfilipino.com/magazine/analysis-dutertes-pivot-mainly-benefits-china.

Ward, O. (2019), "The Overlooked Casualty in the South China Sea Dispute," ASEAN Today, 31 January, https://www.aseantoday.com/2019/01/the-overlooked-casualty-in-the-south-china-sea-dispute/.

CHAPTER 5

The South China Sea in Multilateral Forums: Five Case Studies

Carlyle A. Thayer

INTRODUCTION

This chapter examines whether or not multilateral forums have had any discernible impact on the behavior of claimant states involved in the South China Sea maritime disputes. It explores the research question: Do multilateral settings help restrain different parties' behavior and provide a conductive environment and mechanisms to foster the management and resolution of existing disputes? It reviews five case studies to evaluate how multilateral forums may or may not have contributed to moderating state behavior in the South China Sea. The five case studies include:

45th ASEAN Ministerial Meeting (July 2012),
Third ADMM-Plus Meeting (November 2015),
Special China–ASEAN Foreign Ministers Meeting (June 2016),

C. A. Thayer (✉)
University of New South Wales, Canberra, NSW, Australia
e-mail: carlthayer@webone.com.au

© The Author(s), under exclusive license to Springer Nature Switzerland AG 2021
L. Buszynski and D. T. Hai (eds.), *Maritime Issues and Regional Order in the Indo-Pacific*, Palgrave Studies in Maritime Politics and Security, https://doi.org/10.1007/978-3-030-68038-1_5

Mid-Term Meeting of the Non-Aligned Movement (April 2018), and
32nd ASEAN Summit (April 2018).

This chapter also provides a brief overview and analysis of developments in 2019 with a particular focus on the response by the international community to play a greater role in settling the South China Sea maritime disputes.

Case Study 1: 45th ASEAN Ministerial Meeting (July 2012)

Cambodia, as the ASEAN Chair for 2012, hosted the 45th Association of Southeast Asian Nations Ministerial Meeting (AMM) in Phnom Penh from 8 to 13 July (this section draws on Thayer 2012).[1] Prime Minister Hun Sen stated in his opening address that "we should give emphasis to the implementation of the DOC [Declaration on Conduct of Parties in the South China Sea], including the eventual conclusion of '*Code of Conduct (COC) in the South China Sea*' [emphasis in original] (Abbugao 2012; Agence France Presse 2012)." When the 45th AMM concluded, Cambodia's Foreign Minister, Hor Nam Hong, assigned responsibility for drafting the joint communiqué summarizing the AMM deliberations to a working party of four foreign ministers: Marty Natalegawa (Indonesia), Anifah Aman (Malaysia), Albert del Rosario (Philippines), and Pham Binh Minh (Vietnam) (Bower 2012). Their 132-paragraph draft summarized the wide range of issues taken up including the South China Sea. During the AMM the Philippines expressed its concerns at the standoff with China at Scarborough Shoal. Vietnam also expressed its concerns about the award of oil exploration leases by the China National Offshore Oil Company in Vietnam's Exclusive Economic Zone (EEZ). The wording of the South China Sea section of the joint communiqué (paragraphs 14–16) became such a sticking point between Cambodia and the drafters of the joint communiqué that no communiqué was issued at the prerogative of Cambodia as ASEAN Chair. This was unprecedented in ASEAN's forty-five-year history.

---

[1] The following meetings were also held: ASEAN Post-Ministerial Conference with dialogue partners, the 19th ASEAN Regional Forum, ASEAN Plus Three Foreign Ministers Meeting, and the 2nd East Asia Summit Foreign Ministers Meeting.

Cambodia argued that the matters raised by the Philippines and Vietnam were bilateral and should not be included in an ASEAN joint communiqué. Cambodia further argued that the insistence by the Philippines and Vietnam on including references to Scarborough Shoal and Vietnam's EEZ prevented a consensus from being reached and Cambodia had no recourse but to withhold the joint communiqué. The leaked record of the foreign ministers' retreat held after the AMM reveals a different story. Discussion on the South China Sea took place in the plenary session. All ten foreign ministers spoke in turn. Cambodia's Foreign Minister Hor Namhong rounded off this part of the discussion on the South China Sea by bluntly declaring, "[t]here is no consensus, [we should] bracket the entire paragraph 14…17 for our decision. The most difficult is paragraph 16. It is a complex problem (quoted in Thayer 2012)."[2] The draft paragraph 16 read as follows:

> In this context, we discussed in-depth recent developments in the South China Sea, including the situation in the affected Shoal/disputed area, exclusive economic zones and continental shelves of coastal states, particularly those contrary to the provisions of the 1982 UNCLOS. In this connection, we call upon all parties to respect the universally recognized principles of international law including the 1982 UNCLOS. Further [we call] upon all the parties to resolve the disputes in accordance with universally recognized principles of international law.

The remarks by Hor Namhong as ASEAN Chair provoked an interchange with the foreign ministers of Indonesia, Malaysia, Vietnam, and the Philippines. After each foreign minister spoke, Hor Namhong shot back rejecting each suggestion to move forward. Then the foreign ministers of Indonesia, the Philippines, Malaysia, and Vietnam spoke up again and the same pattern was repeated. Hor Namhong once again rejected all their proposals. According to the Summary of Cambodia Chair's intervention at the AMM Retreat, Hor Namhong made the following points:

---

[2] Cambodia's Ambassador to the Philippines also claimed that "eight out of ten ASEAN Member States agreed to all 132 points in the Joint Communique of the AMM, including the three paragraphs (14, 15, 17) related to the South China Sea, except paragraph 16 which is the bilateral dispute between the Philippines and China and Vietnam and China," See: Sereythonh 2012.

> *On Scarborough Shoal*, we all know it is situated in the South China Sea, and we are talking here about the South China Sea. So why should we specify the Scarborough Shoal precisely in the South China Sea. Up to now, we all know the disputes among the concerned parties [are] in Spratlys and Paracels, but we never mention these name[s] in our talks with China. We always mention only the South China Sea.
>
> *On the inclusion of the wording on EEZ and continental shelf*, we believe that every one is perfectly aware that the 1982 UNCLOS have precisely defined the EEZ and continental shelf, and other issues related to the sea. Why should we repeat again?"
>
> In case we not find a way out, Cambodia as Chair has no more recourse to deal with this issue. So the problem we are facing now is either we have compromise text, [that will] not satisfy[y] everyone. If we cannot agree on [the] text, there should be no text at all. For the Joint Communiqué, countries should not try to impose [their] national position, but the common view in spirit of compromise.

Discussions on the wording of the South China Sea paragraphs continued until Friday morning, July 13, without breaking the impasse (Peter and Naren 2012). Ernest Bower, who spoke to diplomats in Phnom Penh, wrote,

> Repeatedly, however, after taking the draft under consideration, Hor Nam Hong consulted with advisers outside of the meeting room and came back rejecting language referring to Scarborough Shoal and the EEZs, even after multiple attempts to find compromise. He said Cambodia's view was that those were bilateral issues and therefore could not be mentioned in the joint statement. (Bower 2012)

During the days following the AMM Retreat, the Indonesian and Singaporean foreign ministers made a last-ditch effort to broker a compromise. They persuaded Vietnam and the Philippines to agree on a compromise on the wording. But repeated attempts to persuade Cambodia's Hor Namhong failed. At their last meeting, Foreign Minister Hor Namhong "picked up his papers, and stormed out of the room" arguing it was a matter of principle for ASEAN not to take sides in bilateral disputes (Perlez 2012). According to the Philippines Undersecretary for Foreign Affairs Erlinda Basilio who attended the meetings in Phnom Penh: At the 45th ASEAN Ministerial Meeting, Secretary del Rosario discussed the situation in Scarborough Shoal. The text of the proposed Joint Communiqué's item/subhead on the "South China Sea" was drafted by the ASEAN foreign ministers, and several revisions were made to make the text acceptable to all. However, the Cambodian Chair consistently rejected any proposed text that mentions Scarborough Shoal (Basilio 2012a, b).

As a result of ASEAN's lack of consensus, as of this writing, China continues to invest in the military sense of surround and occupy Scarborough Shoal and deny access to the lagoon to Filipino fishermen.

Case Study 2: Third ADMM-Plus (November 2015)

The Third ADMM-Plus meeting was held in Kuala Lumpur in November 2015. Discussions on the South China Sea reached an impasse over whether or not to include a reference to the construction of artificial islands in the South China Sea in the meeting's joint statement. Because of the opposition of China and Russia, reference to artificial islands was dropped from the draft joint statement. The United States then took the following position, "[i]n our view, no statement is better than one that avoids the important issue of China's land reclamation and militarization in the South China Sea" (Parameswaran 2015). Five other Plus states and all ten ASEAN members supported the United States. No joint statement was issued (Tan 2015). China sought to escape culpability by charging that, "Certain countries from outside the region try to cram irrelevant content into joint declaration [sic] despite existing consensus (Parameswaran 2015)." At the conclusion of the Third ADMM-Plus, Malaysia issued a Chairman's Statement that included general reference to the South China Sea but not the specific details sought by the United States and other Plus members. Paragraph 9 of the Chairman's Statement read:

> The meeting noted the joint efforts of the ADMM-Plus countries in promoting practical cooperation and collaboration on maritime security. The Meeting also noted the importance of the effective implementation of the Declaration on the Conduct of Parties in the South China Sea (DOC) and the early conclusion of the Code of Conduct in the South China Sea (COC), in order to build mutual trust and confidence and maintain peace, security, and stability in the region. (Chairman's Statement of the 3rd ASEAN Defence Ministers' Meeting-Plus 2015)

As of this writing, China has continued to deploy advanced weapons systems on its seven artificial islands.

Case Study 3: Special China–ASEAN Foreign Ministers Meeting (June 2016)

On 14 June 2016, China and Singapore co-chaired the Special China–ASEAN Foreign Ministers Meeting in Kunming, Yunnan province. The Special Meeting discussed preparations for the 25th anniversary commemorative ASEAN–China summit, other ASEAN–China-related issues, and the South China Sea (Thayer 2016a, b). Originally the co-chairs of the special meeting, China's Wang Yi, the host, and Singapore's Foreign Minister Vivian Balakrishnan, were to have addressed a press conference at the end of the Special Meeting. According to *The Straits Times*, all ten ASEAN ministers reached prior consensus on an ASEAN statement to be read out to a joint press conference by Balakrishnan, as ASEAN country coordinator for dialogue relations with China (Goh and Sim 2016). "But at the last minute," the report continues, "the Chinese presented the ASEAN ministers instead with a 10-point consensus, which ASEAN could not accept." The Special Meeting ended five hours late. ASEAN ministers decided that Balakrishnan "would not attend any joint press briefing as it would be rude to disagree with the Chinese minister in public." Balakrishnan abruptly left Kunming.

ASEAN ministers also decided to issue their media statement separately to the press.[3] According to *The Straits Times*, "That, too, was scuttled by the Chinese who lobbied its friends in the grouping to block the statement." Media reports suggest that China applied diplomatic pressure on Cambodia and Laos to get them to back away from their earlier endorsement of the media statement. ASEAN ministers then decided that each member could "issue their own statement as they saw fit." There was also confusion over how the original ASEAN media statement was to be disseminated. It was in this context that Malaysia, frustrated "over the immense pressure China has put on ASEAN," released the text of the original joint statement to *Agence France Presse*. According to one

---

[3] On 16 June 2016, the official Vietnam News Agency released the complete text of the media statement drawn up by ASEAN foreign ministers. The text of this statement confirms that "the ASEAN member states consented to the content of the Press Statement of their Foreign Ministers."

ASEAN diplomat quoted by *The Straits Times*, "Malaysia releasing it [the joint press statement] was a manifestation of the extreme frustration of the original five ASEAN members plus Vietnam at the particularly crude and arrogant behaviour of the Chinese."

When the media statement was published, Chinese foreign ministry officials sought clarification from Laos as ASEAN Chair. The ASEAN Secretariat then instructed Malaysia to rescind the document, which it did three hours after its release. By this time ASEAN ministers had dispersed. Chinese officials then claimed that the document in question was not an official ASEAN statement. After the special meeting at least four other ASEAN foreign ministries—Indonesia, Philippines, Singapore, and Vietnam—issued separate statements. What is most striking about the media statement was that it was quite forthright in linking ASEAN–China relations to the South China Sea dispute despite China's insistence there was no linkage. The media statement read:

> We noted that 2016 is a milestone for ASEAN-China relations as it marks the 25th Anniversary of ASEAN-China dialogue relations. We look forward to working together with China to bring ASEAN-China cooperation to the next level. *But we also cannot ignore what is happening in the South China Sea as it is an important issue in the relations and cooperation between ASEAN and China.* [emphasis added]

The rest of the media statement repeated standard ASEAN declaratory policy on the South China Sea.

Case Study 4: Non-Aligned Movement Meeting (April 2018)

The 18th Mid-Term Ministerial Meeting of the Non-Aligned Movement (NAM) was held in Baku. Azerbaijan from 3 to 6 April 2018. For the second time in a row ASEAN's proposed update to the Southeast Asia section of the Final Document was not included (Thayer 2018b). In 2016, ASEAN filed a reservation on the wording of the Southeast Asian section (paragraph 449) of the Final Document at the 17th NAM Summit because its update was not incorporated in the final statement.[4] NAM

---

[4] Laos, as ASEAN Chair, sought to include this update, "concerns expressed by some ministers/leaders on the land reclamations and escalation of activities in the area, including

protocol would normally incorporate the views of ASEAN as the recognized regional organization for Southeast Asia. In 2016, the NAM bowed to Chinese pressure to delete references to the South China Sea. In 2018, ASEAN was once again unsuccessful in its attempt to include an update on the South China Sea in the Southeast Asia section (paragraph 526) of the Final Document. The wording that ASEAN sought to include in paragraph 526 of the Final Document of the 18th NAM Mid-Term Meeting was exactly the same as point 14 of the Zero Draft of the Chairman's Statement of 32nd ASEAN Summit and was the only point from the Zero Draft to be included in the official Chairman's Statement of the 32nd ASEAN Summit on 28 April.

Point 14 in the Zero Draft largely repeated past ASEAN policy. It reaffirmed the importance of freedom of navigation, the full implementation of the Declaration on Conduct of Parties in the South China Sea (DOC), and "warmly welcomed the improving cooperation between ASEAN and China, and were encouraged by the official commencement of the substantive negotiations towards the early conclusion of an effective COC (Code of Conduct) on a mutually-agreed timeline."

Point 14 also welcomed practical measures such as the hotline between the foreign ministries of China and ASEAN members, and the operationalization of the Code for Unplanned Encounters at Sea (CUES).

Point 14 "took note of the concerns expressed by some Leaders on the land reclamations and activities in the region, which have eroded trust and confidence, increased tensions and may undermine peace, security and stability in the region."

Finally, Point 14 "emphasised the importance of non-militarisation and self-restraint in the conduct of all activities by claimant and all other states, including those mentioned in the DOC that could further complicate the situation and escalate tensions in the South China Sea." Basically, Point 14 and the ASEAN update to the Southeast Asia section of the NAM Final Document were a repeat of past ASEAN declaratory statements.

Case Study 5: 32nd ASEAN Summit (April 2018)

ASEAN convened its 32nd Summit in Singapore on 28 April 2018 (this section draws on Thayer 2018a, b). Prior to the summit, on 20 April,

the increased presence of military assets and the possibility of further militarization of outposts in the South China Sea."

ASEAN officials drew up a consolidated Zero Draft of the Chairman's Statement on the 32nd ASEAN Summit to guide discussions. The Zero Draft was divided into four major sections, Key Deliverables, ASEAN's External Relations, Regional and International Issues and Developments, and Other Matters. The draft totaled twenty-five points. The Preamble of the Zero Draft touched indirectly on the South China Sea; it stated that ASEAN leaders reaffirmed their "full respect for legal and diplomatic processes, without resorting to the threat or use of force, in accordance with universally recognised principles of international law" including the 1982 UNCLOS. Since the 2016 Arbitral Tribunal Award in the case brought by the Philippines against China, ASEAN has used the circumlocution "legal and diplomatic processes" to refer to the Arbitral Tribunal. This expression was taken out of the section on the South China Sea and moved to the opening of the ASEAN Chair's statement to emphasize its importance.

The Zero Draft's section on Regional and International Issues and Developments contained seven points on the South China Sea. As a result of discussions among ASEAN senior officials and ministers the Zero Draft of the Chairman's Statement was revised on 26 April. The Zero Draft was annotated with the interventions by member states indicating their support, rejection, or other comments on the wording. The seven points related to the South China Sea, for example, contained sixteen annotations from six of ASEAN's ten members. Cambodia topped the list with seven interventions or nearly forty-four percent of the total, followed by the Philippines with three interventions, Malaysia and Vietnam with two each, and Indonesia and Singapore only one intervention each. There were no comments by Brunei, Laos, Myanmar, or Thailand. A review of annotated Zero Draft reveals that four of the original seven points (numbers 15–20) were deleted in their entirety. For example, ASEAN leaders deleted point 17 in the Zero Draft that included reference to "legal and diplomatic processes" and a proposal by Vietnam and the Philippines to welcome the "award by the Arbitral Tribunal constituted under Annex VII to the UNCLOS." These deletions were confirmed with the official release of the Chairman's Statement on the official ASEAN Secretariat website after the summit (Chairman's Statement of the 32nd ASEAN Summit Singapore 2018). Only three points in the Zero Draft, numbers 14, 19, and 20, were left unchallenged.

Point 15 referred to "candid discussions" on the South China Sea and expressed serious concern "over recent and ongoing developments, *including large scale/all land reclamations and militarization* in the area." Cambodia and Malaysia requested that the words in italics be deleted. In the following sentence, the Philippines requested the insertion of the words in italics: "We took note of *serious* concerns expressed by some Ministers on land reclamations and escalation of activities in the area, *massive* island building, construction of outposts, and deployment of military assets in the disputed areas...." Cambodia moved to retain the original wording. In other words, Cambodia sought to water down the language.

Point 16 reaffirmed "the importance of maintaining and promoting peace, security, stability, *safety* and freedom of navigation in and overflight above the South China Sea." Cambodia queried the word *safety* and stated it would get back on that point. Point 16 also called for "full respect for legal and diplomatic processes." Cambodia called for this wording to be deleted, while Indonesia, Malaysia, Philippines, Singapore, and Vietnam called for its retention.

In Point 17, Cambodia queried the following words in italics and stated it would get back, "We emphasized the importance of non-militarisation and self-restraint in the conduct of activities, *including land reclamation* that could further complicate the situation and *disputes* or escalate tensions in the South China Sea." The Philippines and Vietnam requested that the following words (in italics) be inserted in the text as follows, "We articulated ASEAN's commitment to full respect for legal and diplomatic processes. *In this regard, we welcomed the issuance of the 12 July award by the Arbitral Tribunal constituted under Annex VII to the UNCLOS.*" The intervention by the Philippines is notable since President Duterte declared he would not press China on the implementation of the Award. Finally, Cambodia queried Point 18 in its entirety and stated it would get back. Point 18 in the draft read, "We highlighted the urgency to intensify efforts to achieve further substantive progress in the implementation of the DOC in its entirety, particularly Articles 4 and 5 as well as substantive negotiations for the early conclusion of the COC including the outline and time line of the COC." Article 4 called for the resolution of territorial disputes by peaceful means without the resort to the threat of force through consultations and negotiations by the parties directly concerned on the basis of international law and UNCLOS. Article 5 called for the parties to exercise self-restraint in activities "that would complicate or escalate disputes and affect peace and stability...."

The deletion of four points stands in marked contrast to the statement issued by the ASEAN Chair giving fulsome endorsement of "an ASEAN-centric regional architecture that is open, transparent, inclusive and rules-based" and ASEAN's commitment to "full respect for legal and diplomatic processes… in accordance with the universally recognized principles of international law, including the 1982 United Nations Convention on the Law of the Sea (UNCLOS) (Chairman's Statement of the 32nd ASEAN Summit Singapore 2018)." ASEAN policy on the South China Sea, Point 23 of the official Chairman's Statement (formerly Point 14 in the Zero Draft), did not mention the Arbitral Tribunal or legal and diplomatic process. In sum, ASEAN policy on the South China Sea was boiled down to seven points by the 32nd Summit:

> First, ASEAN reaffirms "the importance of freedom of navigation and overflight above the South China Sea."
> Second, ASEAN underscores the importance of "the full and effective implementation of the 2002 Declaration on the Conduct of Parties in the South China Sea (DOC) in its entirety."
> Third, ASEAN warmly welcomes "the improving cooperation between ASEAN and China" specifically "the official commencement of the substantive negotiation towards the early conclusion of an effective Code of Conduct in the South China Sea (COC) on a mutually-agreed timeline."
> Fourth, ASEAN also welcomes practical measures that could reduce tensions, accidents, misunderstandings, and miscalculation such as the successful testing of the hotline between ASEAN members and China "to manage emergencies in the South China Sea" and the operationalization of the Code for Unplanned Encounters at Sea (CUES).
> Fifth, ASEAN takes "note of the concerns expressed by some Leaders on the land reclamations and activities in the area, that have eroded trust and confidence, increased tensions and many undermine peace, security and stability in the region."
> Sixth ASEAN "reaffirmed the need to enhance mutual trust and confidence, exercise self-restraint in the conduct of activities and avoid actions that may further complicate the situation and pursue peaceful resolution of disputes in accordance with international law, including the 1982 UNCLOS."

Seventh, ASEAN "emphasized the importance of non-militarisation and self-restraint in the conduct of activities by claimants and all other states, including those mentioned in the DOC that could further complicate the situation and escalate tensions in the South China Sea" (This is a reference to China).

CHINA PRESSES ON

In early July, China's geological survey vessel *Haiyang Dizhi 8* and its escorts entered Vietnam's EEZ without permission to commence a seismic survey. At the same time, the China Coast Guard harassed the oil drilling rig the *Hakuryu-5* and its service vessels on contract with Russia's Rosneft Vietnam in adjacent waters. These actions precipitated a three-month standoff that ended in October. On 17 July, two weeks after the commencement of the standoff, Le Thi Thu Hang, spokesperson for Vietnam's Ministry of Foreign Affairs, significantly called on "related countries and the international community to work together to contribute to the protection and maintenance of [order, peace and security in the South China Sea]." The United States was the first country to respond. The Department of State issued two strongly worded press statements, the first on 20 July and the second on 22 August. Vietnam's call for support from the international community also received support from Trilateral Security Dialogue (TSD), comprising the United States, Japan, Australia, and the European Union. But, unlike the United States, neither the TSD nor the EU mentioned China by name. Nonetheless, the international community identified three new themes: concern about threats to oil and gas production, the need for China and the Philippines to comply with the Award of the Arbitral Tribunal, and the interests of third parties in the outcome of ASEAN–China negotiations on a Code of Conduct in the South China Sea. Vietnam, for its part, took the unusual step of raising China's actions at the 69th United Nations General Assembly (28 September 2019) and the Non-Aligned Movement Summit in Baku, Azerbaijan (25–26 October 2019). When ASEAN convened its 35th Summit in Bangkok on 3 November 2019, the Chairman's Statement made no mention of the three-month standoff between China and Vietnam. The Chairman's Statement repeated past ASEAN formulations by taking note of "some concerns on... activities in the area which have eroded trust and confidence, increased tensions and may undermine peace, security and stability in the region." The Chairman's Statement repeated ASEAN's long-standing call for "self-restraint in the conduct of activities... that may further complicate this situation...." ASEAN's call for self-restraint went unheeded by China. In April the following year, in a repeat of the events of 2019, the *Hai Yang Dizhi 8* accompanied by escorts sailed into waters off the East coast of Malaysia to contest the operations of the *West Capella*, a survey ship under contract with Petronas, the state oil company.

Conclusion

Five case studies were examined to determine whether multilateral forums may or may not have contributed to moderating state behavior in the South China Sea: 45th ASEAN Ministerial Meeting (July 2012), Third ADMM-Plus Meeting (November 2015), Special China–ASEAN Foreign Ministers Meeting (June 2016), Mid-Term Meeting of the Non-Aligned Movement (April 2018), and 32nd ASEAN Summit (April 2018). The five case studies, while not necessarily representative of all the multilateral forums convened by ASEAN and the Non-Aligned Movement, provide compelling evidence that multilateral forums did not moderate China's behavior with respect to the maritime disputes in the South China Sea nor did multilateral forums mitigate major power rivalry within multilateral forums. The case studies revealed that internal divisions within ASEAN, exacerbated by Chinese interference, undermined the ability of multilateral forums to moderate state behavior as evidenced by the three-month standoff between Vietnam and China in the waters near Vanguard Bank. The multilateral forums discussed in this chapter operate on the basis of consensus. This results in watering down contentious issues between member states. In addition, multilateral forums issue non-binding statements that may bring some measure of political and moral pressure on states to comply but do not contain any enforcement mechanism or penalty for non-compliance. Thus, ASEAN's October 2012 call on China "to exercise self-restraint in the conduct of activities that would complicate or escalate disputes and affect peace and stability including, among others, refraining from action of inhabiting on the presently uninhabited islands, reefs, shoals, cays, and other features..." (Declaration of conduct 2002) has not restrained China from occupying uninhabited features in the Spratlys and transforming them into militarized artificial islands. In summary, national security and national sovereignty of ASEAN member states continues to override attempts to move beyond consensus decision-making in matters that affect the region to adopt some form of qualified majority voting that parallels the N–x in economic decision-making (Thayer 2017; Heydarian 2018).[5]

References

Abbugao, M (2012), 'ASEAN Pushed on South China Sea Code', *The Advertiser*, 9 July, viewed 29 May 2020, https://www.adelaidenow.com.au/news/world/asean-pushed-on-south-china-sea-code/news-story/5ed7f60d854565fb02e1cbb936f2f60b.

Agence France-Presse (2012), 'Hun Calls for ASEAN South China Sea Code', *The Australian*, 10 July, p. 12 (online Dow Jones Factiva).

Basilio, EL (2012a), 'Why There Was No ASEAN Joint Communiqué?' *Official Gazette*, 18 July, viewed 29 May 2020, https://www.officialgazette.gov.ph/2012/07/18/why-there-was-no-asean-joint-communique/.

Basilio, EL (2012b), "What Happened in Phnom Penh?" *The Philippine Star*, 19 July, viewed 29 May 2020, https://www.philstar.com/headlines/2012/07/19/829282/what-happened-phnom-penh.

Bower, EZ (2012), 'China Reveals Its Hand on ASEAN in Phnom Penh', Southeast Asia from the Corner of 18th and K Streets, 19 July. Retrieved from https://csis-website-prod.s3.amazonaws.com/s3fs-public/legacy_files/files/publication/120719_SoutheastAsia_Vol_3_Issue_14.pdf.

Chairman's Statement of the 3rd ASEAN Defence Ministers' Meeting-Plus (3rd ADMM-Plus) Kuala Lumpur (2015, November 4). Retrieved from https://www.asean.org/wp-content/uploads/images/2015/November/statement/Chairmans%20Statement%20of%20the%203rd%20ADMM-Plus.pdf.

Chairman's Statement of the 32nd ASEAN Summit Singapore (2018, April 28). Retrieved from http://asean.org/storage/2018/04/Chairmans-Statement-of-the-32nd-ASEAN-Summit.pdf.

Declaration on Conduct of Parties in the South China Sea (2012, October 17). Retrieved from https://asean.org/?static_post=declaration-on-the-conduct-of-parties-in-the-south-china-sea-2.

---

[5] In the $N - x$ formula, N stands for two or more ASEAN countries who agree to trade liberalization measures. The x stands for the remainder of ASEAN countries. Under this formula the N countries can proceed and the x countries can join later. As early as 2014, ASEAN officials initiated informal discussions on altering ASEAN's consensus decision-making outside the economic sector by adopting a qualified majority voting system. This system would operate below the ASEAN Summit which would continue to make decisions by consensus. The idea of a qualified majority system has surfaced from time to time without any action.

Goh, SN & Sim, W (2016), 'China "Consensus" Statement Left Asean Divided', *The Straits Times*, 16 June, viewed 29 May 2020, https://www.straitstimes.com/asia/se-asia/chinas-consensus-statement-left-asean-divided.

Heydarian, RJ (2018), 'The Asean Way Needs Modifying', *The Straits Times*, 25 January, viewed May 30, 2020, https://www.straitstimes.com/opinion/the-asean-way-needs-modifying.

Parameswaran, P (2015, November 4), 'China Blocked Asean Defense Meeting Pact Amid South China Sea Fears: US Official', *The Diplomat*. Retrieved from https://thediplomat.com/2015/11/china-blocked-asia-defense-meeting-pact-amid-south-china-sea-fears-us-official/.

Peter, Z & Naren, K (2012), 'Cambodia Criticized for Asean Meeting Failure', *The Cambodian Daily*, 14–15 July, viewed 29 May 2020 https://opendevelopmentcambodia.net/news/cambodia-criticized-for-asean-meeting-failure/.

Perlez, J (2012), 'Asian Leaders at Regional Meeting Fail to Resolve Disputes Over South China Sea', *The New York Times*, 12 July, viewed https://www.nytimes.com/2012/07/13/world/asia/asian-leaders-fail-to-resolve-disputes-on-south-china-sea-during-asean-summit.html.

Tan, SS (2015), 'The 3rd ADMM-Plus: Did the Media Get It Right?' RSIS Commentary, No. 257, 26 November. Retrieved at https://www.rsis.edu.sg/rsis-publication/rsis/co15257-the-3rd-admm-plus-did-the-media-get-it-right/#.Xbt63i1L1QI.

Sereythonh, H (2012), 'Letter to Ms. Ana Marie Pamintuan, Editor-in-Chief', *The Philippines Star*, 26 July, viewed 29 May 2020, http://www.akp.gov.kh/?p=22903&print-1.

Thayer, C (2012, August 20), 'ASEAN'S Code of Conduct in the South China Sea: A Litmus Test for Community-Building?', *The Asia-Pacific Journal*, 10(4), Issue 3. 1–23. Retrieved from https://apjjf.org/2012/10/34/Carlyle-A.-Thayer/3813/article.html.

——— (2016a, June 17), 'The ASEAN-China Special Meeting Mystery: Bureaucratic Snafu or Chinese Heavy-Handedness?', *The Diplomat*. Retrieved from http://thediplomat.com/2016/06/the-asean-china-special-meeting-mystery-bureaucratic-snafu-or-chinese-heavy-handedness/.

——— (2016b, June 19), 'Revealed: The Truth Behind ASEAN's Retracted Kunming Statement', *The Diplomat*. Retrieved from: http://thediplomat.com/2016/06/revealed-the-truth-behind-aseans-retracted-kunming-statement/.

——— (2017), 'ASEAN at 50: Still a Work in Progress', Chennai Centre for China Studies C3S Article, no: 75, pp. 1–4, viewed 30 May 2020, http://www.c3sindia.org/geopolitics-strategy/asean-at-50-still-a-work-in-progress-by-carlyle-a-thayer/.

―――― (2018a, April 26), 'The South China Sea and ASEAN's 32nd Summit Meeting', *The Diplomat*. Retrieved from https://thediplomat.com/2018/04/the-south-china-sea-and-aseans-32nd-summit-meeting/.

―――― (2018b, April 30), 'Consensus by Deletion: Reviewing the 32nd ASEAN Leaders' Summit and the South China Sea', *The Diplomat*. Retrieved from https://thediplomat.com/2018/05/consensus-by-deletion-reviewing-the-32nd-asean-leaders-summit-and-the-south-china-sea/.

CHAPTER 6

Blue Solutions to South China Sea Environmental Problems

Nguyen Chu Hoi

INTRODUCTION

The South China Sea (SCS) is a high-value marine area in terms of marine resources, environmental conservation, and ecosystem services, which are necessary for sustainable blue marine economic development. However, the SCS is facing numerous and increasingly complex challenges such as environmental and marine resource problems, maritime safety and security issues, and destructive human behavior. Human activities and natural hazards have had a destructive impact and have been accelerating at an alarming rate in the sea region. This can be seen in the overexploitation of marine resources, notably overfishing, the loss of marine biodiversity, the degradation of coastal and marine ecosystems, the reduction in area of coral reefs and other habitats; an increase in the risk of climate change and marine waste, especially plastic debris, as well as other waste dumped at sea. There is an urgent and practical need to protect the marine environment, conserve the marine biodiversity and ecosystems, as well as maintain

N. C. Hoi (✉)
Vietnam Fishery Society (VINAFISH), Hanoi, Vietnam

© The Author(s), under exclusive license to Springer Nature Switzerland AG 2021
L. Buszynski and D. T. Hai (eds.), *Maritime Issues and Regional Order in the Indo-Pacific*, Palgrave Studies in Maritime Politics and Security, https://doi.org/10.1007/978-3-030-68038-1_6

the marine natural assets to ensure environmental security for a blue and healthy SCS. Boosting regional cooperation over the SCS will be necessary to address common environmental interests, to manage shared fishery stocks, and to promote confidence-building measures between ASEAN countries and China.

The Resources of the South China Sea

The SCS is rich in marine resources important for sustainable and blue marine economy development. The SCS is considered as one of 64 Large Marine Ecosystems (LME) with a diverse range of habitats including mangroves, seagrass meadows, coral reefs and soft bottom communities, representing the world's most diverse shallow marine ecosystems (Morton and Blackmore 2001). It is one of the world's marine biodiversity centers (Talaue-McManus 2000). The SCS is a highly productive (150–300 g $C.m^{-2} yr^{-1}$) region based on global primary productivity estimates and has 1,443 species of sea algae (Phang et al. 2016). The sea is also a public home to marine living resources, including waterbirds and especially fishery resources most of which are shared stocks with seasonally high migratory species (Nguyen Chu Hoi and Vu Hai Dang 2015, p. 131). Approximately 12% (some 2 million hectares) of the world's and 30% of Asia's mangrove forests are located in the countries bordering the SCS LME (UNEP 2004b, p. 2). Products and ecological services provided by the mangrove ecosystem of the SCS are estimated to be worth about $15.984 million a year. Similarly, the estimated value of the tidal wetlands and estuaries normally associated with seagrass beds in the sea is $190.726 million a year (Nass 2002, p. 45). The SCS contains 7.04% of the world's and about 20% of Southeast Asia's coral reefs with an economically average value of some $350,000/ha/year (de Groot et al. 2012). The SCS has 0.93% of the world's seamounts, with 0.31% of the sea surface being protected (Heileman 2008). About 18 seagrass species among 58 species of the world are recorded within and adjacent to the coastal waters of the SCS (UNEP 2004a, p. 2), with an average value of $212,000/ha/year (UNEP 2004c). The presence of large-scale offshore coral reef systems is a key feature of the SCS, including the Spratly, Paracel, Natuna, and Anambas islands and the Pratas, Macclesfield, and Scarborough reefs. These islands and coral reef systems play an important role in the ecosystems of the SCS (Map 6.1). They have been formed on ancient volcanic rock formations, taking the shape of island clusters

Map 6.1 The large coral systems or offshore islands groups in the SCS (East Sea in Vietnamese)

consisting of various natural features like small islands (<1 km^2), rocks, shoals, and lagoons within atolls. As vulnerable ecosystems, these islands and coral reef systems are a haven for over 3,000 associated organism species in the SCS.

The SCS has a high level of marine biodiversity and is one of five fishing areas in the world with the highest productivity rating with some 12% of the global total catch in 2015. According to the United Nations Environment Program (UNEP), the SCS accounts for one-tenth of the total fish catch in the world and by 2030, China is expected to account for 40% of global fish consumption (Borton 2016). Over half of fishing vessels in the world is operated in the SCS (about 1.72 million fishing boats and vessels) which provide employment for 3.7 million fishermen (CSIS Expert Team of the SCS 2017). Thus, the fishery resources are very important for 190 million people living in the coastal areas of the SCS where about 77% rely on pelagic fishery resources for their daily protein intake and livelihood (Zhang 2018). Such richness of the marine living resources of the SCS depends very much upon the biodiversity and the health of its coastal and marine ecosystems. Healthy marine and coastal ecosystems are highly productive and provide a multitude of valuable goods and services. These range from food, medicine, climate regulation and coastal protection to recreational opportunities and spiritual benefits.

Environmental Issues

With fast economic growth in the SCS region, various threats to the marine environment have arisen. Thus, the SCS environment is now facing challenges from land-based sources and include plastic debris and oil pollution which are highly noticeable. In general, the concentration of marine contaminants is on the rise, mainly from organic components, nitrate, grease, and total suspended solids (TSS). This trend is evident in nearshore bottom sediments due to the increase in accumulated pollutants with persistent toxicity in the marine environment, such as heavy metals and persistent organic pollutants (POPs). Besides that, in certain areas, maritime shipping has caused coastal marine pollution from organic substances and the amount of waste dumped into the sea through both legal and illegal dumping activities is on the rise. This means that the SCS is increasingly being poisoned by environmental incidents and the consequences will be catastrophic. For example, the total amount of solid waste generated throughout Vietnam's coastal areas is 14.03 million tons; the figure for oil, nitrogen, total ammonium is about 35,160 tons/day, 26–52 tons/day, and total 15–30 tons/day (2010), respectively. Coastal tourism activities alone generated 32,273 tons of waste and 4,817,000 m^3 of wastewater per year (Tran Dinh Lan and Nguyen Thi Phuong Hoa 2010). Annually, shrimp farming activities, which cover an area of 600,000 hectares, will generate 3 million tons of solid waste into the environment. These activities along coastal provinces generate daily: 5,200–10,300 tons of solid waste, including plastic debris, 11.8 million tons of wastewater, and 150–440 tons of oil and grease (Vietnam Administration of Seas and Islands 2011). Oil spills stemming from shipping in crowded maritime lanes are also on the rise, especially as tensions related to sovereignty disputes rise. The amount of oil transiting the SCS is around 2.1 billion tons annually, and at any given time, there are approximately 51 large oil tankers operating at the sea. Transboundary pollution is a concern due to the use of the pesticides and possible radioactive contamination from China's nuclear power plants, located in Yangjiang (Guangdong), Changjiang (Hainan Island), and Fangcheng (Guangxi). China's planned floating nuclear power plant in the SCS is also worrying (Nguyen Chu Hoi 2019b).

The management of waste generated from production activities in economic zones, industrial parks, and coastal export processing zones seems to be poor, and environmental incidents in coastal areas occur regularly. The most notable case is the Hung Nghiep Taiwan Company (Formosa) incident when the company, located at Vung Ang Economic Zone (Ha Tinh), was found illegally dumping waste into the sea in April 2016. As a result, four Vietnamese coastal provinces, namely Ha Tinh, Quang Binh, Quang Tri, and Thua Thien Hue, were seriously impacted due to coastal pollution and the degradation of nearly 50% of coral reefs in area to a depth of 10–20 m caused by phenol and cyanide, resulting in a dense mass of fish death. To date, there are positive signs showing the recovery of small size fish and large size benthos. The red tide phenomenon appears quite frequently in the coastal areas of countries bordering the SCS. This phenomenon has had serious consequences for biological resources, and the marine environment in the nearshore and along the beaches of Khanh Hoa, Ninh Thuan, and Binh Thuan provinces of Southern Central Vietnam. The main causes are related to coastal and island urbanization, tourism, agricultural and industrial activities, which generate overly enriched organic waste and nutrients to the marine waters (eutrophication) (Map 6.2).

The countries of the SCS are in the top range when it comes to mismanaging plastic waste, this includes Vietnam with 1.8 million tons of plastic waste per year (including microplastics) (Jambeck and Geyer 2015). However, this issue has not been prioritized in the region as it has been in other parts of the world. The Coordinating Body on the Seas of East Asia (UNDP COBSEA) conducted a review on marine waste and showed gaps in the awareness and knowledge of this critical issue. Partnership networks to properly deal with this issue are absent. However, most of the recent collected information warns that the situation of marine waste in the SCS is much worse than the rest of the world, and the situation is worsening (Project Aware, no date; UNEP 2012).

Coral reefs, seagrass beds, and other shallow waters ecosystems in the SCS are being destroyed and buried rapidly (Gomez 2015). This seems to

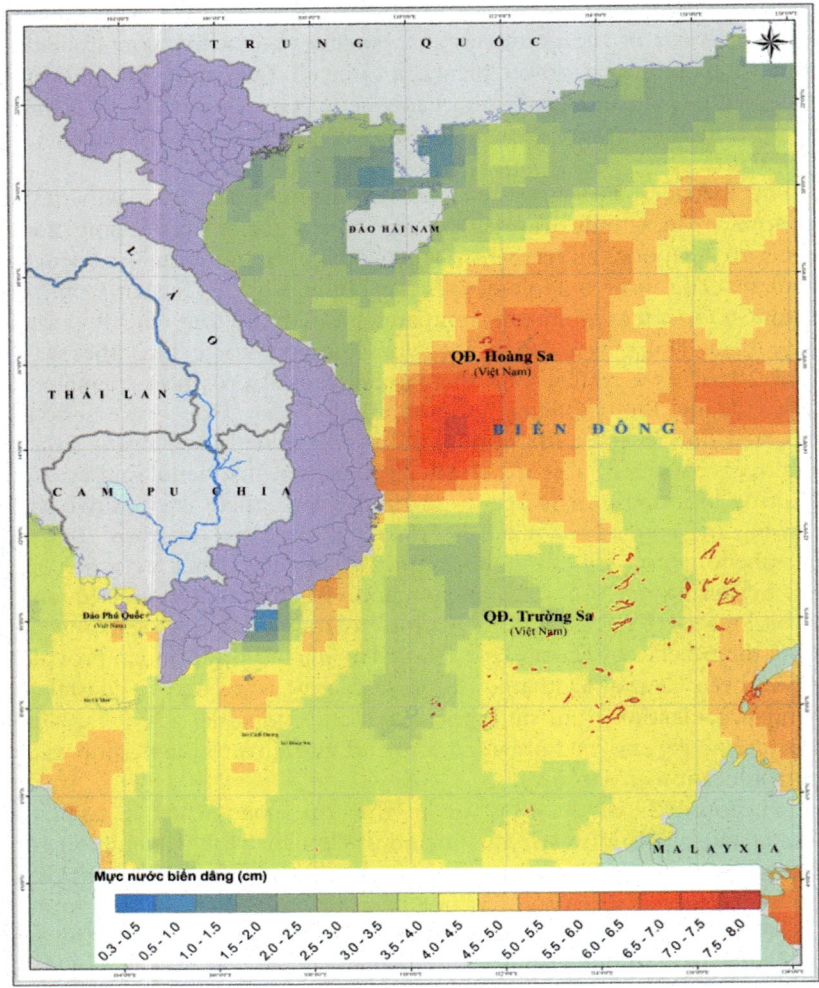

Map 6.2 Increases in sea level of the SCS (according to satellite data) *Source* The Ministry of Natural Resources and Environment of Vietnam

be of little or no concern to Chinese leaders in their rush to gain control of a very important marine ecosystem. Not that other countries have been entirely guiltless, but the proportions are minimal in comparison. In the central part of the SCS, especially the Spratly islands, an area of coral reefs of about 160 square kilometers has been seriously damaged by dredging activities, land reclamation, port construction, and overharvesting of giant clams (Gomez 2015). By the end of 2016, as a result of the construction of artificial islands, China's occupied area expanded by 1,500 hectares of land in coral shoals and rocks in the Spratly islands (1,370 ha) as well as the Paracel islands. China accounted for 95% of the total land reclamation area conducted in the Spratly islands by the other claimants. In fact, Beijing has had the greatest impact on the environment, while the impact made by other claimants is less than 1% than that of China. We are heading to a major disruption in the fisheries industry and this environmental disaster will affect the lives of millions (McManus 2016). China's activities have also caused serious damage to the coastal countries along the SCS, including China itself, the estimated loss is $4 billion (Juinio-Meñez and Gomez 2016, p. 8). For fishermen alone, this estimated loss is around $108.9 million per year (Espejo 2015). Those above-mentioned activities by China not only alter the geographical features and function of shoals, rocks, and atolls in the Spratly islands, but also "cut" the ecological connectivity between the coral islands with the rest of the SCS. This activity has a wider impact on the capacity of the SCS with its coral islands to provide nutrition, seeds and aquatic resources and for the regional countries. Vietnamese, Filipinos, Malaysians, Indonesians, and even the Chinese themselves will suffer (Nguyen Chu Hoi 2016a, p. 62).

In addition, destructive fishing practices in the SCS have caused ecosystem degradation and the risk of extinction of some species, such as sea turtles, some shark species, and other fish species, especially the giant clams. Fisheries resources in the Spratly islands waters and the western areas of SCS belonging to Vietnam have decreased by 16% compared to the period before 2010 (Nguyen Quang Hung and Vu Viet Ha 2015). The destruction of the giant clam population as a result of large-scale poaching in Scarborough Shoal which China took from the Philippines in 2012 has resulted in a prolonged "ecological disturbance" destroying many benthic species. The giant clam shells were carved and sold to tourists and locals in Hainan, China (Juinio-Meñez and Gomez 2016; Nguyen Chu Hoi 2016a). In addition, the number of coral and fish species in disputed waters in the SCS has decreased from 460 down to 261 and the list of endangered species now includes green turtles, giant calms, and hawksbill sea turtles (Espejo 2015). China has seriously violated the relevant international laws, including UNCLOS (Articles 192, 193, 196), especially Article 208 on marine environment pollution; the Convention on Biological Diversity (CBD); the Convention on International Trade in Endangered Species of Fauna and Flora (CITES); and also Article 6 of the Declaration on the Conduct of Parties in the SCS (DOC). China's disregard of international law, and disrespect for bilateral commitments, and ASEAN has provoked strong international responses.

With its unilateral and illegal "nine-dash line" claim (also called U-shaped line, and cow's tongue line) encompassing 80% of the total SCS area, China has step by step illegally occupied the entire Paracel islands (1974) and 7 coral reef shoals within the Spratly islands which are claimed by Vietnam (1988 and 1995). Most recently, while constructing "artificial islands" on coral reef shoals in the Spratly islands and Paracel islands, China destroyed a large area of coral reefs and seagrass beds. In addition, destructive fishing practices in the SCS have led to the ecosystem's degradation, endangering a number of rare marine species and threatening the fisheries of regional countries, including Vietnam. China's behavior has permanently buried these reefs and caused long-term damage to marine habitats and has threatened the environmental security and ecology of the SCS. These violations by China were identified by the Arbitral Tribunal which was established under Annex VII of UNCLOS. The ruling was made public on July 12, 2016 and stated that: China had caused severe and permanent harm to the coral reef environment and violated its obligation to preserve and protect fragile ecosystems and the habitat of depleted, threatened, or endangered species. China's large-scale land reclamation and construction of artificial islands were incompatible with a state's obligations during the dispute resolution proceedings insofar as China inflicted irreparable harm to the marine environment. It built a large artificial island in the Philippines's exclusive economic zone, and destroyed evidence of the natural condition of features in the SCS that were under dispute (Permanent Court of Arbitration 2016). The expansion of infrastructure on these "artificial islands" in the Spratlys and Paracels has increased tensions in the SCS. The face of the SCS region has changed as a result of China's "militarization" and "internationalization" driven by the United States and its allied powers (Nguyen Chu Hoi 2016b).

THE NEED FOR "BLUE SOLUTIONS"

The three most pressing challenges that the sea is facing are: pollution, overfishing, and poor management. If these challenges are not properly resolved, the sustainability of the sea will be significantly affected. To develop a sustainable marine economy, it is necessary for the coastal countries in the SCS to adopt good practices and solutions based on a blue economy which would help overcome the above-mentioned developmental and conservation challenges. According to the World Bank and the UN Department of Economic and Social Affairs, the "blue economy" concept seeks to promote economic growth, social inclusion, and preservation or improvement of livelihoods while at the same time ensuring environmental sustainability. It conceptualizes oceans as "development spaces" where spatial planning integrates conservation and sustainable use of living and non-living resources. The aforementioned practices in the SCS indicate worrying trends of rising environmental incidents and decreasing marine resources which impact upon the blue and sustainable development of the marine economy (Table 6.1). It is necessary to abandon the "old habits" and review blue solutions. According to Professor Gunter Pauli in "Deep Ecology" blue solutions involve a philosophy that considers humankind as an integral part of nature and that the environment also has the right to "live and flourish" according to notions of sustainability. These are the concepts behind "blue thinking" (Pauli 2014, pp. 39–40). Some blue solutions focus on the marine pollution management, marine protected areas, integrating ecosystem services, climate change adaptation, and sustainable financing (GIZ et al. 2017, no

Table 6.1 Environmental trends in the SCS

Reduction trend	Increase trend
Marine natural assets	Marine pollution and environmental incidents
Fishery resources	Marine environmental degradation
Marine biodiversity	Impacts of climate change and sea level rise
Area of marine ecosystems	Coral reef destruction
Area of coastal habitats	Land-based impacts to the sea

date). By contrast, "brown" solutions pollute the environment. Biodiversity destruction should be gradually removed, paving the way for "blue" solutions to ensure environmental security and a peaceful environment in accordance with national and international laws (Borton 2016). In the context of the SCS, environmental, resources, and sovereign issues are considered as "three dimensions of the same issue." The "less sensitive issues" are those in which the parties could cooperate without jeopardizing any sovereignty claims. It means that mitigating tensions will contribute to environmental and food security and vice versa. Given the complicated nature of the SCS disputes, a resolution in the foreseeable future remains highly unlikely. Thus, regional cooperation over the above-mentioned issues can be a tool to facilitate the exchange and sharing of information, not only for marine environmental and biodiversity preservation but also for economic and political purposes. In terms of legal obligations, the duty to protect and preserve the marine environment is well established under international law. This duty extends to rare or fragile ecosystems and the habitats of depleted, threatened, or endangered species and other forms of marine life (Lyons et al. 2019, p. 2). The Declaration on the Conduct of Parties in the SCS (DOC) of 2002 encourages this in Article 6.[1] Environmental protection is a neutral political issue so the claimants in the SCS should be able to sit together at a negotiating table to discuss blue solutions. This is not only an obvious need but also a proper choice to ensure the long-term mutual interests of the claimants in the SCS.

Many of the above-mentioned coral reef features are subject to overlapping sovereignty claims by two or more regional coastal states, including China, Taiwan, the Philippines, Brunei, Malaysia, and Vietnam. Thus, the disputes of the coral islands not only impact on the coral reefs and fisheries sustainability, but also bring about the need for regional cooperation of the shared fisheries development and environmental protection. Excessive claims for fisheries resources and the marine life deterioration contribute to marine disputes and tensions, as the loss of the coral reefs will impact upon the fishery resources and the traditional fishing practices of the regional countries (Nguyen Chu Hoi 2019a). The best approach for managing these disputes is to set aside sovereignty and jointly develop

---

[1] Article 6 says: "Pending a comprehensive and durable settlement of the disputes, the Parties concerned may explore or undertake cooperative activities. These may include the following: (a) marine environmental protection; (b) marine scientific research."

and manage the natural resources, such as fisheries and the associated marine environment (Zhang 2018).

To improve the environment of the SCS, to restore the degraded coastal and marine resources, and to maintain the natural marine assets in accordance with the above-mentioned blue thinking, it is necessary to apply blue solutions with an emphasis on protecting the marine environment. Overfishing of rare species and the increasing number of damaged coral reefs requires a scientific-based policy solution. Expanding scientific cooperation among ASEAN marine scientists, as well as scientific investigations in disputed areas and artificial islands, is a practical, objective need but has not been implemented in the true sense of the word. The Declaration for a Decade of Coastal and Marine Environmental Protection in the South China Sea (2017–2027) was signed at the 20th ASEAN-China Summit in the Philippines in 2017. The governments of China and ASEAN countries considered a *Plan for Strategic Actions to Protect the Marine Environment* as a follow-up to promote regional cooperation on marine environmental management, including actions that are necessary to address the marine environmental degradation and better control land pollutions (Gong and Trajano 2018, p. 4). However, no agreement has been signed. So far, Vietnam's scholars have proposed various solutions to persuade China to comply with the environmental section related to the SCS Arbitral Award. ASEAN and China should develop and update the *Strategic Action Plan* (SAP) which is an outcome of Phase I of the UNEP/GEP Project on "Preventing the trend of environmental degradation in the South China Sea and the Gulf of Thailand" (2002–2008). This SAP plan was completed in 2008, but so far has not been implemented due to sensitive issues related to geopolitical tensions between countries in the SCS region (Vu Hai Dang 2014). ASEAN and China may find ways to form a collaborative management framework in the SCS based on the protection of the marine environment and should establish a Regional Coordinating Unit operating in a cross-sectoral approach. ASEAN and China should also consider some confidence-building measures to implement Article 6 of the DOC.

It is necessary to focus on existing solutions and initiatives, such as establishing a Regional Network of Marine Protected Areas (MPA) throughout the SCS, based on the existing national systems of the MPAs (Vo Si Tuan 2016). Regional countries should also consider establishing a "Marine Peace Park" in the SCS coral islands, especially in the Spratly islands as proposed by John McManus

(2016). James Borton also believes that "in view of an increasing number of incidents between fishing vessels in disputed areas, the leaders of ASEAN and China should find ways to reduce that number by promoting dialogue aimed at establishing a Marine Peace Park in the SCS, instead of by sending more ships to the area" (Borton 2016). In addition, regional actors should also consider establishing a number of "Ecologically and Biologically Significant Marine Areas – EBSAs" on coral reef systems located in the SCS in order to implement management measures in accordance with the Convention on Biological Diversity which was effective from 29 December 1993. Recently, some scientists proposed that there is a compelling case for the claimant States to cooperate in the identification of the Spratly seamounts as an EBSA, so long as it is agreed by all the claimant States that such cooperation is on a "without prejudice" basis (Lyons et al. 2019). For some areas with a high economic potential and high marine conservation value, it is necessary to designate them as "Particularly Sensitive Sea Areas" (PSSA). These measures would be in accordance with the IMO International Convention for the Prevention of Pollution from Ships (MARPOL). To minimize the effect of climate change, disaster risks, and plastic waste, the regional countries should spare no effort in promoting regional initiatives in the Asia-Pacific, including the ocean science and technology initiatives of the Intergovernmental Oceanographic Commission for the Western Pacific (IOC WESTPAC). They should adopt the commission's recommendations on the reduction of marine debris, including micro plastics, etc.

Conclusion

The SCS is now facing a number of environmental challenges. The littoral states are aware of the prospect of marine environmental incidents and disasters and recognize the duty to cooperate under UNCLOS with regard to the protection of common goods in the semi-closed sea. However, smaller claimants are concerned about China's geopolitical intentions and its relentless pursuit of its unlawful claims. Because of the serious harm done to offshore coral reef systems and destructive and illegal fishing practices in overlapping waters, regional cooperation on marine biodiversity conservation and fisheries management between the claimants is necessary. However, as trust recedes, they have been reluctant to cooperate for fear of being further exposed to Chinese coercion and manipulation. Consequently, marine-based sustainable development including environmental protection in the maritime domain has not been a regional priority, though it is of critical importance to all coastal communities and future generations. What has happened in the SCS environmentally is also happening in other locations across the Indo-Pacific region, as politics are being driven by events in the South China Sea.

The Indo-Pacific region, including the SCS, is one of the most significant drivers of global economic growth and is now considered the center of gravity of the global political economy that has been shifting from the western to the eastern hemisphere. There is a common interest among regional countries in marine resources and to rely on the maritime commons including the sea lanes, for the purposes of trade and energy supplies. But there are major disputes between China and other regional countries about how to protect the marine environment and ecology. In this context, it is urgent to introduce "blue solutions" into the existing Indo-Pacific vision to promote region-wide cooperation based on UNCLOS and with the participation of all stakeholders. Blue solutions are required which are adaptable to the SCS to protect the environment and the ecosystems's health. Blue solutions are also peaceful solutions to ensure trust between the parties in managing complex sovereignty disputes because sovereignty, marine resources, and environmental protection in the SCS are intertwined. This is the only feasible way to gain trust and to reverse the current deteriorating trend in the marine environment and ecosystems of the SCS

REFERENCES

Borton, J. (2016) 'Environmental Issues and the South China Sea Arbitral Award', *Tien Phong Newspaper*.

CSIS Expert Team of the SCS (2017) 'The Action Plan of Fisheries Management and Environmental Cooperation in South China Sea'. Available at: http://www.nghiencuubiendong.vn/nghien-cuu-nuoc-ngoai/6734-ke-hoach-hanh-dong-ve-quan-ly-nghe-ca-va-moi-truong-o-bien-dong.

Espejo, E. (2015) 'Philippines Counts the Cost of China Build-Up in Disputed Sea', *Asia Correspondent*.

GIZ et al. (2017) 'Blue Solutions: Learning from Inspiring Experiences Worldwide', *Blue Solutions Newsletter*, 7.

GIZ et al. (no date) *Blue Solutions: From Asia and the Pacific*.

Global Agenda Councils (no date) *The Future of Our Oceans, the World Economic Forum*. Available at: http://www.weforum.org/community/global-agenda-councils/future-of-our-oceans.

Gomez, E. D. (2015) 'Potential Risk to Biodiversity and Economic Performance in the South China Sea', in *Scientific Conference 'South China Sea and Human Behavior'*. Hai Phong.

Gong, L., and Trajano, J. C. (2018) 'Advancing Marine Environmental Protection in the South China Sea', *Policy Report of RSiS Nanyang Technological University*.

de Groot, R., et al. (2012) 'Global Estimates of the Value of Ecosystems and Their Services in Monetary Units', *Ecosystem Services*, 1, pp. 51–60.

Heileman, S. (2008) 'South China Sea LME', *The UNEP Large Marine Ecosystem Report: A Perspective on Changing Conditions in MEs of the World's Regional Seas*, 182, pp. 297–308.

Jambeck, J. R., and Geyer, R. (2015) 'Science Research Reports', 347(6223). Available at: sciencemag.org.

Juinio-Meñez, M. A., and Gomez, E. D. (2016) 'Rock-Island-Reef: The High Stakes in the South China Sea', in *2nd International Seminar on Environmental and Maritime Security for a Blue SCS*. Hai Phong.

Lyons, Y., et al. (2019) 'Moving from MPAs to Area-Based Management Measures in the South China Sea', *The International Journal of Marine and Coastal Law*, 35, pp. 1–31. https://doi.org/10.1163/15718085-23521101.

McManus, J. W. (2016) 'Offshore Coral Reef Damage, Overfishing, and Paths to Peace in the South China Sea', in *E-Proceedings of Scientific Seminar on Environmental and Maritime Security for a Blue South China Sea*. Hai Phong.

Morton, B., and Blackmore, G. (2001) 'South China Sea', *Marine Pollution Bulletin*, 42(12), pp. 1236–1263.

Nass, T. (2002) 'Chapter 4: Dangers to Environment', in T. Kivimaki (ed.) *War or Peace in the South China Sea?* Great Britain: Nordic Institute of Asia Studies (NIAS) Press.

Nguyen Chu Hoi (2016a) 'Environmental Section of the South China Sea Arbitral Award', *Vietnam Journal of Science and Technology*, 11.

Nguyen Chu Hoi (2016b) 'How Does China "Wait" for the "U-Shaped Line" Award Decision?', *The Gioi Toan canh Newspaper* No. 65, pp. 7–9.

Nguyen Chu Hoi (2019a) *Sustainable Fisheries of Vietnam in the South China Sea: Threats and Possible Cooperation*.

Nguyen Chu Hoi (2019b) *Sustainable Management of Islands and Seas in Vietnam*. Ha Noi: Publishing House of National Politics.

Nguyen Chu Hoi and Vu Hai Dang (2015) 'Building a Regional Network and Management Regime of Marine Protected Areas in the South China Sea for Sustainable Development', *Journal of International Wildlife Law & Policy*, 18, pp. 128–138. https://doi.org/10.1080/13880292.2015.1044797.

Nguyen Quang Hung and Vu Viet Ha (2015) 'Marine Resources in Vietnam and Its Relevance to the Ability to Regenerate Resources', in *Scientific Conference 'South China Sea and Human Behavior'*. Hai Phong.

Pauli, G. (2014) *Blue Economy-10 Years, 100 Innovations, 100 Million Jobs*. Ha Noi: Phuong Nam, Thoi Dai Publishing Company.

Permanent Court of Arbitration (2016) *Press Release of the South China Sea Arbitration*.

Phang, S.-M., et al. (2016) 'Marine Algae of the South China Sea Bordered by Indonesia, Malaysia, Philippines, Singapore, Thailand and Vietnam', *Raffles Bulletin of Zoology Supplement*, 34, pp. 13–59. https://doi.org/10.1007/a43c-165932685f02.

Project Aware (no date) *Marine Debris, Project Aware*. Available at: http://www.projectaware.org.

Talaue-McManus, L. (2000) 'Transboundary Diagnostic Analysis for the South China Sea', *EAS/RCU Technical Report Series No. 14*.

Tran Dinh Lan and Nguyen Thi Phuong Hoa (2010) 'Rapid Assessment of Land-Based Sources of Coastal and Marine Pollution of Vietnam', *The UNEP GPA/VASI Report*.

UNEP (2004a) 'Coral Reefs in the South China Sea', *UNEP/GEF/SCS Technical Publications No. 2*, pp. 315–322.

UNEP (2004b) 'Mangroves in the South China Sea', *UNEP/GEF/SCS Technical Publication No. 1*.

UNEP (2004c) 'Seagrass in the South China Sea', *UNEP/GEF/SCS Technical Publications No. 3*.

UNEP (2012) *Progress in the Implementation of UNEP's Marine Litter Activities 2007–2011 and the Way Forward from 2012 to 2016*. Manila.

United Nations (no date) *Oceans*. Available at: http://www.un.org/en/sustainablefuture/oceans.shtml.

Viet Nam Administration of Seas and Lands (2011) *Report on the Current State of Vietnam's Marine Environment Till 2010*.

Vo Si Tuan (2016) 'Regional Efforts for Biodiversity Conservation in the SCS', in *2nd International Seminar on Environmental and Maritime Security for a Blue SCS*. Hai Phong.

Vu Hai Dang (2014) 'The GEF/UNEP Project "Reversing the Environmental Degradation Trend in the South China Sea and Gulf of Thailand', in R. Prime et al. (eds.) *The GEF/UNEP Project "Reversing the Environmental Degradation Trend in the South China Sea and Gulf of Thailand*. Martinus Nijhoff Publishers, pp. 150–156.

Zhang, H. (2018) 'Fisheries Cooperation in the South China Sea: Evaluating the Options', *Marine Policy 89*.

CHAPTER 7

Assessing Europe's Perspectives on the South China Sea

Nicola Casarini

INTRODUCTION

Europe—like the rest of the world—has a strategic interest in a peaceful environment in and around the South China Sea. A large part of Europe's global trade passes through the Sea's international waters to reach some of the EU's most important trading partners: China, Japan, and the Association of Southeast Asian Nations (ASEAN). The security situation in the South China Sea has deteriorated in recent times, mainly due to China's decision to step up territorial and maritime claims over large areas of the Sea. Beijing continues to challenge the rules-based order in the area by building artificial islands with military facilities and weapons systems, drilling for oil and gas, and chasing off its Southeast Asian neighbors' fishing vessels from waters where they have the rights to fish in accordance with the United Nations Convention on the Law of the Sea (UNCLOS). China's militarization of the South China Sea has been a

---

N. Casarini (✉)
Institute of International Affairs, Rome, Italy
e-mail: n.casarini@iai.it

© The Author(s), under exclusive license to Springer Nature Switzerland AG 2021
L. Buszynski and D. T. Hai (eds.), *Maritime Issues and Regional Order in the Indo-Pacific*, Palgrave Studies in Maritime Politics and Security, https://doi.org/10.1007/978-3-030-68038-1_7

wakeup call for the EU and its member states which have stepped up their involvement in the area. Brussels has made itself available to find a solution to the ongoing tensions in the area, in line with its normative approach to security issues. At the same time, some EU European states, in particular France and the UK, have sailed naval vessels in the Sea's international waters to send the message that European powers care about stability and the rules-based order in the South China Sea. This chapter examines Europe's perspectives on the South China Sea. It begins by examining the EU's strategic interests in and around the South China Sea. It subsequently assesses the response of the EU and its member states to the region's deteriorating security environment, including discussion of Europe's naval diplomacy in the Indo-Pacific region. The study argues that Europe is gradually shedding its traditional neutrality stance vis-à-vis territorial and maritime disputes in the South China Sea toward a general hardening of positions vis-à-vis Beijing. There is, in fact a growing willingness within the EU and among member states not only to issue diplomatic protests but also to take actions to defend the rules-based order in the region.

THE EVOLUTION OF EUROPE'S POSITION ON THE SOUTH CHINA SEA, FROM NEGLECT TO CONCERN

A distinctive EU position on the South China Sea's territorial and maritime disputes emerged only in the early 2010s. The EU's European Security Strategy (ESS) issued of 2003 acknowledged the importance of building relationships with Asia—in particular of developing strategic partnerships with Japan, China, and India—but did not refer to the South China Sea disputes at all (European Council 2003). In December 2007, the EU Council adopted the *Guidelines on the EU's Foreign and Security Policy in East Asia*. The document focused on North East Asia and in particular North Korea's nuclear program and Taiwan as issues of concern to the EU and where Europe was committed to play a more active role. The 2007 *Guidelines* made no reference to the South China Seas dispute and said little about Southeast Asia, beyond the EU's desire to deepen its engagement with the ASEAN grouping. The document underlined, however, the dangers of "competitive nationalism in the region" and specifically argued that the EU should "promote confidence-building measures and encourage peaceful and cooperative solutions to disputes over territory and resources" (EU Council 2007).

By the early 2010s, the South China Sea disputes had gained international attention. In this context, in June 2012 the EU adopted a revised version of the *Guidelines*. Much of the text was the same as the 2007 version. However, the 2012 version included Southeast Asia, making clear reference to the South China Sea, stating that "the recent increase in tensions in the South China Sea …could if unchecked have implications for navigation across the broader region, including for EU trade and investment interests". According to the 2012 *Guidelines*, the EU should "encourage the parties concerned to resolve disputes through peaceful and cooperative solutions and in accordance with international law (in particular UNCLOS), while encouraging all parties to clarify the basis for their claims," "recall previous work to build a collaborative diplomatic process on these issues at the regional level; and encourage ASEAN and China to build on this foundation and agree a Code of Conduct" (EU Council 2012).

Western Unity—Asian Division

The updated *Guidelines* served to prepare the way for the joint EU–US statement on the Asia-Pacific made by the Western allies at the margin of the ASEAN Regional Forum (ARF) meeting in Phnom Penh in July 2012. The Ashton-Clinton statement was the culmination of diplomatic efforts and consultations that had occurred between the transatlantic allies since autumn 2011, when the final declaration of the US–EU summit mentioned for the first time the Asia-Pacific as a region where dialogue and cooperation should be furthered between Washington and Brussels. In preparation for the joint EU–US statement, the European External Action Service (EEAS) released an updated and revised version of the *Guidelines* so as to send a reassuring message to the United States about EU intentions in a region where security and public goods are guaranteed by Washington but where the EU is politically absent. With the revised *Guidelines* and the joint EU–US statement, Brussels aligned its position on the Asia-Pacific with that of Washington. The joint EU–US statement on the Asia-Pacific region focuses on three areas of concern for the transatlantic allies: security, sustainable development, and trade (State Department 2012). Clear wording is used with regard to territorial and maritime disputes in the South China Sea which have the potential to affect the security of the sea lanes upon which US and EU trade with the region depend. In this context, the EU–US joint declaration contains an expression of encouragement for "ASEAN and China to advance a Code of Conduct and to resolve territorial and maritime disputes through peaceful, diplomatic and cooperative solutions."

In their joint statement, the EU and the US also pledge their commitment "to work with Asian partners on increasing maritime security based on international law as reflected in the UN Convention on the Law of the Sea" (State Department 2012). These are important passages that show the commitment of the transatlantic allies to the promotion of a stable and peaceful environment in a region which has been put at risk by conflicting territorial and maritime claims between a powerful and more assertive China and its smaller and weaker neighbors of Southeast Asia. Remarkably, while the West appeared united over sending a message to Beijing, during the 2012 ARF meeting a division emerged among Southeast Asian countries precisely on the same subject, i.e., what kind of approach to adopt vis-à-vis an economically important—but also increasingly assertive—China? For the first time in ASEAN's 45-year history, the foreign ministers of the 10-member bloc did not issue the traditional final communiqué which was expected in 2012 to endorse the grouping's position on a range of regional issues, most of all on the hotly debated topic of conflicting territorial and maritime claims between China and some members of ASEAN. At the 2012 ARF summit, Cambodia—the chair holder—refused to allow the Philippines, supported by Vietnam (and unofficially by the US), to include a reference in a communiqué to a stand-off between Manila's naval vessels and Beijing's ships over a reef claimed by both countries. Cambodia—supported by other ASEAN members—turned down the request by the Philippines on the ground that the question was a bilateral one—which is China's policy line—and that as such the 10-member bloc should not involve itself. The episode was a glaring demonstration of the increasing divisions within ASEAN—a division that continues today as the bloc's members are torn as to the approach to adopt vis-à-vis China.

The South China Sea Arbitration

In response to escalating tensions in the South China Sea due to Chinese land reclamation and militarization, in March 2016 the EU issued its first statement on the South China Sea arbitration, expressing the EU's neutrality regarding the various claims to land territory and maritime space in the region. The document underlined the EU's support for "maintaining a legal order for the seas and oceans based upon the principles of international law" especially UNCLOS, and urged 'all claimants to resolve disputes through peaceful means, to clarify the basis of their claims, and to pursue them in accordance with international law' and encouraged "further engagement in confidence building measures which seek to build trust and security in the region." While not explicitly referring to China, the statement noted that the EU was "concerned about the deployment of missiles on islands in the South China Sea," described "the temporary or permanent deployment of military forces or equipment on disputed maritime features which affects regional security and may threaten freedom of navigation and overflight" as "a major concern" and called on "all claimants to refrain from militarization in the region, from the use or threat of force, and to abstain from unilateral actions" (EU Council 2016a).

When the UNCLOS tribunal issued its ruling in favor of the Philippines in July 2016, the EU issued a further statement noting that "the European Union and its Member States …acknowledge the Award rendered by the Arbitral Tribunal," expressing "the need for the parties to the dispute to resolve it through peaceful means, to clarify their claims and pursue them in respect and in accordance with international law, including the work in the framework of UNCLOS," underling "the fundamental importance of upholding the freedoms, rights, and duties established in UNCLOS, in particular the freedoms of navigation and overflight," and recalling its March 2016 statement, called "upon the parties concerned to address remaining and further related issues through negotiations and other peaceful means and refrain from activities likely to raise tensions" (EU Council 2016b). The July 2016 statement was widely viewed as relatively weak, since it only 'acknowledged' the tribunal's decision, rather than calling for China to respect that decision. Beijing had tried to block the statement by putting pressure on some EU member states that had received significant Chinese investments. In the end, the declaration's final version was watered down by Greece, Hungary, and Croatia (Reuters 2016).

Other EU member states had taken a different—and a more principled—approach to the issue. The Foreign Ministers of France, Germany, Italy, and the United Kingdom—together with the Union's High Representative for Foreign Affairs and Security Policy—signed a declaration when the G7 met on maritime security in April 2015 which was, essentially, a response to Chinese assertive behavior in the East and South

China Sea. The *G7 Foreign Ministers' Statement on Maritime Security* included unusually strong language on the issue, emphasizing support for a rules-based approach to maritime governance and security, based on international law, in particular UNCLOS. The G7 Foreign Ministers' declaration committed the signatories "to the freedoms of navigation and overflight and other internationally lawful uses of the high seas and the exclusive economic zones as well as to the related rights and freedoms in other maritime zones, including the rights of innocent passage, transit passage and archipelagic sea lanes passage consistent with international law" (G7 2015). More recently, France, Germany, and the UK issued a statement on 29 August 2019, expressing the three countries' concern about the situation in the South China Sea and their support for the application of UNCLOS. The three "big" European states did this to reinforce their dissatisfaction with regard to growing Chinese assertiveness in the South China Sea and to send a message to their "like-minded" partners in Asia, in particular Japan and ASEAN. The E3 declaration was bolder compared to the statement issued the day before (28 August) by the EU-28 on the South China Sea with regard to the Haiyang Dizhi 8 incident in the Vietnamese Exclusive Economic Zone (EEZ) (E3 2019). Notwithstanding the varying degrees (and strengths) of their declarations, the EU and its member states are all concerned that growing tensions in the area could jeopardize Europe's significant economic interests in Asia.

Europe's Strategic Interests in and Around the South China Sea

In the Far East there are, in fact, some of Europe's biggest commercial partners—China, Japan, and the ASEAN grouping—as well as countries with which Brussels has signed important Free Trade Agreements (FTAs)—South Korea and Japan. Any turbulence in and around the South China Sea would thus have an immediate impact on Europe's prosperity and well-being. China is the EU's second largest trading partner. In 2018, two-way trade amounted to more than €580 billion. China and the EU currently trade more than 1.5 billion euros in goods each day. ASEAN as a whole represents the EU's third largest trading partner outside Europe (after the US and China) with more than €240 billion of trade in goods in 2018, while trade in services amounted to almost €80 billion. The EU is for China the largest and for ASEAN the second largest trading partner as well as the main source of investment. The EU has stepped up its economic engagement with Southeast Asia. Negotiations for a region-to-region FTA with ASEAN were launched in 2007 and paused in 2009 to give way to bilateral FTA negotiations, conceived as building blocks toward a future region-to-region agreement. Negotiations with Singapore and Malaysia were launched in 2010, with Vietnam in June 2012, with Thailand in March 2013, with the Philippines in December 2015, and with Indonesia in July 2016. Negotiations of an investment protection agreement are also under way with Myanmar (Burma). The European Commission finalized negotiations for trade and investment agreements with Singapore in October 2014 and with Vietnam in December 2015. At the regional level, the European Commission and the ASEAN member states have undertaken a stocktaking exercise to explore the prospects of the resumption of region-to-region negotiations. A joint EU–ASEAN Working Group for the development of a Framework setting out the parameters of a future ASEAN–EU FTA meets on a regular basis. The EU has also deepened security relations with ASEAN. After establishing a high-level dialogue on maritime security some years ago, the two groupings decided in January 2019 to upgrade their relationship to a strategic partnership. EU–ASEAN cooperation currently includes exchanges on anti-piracy techniques, maritime surveillance, port security, disaster relief, and capacity building. The EU is also training members of the ASEAN Regional Forum in preventive diplomacy and mediation. The peace, regional stability, and freedom of navigation and overflight in the South China Sea are of crucial importance for the EU and its member states.

Worsening Security Situation in the South China Sea

The security situation in the South China Sea has been deteriorating in recent years, mainly due to China's decision to step up territorial and maritime claims over large parts of the Sea. Since 2010, Beijing has adopted a more assertive posture over territorial and maritime disputes with its maritime neighbors, including statements from representatives of the People's Liberation Army (PLA) that the South China Sea is now a "core issue," giving the impression that the Sea is being elevated to the same strategic significance as Taiwan or Tibet. The US responded with a policy of re-engagement to Asia, encapsulated in the notion of the US "pivot" announced by Barack Obama during his visit to the region in November 2011 (Campbell 2016). This stance has been subsequently backed by the US new Defense Strategic Guidance in January 2012 which included plans to realign US forces and set up a new US Marine Corps base in Darwin, Australia, responsible for the South China Sea and the Indian Ocean, with the aim to keep China's claims in the region in check. Chinese claims are not only based on economic and security considerations, but also on national identity and the renewal of China's past glories. Chinese President Xi Jinping's speech at the 2019 National People's Congress cited China's island-building campaign in the South China Sea as one of the key accomplishments of his Presidency. This implicitly linked his China dream and plan for the rejuvenation of the country with the idea of restoring the glory of ancient times when China presided over a Sino-centric order in East Asia. President Xi's vision of the South China Sea goes to the very heart of China's national identity. In geography classes across the country, Chinese school children study maps of China's territory including the entire South China Sea, where the "nine-dash line" is clearly highlighted. The so-called "nine-dash line" is the border drawn around what China considers to be its sovereign rights in the South China Sea. It includes the islands, banks, and shoals as well as the surrounding waters of the Paracels, Spratlys, Scarborough Shoal, and Macclesfield Bank, and the Pratas Islands all the way down to James Shoal as its southernmost tip—1,800 miles from Mainland China. Chinese claims emphasize its sovereignty over territorial "features" (i.e., islands) within the area demarcated by the dashed lines. It follows that overlapping claims, and alternative interpretations, by other countries in the region—in particular Brunei, Malaysia, the Philippines, Taiwan, and Vietnam—are not recognized by Chinese authorities. The hard-line approach taken by the Chinese Communist Party is supported by Chinese public opinion, which has come to view Beijing's construction of artificial islands as perfectly within its rights, since it occurs within Chinese territory. The overwhelming view in China is that these are "our islands" (Financial Review 2016).

Competing Visions of a Rules-Based Order

There appears to be a glaring division between China, on the one hand, and Japan and the West, on the other, when it comes to the application of international law to sovereignty disputes in the South China

Sea. In July 2016, after more than three years of deliberation, the Arbitral Tribunal ruled on the dispute between the Philippines and China, making it clear that China's extensive claims to maritime areas within the so-called "nine-dash line" are incompatible with UNCLOS and therefore illegitimate (Permanent Court of Arbitration 2016). The tribunal also underscored that none of the land features claimed by China qualify as "islands"—something that would in turn warrant the claiming of an exclusive economic zone under UNCLOS. Following the ruling by The Hague Tribunal, the United States and Japan issued strong declarations condemning China. The EU—through Federica Mogherini, the EU's High Representative for Foreign Affairs and Security Policy—issued a milder declaration stressing the need for the parties to resolve the dispute in accordance with international law (EU Declaration 2016). China strongly condemned the ruling, declaring it "null and void" and questioned the legitimacy of the tribunal itself. This prompted other countries with interests in the South China Sea to reiterate their claims and the United States to intensify its freedom of navigation operations—deliberately sailing into waters claimed by China without notification to assert that they remain international waters—to deter Beijing from adopting more confrontational policies.

THE EU'S RESPONSE

The EU has responded to Chinese claims and assertive behavior toward the smaller neighbors in Southeast Asia in two ways: on the one hand, the EU has made itself available to facilitate ASEAN–China dialogue on devising a code of conduct for the South China Sea. On the other, it has lent support to EU member state naval operations that are aimed at reaffirming the rule of law. At the Shangri-La Dialogue in Singapore in June 2016, France's Defence Minister Jean-Yves Le Drian declared that Paris would encourage the EU to undertake "regular and visible" patrols in the area. In June 2018 there was an official from COASI—the EU Council's Working Group on the Asia-Pacific—on board one of the French vessels that joined the United States and other countries sailing through international waters in the South China Sea. The EU is scaling up its security engagement in and with Asia, in line with EU's global strategic objective to support a rules-based international order (EU Shared Vision 2016). In its Conclusions on *Enhanced EU Security Cooperation in and with Asia* adopted by the Council of the EU (*Foreign Affairs*) on 28 May 2018, the EU states its commitment to exploring possibilities to deepen security cooperation with its Asian strategic partners, in areas such as maritime security, cyber security, counter-terrorism, hybrid threats, conflict prevention, and the development of regional cooperative orders (EU Council 2018a). Following up on this, the European External Action Service (EEAS) and the European Commission have launched a pilot project in December 2018 to support tailor-made security cooperation with an initial set of five countries: India, Indonesia, Japan, Republic of Korea, and Vietnam, with a particular focus in four areas: maritime, counter-terrorism, crisis management (peacekeeping/CSDP), and cybersecurity (EU Council 2018b).

The pilot project builds on—and aims to expand—security cooperation initiatives already established between the EU and these five countries. Of particular relevance for the South China Sea is the high-level dialogue on maritime security that the EU and ASEAN have established some time ago. Their cooperation now includes exchanges on piracy lessons, maritime surveillance, port security, disaster relief, and capacity building. The EU is also training members of the ASEAN Regional Forum on preventive diplomacy and mediation. China does not feature in the pilot project, notwithstanding that Beijing is one of the EU's strategic partners in Asia. Recent developments seem thus to indicate that Europe is gradually shedding its neutrality stance vis-à-vis the South China Sea—based on the assumption that the EU should not confront China openly for fear of commercial reprisals—adopting instead a firm posture—backed up by concrete initiatives—in support of a rules-based order in the region and against Chinese behavior that seeks to impose its maritime claims by force. Naval diplomacy undertaken by some EU member states is possibly the most visible activity in this direction undertaken so far by Europe.

European Powers' Naval Diplomacy in and Around the South China Sea

Since 2014 French naval vessels have regularly patrolled the South China Sea and made port calls in regional states as well as in French territories in the area. France is the only European power with a geographical presence in the Indo-Pacific. The country is in fact rooted in the southern part of the Indian Ocean with the islands of Mayotte and La Réunion, the Scattered Islands, and the French Southern and Antarctic Territories. France is also anchored in the Pacific Ocean with its territories in New Caledonia, Wallis and Futuna, French Polynesia, and Clipperton Island. At the Shangri-La Dialogue in Singapore in June 2016, French minister of defense Jean-Yves Le Drian called on the European navies to coordinate their activities to ensure a presence as regular and visible as possible in the Indo-Pacific. The UK secretary of state for defense of that time, Michael Fallon, added that London was increasingly operating in combined formations, having tested the British expeditionary force with France. Following Le Drian's announcement for coordinated European maritime efforts, in 2016 France deployed a frigate to sail through the South China Sea with personnel from other EU member states on board, including Denmark, Italy, and Germany. In 2017 and 2018, the UK also sent a naval vessel to conduct operations in support of freedom of navigation. Europe's naval diplomacy—with several EU member states contributing, including the four major powers: France, the UK, Germany, and Italy, has allowed Europe to demonstrate support for the core values shared with the US and its Asian allies, but from an independent position based on distinctive European interests.

In the South China Sea there are hundreds of maritime features such as islands, atolls, rocks, cays, banks, shoals, and reefs, many of which are partly or completely submerged at high tide and uninhabitable. They are collectively known as the Pratas Islands, the Paracel Islands, Macclesfield Bank, and the Spratly Islands. The Europeans countries—in particular France—have generally tended to avoid challenging the Chinese presence in an area where there are still some international legal gray zones. However, a British warship did challenge China's straight baselines in the Paracel Islands. The legal status of the Spratly features and Scarborough Shoal was determined by the Arbitral Tribunal on 12 July 2016 and before the Shangri-La Dialogue in June 2018, Britain and France conducted a FONOP in the Spratly Islands near Subi, Mischief and Fiery Cross reefs. In those cases where the legal status of the South China Sea features remains unclear, the Europeans have tended to avoid challenging China with regard to the requirements for prior notification, in contrast with the US navy which has sometimes sailed through waters near features claimed by China without prior notification. A possible explanation of this difference between the Western allies is that the Europeans—in particular France whose vessels have sometimes had on board representatives of other EU member states and EU institutions—prefer to avoid provoking China for fear of commercial reprisals.

The 2017 French operation in support of freedom of navigation in the South and East China Sea encompassed five French navy vessels, including a transit in the Taiwan Strait, and was combined with a port call in Shanghai to demonstrate that the actions are not directed against China. The 2018 operation, which encompassed three British and two French naval vessels, omitted a port call in China. The decision not to visit China reflected growing European dissatisfaction with continued Chinese militarization in the area as well as with China's plans to negotiate a code of conduct for the Sea without including third countries such as the EU. This contributed to Western fears that a prospective code of conduct will include restrictions on the free movement of military vessels and aircraft. In 2019, Europe's naval diplomacy in the Indo-Pacific centered on the Indian Ocean. The capabilities that formed part of the operations were more important than before. France deployed the aircraft carrier Charles de Gaulle with a rotating cast of allied ships from the UK, Portugal, Denmark, Italy, Australia, and the United States. The carrier group sailed from the eastern Mediterranean off the Middle East via the Suez Canal to Bab-el-Mandep, the Horn of Africa and Yemen, then across the Indian Ocean and via the Malacca Strait to Singapore. During the deployment, the carrier group participated in maritime exercises with the Egyptian, Indian, and Japanese navies. It also included the passage of a French warship, the frigate Vendemiaire, through the Taiwan Strait. As a consequence, France was disinvited to a naval parade in Qingdao in April 2019 marking the 70 years since the founding of China's People's Liberation Navy (PLA-N). Europe's naval diplomacy represents concrete efforts by European powers to side with the United States and its Asian allies in countering a growing Chinese military presence across the Indo-Pacific and help defend common values and interests.

However, EU European states continue to sell military equipment in the region. French, German, British, and Italian arms manufacturers have developed a strong market presence in Southeast Asia, especially in sales of naval units (submarines, frigates, corvettes) and jet fighters. Competition exists among European defense companies, of course, but even more so between EU and US defense manufacturers for acquiring shares of Asia's buoyant procurement budgets. European defense companies also benefit from China's defense procurement budget, notwithstanding the persistence of the 1989 arms embargo against Beijing. According to SIPRI, Asia imports almost 20% of its armaments from Europe and around

30% from the United States. European arms sales represent an excellent example of the dilemma facing EU policymakers. On the one hand, Europe's defense sector is the source of highly paid jobs, contributing to the bloc's competitiveness and international technological excellence. To survive, the sector needs market outlets. Yet, the sale of arms, weapons systems, and dual-use goods has the potential to produce destabilizing effects in a part of the world such as the South China Sea where tensions between China, on the one hand, and the United States and its Asian allies, on the other hand, are increasing.

Conclusion

This chapter has examined Europe's perspectives on the South China Sea, including an examination of the EU's strategic interests in and around the South China Sea and the response to the region's deteriorating security environment. It has argued that China's militarization of the South China Sea has been a wakeup call for the EU and its member states which have stepped up their involvement in the area in recent times. Brussels has made itself available to find a solution to the ongoing tensions in the area, in line with its normative approach to security issues. At the same time, some EU European states, in particular France and the UK, have sailed naval vessels in the South China Sea's international waters to send the message that European powers care about stability and the rules-based order in the Sea. There is a growing willingness within the EU and among member states not only to issue diplomatic protests but also to take concrete actions to defend the rules-based order in the region. These dynamics open up new perspectives for collaboration between Europe and Asia, in particular between the EU and the ASEAN—as both regional groupings seek to defend the rules-based order and to avoid being squeezed by growing rivalry between the United States and China.

References

Campbell, Kurt 2016, *The Pivot: The Future of American Statecraft in Asia*, New York: Twelve.

EU Council 2003, *European Security Strategy—A Secure Europe in a Better World*, Brussels, December, p. 14. https://www.consilium.europa.eu/en/documents-publications/publications/european-security-strategy-secure-europe-better-world/.

EU Council 2007, *Guidelines on the EU's Foreign and Security Policy in East Asia*, Brussels, July, https://www.consilium.europa.eu/ueDocs/cms_Data/docs/pressdata/en/misc/97842.pdf.

EU Council 2012, *Guidelines on the EU's Foreign and Security Policy in East Asia*, Brussels, 15 June, http://eeas.europa.eu/archives/docs/asia/docs/guidelines_eu_foreign_sec_pol_east_asia_en.pdf.

EU Council 2016a, *Declaration by the High Representative on Behalf of the EU on Recent Developments in the South China Sea*, Brussels, 11 March, https://www.consilium.europa.eu/en/press/press-releases/2016/03/11/hr-declaration-on-bealf-of-eu-recent-developments-south-china-sea/.

EU Council 2016b, *Declaration on the Award rendered in the Arbitration Between the Philippines and China*, 15 July, https://eeas.europa.eu/delegations/cuba/6873/declaration-on-the-award-rendered-in-the-arbitration-between-the-philippines-and-china_fr.

EU Council 2018a, *Conclusions on Enhanced EU Security Cooperation in and with Asia*, Brussels, 28 May, https://www.consilium.europa.eu/en/press/press-releases/2018/05/28/deepening-eu-security-cooperation-with-asian-partners-council-adopts-conclusions/pdf.

EU Council 2018b, *EU Security Cooperation in and with Asia Under the Partnership Instrument*, Brussels, 3 December, General Secretariat (Working Paper) (WK 15000/2018 INIT).

EU Declaration 2016, *Declaration by the High Representative on behalf of the EU on the Award Rendered in the Arbitration Between the Republic of the Philippines and the People's Republic of China*, Brussels, 15 July, https://eeas.europa.eu/delegations/tunisia/6873/declaration-award-rendered-arbitration-between-philippines-and-china_en.

EU Shared Vision 2016, Common Action: A Stronger Europe. A Global Strategy for the European Union's Foreign And Security Policy, Brussels, June, https://europa.eu/globalstrategy/sites/globalstrategy/files/pages/files/eugs_review_web_13.pdf.

Financial Review 2016, Lisa Murray and Angus Grigg, 'Chinese Public Opinion Firmly Behind Beijing's Actions in the South China Sea', 16 July, http://www.afr.com/brand/special_reports/asia_trade/chinese-public-opinion-firmly-behind-beijings-actions-in-the-south-china-sea-20160714-gq5v56.

G7 2015, *G7 Foreign Ministers' Statement on Maritime Security*, Lübeck, 15 April, https://www.mofa.go.jp/files/000076378.pdf.

Nine Dash Line, http://www.southchinasea.org/maps/territorial-claims-maps/; also: Marina Tsirbas, 'What Does the Nine-Dash Line Actually Mean?', *The Diplomat*, 2 June 2016, https://thediplomat.com/2016/06/what-does-the-nine-dash-line-actually-mean/.

Permanent Court of Arbitration (PCA) 2016, The South China Sea Arbitration (The Republic of Philippines v. The People's Republic of China), https://www.pcacases.com/web/view/7.

Reuters 2016, Robin Emmott, 'EU's Statement on South China Sea Reflects Divisions', *Reuters*, 15 July, https://www.reuters.com/article/us-southchinasea-ruling-eu/eus-statement-on-south-china-sea-reflects-divisions-idUSKCN0ZV1TS.

State Department 2012, *Joint EU-US Statement on the Asia Pacific Region*, Phnom Penh, 12 July, https://2009-2017.state.gov/r/pa/prs/ps/2012/07/194896.htm.

CHAPTER 8

Nexus of the East and South China Seas: A Japanese Perspective

Tomotaka Shoji

INTRODUCTION

This chapter discusses the security situation in two seas in East Asia (including Southeast Asia), namely the East and South China Seas, from a Japanese perspective. Both seas are currently facing serious security challenges and are in a volatile security situation. For Japan, the security situations in the East and South China Seas are qualitatively different, and Tokyo has been addressing them accordingly. However, the two seas share some features and are causally associated, primarily due to China's assertive activities. Thus, this paper discusses the association between the two seas from Japan's perspective and the distinctive way the county has been addressing the security challenges in the two seas. First, it outlines recent improvements in Japan–China diplomatic relations. Second, it describes a deteriorating situation in the East China Sea despite the apparent amelioration in relations between Tokyo and Beijing. Third, it

T. Shoji (✉)
National Institute for Defense Studies, Tokyo, Japan
e-mail: t-shoji@nids.go.jp

© The Author(s), under exclusive license to Springer Nature Switzerland AG 2021
L. Buszynski and D. T. Hai (eds.), *Maritime Issues and Regional Order in the Indo-Pacific*, Palgrave Studies in Maritime Politics and Security, https://doi.org/10.1007/978-3-030-68038-1_8

tries to associate the East China Sea with the South China Sea by examining policy documents issued by the Japanese government, referring to its vision on a Free and Open Indo-Pacific (FOIP). Japan believes that the FOIP functions as an effective vision on regional order not only for economic development but also addressing maritime security. Fourth and finally, it explores Japan's South China Sea policy, both in multilateral and bilateral terms.

IMPROVEMENT IN JAPAN–CHINA RELATIONS

Recently, political relations between Japan and China have been improving remarkably. For his first visit to Japan, President Xi Jinping attended the G20 Summit in Osaka in June 2019, and during his stay in Osaka, President Xi held a bilateral meeting with Prime Minister Shinzo Abe. During this summit meeting, the two leaders agreed that Japan and China entered a "new era" establishing a new bilateral relationship. To consolidate this renewed relationship, Abe invited Xi to pay a state visit to Japan the following spring, and Xi accepted Abe's invitation (however, due to the spread of the coronavirus, Xi's planned visit was postponed). Regarding maritime security, they agreed to build "constructive relations" (Ministry of Foreign Affairs of Japan 2019b). At a working level, a coordination mechanism regarding cooperation in the Mekong sub-region was re-established. A meeting of the Japan–China Policy Dialogue on the Mekong Region was held in Tokyo in September 2019, and was attended by deputy director-general-level officials from the foreign ministries on both sides. The last time the meeting had been held was in December 2014. At the meeting, both countries shared information on their respective frameworks for cooperation in the Mekong sub-region and agreed on the importance of coordination with the Mekong countries, external supporting countries, and international institutions (Ministry of Foreign Affairs of Japan 2019d). Cooperative relations between Japan and China were symbolically resumed in the Mekong sub-region, where the two countries have long competed for regional leadership (Thitinan 2016).

In the maritime domain, bilateral cooperation is making progress. In May 2018, Japan and China signed a memorandum on a maritime and aerial communication mechanism between their defense authorities (Ministry of Foreign Affairs of Japan 2018). Furthermore, in February 2019, an agreement on maritime search and rescue came into effect after completion of the ratification process in both countries (Ministry of Foreign Affairs of Japan 2019a). Defense exchanges also are back on track, and various exchange programs have been conducted. For example, the Chief of Staff of the Japan Maritime Self-Defense Force (JMSDF) visited China for the first time in five years, and JMSDF vessels made a port call to China for the first time in eight years. During a side-line meeting at the 2019 Shangri-La Dialogue in Singapore, Defense Ministers Takeshi Iwaya and Wei Fenghe reconfirmed a continuation of their efforts to promote technical coordination toward the early establishment of a hotline between the two defense authorities, based on the maritime and aerial communication mechanism (Ministry of Defense of Japan 2019b).

Current Situation in the East China Sea

In contrast to the apparent, comprehensive developments in Japan–China diplomatic relations, the situation in the East China Sea is far from stable and has deteriorated. Japan is facing a serious security challenge from China in the sea, especially since the Japanese government's nationalization of the Senkaku Islands in 2012. China's assertiveness has since escalated, and Chinese government ships have repeatedly intruded into Japanese territorial waters around the Senkaku Islands, violating Japan's territorial sovereignty. China's assertiveness in the East China Sea in 2019 was much more apparent than in previous years. Until June, China regularly intruded into Japan's territorial waters around the Senkaku Islands three or four times a month, with the number of intrusions in January–June 2019 amounting to the total number of intrusions in 2018. Furthermore, Chinese government ships sailed in the contiguous zone of the Senkaku Islands for 64 consecutive days in April–June 2019, which was their longest time in the zone (Onihara et al. 2019). The Xi Jinping administration has actively implemented the dual principles of its foreign policy: promotion of the "path of peaceful development" and protection of its "core interests" (National Institute for Defense Studies 2019: 7). China continued to be extremely assertive and provocative in the East China Sea in 2020. In May, two large vessels of the China Coast Guard entered Japan's territorial waters near the Uotsuri Island of Senkaku, and attempted to chase a Japanese fishing boat within the water to demonstrate its territorial claim (Niekawa 2020).

The Japan Coast Guard (JCG), the frontline protector of Japan's territorial sovereignty and maritime interests, incessantly reinforces its operations in the East China Sea. In patrolling, the JCG warns Chinese government ships not to enter Japan's territorial waters, and if they do despite the warning, the JCG repeatedly makes a retreat request and controls the ships' route such that they can be moved out of the waters. Furthermore, as a law-enforcement agency founded on international law and Japan's domestic law, the JCG responds calmly but with a resolute attitude toward foreign fishing vessels and activist ships that make their own specific claims regarding territorial rights. Moreover, the JCG is further reinforcing its operational capabilities by establishing an exclusive unit for operations in the Senkaku waters and deploying more patrol vessels to this unit (Sankei Shimbun 2016a, 2019a). Regarding military activities, the Chinese military has been steadily expanding and intensifying its activities in the East China Sea. The Chinese military is emphasizing the continued improvement of its operational capabilities, which has resulted in its assertive activities, such as the "struggle" against the Senkaku Islands, the establishment of the East China Sea Air Defense Identification Zone (ADIZ) in 2013, and "regular patrols" by its navy and air force. It is highly probable that China is not only planning to make such activities routine, but to expand further and intensify them both qualitatively and quantitatively (Ministry of Defense of Japan 2019c: 71).

The operational area of the Chinese military is not confined to the East China Sea. Recently, China's PLA Navy (PLA-N) has been expanding the area of its regular activities southward. Its vessels are continuously operating in the area near the Senkaku Islands. In June 2016, a PLA-N frigate entered Japan's contiguous zone around the Senkaku Islands. This was the first time that a PLA-N combatant vessel entered the zone. PLA-N intelligence-gathering vessels (AGIs) have also been conducting activities near the Senkaku Islands. In January 2018, a submerged Chinese submarine entered the contiguous zone. This was the first time that the Ministry of Defense of Japan confirmed and announced such an incident. On the same day, a Chinese frigate entered the contiguous zone (Ministry of Defense of Japan 2019c: 71–72). The Japan Self-Defense Forces (JSDF) are actively engaged in the defense of remote islands. To effectively respond to a "gray-zone" situation, the JSDF is active in conducting joint exercises and port calls to demonstrate Japan's will and ability to address the situation. It is also critical to ensure maritime and air superiority through early-stage detection via persistent intelligence, surveillance, and reconnaissance (ISR) operations. If signs of an attack are picked up in advance, JSDF troops are immediately deployed to the area expected to be invaded ahead of the invading forces to block their access. In the event of a partial occupation of the territory, the JSDF will retake the territory by employing all necessary measures, such as bringing the enemy under control with ground fire from aircraft and vessels, followed by the landing of Japan Ground Self-Defense Force (JGSDF) units (Ministry of Defense of Japan 2019c: 277).

The JSDF is continuously making efforts to enhance its defense capabilities in the southwestern region. For example, the Japan Air Self-Defense Force (JASDF) established the 9th Air Wing in January 2016 and the Southwestern Air Defense Force in July 2017. In addition to the establishment of the Yonaguni Coast Observation Unit in March 2016, the JGSDF established the Amphibious Rapid Deployment Brigade with full-fledged amphibious operation capabilities in March 2018. Furthermore, the JGSDF deployed an area security unit to Amami Oshima and Miyakojima Islands in March 2019. The JGSDF will also deploy an area security unit responsible for an initial response to Ishigaki Island (Ministry of Defense of Japan 2019c: 277). The JMSDF is also strengthening its cooperation with the US navy based on the Japan–US alliance. The two naval forces are frequently engaged in joint activities in the broad Indo-Pacific region to enhance the efficiency and effectiveness of their ISR operations. The expansion of these ISR activities will serve to improve deterrence capabilities and ensure information superiority. It also enables the establishment of a seamless cooperation structure between Japan and the United States in all phases, from peacetime to contingencies. In accordance with the Guideline for Japan–United States Defense Cooperation, the two governments will cooperate closely with each other on measures to maintain maritime order in keeping with international law, including freedom of navigation. The JSDF and the US military will cooperate, as appropriate, in various efforts such as maintaining and enhancing bilateral presence in the maritime domain through ISR and joint exercises, while further developing and enhancing shared maritime domain awareness (MDA) (Ministry of Defense of Japan 2019c: 323).

Japan's Vision for Maritime Security

In the international community, interdependence among nations is progressively expanding and deepening. Concurrently, the emergence of new powers, including China, is significantly shifting the balance in international relations, which is consequently becoming more complicated with increasing uncertainty over the existing order. Against this backdrop, there is the notable emergence of inter-state rivalries across the political, economic, and military spheres, with states seeking to shape global and regional order to their advantage as well as increase their influence (Ministry of Defense of Japan 2018: 3). China is unilaterally engaging in coercive attempts to change the status quo based on its own specific assertions, which are incompatible with the existing international order. According to its assertions, Beijing has been expanding and intensifying military activities in the maritime and aerial domains, particularly in the East China Sea. Regarding the South China Sea, the "historic rights" claimed by China within the so-called nine-dash line were rejected in the Philippines–China arbitration issued in July 2016. Furthermore, in recent years, it has been pointed out that China is drawing baselines in the South China Sea that are in conflict with the United Nations Convention on the Law of the Sea (UNCLOS) by applying its own interpretations of the treaty (Ministry of Defense of Japan 2019c: 58). China has forcibly conducted large-scale, rapid reclamation of maritime features in the South China Sea, which are being converted into military footholds. The country is also expanding and intensifying its maritime and air activities in the South China Sea. The capability enhancement of the Chinese military serves to improve its anti-access/area denial (A2/AD) capabilities, enabling it to deny access and prevent the deployment of other militaries to its surrounding areas, to disrupt their military operations therein, and build capabilities with which to conduct military operations over greater distances (Ministry of Defense of Japan 2018: 5).

For Japan, the South China Sea is related to the task of dealing with a powerful and assertive China in the East China Sea. Within the context of increasing tensions in the East China Sea, the Japanese government is addressing the South China Sea in tandem with the East China Sea. More concretely, Japan is pursuing cooperation with the Association of Southeast Asian Nations (ASEAN) in multilateral dialogues as well as fostering bilateral cooperation with ASEAN claimants, like Vietnam and the Philippines, aiming to jointly address China's assertiveness (Shoji 2014: 128). To deal with China's maritime expansion, Japan's vision of a Free and Open Indo-Pacific (FOIP) ties the East China Sea to the South China Sea. In this vision, Japan aims to promote peace, stability, and prosperity across the Indo-Pacific region to make the region "free and open" for international public goods. As Kei Koga correctly pointed out, Japan's FOIP initially included many "conceptual ambiguities." However, Japan has gradually evolved the concept and made the FOIP more strategically sophisticated (Koga 2019: 288). The vision is composed of three pillars: (1) promotion and establishment of the rule of law, freedom of navigation, and free trade; (2) pursuit of economic prosperity by improving connectivity and strengthening economic partnerships; and (3) commitment to peace and stability, encompassing capacity building in maritime law enforcement (Ministry of Foreign Affairs of Japan 2019e).

Tokyo claims that the Indo-Pacific region is facing various security challenges such as non-traditional threats and "attempts to change the status quo," referring to China's maritime expansion in the East and South China Seas. Based on the vision, Japan has increased its commitment to peace and stability, including the promotion of strategic communication in the international arena through the media. Furthermore, Tokyo is keen on lending capacity-building assistance to countries in the Indo-Pacific region, including strengthening the capacity of maritime law enforcement and MDA, coupled with cooperation in humanitarian assistance and disaster relief (HA/DR), anti-piracy, counter-terrorism, and non-proliferation (Ministry of Foreign Affairs of Japan 2019e). In the defense domain, Japan's approach toward maritime security is embedded in the Vientiane Vision. In November 2016, the second ASEAN–Japan Defense Ministers' Informal Meeting was held in Vientiane. During this meeting, Defense Minister Tomomi Inada proposed Japan's initiative called the "Vientiane Vision: Japan's Defense Cooperation Initiative with ASEAN" as a guideline for Japan–ASEAN defense cooperation. The Vientiane Vision is the first document on Japan's defense policy to clearly present an overall picture of the areas of priority for the future direction of Japan–ASEAN defense collaboration. In this vision document, in addition to bilateral defense cooperation with ASEAN member states, Japan will promote multilateral defense cooperation with ASEAN that contributes to the association's capacity building by focusing on three points: (1) consolidating the regional/maritime order in line with the principles of international law; (2) reinforcing maritime security cooperation; and (3) effectively addressing increasingly diversifying and complex security issues.

The Vientiane Vision contains two important elements. First, it clarifies Japan's attitude toward ASEAN in defense cooperation. For Japan, ASEAN is undoubtedly an important strategic partner. Second, as Defense Minister Inada mentioned, Japan should cooperate with ASEAN in maritime security in East Asia, including both the East and South China Seas, which are getting more complicated and are deteriorating

(Ministry of Defense of Japan 2016). With China's aggressive maritime expansion, Japan has expressed its active involvement in maintaining order based on the rule of law in Southeast Asia. Japan is aiming to promote understanding of international law on sea and in the air, improve information gathering, and search and rescue capabilities. The objective is to spread awareness of international law and strengthen maritime security throughout ASEAN through various means of cooperation (Nishida 2018).

Pursuing Maritime Security in the South China Sea

Despite not being a claimant, Japan has been greatly interested in the South China Sea in terms of trade and energy security. For Japan, the sea is the main route for energy supply from the Middle East. Tokyo is concerned about freedom of navigation in the South China Sea being threatened in the event of escalation in confrontations between the countries involved. The South China Sea is closely tied to the East China Sea. Japan's engagement in the South China Sea is aimed at preventing China from enforcing its unilateral claim to the sea, and from making bilateral deals with ASEAN claimants regardless of the current maritime order based on international law (Sato 2016: 273). Japan's perception of the South China Sea is that the dispute is of great concern to the entire international community due to its direct implications for peace and stability of the Indo-Pacific region. The countries involved, including China, are urged to refrain from taking unilateral actions that heighten tension and to act in accordance with the rule of law (Ministry of Defense of Japan 2019c: 77). In this regard, it is crucial for Tokyo to collaborate with ASEAN, both multilaterally and bilaterally, aiming at demonstrating a unified will to jointly tackle China's assertiveness and check its unilateral and aggressive behavior. The Japanese government has utilized multilateral security dialogues to try to establish rules and coordination mechanisms to manage the South China Sea dispute. Since 2010, Japan has consistently expressed its concerns at multilateral settings and emphasized the need to maintain the current maritime order (Storey 2013: 151).

In a broader context, the maritime disputes and China's assertiveness are related to China's challenge of the long-held regional order. Tokyo aims to protect and strengthen the US-led liberal order in East Asia.

Japan's growing strategic interest in ASEAN is reinforced by Tokyo's desire to protect the existing regional order. To achieve this objective, the Japanese government under Prime Minister Abe tried to collaborate with ASEAN to check China's rise, not only in military terms but also in the strengthening of maritime law-enforcement agencies, providing "greater hedging and balancing options" for ASEAN countries (Lee 2015: 4). Tokyo's basic approach in multilateral arenas is to put maritime security on the agenda, reiterating the importance of resolving territorial disputes in a peaceful manner and securing freedom of navigation based on the rule of law, as universal rules that every country should observe. This approach aims to check China's unilateral behavior in the South China Sea by garnering support from as many regional countries as possible, including ASEAN members. It also implies an attempt to encourage China to refrain from taking assertive actions in the East China Sea (Shoji 2014: 132). In the East Asia Summit's Foreign Ministers' Meeting held in August 2019, Foreign Minister Taro Kono stressed the importance of upholding the rule of law in every sea including the East and South China Seas and stated that Japan shares with the East Asian Summit (EAS) participating countries a serious concern over the worsening situation in the East and South China Seas. He expressed his strong opposition to attempts to unilaterally change the status quo as well as acts of intimidation against other parties and called for the demilitarization of disputed features and peaceful resolution of disputes in accordance with international law as reflected in UNCLOS. He also emphasized that the Code of Conduct in the South China Sea (COC) must uphold the principles of freedom of the seas, and must not prejudice the interests of third parties or the rights and freedoms of all states under international law (Ministry of Foreign Affairs of Japan 2019c).

Compared to its approach toward multilateral dialogues, Japan's bilateral support to ASEAN countries focuses more on the strengthening of their coastal defense capabilities. Since the re-intensification of the South China Sea disputes, ASEAN claimants such as Vietnam and the Philippines have sought to reinforce security cooperation with external powers. Whereas the foremost partner might be the United States, Japan is also considered to be a reliable partner. These ASEAN claimants need substantial support from Japan for modernizing equipment as well as promoting capacity building. Since the re-inauguration of the Abe administration in December 2012, Japan has become remarkably active in providing substantial support to Hanoi and Manila. This support also demonstrates

Japan's will to form a unified stance between Japan and the ASEAN claimants for checking China's assertiveness in maritime areas.

The Japanese government officially expressed its intention to begin talks with Hanoi on the provision of patrol vessels at a meeting between the prime ministers of the two countries in December 2013 (Ministry of Foreign Affairs of Japan 2013b). Further in August 2014, Japan signed with Vietnam an exchange of notes concerning Japan's non-project aid to Vietnam, in which the Japanese government pledged to provide six used vessels and equipment related to maritime safety, aiming at enhancing Vietnam's maritime law-enforcement capabilities (Ministry of Foreign Affairs of Japan 2014). Furthermore, in January 2017, Prime Minister Abe agreed with Prime Minister Nguyen Xuan Phuc that Japan should provide six more newly constructed patrol vessels to Vietnam's Coast Guard (Ministry of Foreign Affairs of Japan 2017). In defense cooperation, capacity-building assistance is being strongly promoted by the Japan Ministry of Defense (MOD). In fact, the MOD has been implementing projects on capacity-building assistance to Vietnam most intensively. Regarding maritime security, since 2012 Japan has quite regularly conducted a seminar with its Vietnamese counterpart on underwater medicine. This project seems to contribute to submarine operations conducted by the Vietnamese Navy. The seminars have often been conducted together with the United States and Australian navies, which clearly contributes to the strengthening of trilateral/quadrilateral defense cooperation on maritime security with Vietnam and its partners (Ministry of Defense of Japan 2020). Furthermore, the JMSDF frequently made "strategic" port calls in Vietnam to enhance its naval presence in the South China Sea. For example, two JMSDF vessels visited Cam Ranh Bay in April 2016 as their first visit to this strategic chokepoint for Vietnam, followed by the visit of the submarine Kuroshio in September 2018. In June 2019, two destroyers (Izumo and Murasame) made a port call to Danang to develop friendship with the Vietnamese Navy (Sankei Shimbun 2016b, 2018, 2019b). Japan and Vietnam are also increasingly cooperating in defense technology and equipment: a memorandum of understanding (MOU) on promoting cooperation in the defense industry was signed between the two countries in May 2019 (Ministry of Defense of Japan 2019a).

Bilateral cooperation in maritime security between Japan and the Philippines has developed significantly over the last few years, even under the Duterte administration, which often takes a conciliatory stance toward

China regarding the South China Sea. Collaboration between Tokyo and Manila reflects a convergence of their shared concern over the South China Sea, or more broadly, a shared security concern about maritime issues against the backdrop of China's assertiveness. Under the Abe administration, Tokyo vigorously supported Manila's efforts to enhance its coastal defense capabilities in various respects. First, the provision of patrol vessels should be noted. During the bilateral summit meeting held in July 2013, Abe pledged to provide ten patrol vessels through a yen loan, as a "strategic use" of official development assistance (ODA) to enhance the capabilities of the Philippine Coast Guard (Ministry of Foreign Affairs of Japan 2013a). The first ship arrived in Manila in August 2016. The coast guards of Japan and the Philippines conducted a joint exercise in May 2017, in which a Philippine patrol vessel provided by Japan participated.

Moreover, capacity-building assistance has been implemented. In February 2015, Japan's MOD commenced support for the Philippine Air Force through a project on air transport, inviting Filipino military officers to JSDF bases (Ministry of Defense of Japan 2015). Projects on capacity building between Japan and the Philippines have been further accelerated and diversified since the June 2015 joint declaration highlighted the strengthening of security cooperation. The annex Action Plan to implement the strengthening of the strategic partnership mentioned items of cooperation including information sharing, HA/DR, maritime security, cooperation in defense equipment and technology, and capacity-building assistance (Ministry of Foreign Affairs of Japan 2015). Moreover, the Japanese government provided patrol aircraft (TC-90) to the Philippines as the first case of provision of JSDF equipment to ASEAN based on the Three Principles on Transfer of Defense Equipment and Technology, newly defined by the Japanese government (Ministry of Foreign Affairs of Japan 2016). The JMSDF and the Philippine Navy have embarked on bilateral joint exercises. In January 2015, Defense Ministers of Japan and the Philippines signed an MOU on defense cooperation and exchanges. Based on this MOU, the two navies conducted their first bilateral joint exercise in the South China Sea. In July of the same year, they also conducted a joint ISR exercise in Palawan Island facing the South China Sea, using P-3C patrol aircraft. In addition to participation in US–Philippine joint exercises like "CARAT" and "PHIBLEX," Japan reinforces cooperation between "spokes" based on the system of US alliances in the Indo-Pacific region. Also, the Philippine Air Force participated in the "2015 Cope North Guam," a joint exercise between Japan, the United States, and Australia. The trend continues even under the Duterte administration: in May 2019, a quadrilateral joint training exercise among the navies of Japan, the United States, India, and the Philippines was conducted in the South China Sea. Japan's promotion of joint training and exercises with ASEAN countries in cooperation with its ally and security partners in the Indo-Pacific is a part of its efforts to reinforce Quad cooperation. Tokyo is trying to combine and synergize various bilateral activities of defense cooperation among "like-minded" ASEAN countries and ASEAN's dialogue partners.

Conclusion

Despite the apparent and comprehensive development of Japan–China diplomatic relations, the security situation in the East China Sea is volatile. To effectively deal with the East China Sea, in addition to reinforcing self-reliance measures as well as cooperation with the United States based on their alliance, Japan is keen to collaborate with ASEAN in the South China Sea. Security cooperation between Japan and ASEAN is both multilateral and bilateral, covering a variety of activities from cooperation on multilateral dialogues to bilateral capacity-building assistance on maritime security. These initiatives are based on Japan's vision of the Free and Open Indo-Pacific (FOIP) and the Vientiane Vision regarding defense cooperation. The FOIP vision underscores, as one of its three pillars, the promotion and establishment of the rule of law and freedom of navigation. Whether Japan can effectively manage maritime issues and regional security cooperation depends on how Tokyo can collaborate with ASEAN as well as the United States, based on their alliance, and involve other regional players.

(The views expressed herein are entirely the author's own and do not represent the official position of his organization.)

References

Koga, K. (2019) Japan's "Free and Open Indo-Pacific" Strategy: Tokyo's Tactical Hedging and the Implications for ASEAN. *Contemporary Southeast Asia* 41 (2): 286–313.

Lee, J. (2015) *Strategic Possibilities and Limitations for Abe's Japan in Southeast Asia*. Trends in Southeast Asia (ISEAS Yusof-Ishak Institute) 8.

Ministry of Defense of Japan (2015) *Hesei-26-Nendo Firipin niokeru Noryoku Kochiku Shien Jigyo* [Project on Capacity-building Assistance for the Philippines in FY2014], 20 February: https://www.mod.go.jp/j/approach/exchange/cap_build/philippines/h270217.html.

Ministry of Defense of Japan (2016) *Dai 2-kai Nichi-ASEAN Boei Daijin Tanto Kaigo* [Second Japan-ASEAN Defense Ministers' Informal Meeting], 16 November: https://www.mod.go.jp/j/approach/exchange/dialogue/j-asean/admm/02/j-asean_02.html.

Ministry of Defense of Japan (2018) National Defense Program Guidelines for FY 2019 and Beyond, 18 December: www.mod.go.jp/j/approach/agenda/guideline/2019/pdf/20181218_e.pdf.

Ministry of Defense of Japan (2019a) *Nichi-Etsu Boesho Kaidan* [Japan-Vietnam Defense Ministers' Meeting], 2 May: https://www.mod.go.jp/j/approach/exchange/area/docs/2019/05/02_j-viet_gaiyo.html.

Ministry of Defense of Japan (2019b) *Nicchu Boesho Kaidan (Gaiyo)* [Outline of the Japan-China Defense Ministers' Meeting (Overview)], 1 June: https://www.mod.go.jp/j/approach/exchange/area/docs/2019/06/01_j-chin_gaiyo.html.

Ministry of Defense of Japan (2019c) Defense of Japan 2019.

Ministry of Defense of Japan (2020) Capacity Building Assistance: Viet Nam, 10 March: https://www.mod.go.jp/e/d_act/exc/cap_b/vietnam/index.html.

Ministry of Foreign Affairs of Japan (2013a) *Nichi-Firipin Shuno Kaidan (Gaiyo)* [Japan-Philippines Summit Meeting (Overview)], 27 July: http://www.mofa.go.jp/mofaj/kaidan/page3_000326.html.

Ministry of Foreign Affairs of Japan (2013b) Japan-Viet Nam Summit Meeting, 15 December: http://www.mofa.go.jp/region/page23e_000033.html.

Ministry of Foreign Affairs of Japan (2014) Signing on Exchange of Notes Concerning Japan's Non-Project Grant Aid to Viet Nam, 1 August: http://www.mofa.go.jp/press/release/press4e_000386.html.

Ministry of Foreign Affairs of Japan (2015) Action Plan for Strengthening of the Strategic Partnership (Annex of the Joint Declaration), 4 June: www.mofa.go.jp/mofaj/files/000083659.pdf.

Ministry of Foreign Affairs of Japan (2016) *TC-90-to no Firipin eno Iten* [Transfer of TC-90 to the Philippines], 6 September: www.mofa.go.jp/mofaj/s_sa/sea2/ph/page3_001796.html.

Ministry of Foreign Affairs of Japan (2017) Japan-Viet Nam Summit Meeting, 16 January: https://www.mofa.go.jp/s_sa/sea1/vn/page4e_000577.html.

Ministry of Foreign Affairs of Japan (2018) Premier of the State Council of China Li Keqiang Visits Japan: Japan-China Summit Meeting and Banquet, 9 May: https://www.mofa.go.jp/a_o/c_m1/cn/page3e_000857.html.

Ministry of Foreign Affairs of Japan (2019a) Japan-China Agreement on Maritime Search and Rescue (SAR) Came into Effect, 14 February: https://www.mofa.go.jp/mofaj/press/release/press4_007066.html.

Ministry of Foreign Affairs of Japan (2019b) Japan-China Summit Meeting and Dinner, 27 June: https://www.mofa.go.jp/a_o/c_m1/cn/page3e_001046.html.

Ministry of Foreign Affairs of Japan (2019c) The Ninth East Asia Summit (EAS) Foreign Ministers' Meeting, 2 August: https://www.mofa.go.jp/a_o/rp/page4e_001056.html.

Ministry of Foreign Affairs of Japan (2019d) The Sixth Meeting of the Japan-China Policy Dialogue on the Mekong Region, 13 September: www.mofa.go.jp/s_sa/sea1/page22e_000917.html.

Ministry of Foreign Affairs of Japan (2019e) Free and Open Indo-Pacific, 21 November: https://www.mofa.go.jp/files/000430632.pdf.

National Institute for Defense Studies (2019) *China Security Report 2019: China's Strategy for Reshaping the Asian Order and Its Ramifications.* Tokyo: National Institute for Defense Studies (NIDS).

Niekawa, S. (2020) Chugoku Kosen 2-Seki Nihon Gyosen ni Sekkin-shi Tsuibi Senkaku-Oki no Ryokai [2 Chinese Government Vessels Approached and Chased a Japanese Fishing Boat Within the Territorial Waters of the Senkaku Islands]. *Asahi Shimbun*, 9 May www.asahi.com/articles/ASN593CGWN59UTIL003.html.

Nishida, I. (2018) *Nihon no Tai-ASEAN Boei Gaiko: Bienchan Bijon towa Nanika?* [Japan's Defense Diplomacy with ASEAN: What is the 'Vientiane Vision'?]. In International Information Network Analysis (IINA), Sasagawa Peace Foundation, 24 August: www.spf.org/iina/articles/nishida-asean-economy.html.

Onihara, T, K. Tomina, and N. Fukuda (2019) "Eien no Ringoku" Ayumiyori Kyocho, Kadai mo: Nicchuu Ryoshuno no Omowaku ["Permanent Neighbors": Emphasis on Rapprochement, Further Challenges, and Different Intentions between the Leaders of Japan and China]. *Asahi Shimbun*, 28 June: www.asahi.com/articles/ASM6W7J7GM6WUTFK016.html.

Sankei Shimbun (2016a) *"Senkaku Keibi Senju Butai" Kansei e* [Completion of the "Forces Exclusively for Protecting the Senkaku Islands"], 24 February: https://www.sankei.com/politics/news/160224/plt1602240003-n1.html.

Sankei Shimbun (2016b) *Kaiji-Goekan ga Etsu no Yosho Kamuran-Wan ni Hatsu-Kiko* [A JMJSDF Destroyer Makes its First Visit to the Cam Ranh Bay], 12 April: https://www.sankei.com/politics/news/160412/plt1604120008-n1.html.

Sankei Shimbun (2018) *Kaiji-Sensuikan Minami-Shinakai de Kunren* [A JMJSDF Submarine Trained in the South China Sea], 17 September: https://www.sankei.com/politics/news/180917/plt1809170009-n1.html.

Sankei Shimbun (2019a) *Ishigaki-Jima ni Saidaikyu Junshisen Haibi e* [The Largest Patrol Vessel Deployed to the Ishigaki Island], 13 June: https://www.sankei.com/affairs/news/190613/afr1906130060-n1.html.

Sankei Shimbun (2019b) *Goekan "Izumo" ga Betonamu Gunji-Yosho Kamuran-Wan ni Kiko* [Destroyer "Izumo" visits Cam Ranh Bay, a military chokepoint of Vietnam], 14 June: https://www.sankei.com/politics/news/190614/plt1906140018-n1.html.

Sato, Y. (2016) Japan and the South China Sea Dispute: A Stakeholder's Perspective. In: I. Storey and C. Lin (eds.), *The South China Sea Dispute: Navigating Diplomatic and Strategic Tensions*, Singapore: ISEAS Yusof-Ishak Institute, pp. 272–290.

Shoji, T. (2014) The South China Sea: A View from Japan. *NIDS Journal of Defense and Security* 15: 127–141.

Storey, I. (2013) Japan's Maritime Security Interests in Southeast Asia and the South China Sea Dispute. *Political Science* 65 (2): 135–156.

Thitinan, P. (2016) Thailand: Military Resurgence and Geostrategic Imbalance. In: *Security Outlook of the Asia-Pacific Countries and Its Implications for the Defense Sector* (NIDS Joint Research Series No. 14). Tokyo: NIDS, pp. 73–85.

CHAPTER 9

Misperceptions of China's East China Sea ADIZ: Technical Flaws and Legal Facts

Cao Qun

Since the establishment of China's East China Sea (ECS) Air Defense Identification Zone (ADIZ) in November 2013, some scholars and policymakers have misinterpreted certain legal facts of that zone. They usually describe its rules as being "unlike other ADIZ rules," even though, as this article will demonstrate, China's ADIZ policies fall within international norms. Notable misperceptions include, but are not limited to: first, the ECS ADIZ includes the *disputed* Diaoyu Dao/Senkaku Islands (hereinafter referred to as "Diaoyu Dao Islands"); second, China's ADIZ rules do not distinguish between civil and state aircraft; third, the Chinese rules apply to all aircraft flying in the ADIZ, and make no exception for aircraft not intending to enter Chinese national airspace (Roach 2017). The above misperceptions, which touch on the fundamental nature of China's ECS ADIZ, have received insufficient attention in the media and

---

C. Qun (✉)
China Institute of International Studies, Beijing, China
e-mail: caoqun@ciis.org.cn

© The Author(s), under exclusive license to Springer Nature Switzerland AG 2021
L. Buszynski and D. T. Hai (eds.), *Maritime Issues and Regional Order in the Indo-Pacific*, Palgrave Studies in Maritime Politics and Security, https://doi.org/10.1007/978-3-030-68038-1_9

if left unclarified, could worsen distrust between governments and escalate tensions in the region. While this article does not seek to provide a comprehensive analysis of China's strategy and motivations in the ECS, the author hopes that establishing the basic legal facts regarding the ECS ADIZ can facilitate constructive dialogue between relevant actors going forward.

CHINA'S ECS ADIZ DOES NOT COVER THE TERRITORIAL AIRSPACE OF THE DIAOYU DAO ISLANDS

Quite a few scholars argue that both Japan's ADIZ and China's ADIZ include the Diaoyu Dao Islands. This is not correct. In fact, Japan's ADIZ does cover the islands, but China's ECS ADIZ does not. The November 2013 Chinese Government Statement announcing the ECS ADIZ (*China Daily* 2013a) made it clear that "the zone includes the airspace within the area enclosed by China's *outer limit of the territorial sea* [emphasis author's own] and the following six points: 33°11′N (North Latitude) and 121°47′E (East Longitude), 33°11′N and 125°00′E, 31°00′N and 128°20′E, 25°38′N and 125°00′E, 24°45′N and 123°00′E, 26°44′N and 120°58′E." Because the islands are "an inseparable part of the Chinese territory" and thus generate a territorial sea,[1] China's ADIZ borders the outer limit of the territorial airspace of the islands and therefore *surrounds* the national airspace of the islands, but does not *include* it. This fact can refute the conventional argument that "China's primary purpose in declaring an ADIZ was to advance and strengthen its claim to the islands, most likely as a reaction to the Japanese government's purchase of three of the five islands from private Japanese citizens in late 2012" (Burke and Cevallos 2017). Knowing that the Japanese ADIZ covers the territorial airspace of the *contested* islands, China would not exclude the territorial airspace of the islands from the ECS ADIZ, if the purpose of the ECS ADIZ is to retaliate against Japan for "purchase of the islands." Accordingly, China's establishment of the ECS ADIZ should perhaps be viewed less as primarily a move to strengthen its claim over a *contested* territory, and more to do with China's concerns over protecting its national

---

[1] The baselines of the territorial waters of the Diaoyu Dao Islands have been publicized by the Chinese Government on September 10, 2012. See "Diaoyu Islands Baseline Announcement Significant: Diplomat," *China Daily*, September 13, 2012, http://www.chinadaily.com.cn/china/2012Diaoyu/2012-09/13/content_15756926.htm.

security interests in the ECS, where Japan's ADIZ covers a large area and China formerly had none. Even if the ECS ADIZ includes the islands, establishing an ADIZ that includes "contested territory" does not necessarily legitimize a sovereign claim, and is legally acceptable. From a purely international-law-based perspective, an ADIZ itself has no impact on sovereignty claims at all. The establishment of an ADIZ, whether including or excluding contested territory, is irrelevant to the claim. As an example, Japan's ADIZ does not cover the disputed Takeshima/Dokto Islands, nor does it cover the Northern Territories (Southern Kurils), which does not mean Japan cedes its claims; similarly, South Korea's ADIZ covers Takeshima/Dokto Islands, legally has no relevance for its claim. Taiwan's ADIZ does not cover the Diaoyu Dao Islands, which has no relevance for its sovereignty claim either. As such, it would be unreasonable for China to declare an ADIZ with the primary intent of advancing and strengthening its claim to the islands.

In addition, existing precedents demonstrate that an ADIZ covering *contested* territory does not make it legally unacceptable. Setting aside the fact that Japan's ADIZ covers the same *disputed* islands, there are a couple of precedents for governments establishing an ADIZ over the *indisputable* territory of another country. For example, the South Korean ADIZ—originally established by the United States in 1951, later extended south in 2013—covers a large portion of North Korea (see Map 9.1) (Ikeshima 2016). Another case is the Taiwan authorities' ADIZ, which covers part of Japan's Yonaguni Island. In response, Japan in 2010 unilaterally declared an extended ADIZ line that covered Yonaguni Island completely (China News 2010). Japanese officials with the Ministry of Foreign Affairs told the Taipei Times (Shih 2010) that "ADIZ demarcation is at the discretion of each country, [so] it was natural for Japan not to seek prior approval" from the Taiwan authorities. Taipei denies the validity of that change, and to this day insists on the 123°00'E line established by the United States as the limit of the Japanese ADIZ decades ago. If including the *indisputable* territory of another country in an ADIZ is not contrary to international practice, China's enclosure of *contested* territory should not be criticized either.

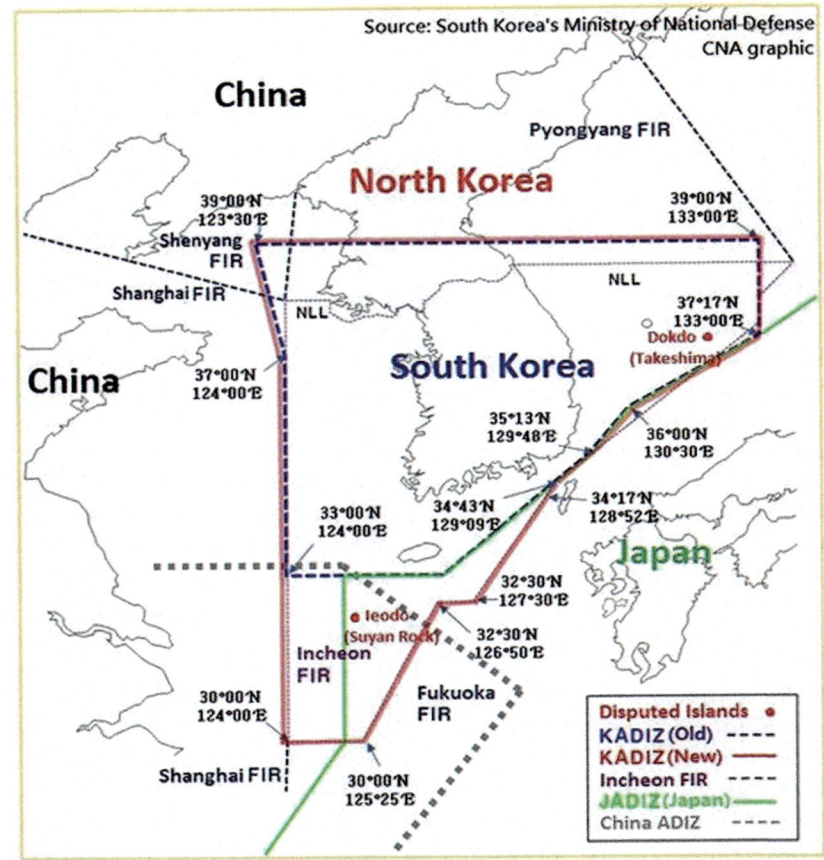

Map 9.1 South Korea's ADIZ

THERE IS NO EVIDENCE THAT CHINA'S ADIZ RULES APPLY TO MILITARY AIRCRAFT

Some American scholars, without sufficient evidence and thorough analysis, criticize China's ECS ADIZ rules for applying not only to civil aircraft, but also to state aircraft,[2] including military, customs, and police aircraft. However, according to the aircraft identification rules for the ECS ADIZ, there is actually no "applicability" clause in China's rules, and the full text (*China Daily* 2013b) does not contain any expression of *civil* or *state* aircraft:

1. Flight plan identification. Aircraft flying in the East China Sea Air Defense Identification Zone should report the flight plans to the Ministry of Foreign Affairs of the People's Republic of China or the Civil Aviation Administration of China.
2. Radio identification. Aircraft flying in the East China Sea Air Defense Identification Zone must maintain two-way radio communications, and respond in a timely and accurate manner to the identification inquiries from the administrative organ of the East China Sea Air Defense Identification Zone or the unit authorized by the organ.
3. Transponder identification. Aircraft flying in the East China Sea Air Defense Identification Zone, if equipped with the secondary radar transponder, should keep the transponder working throughout the entire course.
4. Logo identification. Aircraft flying in the East China Sea Air Defense Identification Zone must clearly mark their nationalities and the logo of their registration identification in accordance with related international treaties.

Such ambiguity in the "applicability" of the Chinese rules is not unique. The United States, as the first country to establish ADIZs and whose ADIZ practices are used as a precedent by other countries, had similarly ambiguous provisions (15 Federal Register 1950) around applicability prior to a 1961 amendment of US ADIZ regulations:

§620.1 *Basis and purpose*. The regulations prescribed in this part contain rules and regulations which have been found necessary in the interest of national security to identify, locate, and control U.S. and foreign aircraft

---

[2] "Aircraft used in military, customs and police services shall be deemed to be state aircraft." See Convention on International Civil Aviation, done at Chicago on the 7th day of December 1944, Article 3(b).

operated within areas designated by the administrator of Civil Aeronautics as air defense identification zones (ADIZ).

The American regulations perhaps intentionally used the expression *U.S. and foreign aircraft* in the above clause (which might make the US ADIZ rules in 1950s "literally" apply to foreign military aircraft). Under US Federal Regulations at that time, a "foreign aircraft" is defined as an aircraft other than a "US aircraft," and the definition of "US aircraft" includes both US civil and military aircraft, which could lead to the interpretation that the definition of "foreign aircraft" includes foreign military aircraft.[3] Considering the fact that the US ADIZs cover airspace over the high seas adjacent to its coast, the possible inclusion of foreign military aircraft under US ADIZ rules would contract the traditional high seas freedoms that the United States claims for military aircraft. The ambiguity surrounding whether military aircraft are subject to the US ADIZ rules was seemingly clarified in the late 1950s. The related provisions in *14 CFR* had listed "Sec.1202. Security Control of Air Traffic" of the *Federal Aviation Act of 1958* as one of the legislative authorization clauses, which stated very clearly that the rules or regulations only apply to civil aircraft.[4] The ambiguous provision in "applicability" was officially amended in the Federal Register on October 14, 1961 (this amendment became effective

---

[3] See 15 Fed. Reg. (1950), December 27, 1950, Title 14—Civil Aviation, Part 620—Security Control of Air Traffic, pp. 9319–9321.

§620.2 *Definitions*. As used in this part the words listed below shall mean:

(f) *Foreign aircraft*. An aircraft other than a United States aircraft defined in paragraph (1) of this section.

(1) *United States aircraft*. (1) An aircraft registered with the Administrator of Civil Aeronautics as a "civil aircraft of the United States" (2) an aircraft of the national-defense forces of the United States, or (3) an aircraft of the Federal Government, or of a State, Territory or Possession of the United States, or the District of Columbia, or of any political subdivision thereof which has been registered with the Administrator of Civil Aeronautics.

[4] Sec. 1202 of Federal Aviation Act of 1958: "In the exercise of his authority under section 307 (a) of this Act, the Administrator, in consultation with the Department of Defense, shall establish such zones of areas in the airspaces of the United States as he may find necessary in the interests of national defense, and by rule, regulation, or order restrict or prohibit the flight of **civil aircraft**, which he cannot identify, locate, and control with available facilities, with such zones or areas." See Federal Aviation Act of 1958, Public Law 85-726, Aug. 23, 1958, Sec. 1202.

on November 16, 1961)—according to §620.1, the former expression *U.S. and foreign aircraft* was amended to *all civil aircraft*.[5]

From 1961 to 2003 the United States made it clear that the ADIZ rules only applied to civil aircraft. Though in 2004 US ADIZ regulations were amended to indicate that the rules apply to "all aircraft," it can be inferred from practice and related domestic legal documents that the regulations are not applicable to military aircraft in the "international airspace" part of US ADIZs.[6] According to the Federal Register on 30 March 2004, the definition of an ADIZ has been amended as "an area of airspace over land or water in which the ready identification, location, and control of all aircraft (except for Department of Defense and law enforcement aircraft) is required in the interest of national security" (14 CFR 2005–2018). The only difference from the previous version is the change from *civil aircraft* to *all aircraft* (except for Department of Defense and law enforcement aircraft). According to the FAA official interpretation (69 Federal Register 2004), this amendment was made to cover all *civil* and *public* aircraft in the definition except for the US DoD and law enforcement aircraft. Under American law, *public aircraft* can be briefly summarized as aircraft used by American armed forces and any subdivision of the Government of the United States or a State in relevant public services (the definition *of public aircraft* does not mention aircraft used by any Government of foreign countries other than the United States).[7] Further, according to an Advisory Circular issued by the

---

[5] §620.1 *Purpose*—"This part establishes rules which have been found necessary in the interest of national security to identify, locate and control **all civil aircraft** operated within areas designated as Air Defense Identification Zones (ADIZs) or Defense Areas." See 26 Fed. Reg. (1961), October 14, 1961, Title 14—Civil Aviation, Part 620—Security Control of Air Traffic, pp. 9709–9711.

[6] The US ADIZs (including the *Defense area* in the Contiguous United States) not only cover *international airspace*, but also the *territorial airspace* of the United States.

[7] See 49 U.S. Code, §40102. Definitions.

(41) "Public aircraft" means any of the following: (A) Except with respect to an aircraft described in subparagraph (E), an aircraft used only for the United States Government, except as provided in section 40125(b). (B) An aircraft owned by the Government and operated by any person for purposes related to crew training, equipment development, or demonstration, except as provided in section 40125(b). (C) An aircraft owned and operated by the government of a State, the District of Columbia, or a territory or possession of the United States or a political subdivision of one of these governments, except as provided in section 40125(b). (D) An aircraft exclusively leased for at least 90 continuous days by the government of a State, the District of Columbia, or a territory or possession

FAA (Federal Aviation Administration 2014), *public aircraft* status exists only within US airspace; an aircraft operating outside of the United States loses its PAO (Public Aircraft Operations) status and is either civil or state (including military), depending on its official designation. As such, the 2004 amendment has no substantial impact on foreign military aircraft, to which the US ADIZ rules still do not apply, especially in "international airspace."

Compared to the 70-year-old US ADIZ regime, China's ADIZ is still in development. Some allowance should be made for ambiguities in Chinese ADIZ rules as detailed regulations have not yet been announced. Therefore, at least for now, it is not reasonable to assume that Chinese ADIZ rules apply to "all aircraft," or that there are substantial differences between the Chinese and American ADIZ rules in this regard. If American rules may be allowed to use relatively vague terms such as "U.S. and foreign aircraft" and "all aircraft" that could be interpreted otherwise as "civil aircraft" and received little criticism ever since, it is unfair to criticize Chinese rules for using the term "aircraft" without distinguishing between civil and state aircraft. Moreover, according to an American research report (Rinehart and Elias 2015), South Korea's ADIZ rules apply to military aircraft (a state aircraft that transits South Korea's ADIZ without entering sovereign airspace is required to file a flight plan). Though this kind of ADIZ regime is contrary to the traditional high seas freedoms that the United States claims for military aircraft, the United States has never criticized it.

---

of the United States or a political subdivision of one of these governments, except as provided in section 40125(b). (E) An aircraft owned or operated by the armed forces or chartered to provide transportation or other commercial air service to the armed forces under the conditions specified by section 40125(c). In the preceding sentence, the term "other commercial air service" means an aircraft operation that (i) is within the United States territorial airspace; (ii) the Administrator of the Federal Aviation Administration determines is available for compensation or hire to the public, and (iii) must comply with all applicable civil aircraft rules under title 14, Code of Federal Regulations. (F) An unmanned aircraft that is owned and operated by, or exclusively leased for at least 90 continuous days by, an Indian Tribal government, as defined in section 102 of the Robert T. Stafford Disaster Relief and Emergency Assistance Act (42 U.S.C. 5122), except as provided in section 40125(b).

Requiring an Aircraft not Entering Territorial Airspace to Identify Itself—Not Just China

China's ADIZ rules apply to all aircraft flying in the ADIZ, and make no exception for aircraft not intending to enter national airspace. In the opinion of some American scholars, this is contrary to "international norms," and unlike China's ADIZ rules, US ADIZ rules do not apply to aircraft not intending to enter national airspace. When discussing ADIZ, US officials usually argue that (The Commander's Handbook on the Law of Naval Operations, Department of the Navy & Department of Homeland Security 2017):

> The legal basis for ADIZ regulations is the right of a State to establish reasonable conditions of entry into its territory. Accordingly, an aircraft approaching national airspace can be required to identify itself while in international airspace as a condition of entry approval. ADIZ regulations promulgated by the United States apply to aircraft bound for U.S. territorial airspace and require the filing of flight plans and periodic position reports. The United States does not recognize the right of a coastal State to apply its ADIZ procedures to foreign aircraft not intending to enter national airspace nor does the United States apply its ADIZ procedures to foreign aircraft not intending to enter U.S. airspace.

However, the above policy is surprisingly inconsistent with current American ADIZ rules, specifically "§99.1 Applicability" of *14 CFR part 99* as below (14 CFR 2018):

> (a) This subpart prescribes rules for operating all aircraft (except for Department of Defense and law enforcement aircraft) in a defense area, or into, within, or out of the United States through an Air Defense Identification Zone (ADIZ) designated in subpart B.

The US ADIZ rules "literally" apply to not only aircraft bound for US territorial airspace, but also aircraft operating out of the United States (whose point of departure is within the United States) bound for any other country through its ADIZs.[8] What accounts for this seeming

---

[8] According to the *Aeronautical Information Manual* (12 October 2017, see 5-6-2.b. & 5-6-3.e.), "Aircraft operations to or from, within, or transiting U.S. territorial airspace must also comply with all other applicable regulations published in 14 CFR"; and "*From*

inconsistency? From my perspective, the drafters of *The Commander's Handbook on the Law of Naval Operations* made a mistake in terms of its emphasis on "aircraft bound for U.S. territorial airspace" and may have paid too much attention to the "position reports" (perhaps the most important provision in their opinion) that was the only part of American ADIZ rules (15 Federal Register 1950) which had been specifically restricted (before the 1988 amendment[9]) to only apply to aircraft operating within the United States or entering the United States through an ADIZ. The drafters may have overlooked other provisions of the US ADIZ rules, including "ADIZ flight plan requirements," "Radio requirements," "Transponder-on requirements," and "Special security instructions," which are applicable for operating aircraft "in a defense area,[10] or into, within, or out of the United States through an Air Defense Identification Zone." As such, aspects of US ADIZ rules appear to be inconsistent with the US position that a coastal States does not have the right to apply its ADIZ procedures to foreign aircraft not intending to enter national airspace.

In actuality, Canada,[11] South Korea, Japan, the Philippines, Australia, and Taiwan authorities similarly do not make a clear distinction in their published identification procedure rules between aircraft entering their territorial airspace and aircraft merely passing through their ADIZ. (Burke and Cevallos 2017) Perhaps, they have taken as precedent US ADIZ rules

---

U.S. territorial airspace means any flight that exits U.S. territorial airspace after departure from a location in the U.S., its territories or possessions, and lands at a destination outside the U.S., its territories or possessions."

[9] Before the 1988 amendment, the "Position reports" requirements only applied to aircraft "entering the US," but this restriction has been deleted (maybe because of carelessness) by the *Federal Register* on May 20, 1988. See 53 Fed. Reg. (1988), May 20, 1988, 14 CFR Part 99, pp. 18217–18218.

[10] See 14 CFR (2018), §99.3:

Defense area means any airspace of the contiguous United States that is not an ADIZ in which the control of aircraft is required for reasons of national security.

[11] See Canadian Aviation Regulations (CARs), §602.145 (1):

This section applies in respect of aircraft before entering into and while operating within the ADIZ, the dimensions of which are specified in the Designated Airspace Handbook.

from before 1961. Pre-1961 American ADIZ rules had broad "applicability" (the rules not only applied to aircraft operating into or from the national airspace of the declaring country through its ADIZ, but also aircraft merely passing through its ADIZ) (15 Federal Register 1950):

> §620.1 *Basis and purpose.* The regulations prescribed in this part contain rules and regulations which have been found necessary in the interest of national security to identify, locate, and control U.S. and foreign aircraft operated within areas designated by the administrator of Civil Aeronautics as air defense identification zones (ADIZ).
> §620.10 *Scope.* Aircraft shall not be operated into or within an Air Defense Identification Zone (ADIZ) prescribed by the Administrator in Subpart C of this part, in violation of the following rules.

Interestingly, although the applicability criteria of the original American rules were restricted in the 1961 amendment,[12] other countries which had declared ADIZs before or after 1961 did not follow suit and make their own ADIZ rules match with the updated US ADIZ rules, but stuck to the provisions of the original, broadly applicable, American ADIZ rules. If American scholars want to criticize China's ADIZ rules for being applicable to aircraft not intending to enter territorial airspace, they should perhaps clarify whether the broad applicability of pre-1961 American ADIZ rules (which were copied by many countries and continues to be in use) may be in line with "international norms," and why the current American ADIZ rules (which other countries have not followed) can be representative of "international norms."

Conclusion

Though a common legal framework governing the establishment or enforcement of ADIZs does not exist, in my opinion, scholars should work together to help policymakers develop an international-law-based comprehensive understanding about the theory and practice of ADIZs,

---

[12] §620.10 *Application*—"No person shall operate a civil aircraft **within the defense areas or into, within, or out of the United States through the ADIZs** prescribed in Subpart C of this part in violation of the rules provided in this part." See 26 Fed. Reg. (1961), October 14, 1961, Title 14, Part 620, pp. 9709–9711.

especially the history of US ADIZs and the significant amendment of those rules in 1961. After carefully studying the US ADIZ rules and other countries' ADIZ practices, we find that the ECS ADIZ rules are not unlike those of other countries, and that a lack of knowledge of China's ADIZ policies has fueled misperceptions in the international community.

References

14 CFR (2018), §99.1(a).
14 CFR (2005–2018), §99.3.
15 Federal Register. (1950), December 27, 1950, Title 14—Civil Aviation, Part 620—Security Control of Air Traffic, pp. 9319, 9320, 9319–9321.
69 Federal Register (2004), March 30, 2004, Rules and Regulations, pp. 16754–16756.
Burke, E. J., and Cevallos, A. S. (2017). *In Line or Out of Order? China's Approach to ADIZ in Theory and Practice*. RAND Corporation, 10 November, pp. 5–6, 6–8.
China News 2010, "日本执意扩大防空识别区 台方重申不接受立场," 中国新闻网, June 25, http://www.chinanews.com/tw/tw-jsdt/news/2010/06-25/2362121.shtml.
China Daily 2013a, "Statement by the Government of the People's Republic of China on Establishing the East China Sea Air Defense Identification Zone," November 23, http://www.chinadaily.com.cn/china/2013-11/23/content_17126611.htm.
China Daily 2013b, "Announcement of the Aircraft Identification Rules for the East China Sea Air Defense Identification Zone of the People's Republic of China," November 23, http://www.chinadaily.com.cn/china/2013-11/23/content_17126618.htm.
Department of the Navy & Department of Homeland Security, *The Commander's Handbook on the Law of Naval Operations*, NWP 1-14 M/MCTP 11-10B/COMDTPUB P5800.7A, EDITION AUGUST 2017, 2–14.
Federal Aviation Administration, U.S. Department of Transportation, Advisory Circular, Subject: Public Aircraft Operations—Manned and Unmanned, Date: 9/21/14, AC No: oo-1.1B, p. 4.
Ikeshima, T. (2016), "China's Air Defense Identification Zone (ADIZ) and its Impact on the Territorial and Maritime Disputes in the East and South China Seas," *Transcommunication*, 3(1), p. 159.
Rinehart, I. E., and Elias, B. (2015). *China's Air Defense Identification Zone (ADIZ)*. CRS Report R43894, Congressional Research Service, 30 January, p. 4.

Roach, J. A. (2017). Air Defence Identification Zones. In: R. Wolfrum (ed.), *The Max Planck Encyclopedia of Public International Law*. Article last updated: March 2017, para. 14, https://opil.ouplaw.com/view/10.1093/law:epil/9780199231690/law-9780199231690-e237?rskey=KFhpz0&result=1&prd=MPIL.

Shih, H. (2010). "Japan Extends ADIZ into Taiwan Space," *Taipei Times*, June 26, http://www.taipeitimes.com/News/front/archives/2010/06/26/2003476438/1.

CHAPTER 10

The Legal Contest in the East China Sea

Yann-huei Song

INTRODUCTION

Maritime disputes are extremely common in the world's oceans and seas. Worldwide, over 400 maritime disputes have occurred, with less than half of them have been resolved (Chatham House 2006). In East Asia, the maritime boundaries in the Sea of Japan, Yellow Sea, East China Sea (ECS), and South China Sea (SCS) overlap and remain unsettled. Under international law, all countries have the duty to cooperate in good faith and resolve maritime disputes by a variety of peaceful means including negotiation. Negotiations can lead to agreements on maritime boundaries, fisheries cooperation, law enforcement measures, joint development of resources, scientific exploration, and environmental protection. Provisional arrangements, *modus vivendi*, or provisional boundaries are also possible outcomes. This is the case with regard to the maritime dispute between Japan and the People's Republic of China (PRC) over the boundary of the Exclusive Economic Zone (EEZ) and the continental shelf in the ECS. This chapter discusses the maritime disputes in the ECS

Y.-h. Song (✉)
Academia Sinica, Taipei, Taiwan
e-mail: yhsong@gate.sinica.edu.tw

by focusing on the disputants' duty to cooperate and their obligation to settle disputes by peaceful means in accordance with the provisions contained in the UN Charter and UNCLOS.

Maritime Boundary Dispute in the ECS

Japan and the PRC signed the UNCLOS on 10 December 1982 and ratified the Convention in May and June 1996, respectively. In June 1996, Japan enacted the Law on the Exclusive Economic Law and Continental Shelf (Law No. 74) (Japan 1996). Under Article 1 of the law, Japan established the EEZ that comprises the areas of the sea extending from the baseline of Japan and to the line every point of which is 200 nautical miles from the nearest point on the baseline of Japan and its subjacent seabed and its subsoil. Paragraph 2 of Article 1 provides that "where any part of that line lies beyond the median line ... as measured from the baseline of Japan, the median line (or the line which may be agreed upon between Japan and a foreign country as a substitute for the median line) shall be substituted for that part of line." The regulation is also applied to the Japanese claim to continental shelf.

As far as the PRC is concerned, its law on EEZ and continental shelf was adopted on 26 June 1998 (PRC 1998). Under Article 2 of the law, the PRC's EEZ is "an area beyond and adjacent to the territorial sea" of the PRC "extending to a distance of 200 nautical miles from the baselines from which the breadth of the territorial sea is measured." Under the same article, its continental shelf "comprises the seabed and subsoil of the submarine areas that extend beyond its territorial sea throughout the natural prolongation of its land territory to the outer edge of the continental margin, or to a distance of 200 nautical miles from the baselines from which the breadth of the territorial sea is measured where the outer edge of the continental margin does not extend up to that distance." The two countries' EEZ and continental shelf laws give rise to four legal issues: (1) the legitimacy of Japan's use of the median line to delimit maritime boundaries in the ECS, (2) the applicability of the natural prolongation of land territory principle, as the PRC insists, in drawing the limit of its continental shelf. Another two issues are related to the PRC–Japan maritime boundary; (3) territorial sovereignty disputes over the eight maritime features of the Diaoyu/Senkaku island group, and (4) the legal status of Diaoyu/Senkaku Islands and their role in maritime boundary delimitation.

THE ECS AND ITS ESTIMATED OIL AND GAS RESERVES

The ECS is a semi-enclosed sea as defined in Article 122 of the UNCLOS. It has a total area of about 770,000 square kilometers with average water depth of 370 meters, of which the continental shelf covers 460,000 square kilometers with average depth of 72 meters (Guo 2005). The continental shelf basin of the ECS is the largest Cenozoic sedimentary basin in offshore Chinese mainland, covering 2.4 million square kilometers. Oil and gas deposits in the ECS are difficult to estimate. The overlapping and disputed areas in the sea are underexplored, and the territorial and maritime claims precluded further development. However, the U.S. Energy Information Administration (EIA) estimates that the ECS contains around 200 million barrels of oil in proved and probable reserves and between 1 and 2 trillion cubic feet of proved and probable natural gas reserves. But Chinese sources claim that the oil reserves in the entire ECS can be as high as 70–160 billion barrels of oil, mostly in the Okinawa Trough and 250 trillion cubic feet of natural gas resources, also mostly in the Okinawa Trough (U.S. EIA 2014). Proven hydrocarbon reserves are closer to the mainland Chinese coast and more readily accessible by a Chinese undersea pipeline that runs from the Pinghu gas field to Shanghai. Proven gas reserves are farther from Japan's main islands and because of the depth of the Okinawa Trough, pipeline transportation to Japan is expensive and technically challenging. According to a report by Offshore Technology in November 2018, the China National Offshore Oil Corporation (CNOOC) produced 22.3 billion cubic feet of natural gas and 1.6 million barrels of oil in the ECS area in 2017. From 2013 to 2017, the corporation's production in the area has increased by approximately 260% despite ongoing clashes between Japan and the PRC (Offshore Technology 2018).

OBLIGATIONS OF STATES IN THE OVERLAPPING/UNDELIMITED MARITIME AREAS

Articles 74 and 83 of the UNCLOS regulate the legal issues concerning delimitation of the EEZ and continental shelf between states with opposite or adjacent coasts. Under these two provisions, the delimitation of the EEZ and continental shelf "shall be effected by agreement on the basis of international law, as referred to in Article 38 of the Statute of the International Court of Justice, in order to achieve an equitable solution"

(UNCLOS 1982). If no agreement can be reached within a "reasonable period of time," they "shall resort to the procedures provided for in Part XV" of the Convention. However, agreement is subject to what is regarded as a "reasonable" period of time. Under paragraph 3 of Articles 74 and 83, pending agreement, the states concerned, "in a spirit of understanding and cooperation, shall make every effort to enter into provisional arrangements of a practical nature and, during this transitional period, not to jeopardize or hamper the reaching of the final agreement. Such arrangements shall be without prejudice to the final delimitation" (UNCLOS 1982). Finally, where there is an agreement in force between the states concerned, questions relating to the delimitation of the EEZ and continental shelf should be determined in accordance with the provisions of the agreements they concluded. These two provisions implicitly stipulate that the states concerned should show self-restraint and carry out any activities in the overlapping/undelimited areas in good faith. They are required not to conduct activities that jeopardize or hamper the reaching of a final delimitation agreement in respect of overlapping EEZ or continental shelf in the areas where no provisional arrangements apply. However, it is debatable as what kind of actions should be taken and exactly where. If taken by a country in or near the undelimited area it could affect the efforts to enter into provisional arrangements. If bordering a semi-enclosed sea the states concerned also bear the obligation to cooperate with each other in the exercise of their rights and in the performance of their duties under UNCLOS.[1]

Professor Robin Churchill (BIICL 2016) raised a number of questions concerning the interpretation and application of Article 74(3) and Article 83(3) of the UNCLOS: (1) What is the substantive scope of the obligation not to jeopardize or hamper, and is it a subjective or an objective standard? (2) Is the obligation geographically limited, and, if so, what is its geographical scope? (3) What is the temporal scope of the obligation? and (4) Should the proclamation of a continental shelf or EEZ on the basis of the median line could itself be interpreted as practice relating to the obligations under Articles 74(3) and 83(3). According to Churchill, none of these questions can be answered adequately by recourse to the drafting history of the UNCLOS, or by the scarce judicial practice. But he suggested that certain activities conducted in undelimited areas "seem

---

[1] Article 123 of the UNCLOS.

to be clearly in violation of the obligation" under Articles 74 (3) and 83(3) of the UNCLOS, "especially exploitation activities and exploratory activities involving drilling." However, as pointed out by Nuno Antunes, there exists a need to distinguish between an "undelimited area" and a "disputed area" because it is possible for a party concerned to claim a maritime area as undelimited without there being a dispute, but the other party concerned may take a different view (BIICL 2016). The dispute between Japan and the PRC in the ECS covers both undelimited and disputed areas, since the two countries had ratified UNCLOS they are bound by the provisions mentioned above.

OBLIGATIONS OF STATES TO COOPERATE AND SETTLE DISPUTES BY PEACEFUL MEANS

Implicitly, the duty to cooperate is found in Articles 74(3) and 83(3) of the UNCLOS. In addition, under Article 123 of the same Convention, states that are bordering enclosed or semi-enclosed seas bear the duty to cooperate (1) for management, conservation, exploration, and exploitation of the living resources of the sea; (2) for the implementation of their rights and duties with respect to the protection and preservation of the marine environment, and (3) for policy-making and activities in relation to marine scientific research in the sea. As far as the obligation to settle disputes by using peaceful means is concerned, in accordance with Article 279 of the UNCLOS, the states concerned should settle their disputes with regard to the delimitation of the EEZ and continental shelf. This provision provides that "States Parties shall settle any dispute between them concerning the interpretation or application of this Convention by peaceful means in accordance with Article 2, paragraph 3, of the Charter of the United Nations and, to this end, shall seek a solution by the means indicated in Article 33, paragraph 1, of the Charter." Under Article 280, the states concerned have the right to settle their maritime boundary disputes by "any peaceful means of their own choice." In accordance with Article 2, paragraph 3, of the UN Charter, the countries concerned should settle their disputes by peaceful means in such a manner that international peace and security, and justice, are not endangered. Under Article 33, paragraph 1, of the Charter, the methods of peaceful settlement of disputes include "negotiation, enquiry, mediation, conciliation, arbitration, judicial settlement, resort to regional agencies or arrangements, or other peaceful means of their own choice" (UN Charter 1945).

In an undelimited area disputants may have recourse to compulsory dispute settlement in relation to disputes as seen in Articles of 74(3) and 83(3) of the UNCLOS. This may be particularly the case when a dispute regarding the obligation not to jeopardize or hamper the reaching of the final agreement arises during the transitional period. According to Naomi Burke, the desirability of recourse to Section 2 (Compulsory Procedures Entailing Binding Decisions) of Part XV of the UNCLOS depends on whether the states concerned "seek to stop the prejudicial conduct, delimit the maritime boundary, or both" (BIICL 2016). In principle, maritime boundary delimitation disputes are subject to the compulsory settlement system in Part XV of the Convention. If a delimitation dispute were submitted to a competent court or tribunal, parties could seek to stop any activity pending delimitation by requesting provisional measures under Article 290 of UNCLOS. However, it should be noted that the provisions of Articles 74(3) and 83(3) are covered by the opt-out provision of the UNCLOS, namely, Article 298.[2] Currently, around one-fifth of states which are parties to the Convention have made declarations under Article 298 to exclude the maritime boundary delimitation dispute from the compulsory settlement procedures of Part XV (BIICL 2016). The PRC made the declaration in accordance with Article 298 on 25 August 2006 (PRC 2006).

POSITIONS OF PRC AND JAPAN ON DEVELOPMENT OF RESOURCES IN THE UNDELIMITED AREAS

As the ECS is less than 400 nautical miles or 741 kms in width, the EEZs and continental shelves of both Japan and the PRC overlap and there is a need for delimitation between the two countries. However, no delimitation agreement has been concluded so far. The 2008 Agreement/Principled Consensus is not a treaty or delimitation agreement. However, if agreed and implemented, it should be considered as a provisional arrangement under Articles 74(3) and 83(3) of the UNCLOS. Japan insists on the equidistant line for delimitation in the ECS area, which Beijing cannot accept. The PRC argues that the unique feature of the ECS, such as the natural prolongation of the continental shelf and

---

[2] Paragraph 1 of this Article allows states and entities to declare that they exclude the application of the compulsory binding procedures for the settlement of disputes under the Convention in respect of certain specified categories kinds of disputes.

contrasting geographic formulation of the continent and islands, should be taken into account for the delimitation. Japan argues that the Chinese claim and position is baseless under current international law. In addition, pending final delimitation, Japan is holding the position that in accordance with the relevant provisions of the UNCLOS, it can exercise sovereign rights and jurisdiction on the Japanese side of the equidistance line in the ECS and this does not mean that it has given up its entitlements beyond the equidistance line in any way.

Currently, Japan temporarily limits its exercise of sovereign rights and jurisdiction over the Japanese side of the equidistance line pending delimitation under international law. Given that maritime boundaries in the ECS are not yet delimited between Japan and the PRC, and that Beijing rejects Japan's use of the median line to delimit the overlapping maritime zones, Japan claims that it is entitled to an EEZ and continental shelf in the ECS up to 200 nautical miles measured from its territorial sea baselines (MOFA, Japan 2015). In March 2019, Japan's Ministry of Foreign Affairs issued a statement on the current status of the PRC's oil and gas development activities in the ECS, in which Tokyo confirmed that there are 16 structures in total on the Chinese side of the geographical equidistance line between Japan and the PRC. In addition, the statement updated Japan's position on the dispute.

As far as the position of the PRC is concerned, Beijing claims EEZs measured from its territorial baselines seaward up to or 200 nautical miles limit and 350 nautical miles for its continental shelf (PRC 1998). The Chinese maritime zones overlap with Japan's and there is a need for maritime boundary delimitation. Under Article 2, paragraph 3, of the Chinese EEZ and continental shelf law, "Where the claim of the People's Republic of China for the exclusive economic zone and the continental shelf overlaps with that of other country adjacent or opposite in their seacoasts, a boundary shall be determined under the principle of equity and based on the international law." In May 2009, the PRC submitted preliminary information to the Secretary-General of the United Nations, indicative of the outer limits of its continental shelf beyond 200 nautical mile. It claimed that the natural prolongation of the continental shelf in the ECS extends beyond 200 nautical miles from the baselines from which the breadth of the territorial sea is measured. It added that the outer limits of the shelf as delineated by reference to a distance of 60 nautical miles from the foot of the continental slope do not exceed 350 nautical miles from the baselines from which the breadth of the territorial sea is measured (United Nations 2009). Accordingly, Beijing claims that the outer limits of its continental shelf extend beyond 200 nautical miles in the ECS as located on the axis of the Okinawa Trough. It is also stated in the Preliminary Information that, following its consistent position, the PRC will, through peaceful negotiation, delimit the continental shelf with states with opposite or adjacent coasts by agreement on the basis of the international law and the principle of equity.

The same position was outlined in December 2012 when the PRC submitted its application for outer limits of the continental shelf beyond 200 nautical miles in the ECS, through the UN Secretary-General to the Commission on the Limits of the Continental Shelf (hereinafter. CLCS United Nations 2012b). In July 2015, the PRC government responded to a Japanese document by posting a statement titled "China's Oil and Gas Development in the East China Sea is Justified and Legitimate" in its Foreign Ministry website, in which Beijing pointed out that the two countries have yet to reach agreement on maritime delimitation in the ECS, and that it "does not recognize the so-called median line unilaterally claimed by Japan, nor Japan's position of delimitating the East China Sea on the basis of the so-called median line" (MOFA, PRC 2015). The Chinese government proposed joint development with Japan without prejudice to the respective legal positions. It is worth noting that in the statement, the PRC accused Japan of misinterpreting the 2008 Agreement/Principled Consensus creating obstacles to its implementation. But at the same time Beijing stressed that it is ready to have dialogue and communication with Japan on ECS issues through various channels, including the High-level Consultation Mechanism on Maritime Affairs.

In December 2018, Japan lodged a protest with the PRC over new oil and gas drilling activities in the area near Tokyo-proposed median line in the ECS (Ryall 2018). In response, Geng Shuan, spokesman of the Chinese Foreign Ministry, stated at a regular press conference in December 2018 that the activities were conducted in waters "indisputably under China's jurisdiction and are therefore within our sovereign right and right of jurisdiction." He added, the Japan-proposed median line "is just a unilateral claim by the Japanese side" and the PRC "firmly opposes it and never acknowledges it." In addition, the working teams of the two countries will follow the spirit of the 2008 Principled Consensus to conduct the relevant work in the future, he said (MOFA, PRC 2018). The same PRC position was expressed again in March 2019 (MOFA, PRC 2019).

SINO-JAPANESE NEGOTIATIONS ON THE ECS

Between 2003 and 2008, Japan and the PRC were at odds over the right to explore and exploit oil and gas resources in the ECS. In August 2003, a Chinese oil company set up a production platform at the *Chunxiao* oilfield, which prompted Japan to lodge a strong protest, asserting that the Chinese drilling in the area about 5 kilometers west of the Japanese claimed median line in the ECS would siphon off oil and gas reserves from Japan's side. Japan called on the PRC to suspend production close to the median line pending a diplomatic resolution of the dispute. In June 2008, after 11 rounds of serious consultations, Japan and the PRC finally reached *the Principled Consensus on the East China Sea Issues*, where the two countries agreed to cooperate in the transitional period prior to delimitation without prejudicing their respective legal positions in the areas concerned. As the first step, Japan and the PRC agreed to establish a block in the ECS for the joint development of oil and gas resources. In addition, they also agreed to continue consultations for the early realization of joint development in other parts of the ECS (*China Daily* 2008).

The consultation on implementation of the 2008 Agreement/Principled Consensus came to a halt when Japan and PRC relations deteriorated as a result of several incidents. In September 2010, Japan's Coast Guard arrested the captain of a Chinese fishing boat near the Diaoyu/Senkaku Islands despite China's protests. According to the understanding reached between the two sides in November 2011, Japan–PRC high-level meetings on maritime affairs were free to discuss any topics, including the 2008 Agreement/Principled Consensus and ECS-related issues. However, later in September 2012, the Japanese government decided to "nationalize" three islands in the disputed island group. In the same year, the PRC government deposited a chart and a list of geographic coordinates on the baselines of the territorial sea of Diaoyu Dao (Uotsuri Shima in Japanese) and its affiliated islands to the UN Secretary-General (United Nations 2012a), The PRC dispatched its Coast Guard vessels to the waters surrounding the Diaoyu/Senkaku island group (Fackler 2012), and published a white paper titled "Diaoyu Dao, an Inherent Territory of China" (PRC 2012). In December 2012, the PRC government submitted its application for an outer continental shelf in the ECS to the UN CLCS (United Nations 2012b). Beijing also suspended the second round of Japan–PRC high-level consultations on maritime affairs that was scheduled for the second half of 2012.

Unilateral Actions Taken by PRC and Japan's Response: 2017–2019

In August 2017, Japan's top government spokesman Yoshihide Suga told reporters it was "extremely regrettable that China is unilaterally continuing its development activity" by stopping mobile drilling ships near the median line (*The Straits Times* 2017). Japan asked the PRC to cease its unilateral development and to resume negotiations as soon as possible based on the "2008 Agreement." In response, the Chinese Foreign Ministry stated that "China's oil and gas activities in the East China Sea are all located in maritime areas indisputably under Chinese jurisdiction" and that "[t]he so-called issue of 'unilateral exploitation' does not exist." Japan lodged its protests again in June and November 2018, respectively (Reuters 2018). In March 2019, in a report on the current status of PRC's unilateral development of natural resources in the ECS, the Japanese Ministry of Foreign Affairs stated that "[i]n recent years, China has accelerated its development activities of natural resources in the East China Sea, and the government of Japan has confirmed that there are 16 structures in total on the Chinese side of the geographical equidistance line between Japan and China" (MOFA, Japan 2019a). According to the report, maritime boundary delimitation in the ECS should be conducted based on the geographical equidistance line between Japan and China. The Japanese government "strongly requests China to cease its unilateral development and to resume negotiations as soon as possible on the implementation of the 2008 Agreement."

In addition to the unilateral development of oil and gas resources in the undelimited areas, Tokyo also lodged protests against PRC research activities conducted inside the Japanese claimed EEZs in the ECS. In July 2017, Japan lodged protests when the Chinese research vessels sailed into the Japanese claimed EEZs surrounding the Diaoyu/Senkaku Islands. In April 2018, Japan's Coast Guard warned the *Xiangyanghong No. 10*, a Chinese research vessel that was conducting "unauthorized activities" in Japan's EEZ in the ECS (Panda 2018). This was followed by another report in October 2018, saying that a Chinese oceanographic research vessel conducted activities in Japan-claimed EEZ without prior notice (Shim 2018). In March 2019, Japan protested a Chinese research vessel entering into its EEZ surrounding *Okinotorishima*, which is a maritime feature claimed by Japan as a full-fledged island in accordance with Article 121 of the UNCLOS and therefore is entitled the right to generate 200-nautical mile EEZ and continental shelf. But the PRC opposes the Japanese position, arguing that it is not an island but a "rock" according to Article 121, paragraph 3, of the Convention. Because *Okinotorishima* cannot sustain human habitation or has its own economic life, it does not have the right to claim an EEZ or continental shelf (PRC 2009). In July 2019, a Japan Coast Guard vessel warned a Chinese vessel that no research is allowed without prior consent in Japan's EEZ. According to a report by *Nikkei Asian Review*, it was the fourth time since the beginning of 2019 that a Chinese research vessel had entered Japan's EEZ (Nagai 2019).

Positive Developments in PRC–Japan Relations Regarding ECS Issues

In recent years, there have been some positive developments that have led the PRC and Japan to talk about the joint development of oil and gas resources in the ECS. Starting in September 2016, at the 5th round meeting of PRC–Japan high-level consultation on maritime affairs, held in Hiroshima, Japan, the two sides began to talk about the 2008 Principled Consensus and the need to promote maritime cooperation in the ECS (MOFA, Japan 2016). During the 11th round meeting, both sides agreed to adhere to the principles and consensus reached in June 2008 concerning the ECS and agreed to further strengthen communication and exchanges (Xinhuanet 2019). Due to the coronavirus disease outbreak (COVID-2019), the 12th round meeting, scheduled to be held in mainland China at the end of 2019, was postponed. Meetings of state leaders and top government officials also point to the same positive direction with regard to possible cooperation between the two countries on the ECS. During his visit to Beijing in October 2018, Prime Minister Abe stated that there will be no genuine improvement in the Japan–PRC relationship without stability in the ECS. At the meeting, the two sides reaffirmed their complete adherence to the 2008 Principled Consensus regarding the development of resources in the ECS and shared the view that they will further increase communication with the aim of an early resumption of negotiations to implement the consensus reached in 2008. The leaders also welcomed the signing of the Japan–China Maritime Search and Rescue (SAR) Agreement (MOFA, Japan 2018).

More importantly, Prime Minister Abe and President Xi met at the sidelines of the G-20 Summit held in Osaka in June 2019. Regarding the ECS issues, Abe reiterated that "there will be no genuine improvement in Japan–PRC relations without stability in the East China Sea" (MOFA, Japan 2019b). He also requested self-restraint in PRC's activities in the ECS, particularly the waters surrounding the Diaoyu/Senkaku Islands, based on a broad perspective of Japan–PRC relations and peace and stability in the region and international community. The ten-point consensus reached at the Japan–PRC summit noted that the two leaders agreed to properly handle sensitive issues and manage disputes and differences constructively. They said that the two sides shared the view on promoting and implementing the Principled Consensus on the East China Sea Issues (the abbreviation "2008 Agreement" is used by Japan, but the Chinese term is "Principled Consensus") (Hayashi 2012) and make joint efforts to safeguard peace and stability of the ECS, so as to turn it into a "sea of peace, cooperation and friendship" (*China Daily* 2019). The two leaders agreed on the idea of resource development in order to achieve the goal of making the ECS a "sea of peace, cooperation and friendship" (MOFA, Japan 2019b). In August 2019, during his visit to mainland China, Japanese foreign minister Taro Kono underscored the importance of making substantive progress on the ECS in order to develop Japan–PRC relations in a stable manner after President Xi's visit to Japan which was scheduled for April 2020 (MOFA, Japan 2019c). However, the coronavirus disease (COVID-19) outbreak delayed the progress in managing and resolving the dispute.

A Possible Way Out

The possibility of a resolution of the maritime boundary dispute is increasing as the leaders of the two countries hold the view that there will be no genuine improvement in their bilateral relations without stability in the ECS. In addition, they reiterate the common policy commitment on making the ECS a "sea of peace, cooperation and friendship." Given that Japan had made its position clear and requested a restart to the negotiations on the dispute, the success of managing or resolving the Sino-Japanese maritime boundary disputes in the ECS is hinged on Chinese acceptance of the principles and consensus reached between the two sides in 2008. During the negotiation process, Beijing and Tokyo should exercise restraint, in particular, no unilateral oil and gas development activities should be allowed in the undelimited areas. Once serious negotiations begin, the best possible outcome could be a joint hydrocarbon development agreement between the two sides, based on the principles and consensus agreed in 2008. It should further expand the geographical scope for joint development in the ECS. Japan and PRC should agree to put aside sovereignty over the Diaoyu/Senkau Islands and move forward to maritime cooperation not only for exploration and exploitation of non-living resources, but also for fisheries resources, environmental protection, and scientific research. In return, Beijing should stop its unilateral development activities in the undelimited areas near the Japanese proposed median line. Although the possibility is slim, a legal approach, if adopted, could help resolve the maritime boundary disputes between the two countries in the ECS. For Japan, it could mean appealing to an international tribunal to resolve the dispute with the PRC over Beijing's obligation not to jeopardize or hamper the reaching of an agreement on final maritime boundary delimitation. The PRC could argue that the Japanese proposal of using the median line in delimiting maritime boundaries in the ECS is not consistent with Articles 74 and 83 of the UNCLOS, and that it has the right to conduct oil and gas development activities in the areas that are outside the Japanese claimed median line. The adoption of the legal approach is hinged on Chinese consent to resolve maritime dispute before a judicial body. However, two key challenges need to be overcome: first, it is PRC's consistent position to settle its disputes with other countries by peaceful negotiation; and second, China issued a declaration in accordance with Article 298 of the UNCLOS to exclude the EEZ and continental shelf boundary disputes from the compulsory judicial settlement mechanism under Part XV of the Convention. This means that for legal arbitration to proceed, Beijing must modify its policy position with respect to the resolution of maritime disputes, which, if not entirely impossible, is very difficult.

References

BIICL. (2016) Obligation of States Under Articles 74(3) and 83(3) of UNCLOS in respect of Undelimited Maritime Areas. Report of Conference, British Institute of International and Comparative Law 22 July, pp. 12–14 and 167–168. https://www.biicl.org/documents/1296_obligations_of_states_in_und

elimited_maritime_areas_final_event_report.pdf?showdocument=1 (Accessed: 20 September 2019).
Chatham House. (2006) *Methods of Resolving Maritime Boundary Disputes*. Summary of a Meeting of the International Law Discussion Group, pp. 728–743.
China Daily. (2008) China, Japan reach principled consensus on East China Sea Issue, 18 June. Available at: http://www.chinadaily.com.cn/china/2008-06/18/content_6774860.htm.
China Daily. (2019) Xi, Abe Reach 10-Point Consensus to Promote Bilateral Relations, 27 June. Available at: http://www.chinadaily.com.cn/a/201906/27/WS5d14c3dda3103dbf1432ab0a.html.
Fackler, M. (2012) Chinese Ships Enter Japanese-Controlled Waters to Protest Sale of Islands. *The New York Times*, 13 September. https://www.nytimes.com/2012/09/14/world/asia/chinese-ships-enter-japanese-controlled-waters-to-protest-sale-of-islands.html.
Guo, Z. (2005) Key Issues in the East China Sea: A Status Report and Recommended Approaches. In: S. Harrison (ed.) *Seabed Petroleum in Northeast Asia: Conflict or Cooperation?* Woodrow Wilson International Center for Scholars Asia Program, pp. 36–37. https://www.wilsoncenter.org/sites/default/files/Zhao_Li_Guo.pdf.
Hayashi, M. (2012) The 2008 Japan-China Agreement on Cooperation of the East China Sea Resources. In: Myron H. Nordquist and John Norton Moore (eds.) *Maritime Border Diplomacy*. Leiden and Boston: Martinus Nijhoff, pp. 35–46.
Japan. (1996) Law on the Exclusive Economic Law and the Continental Shelf (Law No. 74 of 1996). Law of the Sea Bulletin (35). https://www.un.org/Depts/los/doalos_publications/LOSBulletins/bulletinpdf/bulletinE35.pdf.
MOFA, Japan. (2015) Japan's Legal Position on the Development of Natural Resources in the East China Sea, 6 August. https://www.mofa.go.jp/a_o/c_m1/page3e_000358.html.
MOFA, Japan. (2016) Fifth Round Meeting and Working Group Meetings of Japan-China High-Level Consultation on Maritime Affairs. News, 15 September. http://www.mofa.go.jp/press/release/press3e_000071.html.
MOFA, Japan. (2018) Prime Minister Abe Visits China. Countries & Regions, 26 October. https://www.mofa.go.jp/a_o/c_m1/cn/page3e_000958.html.
MOFA, Japan. (2019a) The Current Status of China's Unilateral Development of Natural Resources in the East China Sea. Countries & Regions, 28 March. https://www.mofa.go.jp/a_o/c_m1/page3e_000356.html.
MOFA, Japan. (2019b) Japan-China Summit Meeting and Dinner. Countries & Regions, 27 June. https://www.mofa.go.jp/a_o/c_m1/cn/page3e_001046.html.

MOFA, Japan. (2019c) Japan-China Foreign Ministers' Meeting. Countries & Regions, 20 August. Available at: https://www.mofa.go.jp/a_o/c_m1/cn/page3e_001078.html (Accessed: 20 September 2019).

MOFA, PRC. (2015) China's Oil and Gas Development in the East China Sea Is Justified and Legitimate, 25 July. https://www.fmprc.gov.cn/mfa_eng/wjbxw/t1284278.shtml.

MOFA, PRC. (2018) Foreign Ministry Spokesperson Geng Shuang's Regular Press Conference, 3 December. https://www.fmprc.gov.cn/mfa_eng/xwfw_665399/s2510_665401/2511_665403/t1618558.shtml.

MOFA, PRC. (2019) Foreign Ministry Spokesperson Geng Shuang's Regular Press Conference, 22 March. https://www.fmprc.gov.cn/mfa_eng/xwfw_665399/s2510_665401/2511_665403/t1647752.shtml.

Nagai, O. (2019) Japan and China Lock Horns in the East China Sea. *Nikkei Asian Review*, 1 September. https://asia.nikkei.com/Politics/International-relations/Japan-and-China-lock-horns-in-the-East-China-Sea.

Offshore Technology. (2018) From Drillships to Warships: Increasing Tensions in the East China Sea.

Panda, A. (2018) East China Sea: Japan Coast Guard Warns Chinese Survey Ship in Exclusive Economic Zone. *The Diplomat*, 22 April. https://thediplomat.com/2018/04/east-china-sea-japan-coast-guard-warns-chinese-survey-ship-in-exclusive-economic-zone/.

PRC. (1998) Law of the People's Republic of China on the Exclusive Economic Zone and the Continental Shelf. http://www.asianlii.org/cn/legis/cen/laws/lotprocoteezatcs790/.

PRC. (2006) Declaration, 25 August. https://treaties.un.org/Pages/ViewDetailsIII.aspx?src=TREATY&mtdsg_no=XXI-6&chapter=21&Temp=mtdsg3&clang=_en#EndDec.

PRC. (2009) Communication Sent by the Permanent Mission of the People's Republic of China to the United Nations, CML/2/2009, 6 February. https://www.un.org/Depts/los/clcs_new/submissions_files/jpn08/chn_6feb09_e.pdf.

PRC. (2012) Diaoyu Dao, an Inherent Territory of China. The State Council Information Office, 26 September (English translation). http://www.gov.cn/english/official/2012-09/25/content_2232763.htm.

Reuters. (2018) Japan Protests Over China Drilling Vessel in Disputed Waters, 29 June. https://www.reuters.com/article/us-japan-china-gas-idUSKBN1JP0KF.

Ryall, J. (2018) Beijing May Be 'Testing Tokyo's Resolve' with Drilling Missions in Contested Parts of East China Sea. *South China Morning Post*, 4 December. https://www.scmp.com/news/asia/diplomacy/article/2176280/beijing-may-be-testing-tokyos-resolve-drilling-missions.

Shim, E. (2018) Japan Slams Chinese Ship for Oceanographic Research in EEZ. UPI, 8 October. Available at: https://www.upi.com/Top_News/World-News/2018/10/08/Japan-slams-Chinese-ship-for-oceanographic-research-in-EEZ/4441539019430/ (Accessed: 3 October 2019).

Straits Times. (2017) Beijing Defends Oil, Gas Activity in East China Sea, 3 August. https://www.straitstimes.com/asia/beijing-defends-oil-gas-activity-in-east-china-sea.

United Nations. (1945) Charter of the United Nations.

United Nations. (2009) Preliminary Information Indicative of the Outer Limits of the Continental Shelf Beyond 200 Nautical Miles of the People's Republic of China, 11 May. https://www.un.org/Depts/los/clcs_new/submissions_files/preliminary/chn2009preliminaryinformation_english.pdf.

United Nations. (2012a) M.Z.N. 89.2012.LOS (Maritime Zone Notification), 21 September. https://www.un.org/Depts/los/LEGISLATIONANDTREATIES/PDFFILES/mzn_s/mzn89ef.pdf.

United Nations. (2012b) CLCS.63.2012.LOS (Continental Shelf Notification), Receipt of the Submission made by the People's Republic of China to the Commission on the Limits of the Continental Shelf, December 14. https://www.un.org/Depts/los/clcs_new/submissions_files/chn63_12/clcs_63_2012.pdf.

UNCLOS. (1982) United Nations Treaty Collection. https://treaties.un.org/Pages/ViewDetailsIII.aspx?src=TREATY&mtdsg_no=XXI-6&chapter=21&Temp=mtdsg3&clang=_en.

U.S. Energy Information Administration. (2014) East China Sea. https://www.eia.gov/beta/international/regions-topics.php?RegionTopicID=ECS.

Xinhuanet. (2019) China and Japan Held the 11th Round of High-Level Consultation Meeting on Maritime Affairs (in Chinese), 11 May. http://www.xinhuanet.com/world/2019-05/11/c_1124480563.htm.

CHAPTER 11

Historical Continuities, Geopolitical Interests, and Norms in Japan's Free and Open Indo-Pacific

Toshiya Takahashi

INTRODUCTION

Japan's gradual assertion of a geopolitical interest in the Indo-Pacific has become salient since the 2010s in the face of China's increasing security, political, and economic challenges. The Japanese government under Prime Minister Shinzo Abe espoused the idea of the Free and Open Indo-Pacific (FOIP) in 2016. Though it has been broadly used by many countries such as the United States, Australia, India, and ASEAN for their strategies and policy orientations, their contents and intentions are not the same (Cannon and Ash Rossiter 2018; Gyngell 2018). The FOIP is a Japanese version and can be regarded as a key vision for Japan's diplomacy, security policy, and economic cooperation with the region. It was prompted by China's increasing political and economic influence

---

T. Takahashi (✉)
Shoin University, Kanagawa, Japan
e-mail: NSA13921@nifty.com

© The Author(s), under exclusive license to Springer Nature Switzerland AG 2021
L. Buszynski and D. T. Hai (eds.), *Maritime Issues and Regional Order in the Indo-Pacific*, Palgrave Studies in Maritime Politics and Security, https://doi.org/10.1007/978-3-030-68038-1_11

especially under the Belt and Road Initiative (BRI), but reflects the past in Japan's approach to the area. An examination of history would help to understand the meaning of the FOIP and make clear its possibilities and limitations. This chapter will examine Japan's geopolitical interest in the Indo-Pacific from a historical perspective and will clarify the meaning of the FOIP, its diplomatic vision, and the role of norms in Japanese geopolitical interests in the region. It will note Prime Minster Nobusuke Kishi's India and Southeast Asia policy in the 1950s, the 1976 Fukuda Doctrine by Prime Minister Takeo Fukuda, Prime Minister Zenko Suzuki and Yasuhiro Nakasone's sea lane defense in the 1980s, and Japan's value diplomacy in the 2000s which was a harbinger of the FOIP. Observers may regard the FOIP as a clear expression of Japan's counter-strategy against China and claim that Japan has taken a step in geopolitical competition with China. However, the Japanese debate on the FOIP shows ambiguities in relation to competition with China which will be explained from a historical perspective and in the context of the Japanese debate over the Indo-Pacific.

Japan's Geopolitical Interests in the Western Pacific and India in History

Prewar Japan's military expansion was often led by geopolitical thought. The influence of western geopolitics on Japan's strategic thinking can be traced back to the end of the nineteenth century. Alfred Mahan's book, *The Influence of Sea Power upon History 1660–1783*, strongly affected Japan's nascent imperial navy and became a bible for its naval expansion. Modern Japan sought to expand its sphere of influence in the Asian continent and ventured to intervene in the Korean Peninsula. Some Japanese political leaders such as Taro Katsura (Prime Minster in 1901–1906, 1908–1911, and 1912–1913) announced a vison "defend the north, advance to the south" and espoused a shift from Japan's continental expansion to Southeast Asia (Kurono 1996). The 1907 Imperial Defense Policy endorsed Japan's advance to both south and north (ibid.). Geopolitical thinking influenced Japan's diplomacy toward Germany and its war plans, particularly Karl Haushofer's idea of a Eurasian bloc, which finally led to the 1940 Tripartite Pact between Germany, Italy, and Japan (Spang 2001). Two months after Japan raided Pearl Harbor in December 1941, the Japanese imperial army planned a grandiose vison to share the globe with Germany. In this plan, Japanese territories were supposed to expand to the Southern Pacific including Australia and New Zealand, the Eastern Pacific, Ceylon, Alaska, and Central America (Hata 2010). In line with this strategic thinking, the Japanese empire expanded southwards as it attempted to secure natural resources and strategic points in Southeast Asia during the 2nd Sino-Japanese War (1937–1945) and the Pacific War (1941–1945). These geopolitical interests were the objectives of Japanese military strategy and the vision of the Greater East Asia Co-prosperity Sphere, but its overextension was apparent. The dream of the Japanese empire soon vanished with its complete defeat in the war.

Postwar Japan renounced military means as it was restrained by the 1947 constitution which prohibited the use of the Self-Defense Forces (JSDF) outside its territory. Article 9 of the constitution only allows the JSDF to maintain "defensive self-defense (*Senshuboei*)," which justifies Japan's military actions only in response to actual aggression. JSDF units were not allowed to operate overseas until the 1992 UN Peacekeeping Operation in Cambodia even if for non-combatant missions. Since then, the use of the JSDF overseas has been realized but limited to non-combatant operations in multilateral security cooperation such as United Nations peacekeeping operations, joint exercises, defense exchanges, or information sharing. Postwar Japan's strategic reach was necessarily "geo-economic" which shaped its foreign policy toward Southeast Asia and India. Japan's economic relationship with them started with war reparations diplomacy, which was intended to create important export markets for its industrial products, though only Southeast Asia actually became so. Japan's war reparations to Southeast Asian countries took the form of "the services of the Japanese people in production" as Article 14 of the San Francisco Peace Treaty stipulates. During 1950, Japan concluded war reparation agreements with Burma, the Philippines, Indonesia, and (then South) Vietnam. "The services of the Japanese people in production" became the harbinger of Japanese industrial exports to the countries. As for those Southeast Asian countries and India which renounced reparation claims in the San Francisco Peace Treaty, Japan concluded sub-reparation agreements with them during 1950s–1960s. The countries included India, Thai, Laos, Cambodia, Singapore, and Malaysia. Those sub-reparation and economic cooperation agreements allowed Japan to export industrial products, and Japan's presence in Southeast Asia gradually increased through trade and investment, not military power.

Under this "geo-economic" approach, postwar Japan's political presence in Southeast Asia and India was limited, but two Japanese conservative prime ministers, Nobusuke Kishi (1957–1960) and Takeo Fukuda (1976–1978), were exceptions though their ideological backgrounds were considerably different. Kishi is often regarded as the first Japanese leader who initiated an Asia-centric diplomacy. He was a pan-Asian nationalist and opposed the expansion of communism in Asia. He was engaged in Manchukuo as one of the key administrators (1936–1939) before the Pacific War. He showed strong interest in Japan's diplomacy toward Southeast Asia and India and envisaged the reestablishment of Japan as an Asian leader through this. On his way to the United States in 1957, he visited Burma, India, Pakistan, Ceylon (Sri Lanka), Thailand, and Taiwan, all were generous in renouncing or reducing war reparations. He thought that Japan should understand those countries as the leader in the region and this would make Japan's position more equal to the United States in terms of diplomatic bargaining (Kishi 1983). He also regarded a visit to India as important. He appreciated India's skeptical view of the International Military Tribunal for the Far East (the Tokyo War Crimes Tribunal), which treated him as a Class-A War criminal for crimes against the peace. India's refusal to attend the San Francisco Peace Conference of 1951 and its generous attitude to Japan's war reparation also explained his sympathy for this country. According to his memoir written while in prison, Kishi was impressed by Indian Prime Minister Jawaharlal Nehru's movement for an independent Asia and his view of Japan as a model for India's economic development (Hara 2003). Japan initiated economic cooperation with India under the Colombo Plan after it concluded a peace treaty with it in 1952, and started yen loans from 1958. India was one of the largest recipients of Japan's economic cooperation during the 1950s–1960s (Nagano and Kondo 1999). He also initiated economic cooperation with Southeast Asian countries through Japan's war reparations, but his intention included the containment of communism in the region (Kishi 1983). Kishi proposed a Southeast Asia development fund which included the United States as the main sponsor, but failed to obtain its support. Kishi's only diplomatic tool was economic support for the pro-Japan countries in the region as Japan's pacifist diplomacy only allowed economic measures which began with war reparations. His Southeast Asia and India policy soon wilted as there was no follow-up by his successors and Japan's economic capacity was at that time limited.

Prime Minister Fukuda upheld neither pan-Asianism nor anti-communism and adopted a liberal and benevolent stance toward Southeast Asia when concerns over Japan's remilitarization were broadly observed there. Prime Minister Kakuei Tanaka's visits to Southeast Asia in January 1974 provoked anti-Japan demonstrations and the Japanese government had to consider how to mitigate tensions (Edamura 2013). Fukuda showed a strong interest in the political aspect of the Japan–Southeast Asia relationship. According to Sakutaro Yano, then a Director in the Ministry of Foreign Affairs of Japan (MOFA), MOFA observed that China and the Soviet Union increased their influence on Southeast Asian countries and this should be weakened (Yano 2015). Fukuda had the strong view that "Japan should not seek only economic self-interest but also fulfil its international duties commensurate with its position as the second largest economy" (Edamura, ibid.). He announced what became known as the Fukuda Doctrine during his tour of Southeast Asian countries in 1977 to strengthen Japan's relationship with them. The Fukuda Doctrine emphasized that Japan would not become a great military power and would seek "heart-to-heart" mutual understanding with Southeast Asian countries, leaving ideological differences behind. His doctrine upheld Japan's non-militarization and "heart-to-heart" understanding as norms and he hoped to see gradual and autonomous change within Southeast Asia through Japan's economic support. This doctrine obscured the intention to weaken Chinese and Soviet influence in the region though Japan's economic support for the region sometimes had this purpose. According to ex-Prime Minister Yasuhiro Nakasone, Japan's decision to increase aid to Laos in 1983 was intended to increase its presence in Indochina where Vietnam intervened in the civil war in Cambodia at that time. This policy reflected Japan's active political commitment which Fukuda envisaged (Nakasone 2012).

References to Japan's geopolitical interest in the Western Pacific were also found in Japan's defense debate. Postwar Japan stressed the security of the "sea lanes" in the Western Pacific because its commercial imports, especially from the Middle East and the United States, largely depended on them. The defense of sea lanes was studied within Martime Self-Defense Force (JMSDF) before the 1980s, but there was no consensus on its constitutionality and feasibility (Auer 1973). On the other hand, the expanding Soviet naval capability in the Western Pacific and the Sea of Okhotsk became a concern for the US navy. Informed of the JMSDF study, the United States at the end of the 1970s requested that Japan support its maritime operations to protect the sea lanes in the Western Pacific (Agawa 2001). In the press conference after the 1981 summit meeting with US President Ronald Reagan, Prime Minster Zenko Suzuki (1980–1981) stated that Japan would be able to commit itself to JSDF naval operations within some hundreds nautical miles around Japan and in two 1000 nautical mile sea lanes stretching from Japan to the Philippines and to Guam, and he also affirmed this view in the Diet (Suzuki 1982). Despite Suzuki's announcement, there was no domestic consensus on Japan's use of the JSDF for sea lane defense, however. Suzuki was not well informed by his bureaucrats that it might violate Japan's self-imposed ban on the use of the right to collective defense and on the overseas dispatch of the JSDF (Agawa, ibid.). Consequently, his sea lane defense was not realized.

Prime Minister Yasuhiro Nakasone (1982–1987) showed active support for Japan's defense cooperation on sea lanes to bring about an equal partnership with the United States. He decided to purchase P3-C patrol aircraft for supporting US maritime operations in the Western Pacific and strengthened defense cooperation with the United States. His idea of sea lane defense was intended to protect Japanese commercial vessels from unexpected attacks. He sought to defend the sea lanes from Japan to Guam, and then to the Bashi Channel and the Luzon Strait, which formed a fan shape zone whose center was Japan (Nakasone 2012). According to him, Japan's concern in sea lane defense was especially about the Taiwan Strait, which is a Japanese commercial sea lane, and beyond the Bashi Channel, the inclusion of the sea around the Malay Peninsula was also debated (ibid.). He also emphasized that this was not the result of US pressure but Japan's own need (ibid.). This plan for sea lane defense caused a controversy in Japanese domestic politics at that time when pacifist sentiments were strong. The active use of the JSDF beyond Japan's territory even only for escort operations for commercial vessels was regarded as a violation of the constitutional constraint on the use of the JSDF, especially the ban on dispatching the JSDF overseas. In addition, the capability required for sea lane defense was beyond Japan's ability at the time and was not realistic, and there was a negative view of Japan's expanded defense activities beyond Taiwan among the ASEAN countries (ibid.). Nakasone's plan for sea lane defense was also not realized at that time because of the lack of domestic consensus.

Kishi, Fukuda, and Nakasone represented postwar Japan's approach to India and Southeast Asia despite their different leadership styles and promoted interests which are included in the FOIP. Japan had developed its multilateral diplomacy and security cooperation before the FOIP was born, which was a new name for Japan's security and economic cooperation as developed by these leaders. Kishi was the first Japanese leader to bring India into Japan's diplomatic landscape for a strategic purpose. Fukuda stressed the strategic importance of ASEAN or Southeast Asia for Japan and strengthened the political and economic relationship with the region. Nakasone attempted to approach maritime Southeast Asia in terms of Japan's sea lane defense and stressed the protection of Japan's trade routes and oil supply lifelines. The power configuration in the Indo-Pacific has considerably changed and Kishi and Fukuda approached Southeast Asia when the US presence was strong and Soviet and Chinese influence was limited. Nakasone's sea lane defense in the Western Pacific was against the Soviet Union, but the threat to Japan's sea lanes in the East China Sea and the South China Sea today is China's naval expansion. The Indo-Pacific region sees the rise of China which challenges US dominance and Japan has to deal with this new security object. Japan's geopolitical approach to the region has been built on the past, but the object of its security policy has changed.

Japan's China Challenge, Value Diplomacy, and Quadrilateralism

China's security challenges in the East China Sea and the South China Sea have gradually changed the range of JSDF maritime operations. Japan began to show a concern with China's naval expansion in the Western Pacific and its near seas from the late 1990s, and China became an object of Japan's defense operations in the 2000s. Japan started to denounce Chinese naval activities in the South China Sea in its white papers from 2012 and the South China Sea became an important issue for Japan's defense debate. In his article on the "security diamond" in December 2012, Abe called the South China Sea "Beijing's lake" and strongly asserted that Japan's security interest was threatened by China in this sea (Abe 2012). Since the 2010s, Japan has actively dispatched JMSDF vessels to the South China Sea, the Indian Sea, and the Western Pacific for joint exercises and port visits. It began to support Vietnam and the Philippines in capability-building in maritime security. Japan's security cooperation with countries in the Indo-Pacific had already increased before the FOIP was formally announced. Despite the increased security cooperation in the Indo-Pacific, Japan's use of the JSDF is still constrained by Article 9. It has been cautious about its involvement in contingencies beyond its territories while engaged in the use of the JSDF in the South China Sea and the Indian Ocean. Behind this defense posture, there is a cautious attitude to any military confrontation with China. Japan has not participated in US Freedom of Navigation Operations (FONOPs) though it has supported them diplomatically. Article 9 continued to constrain the use of the JSDF and would not support defensive operations beyond Japan's territory and territorial waters.

Japan's diplomacy changed from the middle of the 2000s under the first Shinzo Abe government (2006–2007) as it began to pursue strategy-based diplomacy. This change could be traced to two diplomats, Shotaro Yachi who was then-Deputy Minister of Ministry of Foreign Affairs of Japan (MOFA) and became the first Secretary General of the National Security Secretariat in 2012, and Nobukatsu Kanehara who was then Director of Policy Coordination Division of the Foreign Policy Bureau of MOFA and became Assistant Chief Cabinet Secretary in 2012. One ex-journalist, Tomohiko Taniguchi, was also included. He was a journalist with Nikkei business magazine and became Deputy Press Secretary of MOFA in 2005 and Special Adviser to the Cabinet in 2014 (Suzuki 2017). They changed Japan's diplomacy by promoting two strategic visions, "value diplomacy" which was presented to foreign minister Taro Aso, and "Panoramic Diplomacy (diplomacy that takes a panoramic perspective of the world map) which was presented to Shinzo Abe. The latter was created by Yachi and Kanehara for Abe because Abe considered that value diplomacy was Aso's domain (ibid.). Yachi, Kanehara, and Taniguchi also wrote Abe's speech to Indian parliament in 2007 which was called, "Confluence of the Two Seas" (ibid.). Yachi sought to expand Japan's diplomatic possibilities and wanted to renounce its postwar reactive posture to express national "will" (*kokorozashi*) in Japan's diplomacy (ibid.). According to journalist Yoshikatsu Suzuki, Kanehara was influenced and inspired by Halford Mackinder's geopolitics. Under the leadership of Yachi, he drafted a vision of value diplomacy and later the FOIP (ibid.). The geopolitical ideas in value diplomacy were influenced by Mackinder's proposal for Britain in the first half of the twentieth century such as "the league of democracies" and the "heartland" (ibid.). This "league" should cooperate to prevent the occupation of the "heartland" by land powers. Value diplomacy was announced by then-Foreign Minister Taro Aso during the first Abe government with the concept of the Arc of Freedom and Prosperity, which stretches from Japan to Southeast Asia, India, Central Asia, Eastern Europe, and Western Europe. This reflected the "arc of instability" which was found in the 2001 US Quadrennial Defense Review (QDR) (ibid.). The Arc of Freedom and Prosperity was initially intended to contain Russia as the "heartland" by strengthening Japan's diplomatic ties with countries in the arc, but the "heartland" later became China (ibid.). For Yachi, this was a means of exerting diplomatic pressure against China. This vision disappeared from Japan's diplomacy soon after the first Abe government, but re-appeared as Panoramic Diplomacy at the beginning of the second Abe government.

The Arc of Freedom and Prosperity brought universal values such as democracy and freedom to Japan's diplomacy while its geopolitical target was rather huge. Yachi and Kanehara believed that Japan should be a supporter of the liberal order and the term freedom and prosperity would be good for this vision (ibid.). It was a mid-term or long-term strategic vision to widen Japan's diplomatic horizon by contributing to the countries sharing liberal values with Japan (Yachi and Takahashi 2009). Value diplomacy was Japan's attempt to create a diplomatic vision and to restore national will in diplomacy but its geographical design was influenced by Mackinder's "league of democracies." The Japanese vision also called for bilateral and multilateral dialogues, the extension of Japan's ODA, people-to-people exchanges, and human development as well as emphasizing Japan's diplomatic ties with India. Its tools were norms such as freedom of navigation, the rule of law, and free trade which benefited postwar Japan in the US-led liberal order. Yachi dared to say that the Arc of Freedom and Prosperity was open to China and Russia if they could agree to its principles (ibid.). In addition, Yachi and Kanehara emphasized that the way to achieve this vision was through economic support, and unlike the past the military would not be used (ibid.). Value diplomacy was a mixture of Japanese nationalism and a geopolitical idealism that was shared by Abe and his close political and diplomatic elites.

During his first premiership (2006–2007), Abe initiated a quadrilateral Security Dialogue (Quad) with the United States, Australia, and India to counter China's security challenges, but this dialogue soon failed due to Australia's withdrawal by Australian Prime Minister Kevin Rudd. At the beginning of his second government (2012–2020), he actively asserted his views on the Indo-Pacific. He made clear Japan's strong commitment to the Indo-Pacific in his speech to the Center for Strategic and

International Studies (CSIS) in Washington, D.C., called "Japan is back" and in his speech in Jakarta called "The Bounty of the Open Seas: Five New Principles for Japanese Diplomacy"(Abe 2013a, b). As a personal view, he published in December 2012 his vision of a "security diamond" whose writer was Taniguchi (Suzuki, ibid.). This seemed to suggest the containment of China by Japan, the United States, Australia, and India, but Yachi, who became Secretary General of National Security Secretariat under the Abe government, denied such an intention eight months later (Yachi 2013).

Abe's vision was strongly influenced by his anti-China view at that time and his personal sympathy with India. His anti-China view reflects Japanese neo-conservatism (JNC) of which he has been the key proponent in Japanese politics. The JNC espouses anti-China feelings which come from anti-communism, Japan–China rivalry, and a belief in Japan's supremacy over China (Takahashi 2020). From the 2000s, the LDP moved to the right because of a generational change in which moderate conservative and liberal LDP lawmakers retired and moderate conservative supporter groups lost influence in the party. Instead, rightist groups increased their influence on the LDP and Abe became party leader in this context. On the other hand, Abe's sympathy with India comes from his high respect for his grandfather Kishi. He followed Kishi's stance not only on national security, anti-communism, and constitutional revision, but also on Japan's India policy. In his address to the Indian parliament in August 2007, he referred not only to the confluence of the two seas and an enlarged Asia with India, but also Kishi's strong connection with India (Abe 2007). In addition, Japanese political elites mostly have shown goodwill to India since the 1990s in tandem with India's pro-Japan attitudes (Yano, ibid.). Japan's sympathy may be an outcome of its geographical distance and limited exchanges since China is too close to be a friend while India is too far to be an enemy. The FOIP under Abe's leadership was largely based on his preference to counter China and his sympathy with India.

THE FOIP AND ITS LIMITATIONS

The origin of the FOIP can be found in Abe's speech to Indian parliament in 2007, which was titled as "Confluence of the Two Seas." In his speech, he presented an idea of "broader Asia" and emphasized that "this 'broader Asia' will evolve into an immense network spanning the entirety of the Pacific Ocean, incorporating the United States of America and Australia (Abe, ibid.)." As examined above, the speech was written by Yachi, Kanehara, and Taniguchi, all of whom drafted Japan's value diplomacy. After a decade, the idea of the FOIP was born in Summer 2016 which was intended to counter China's BRI. In the Sixth Tokyo International Conference on African Development (TICAD VI) in August 2016, Abe pledged Japan's active commitment to economic cooperation with Africa by saying that "Japan bears the responsibility of fostering the confluence of the Pacific and Indian Oceans and Asia and Africa into a place that values freedom, the rule of law, and the market economy, free from force or coercion, and making it prosperous" (Abe 2016). Foreign Minister Kono's speech to the 196th Session of the Diet in January 2018 embodied the FOIP for the first time in public speeches. He emphasized "peace and prosperity in the Pacific and the Indian Ocean" and called for "maintaining and strengthening a free and open maritime order of the Indo-Pacific region" as a global commons (Kono 2018).

The FOIP embraces diplomacy, defense policy, and economic cooperation. It includes three policy pillars. The first is the promotion of fundamental principles (rule of law, freedom of navigation, openness, free trade, etc.). It makes clear that "(a) free and open maritime order based on the rule of law is a cornerstone for stability and prosperity of the Indo-Pacific." Japan should have "responsibility for promoting freedom, the rule of law, and the market economy through the confluence of two oceans (ibid.)." It is a normative commitment to the present liberal order in terms of maritime security, trade, and investment which the United States has maintained since the end of the Pacific War. Its target is China's maritime activities especially in the South China and East China Seas and its state-controlled economy. The second pillar is enhancing connectivity through the quality of infrastructure. "(T)he Indo-Pacific region… is the core of global development where more than half of the global population resides (ibid.)." The FOIP in the second pillar is basically the enhancement of economic cooperation with Southeast Asian countries, India and Africa especially through Japanese infrastructure such as roads and bridges. Its assumed target is China's BRI. Japan's stress on quality intends to differentiate its contribution from the BRI and seeks to promote norms for economic infrastructure. The third pillar is peace and stability in maritime security and safety, counterterrorism, and disaster risk reduction by providing equipment and human development for the countries in the region. This is capability-building especially for coast guards and disaster relief in countries around the Western Pacific and the Indian Sea and it entails support for countries showing a concern with China's maritime conduct in the South China Sea or elsewhere. Japan's security cooperation with Vietnam and the Philippines through paramilitary capability enhancement is an example. The third pillar also seeks to enhance governance in countries in the region "including elections, parliamentary affairs, laws, justice, security, tax collection, and immigration control (ibid.)."

The significance of the FOIP lies in the emphasis on the role of norms (Cannon 2018). In his 2018 speech to the 196th Diet, Foreign Minister Kono noted that: "(v)alues which humankind has created in the modern age, including freedom, democracy, human rights and the rule of law, require that governments and peoples make various efforts to establish and maintain them" (Kono, ibid.). "In order to ensure that those values take root in the international community, we must lend a necessary helping hand" (Ibid.). He added that "maintaining and strengthening a free and open maritime order of the Indo-Pacific region as a global commons will bring stability and prosperity equally to all countries in this region (ibid.)." Diplomacy and multinational dialogues are the basis of the FOIP.

Japan's capability may influence East Asia, but it would be different in the Indian Ocean, South Asia, and Africa. Japan stresses diplomacy, security cooperation, economic infrastructure, and support for capability-building in the region, but defense and ODA budgets have not increased to meet the demands of this huge project. As to defense, the FOIP envisages Japan's influence in the Indo-Pacific, but Japanese capability is limited and there has been no clear consensus in Japan's domestic politics as to how Japan's defense capability should be allocated to the Indo-Pacific (Tsuruoka 2018). The defense budget has not been prepared and planned to deploy naval fleets in the Indian Ocean even though Japan decided to increase the number of submarines and commissioned two Izumo-class multi-purpose operation destroyers, one of which is being converted into an aircraft carrier. The 2019–2023 mid-term defense plan outlined procurement for the JSDF in the coming five years, but did not indicate a new capability build-up under the FOIP. The 2018 Japan–US agreement on cooperation on the Indo-Pacific was mainly non-military including maritime capability-building and disaster risk reduction in third countries such as the Marshall Islands, Micronesia, Palau, the Philippines, and Sri Lanka. In relation to economic cooperation, Japan's ODA budget has not increased significantly even after the announcement of the FOIP. Only piecemeal increases were observed from 2016 but the budget was still about half of the 1997 ODA budget. Japan financed large economic projects in India but this did not give it an advantage over other donors which invested as well. The probable impact of these policies on the region would not be so significant for the huge geographical area of the Indo-Pacific.

JAPAN'S NATIONAL WILL AND DEFENSE PREPARATION

The importance of the FOIP lies not in a defense capability, but in Japan's political will to commit itself to security and economic issues in the Indo-Pacific. Under a limited ODA budget, Japan maintains an active stance in the promotion of quality infrastructure in India and Southeast Asia. In defense, Japan showed a strong will to promote a presence in the South China Sea. The JSDF, for the first time, conducted a naval exercise involving a JMSDF submarine (*Kuroshio*) and its escort fleet within the nine-dash line in the South China Sea in September 2018. Abe dared to comment that exercises by JMSDF submarines in the South China Sea actually started fifteen years ago (The Nihon Keizai Shimbun 2018). The JMSDF actively began to use the *Izumo* and *Kaga* (helicopter carriers) for joint exercises and port visits in the South China Sea and the Indian Ocean from 2017. This is a clear political message signaling Japan's presence in the Indo-Pacific region. Japan strengthened the security relationship with India from the 2000s. Both countries announced "the Joint Statement Towards the Japan–India Strategic and Global Partnership" in 2006, in which their strategic partnership, political, security, and comprehensive economic cooperation were confirmed. In September 2014, Japan and India agreed to a joint statement entitled "Tokyo Declaration for Japan–India Special Strategic and Global Partnership," which included security and defense cooperation. For anti-submarine operations, Japan conducted naval exercises, sending *Izumo*, in the Indian Ocean (the Andaman Sea) with the Indian navy in May 2019, and its joint exercise was held close to Aomori (Japan) in July 2019. Japan also joined the Malabar naval exercise with India, the United States, and other countries in the region from 2007. The annual Malabar exercise involving Japan, the United States, and India was conducted in the sea off Sasebo (Kyushu, Japan) in September 2019. Japan and India started a 2 plus 2 meeting (Foreign Minister and Defense Minister meeting) from November 2019, and agreed to an Acquisition and Cross-Servicing Agreement (ACSA) between the two countries in September 2020. Japan's security cooperation with Australia was gradually deepened from the 2000s, and Australia has become a "Special Strategic Partner" for Japan (Ministry of Defense of Japan 2019). They concluded the Japan–Australia Joint Declaration on Security Cooperation in 2007, an ACSA in 2010, and the Japan–Australia Information Security Agreement in 2012. This accumulation of security cooperation with Australia and India gradually created a Japanese domestic consensus on the importance of the Indo-Pacific for Japan's security in the face of China's security challenges.

Japan's will is also demonstrated in its written defense strategy. The 2018 National Defense Program Guidelines (NDPG), which defines Japan's defense policy orientation for the future five or more years, was the first NDPG to refer to the FOIP as a vision for multilateral and multi-layered security cooperation. Japan will strengthen its joint drills and exercises, technical cooperation, support for capability-building for maritime security, and military exchanges. Japan's defense white paper in 2019 put the FOIP in a new sub-heading for this security cooperation. Under this heading, it listed security cooperation with Australia, India, ASEAN, Canada, New Zealand, and the Pacific islands, anti-piracy operations in the Gulf of Aden, and MJSDF exercises in the Indo-Pacific, though the contents were not changed considerably from the previous version (Minister of Defense of Japan 2019). In addition, the priority order of Japan's partners in security cooperation was rearranged. India came in third after the United States and Australia, instead of South Korea. The description of China's naval activities in its defense white papers changed as well, though much was intact. From the 2018 version, a new sub-section titled "Trends in the Indian Ocean and Other Seas" was created in the section on China's "Water and Airspace Activities," which made the description of China's military activities beyond the East China Sea and the South China Sea clearer. The FOIP is also symbolic of security cooperation under the US–Japan alliance in Japan's white papers. A sub-heading "Involvement in the Asia-Pacific Region" in the section on the United States was replaced by "Involvement in the Indo-Pacific Region" in the 2018 and subsequent defense white papers, and the length of this section was increased. The FOIP has not changed Japan's security cooperation drastically, but Japan's defense strategy and its white papers show an increasing use of the FOIP as a "title" for security cooperation in the region. In this sense, the FOIP may be an expression of Japan's "expectations" for better security and economic cooperation within the confines of a limited capability at this stage.

How Will the FOIP Develop?

How will the FOIP shape Japan's commitment to the Indo-Pacific in a geopolitical sense? The FOIP stresses the power of norms, which should be distinguished from military power. It intends to use norms as the means of persuasion, not coercive power. Japan understands that its influence in the region rests upon normative power. It attempts to strengthen this power through multilateral regional and global dialogues and considers that norms in the FOIP are a way of locking China into the regional order and moderating its expansionist naval activities in the South China and the East China Seas. The FOIP would be beneficial for the countries in the region if it is properly implemented to control competition and encourage cooperation between Japan and China. The benefit for small and middle powers is normative support by Japan. The FOIP respects the autonomy of middle and small powers through the support of norms, quality of infrastructure, and capability-building. It seeks to contribute to their own security and economic resources for their autonomous actions based on these norms. It encourages them to invest in durable and financially sound infrastructure projects and develop their maritime capabilities which would support their sovereignty and resist coercion by external powers. Support for their autonomy is the most valuable aspect of the FOIP. Here, we can identify another normative role in the FOIP which is not clearly written but implicitly included.

On the other hand, the limitations of the FOIP should be noticed. First, the FOIP has limited power of persuasion in defense cooperation against China. It will not be the main tool for Japan's defense cooperation in the Indo-Pacific. Japan's military commitment to the Indo-Pacific will continue to be mainly guided by US–Japan defense cooperation as US–Japan joint exercises have expanded in the region and have sent a political message to China in regard to its naval challenges. Japan also has promoted Quadrilateralism (the Quad). The FOIP and the Quad have been regarded as Japan's security initiatives in the Indo-Pacific, but the two are different in their way of competing with China. Japan, the United States, Australia, and India restarted Quadrilateral dialogue from 2017 which was clearly intended to counter China's security challenges in the Indo-Pacific by demonstrating military power in a quasi-coalition. In contrast, the FOIP is a Japanese project stressing security and economic cooperation with countries in the Indo-Pacific which are concerned about China's increasing power. Japan uses a more nuanced posture toward China in the FOIP. In the 2017 Diet, Abe noted that the FOIP can be a basis for cooperation with any country including China if it can accept its values (The Minutes of the Diet of Japan 2017). In his 2019 Diet speech, Abe mentioned the United States, Britain, France, Australia, and India as partners in the FOIP but did not necessarily deny cooperation with China (The Minutes of the Diet of Japan 2019). Both the Quad and the FOIP intend to counter China's influence in the Indo-Pacific, but the former suggests the use of military power in a coalition while the latter stresses political and economic means through norms and economic support.

A second limitation to the FOIP is the probable linkage of China's security challenges between the East China Sea and the South China Sea. Japan's activities in the South China Sea may provoke China in the East China Sea around the Senkaku/Diaoyu islands, though this linkage in China's thinking is not necessarily clear. One Japanese security expert concludes that there was no linkage between Japan's political engagement in the South China Sea, China's naval challenges to the Senkaku/Diaoyu islands, and the South China Sea Arbitration ruling of July 2016 which involved China and the Philippines (Kotani 2017). In contrast, Japanese security expert Bonji Ohara suggests that a link exists between the South China Sea and the East China Sea in Chinese thinking. He points out that China regards Japan as an outsider in the South China Sea and that China views Japan's involvement there as a means to counter its increasing naval presence around the Senkaku/Diaoyu islands by damaging its international reputation (Ohara 2016). If Ohara's observation is correct, Japan's involvement in the South China Sea would lead to intensified China's security challenges against Japan in the East China Sea, which may require Japan to reconsider its military presence in the South China Sea. A crisis might arise if Japan sends JMSDF vessels to a military standoff with China in the Indo-Pacific. China's naval challenges around the Senkaku/Diaoyu islands increased in Spring 2020 despite the cooperative political mood between Japan and China at this time. Controlled competition and cooperation between the two countries is required.

A third limitation is that the gap between the FOIP's geopolitics setting and Japan's actual capability is too large to be bridged. For those countries which feel uneasy or anxious about China's increasing influence, the FOIP may meet their expectations of Japan's commitment to the Indo-Pacific. However, Japan's actual influence, especially in the military field, would be limited because of Article 9. Japan may have geopolitical interests in the Indo-Pacific but, in domestic politics, this interest is not so defensible as to change its postwar identity of pacifism. The confluence of the two oceans as found in Abe's speech of 2007 is rather idealistic and this rhetorical vision may have left substantial policy debates behind. Japan's use of the military in the Indo-Pacific will be limited to joint naval exercises, port visits, or other defense exchanges, all of which are allowed under Article 9. Japan's economic support for the region including the African continent will continue and will have a high priority in its ODA budget, but Japanese business sectors' investment in India and Africa is far behind China and catching up is improbable (JETRO 2019). In contrast, in terms of geography, China is more closely involved in the Indo-Pacific than Japan. It faces the South China Sea and shares boundaries with Vietnam, Laos, Myanmar, Bhutan, Nepal, and India and its geopolitical influence is naturally far larger than that of Japan. China is an "embedded" great power in the region. Because of this, Japan's commitment to the region should not bring the danger of further confrontation. In addition, the writers of the FOIP only reflected part of Japan's political and diplomatic elites and this political base may not be necessarily strong after Abe's premiership. Sakutaro Yano, ex-Ambassador to India, criticized value diplomacy and pointed to negative reactions or concerns from Southeast Asia and India (Yano, ibid.). In terms of the gap between the geographical area and capability, weak domestic support, and probable cautious views from Southeast Asia and India, Japan may face the difficulty of continuing with the FOIP as a working geopolitical strategy or vision in the future. The way to overcome the difficulty lies in Japan's effort to develop multilateral diplomacy in the region for the promotion of norms.

Conclusion

The FOIP was born in 2016 as the manifestation of Japan's geopolitical interest in the Indo-Pacific, but historical continuities can be identified. In the prewar period, Japan pursued its geopolitical interests by military expansion, but this approach was renounced afterwards. Postwar Japan was cautious about the use of military power and ideological confrontation in its approach to the region and sought to secure its political presence through friendly relationships and economic support for the countries in the region. Its use of the JSDF for maritime security remained within a limited area of the Western Pacific under Article 9. In the face of China's rise, Japan announced the FOIP to show its political presence in the Indo-Pacific not in terms of the use of force and ideological confrontation but through the promotion of norms such as freedom of navigation, rule of law, and free trade. Through this, Japan shows a strong political will to counter China's influence in the region and has the expectation that China can be locked into a regional order by the power of norms. The FOIP is Japan's political tool to put psychological pressure on China by non-military means. However, the contents of the FOIP in actual policy are a continuation or at best an incremental step based on Japan's past security and economic cooperation with the region. The strategic use of the JSDF beyond territorial defense is still cautiously restrained by the Japanese government except for naval exercises, port visits, and defense exchanges in the region. Like value diplomacy, the FOIP is a product of Japanese nationalism and geopolitical idealism which envisages competition between the two regional great powers as "Japan versus China." The idealistic elements are only shared by some conservative political and bureaucratic elites such as Abe and Yachi. The gap between its grandiose geopolitical vision and capability is obvious. Japan's defense and ODA budget has not significantly increased to cover the huge geographical area and to compete with China. Given this limited material capacity, Japan should recognize that its influence on the region and on China rests upon coalition making and the "power" of norms. In this sense, the Quad will work better than the FOIP in exerting psychological pressure on China in that it is based upon a coalition which includes US military power. Nonetheless, strengthening multilateralism and active global agenda-setting in Japan's diplomacy would be the key to promote the power of norms in the FOIP. Japan should demonstrate through the FOIP how its path to security and economic cooperation differs from that of China. How sensitively and effectively Japan can promote the power of norms with its partners in multilateral settings over regional issues will determine the success of the FOIP.

References

Abe, S. (2007) Confluence of the Two Seas, Speech by H.E. Mr. Shinzo Abe, Prime Minister of Japan at the Parliament of the Republic of India, August

22, 2007. Ministry of Foreign Affairs of Japan. https://www.mofa.go.jp/region/asia-paci/pmv0708/speech-2.html (accessed April 10, 2020).

Abe, S. (2012) Asia's Democratic Security Diamond. Project Syndicate. https://www.project-syndicate.org/onpoint/a-strategic-alliance-for-japan-and-india-by-shinzo-abe?barrier=accesspaylog (accessed April 9, 2020).

Abe, S. (2013a) Japan is Back By Shinzo Abe, Prime Minister of Japan, February 22, 2013 at CSIS. Ministry of Foreign Affairs of Japan. https://www.mofa.go.jp/announce/pm/abe/us_20130222en.html (accessed April 7, 2020).

Abe, S. (2013b) The Bounty of the Open Seas: Five New Principles for Japanese Diplomacy, Speech and Statements by the Prime Minister, January 18, 2013. Prime Minister of Japan and His Cabinet. http://japan.kantei.go.jp/96_abe/statement/201301/18speech_e.html (accessed 7 April, 2020).

Abe, S. (2016) Address by Prime Minister Shinzo Abe at the Opening Session of the Sixth Tokyo International Conference on African Development (TICAD VI), August 27, 2016. Ministry of Foreign Affairs of Japan. https://www.mofa.go.jp/afr/af2/page4e_000496.html (accessed February 20, 2020).

Agawa, N. (2001) *Umino yujyo: Beikoku kaigun to kaijyo jieitai* (*Friendship on the Sea: US Navy and Maritime Self-Defense Force*). Tokyo: Chuokoron-shinsha, pp. 211–19.

Auer, J. (1973) *Postwar Rearmament of Japanese Maritime Forces, 1945–71.* New York: Irvington Publishers.

Cannon, B. (2018) Grand Strategies in Contested Zones: Japan's Indo-Pacific, China's BRI and Eastern Africa. *Rising Powers Quarterly*, 3(2), pp. 195–221.

Cannon, B. and Rossiter, A. (2018) The "Indo-Pacific": Regional Dynamics in the 21st Century's New Geopolitical Center of Gravity. *Rising Powers Quarterly*, 3(2), pp. 7–17.

Edamura, S. (2013) The Fukuda Doctrine: Diplomacy with a vision. In: L. Peng, ed., *Japan's Relations with Southeast Asia: The Fukuda Doctrine and beyond*. Abingdon: Routledge, pp. 24–25.

Gyngell, A. (2018) To each their own 'Indo-Pacific'. *East Asia Forum*, 23 March.

Hara, Y. (2003) *Kishi Nobusuke shogen roku* (*Kishi Nobusuke's Monologue*). Tokyo: Mainichi Shinbum-sha, p. 55.

Hata, I. (2010) Nichibei no senso shido 1941–43 (Leadership in War in Japan and the United States: 1941–43). The Report of the 8th International Forum on War History. Ministry of Defense of Japan. 28. https://warp.da.ndl.go.jp/info:ndljp/pid/1052049/www.nids.go.jp/event/forum/pdf/2009/03.pdf.

JETRO. (2019) *Jetoro sekai boeki toshi hokokusho 2019* (*JETRO Report on World Trade and Investment, 2019*). Tokyo: The Japan External Trade Organization.

Kishi, N. (1983) *Kaiko roku: Hoshu godo to anpo kaitei* (*Kishi Nobusuke's Memoirs: The Merger of Japan's Conservative Parties and The Revision of the U.S-Japan Mutual Security Treaty*). Tokyo: Kosai-do, pp. 312, 384.

Kono, T. (2018) Foreign Policy Speech by Foreign Minister Kono to the 196th Session of the Diet, Speeches by the Foreign Minister, January 22, 2018. Ministry of Foreign Affairs of Japan. https://www.mofa.go.jp/fp/unp_a/page3e_000816.html (accessed April 5, 2020).

Kotani, T. (2017) Minami shina kai chusai handan go no higashi shina kai: Minami shina kai mondai tono sokan kankei (The East China Sea after the Arbitration of the South China Sea: the Correlation with the South China Sea problem. International Affairs). The Japan Institute of International Affairs, No. 659, March.

Kurono, T. (1996) Teikoku kokubo hoshin seisenryakuko (The Imperial Defense Policy of 1907 Reconsidered). *International Politics* (The Japan Association of International Relations), 112, May, pp. 179–181.

Ministry of Defense of Japan. (2019) *Nihon no bouei 2019* (Defense of Japan 2019). Tokyo: Ministry of Defense, pp. 355–56.

Nagano, S. and Kondo, M. (eds.) (1999) *Nihon no sengo baisho: Ajia Keizai kyoryku no shupatsu (Japan's Postwar War Reparation: The Start of Japan's economic cooperation with Asia)*. Tokyo: Keiso Shobo, p. 205.

Nakasone, Y. (2012) *Nakasone Yasuhiro ga kataru sengo nihon gaiko (Japan's Foreign Policy since 1945, Yasuhiro Nakasone Oral History)*. Tokyo: Shinchosha, pp. 289–90, 320–22, 336–37.

National Diet of Japan. (2017) The Minutes of the Diet, the General Assembly, the House of Representatives, November 20, 2017.

National Diet of Japan. (2019) The Minutes of the Diet, the General Assembly, the House of Representatives, October 4, 2019.

Nihon Keizai Shimbun. (2018) Kaiji sensuikan ga minami shinakai de kunren, Hatsu no kohyo, Chugoku kensei (Announcement on JMSDF Submarine's exercise in the South China Sea as Check against China), September 17, 2018. https://www.nikkei.com/article/DGXMZO35447400X10C18A9PE8000/.

Ohara, B. (2016) Senkaku ni oshiyoseru tairyo no chugoku sen, Higashi shinakai to minami shinakai ga rendosuru riyu (Massive Chinese vessels heading to the Senkaku islands, the reasons of the linkage between the East China Sea question and the South China Sea question) Wedge Infinity, August 12, 2016. https://wedge.ismedia.jp/articles/-/7532.

Spang, C. (2001) Kaaru hausu houfa to nihon no chiseigaku: daiichiji sekaitaisengo no nichidoku kankei no nakade hausu houfa no motuigi ni tuite (Karl Haushofer and Japan's geopolitics: The importance of Haushofer in Japan-German relationship after WWI). *Space, Society and Graphical Thought*, 6, pp. 6–8.

Suzuki, Z. (1982) Prime Minister Zenko Suzuki, "Written Answer (答弁書), Memorandum on Questions (質問主意書)," House of Councilors, The National Diet of Japan, July 13, 1982. https://www.sangiin.go.jp/japanese/joho1/kousei/syuisyo/096/touh/t096024.htm.

Suzuki, Y. (2017) *Nihon no senryaku gaiko (Japan's Strategic Diplomacy)*. Tokyo: Chikuma-shobo, pp. 71–74, 81–98, 102, 137–38,140–41.

Takahashi, T. (2020) In: Takahashi, T. *China in Japan's National Security: Domestic Credibility*. Abington: Routledge, Ch 5.

Tsuruoka, M. (2018) Japan's Indo-Pacific Engagement: The Rationale and Challenges., Italian Institute for International Political Studies, 4 June 2018. https://www.ispionline.it/en/pubblicazione/japans-indo-pacific-engagement-rationale-and-challenges-20691.

Yachi, S. (2013) Chikyu o fukan suru abe gaiko, Yachi Shotaro naikaku kanbo sanyo intabyu (Abe's Diplomacy of Panoramic Views, Interview with Shotaro Yachi), Nippon. Com, July 5, 2013. https://www.nippon.com/ja/currents/d00089/ (accessed April 13, 2020).

Yachi, S. and Takahashi, M. (2009) *Gaiko no senryaku to kokorozashi (Strategy and Will of Diplomacy)*. Tokyo: Sankei Shimbun, pp. 143–45.

Yano, S. (2015) *Gaiko shogen roku Ajia gaiko: kaiko to kosatsu (Testimony on Japan's Asia Diplomacy: Retrospectives and Examinations)*. Tokyo: Iwanami, pp. 45–46, 269–80.

CHAPTER 12

Toward an Improved Understanding of the US Indo-Pacific Strategy

Derek Grossman

INTRODUCTION

On his first trip to the Asia-Pacific in November 2017, President Donald Trump renamed the region to the "Indo-Pacific." Since then, the Trump administration has offered an evolving definition of the term, and countries participating in the Indo-Pacific strategy (Department of Defense 2019) as well as outside observers have expressed confusion over the strategy's objectives and implementation. This chapter attempts to briefly explain Washington's ongoing conceptualization of the Indo-Pacific as a region, and to provide some thoughts on the state of the strategy. It concludes with a discussion of ways in which Washington might strengthen the Indo-Pacific strategy going forward.

D. Grossman (✉)
RAND Corporation, Santa Monica, CA, USA
e-mail: dgrossma@rand.org

America Defines the Indo-Pacific

At its most fundamental level, the Indo-Pacific is a combination of the Indian and Pacific Oceans. But starting in 2007, think tank experts began to consider how states within this enormous region should be interacting with each other. Indian navy captain and maritime strategist Gurpreet S. Khurana, for example, believed the term Asia-Pacific unfairly excluded India, especially as it continued to rise to major power status in the early twenty-first century. From his perspective, India and East Asia should seek to enhance economic interconnectivity across the Indo-Pacific (Khurana 2007, 2017). Additional Indo-Pacific research, however, veered in another direction. Notably, Australian researcher Rory Medcalf in the same year floated the Indo-Pacific as a geostrategic concept to the incoming Australian foreign minister Stephen Smith. Medcalf's view held that like-minded countries should work together across the Indo-Pacific in common causes, such as maritime security (Medcalf 2007). Within this environment of deep thought cross-regionally, Japanese Prime Minister Shinzo Abe in August 2007 visited India and gave a seminal speech to Parliament entitled "Confluence of the Two Seas." Abe pushed for greater economic interconnectivity between the Asia-Pacific and South Asian regions, but also touted the strategic partnership between the two "like-minded" democratic nations of India and Japan to build an "Arc of Freedom and Prosperity" (Abe 2007; Aso 2007). Although "Indo-Pacific" did not appear in Abe's speech, he used the term "broader Asia" several times as a clear antecedent to the concept of the Indo-Pacific. Significantly, Abe noted that Australia and the United States should be involved in broader Asia.

Upon entering office again in 2012 for his second non-consecutive term, Abe penned an important op-ed entitled "Asia's Democratic Security Diamond" (Abe 2012). In a stark departure from his India speech in 2007 which did not discuss China at all, this op-ed specifically criticized China multiple times for its rising assertiveness in the East and South China Seas, questioning whether the free world should tolerate the creation of "Lake Beijing" in Asia. Abe called for enhanced security cooperation among not only Australia, India, Japan, and the United States (known as the Quadrilateral Security Dialogue or the Quad), but also France, Great Britain, and the British Five Power Defense Arrangements including Great Britain, Malaysia, Singapore, New Zealand, and Australia. Notably, Abe's op-ed still did not use the term Indo-Pacific. By August

2016, Abe gave another foundational speech to African nations in which he said: "Japan bears the responsibility of fostering the confluence of the Pacific and Indians Oceans and of Asia and Africa into a place that values freedom, the rule of law, and the market economy, free from force or coercion, and making it prosperous" (Abe 2016). Even though Indo-Pacific was once again not invoked, this speech represented Tokyo's official roll out of the "Free and Open Indo-Pacific" (FOIP) strategy. In 2017, the Japanese Ministry of Foreign Affairs issued a factsheet that referenced the speech and discussed Tokyo's new FOIP strategy, stating: "Under the 'Free and Open Indo-Pacific Strategy,' Japan will enhance 'connectivity' between Asia and Africa to promote stability and prosperity across regions" (Japanese Ministry of Foreign Affairs 2017; Hosoya 2019).

When President Trump traveled to Japan on the first leg of his Asia trip in November 2017, he used the term Indo-Pacific for the first time in their joint statement. He noted that the United States and Japan had "aligned our strategic priorities to a shared vision of a free and open Indo-Pacific" (White House 2017a). Later during his trip, President Trump delivered a major speech on FOIP in Vietnam for the Asia-Pacific Economic Conference (APEC) CEO summit. He referred to his "Indo-Pacific dream" and concluded: "Let us choose a free and open Indo-Pacific" (White House 2017b). Given the identical construction of Prime Minister Abe and President Trump's FOIP concepts and the fact that Abe's predated Trump's by over a decade, it is reasonable to surmise that Abe's version rubbed off on Trump. The two leaders by late 2017 had also developed a close personal friendship, enabling a frank exchange of ideas (Liptak 2017). Although there were certainly other countries, namely, Australia, India, and Indonesia, who had also been conceptualizing a new Indo-Pacific region for years, their versions bore fewer similarities to what became the US version, suggesting Japan had significantly more influence on Trump administration policymaking (Medcalf 2013; Australian Department of Defence 2013; Australian Department of Defence 2016).[1]

An alternative explanation is that Trump had politics in mind when he adopted Indo-Pacific. Prior to President Trump, no US president had

---

[1] For example, Australia by 2013 talked at length about the "Indo-Pacific" within its defense white paper, but never used the "free and open" construct to describe it. By 2016, however, Canberra did start to use "free and open" as a phrase, but only to discuss narrow areas such as trade.

ever uttered the term, and as an unconventional leader, Trump has clearly been willing to break with the past. Perhaps more importantly, his predecessor and rival, President Barack Obama, had his own strategic rebalance or "pivot" to Asia strategy, and so Trump may have sought to strike a contrast with Obama's policy. It is interesting to note, however, that other Obama administration officials, including most notably Secretary of State Hillary Clinton, who also opposed Trump in the 2016 presidential election, used Indo-Pacific once in 2011 in a *Foreign Policy* op-ed. Clinton said "We are also expanding our alliance with Australia from a Pacific partnership to an Indo-Pacific one, and indeed a global partnership" (Clinton 2011). As a bitter political rival to Clinton, Trump would have been loath to repeat the term, so the fact that he did nonetheless suggests President Trump's discussions with Prime Minister Abe were the predominant force in his decision-making.

Yet another possibility is that the US military's Indo-Pacific Command (INDOPACOM), which changed its name from Pacific Command (PACOM) in 2018, influenced President Trump to adopt Indo-Pacific. Indeed, at least the last two PACOM commanders—Admiral Harry Harris and Admiral Samuel Locklear before him—referred to their command's area of responsibility as the "Indo-Asia-Pacific" (Medcalf 2013; Harris 2016). In the case of Admiral Harris, he attended India's annual Raisina Dialogue in 2016 and said: "I'm sometimes asked why I always use the term 'Indo-Asia-Pacific' versus the commonly used term 'Asia-Pacific' by smart people like those in the room today. My answer is simple. Indo-Asia-Pacific more accurately captures the fact that the Indian and Pacific Oceans are the economic lifeblood that links India, Australia, Asia, Oceania, and the United States together" (Harris 2016). It stands to reason, then, that perhaps the US military had some measure of influence on President Trump's thinking as well. After all, President Trump's first stop before Japan in November 2017 was to Hawaii to visit INDOPACOM headquarters. But INDOPACOM had also never used the "free and open" construction, once again giving more weight to the idea that the United States adopted the term primarily from Japan.

Regardless, shortly after his visit, the Trump administration issued its *National Security Strategy* in December 2017 (White House 2017c). The *National Security Strategy* devoted an entire section to the Indo-Pacific, which was defined as encompassing an enormous region stretching from the American to Indian west coast. Unlike Japan's FOIP concept, however, the United States took a far harsher stance on China's role in the Indo-Pacific. For the first time, official US policy became publicly adversarial toward China. The *National Security Strategy* referred to China as a "revisionist power," "rival," "adversary," and "competitor."[2] China, according to the strategy, was no better than fellow revisionist power Russia, pariah states Iran and North Korea, and jihadist terrorist groups because it "is using economic inducements and penalties, influence operations, and implied military threats to persuade other states to heed its political and security agenda." Although the United States pledged to continue cooperation with China when possible, competition and countering China within the Indo-Pacific would now constitute core US strategy. Subsequent key Trump administration reports, including the *National Defense Strategy*, *Indo-Pacific Strategy Report*, and *A Free and Open Indo-Pacific*, all echoed and expanded upon these same themes (Department of Defense 2018; Department of Defense 2019; Department of State 2019).

Finally, since the release of these official documents, the Trump administration has exhibited a continual evolution in its thinking on the region. Significantly, while attending the Raisina Dialogue in January 2020, deputy national security adviser and former senior director for Asia at the National Security Council, Matthew Pottinger, commented that the Indo-Pacific now stretches "from California to Mount Kilimanjaro" (Bagchi 2020). Pottinger's statement ended the previous Indo-Pacific bumper sticker "from Hollywood to Bollywood" in favor of dramatically enlarging further an already very large region. Although his comment may have confused Indo-Pacific allies, partners, and observers, the most logical explanation is that the United States has been trying to better align its geographic conception of the Indo-Pacific to that of key partner India and security ally Japan. India has always believed that the eastern Indian Ocean region was a part of its Indo-Pacific because of historical, cultural, and trade links to east Africa, whereas Abe also values Africa as part of Japan's Indo-Pacific, demonstrated by his FOIP rollout speech to African colleagues. Irrespective of the exact geography, the bottom line is that the United States no longer views the Asia-Pacific as being separate from the Indian Ocean Region. Instead, Washington now has a cross-regional and cross-cutting perspective that concentrates less on cooperation with

---

[2] Notably, "enemy" is used once in a military context as well.

China, and more on working together with allies and partners inhabiting the maritime rim around it.

US Objectives and Strategy in the Indo-Pacific

The Trump administration's Indo-Pacific policy is contained within four key documents including the *National Security Strategy, National Defense Strategy, Indo-Pacific Strategy Report,* and *A Free and Open Indo-Pacific.* The core theme linking all reports is that the Indo-Pacific must remain "free and open" from coercion, and in particular, from Chinese coercion. Notably, according to the *Indo-Pacific Strategy Report,* Washington seeks to uphold the following principles:

- Respect for sovereignty and independence of all nations;
- Peaceful resolution of disputes;
- Free, fair, and reciprocal trade based on open investment, transparent agreements, and connectivity; and
- Adherence to international rules and norms, including those of freedom of navigation and overflight (Department of Defense 2019).

It is telling, however, that none of these reports specifically lay out American "objectives" in the Indo-Pacific. Instead, Washington has a "vision" of a future region that maintains the four aforementioned principles in the face of China's growing assertiveness.[3] In other words, the United States, in concert with allies and partners, is trying to preserve the liberal, rules-based international order that it helped establish following the end of World War II—and the preservation of that order, in essence, *is* the US objective in the Indo-Pacific. Put another way, Washington believes the Indo-Pacific would still be fine today if not for Beijing's interference. The Indo-Pacific would remain US-centric, and even though Japan and India are on the rise militarily and economically, they are friends that share American values of democracy and human rights. China clearly does not, and according to the *National Defense Strategy,* Beijing instead seeks to overturn the regional order in its favor. This excerpt from the

---

[3] Importantly, China is not the only threat mentioned in the Indo-Pacific. Others include Russia, North Korea, and transnational challenges, but China is certainly the primary threat that is the driving force behind the Indo-Pacific strategy.

National Defense Strategy provides additional context for why China is so problematic for the United States:

> China is leveraging military modernization, influence operations, and predatory economics to coerce neighboring countries to reorder the Indo-Pacific region to their [China's] advantage. As China continues its economic and military ascendance, asserting power through an all-of-nation long-term strategy, it will continue to pursue a military modernization program that seeks Indo-Pacific regional hegemony in the near-term and displacement of the United States to achieve global preeminence in the future. (Department of Defense 2018)

Therefore, the United States seeks to preserve rather than reshape the Indo-Pacific. At its core, Washington's mantra to keep the region "free and open" from coercion is also defined in the Indo-Pacific strategy. The strategy notes that a "free" Indo-Pacific "is one in which all nations, regardless of size, are able to exercise their sovereignty free from coercion by other countries" (Department of Defense 2019). Contrary to some of the interactions I have had with Asian interlocutors, the US intention here is *not* to promote or export democracy abroad. Rather, Washington seeks to prevent China from undermining their ability to remain independent. The Indo-Pacific strategy defines "open" as a region that "promotes sustainable growth and connectivity in the region" and in which "all nations enjoy access to international waters, airways, and cyber and space domains, and are able to pursue peaceful resolution of territorial and maritime disputes" (Department of Defense 2019). Washington most often cites the open concept when defending its right, along with the rights of others under the United Nations Convention for the Law of the Sea (UNCLOS), to conduct freedom of navigation operations (FONOPs) in contested waters, such as in the South China Sea.

Washington expands upon its definition of FOIP by explicitly recognizing "the linkages between economics, governance, and security." In this vein, the United States pledged to "uphold the rule of law, encourage resilience in civil society, and promote transparent governance" to ensure that "independent nations can both defend their interests and compete fairly in the international marketplace." As a preferred end state, the United States seeks a region in which "no one nation can or should dominate" (Department of Defense 2019). To maintain a rules-based order, the US Indo-Pacific strategy proposes three interconnected lines of effort: "Preparedness, Partnerships, and Promoting a Networked Region." Washington describes these 3Ps as follows:

- **Preparedness**: The *National Defense Strategy* directs the Department [of Defense] to employ its resources in ways that enhance the lethality, resilience, agility, and readiness of the Joint Force. This resourcing must span near-term force employment activities and longer-term investments to modernize and redesign the US military.
- **Partnerships**: Mutually beneficial alliances and partnerships are crucial to our [Indo-Pacific] strategy, providing a durable, asymmetric strategic advantage that no competitor or rival can match. Expanding our interoperability with allies and partners will ensure that our respective defense enterprises can work together effectively during day-to-day competition, crisis, and conflict.
- **Promoting a Networked Region:** As the Indo-Pacific changes, the United States is augmenting its bilateral relationships with trilateral and multilateral arrangements, and encouraging intra-Asian security relationships for partnerships with purpose. As articulated in the *National Defense Strategy*, the Department of Defense (DoD) will strengthen and evolve our alliances and partnerships into an extended network capable of deterring or decisively acting to meet the shared challenges of our time (Department of Defense 2019).

Following the release of the Indo-Pacific strategy, the US Department of State in November 2019 released an "implementation update" report entitled *A Free and Open Indo-Pacific: Advancing a Shared Vision*. This report repeats the same "free and open" themes from the preceding reports, but also provides a deeper dive into the non-military dimensions of the Indo-Pacific strategy, to include governance and economics. On governance, the report notes that the United States seeks to uphold "…citizen-responsive governance and light-touch regulation that fosters entrepreneurship and the efficient allocation of capital, and institutions that promote transparency, fairness, and the sanctity of contracts." It further states that "To address governance challenges across the Indo-Pacific region, U.S. programs empower the region's citizens and civil societies, combat corruption, and build resilience to foreign influence that threatens nations' sovereignty" (Department of State 2019). Regarding economics, which is referred to as "economic prosperity" in the report, the United States offers the following explanation of its goals:

The United States believes that the role of government is to enable free enterprise while protecting individual rights and empowering people. We respect the sovereignty of every nation, and our economic engagement seeks to equip states to resist coercive economic practices, unsustainable debt burdens, and other dangers. We do this by improving market access and competitiveness, facilitating business-to-business ties, and promoting free, fair, and reciprocal trade.

The rest of *A Free and Open Indo-Pacific* is devoted to detailing US accomplishments thus far in the governance, economics, and security domains. After a close examination of Trump administration strategy reports, it becomes clear that the Trump administration's Indo-Pacific strategy bares many similarities to the Obama administration's strategic rebalance or pivot Asia to policy, and thus should *not* be viewed as a total break from past US Asia policy (Ford 2020). Although the geographic focus of "Asia" has certainly expanded significantly, both President Trump and President Obama prioritize deepening bilateral and multilateral ties with allies and partners to address common threats. However, the Indo-Pacific strategy (and *National Security Strategy* and *National Defense Strategy* before it) is more vocal about the primary threat, which is China, then was the case under Obama's strategic rebalance policy.

IMPLEMENTING THE US INDO-PACIFIC STRATEGY

It is an open secret that US implementation of the Indo-Pacific strategy has been rocky at best. Nagging questions about the strategy's purpose, whether it can be sustained, if it even constitutes a strategy, and why allies and partners apparently must choose between the United States and China in this new era of great power competition hang a dark cloud over Washington's plans (Samaan 2019; Carafano 2019; Cooper and Poling 2019; Voice of America 2019a). Nevertheless, US allies and partners have generally supported Washington's core security objectives of keeping the Indo-Pacific "free and open" from Chinese coercion. Their bottom line is that the maintenance of a rules-based order and international norms of behavior are critical to mitigating the challenges posed by Beijing's growing economic and military power in the region and globally. These include the staunchest of allies Australia, Japan, Taiwan (unofficial ally), and South Korea, as well as those who are quieter on the benefits of the strategy but have likewise endorsed US goals, such as India and Vietnam (Australian Department of Foreign Affairs and Trade 2019; Japanese Ministry of Foreign Affairs 2017; Republic of China (Taiwan) Ministry of Foreign Affairs 2018; White House 2019; Indian Ministry of External Affairs 2018, 2019). American allies and partners that have strenuously sought to avoid picking the United States or China, namely, the Philippines, Malaysia, Indonesia, and Singapore all seem to at least acknowledge the importance of maintaining great power balance in contested regions such as the South China Sea (Vicedo 2018; Kadir 2019; Weatherbee 2019; Chan and Wong 2019).

A distinct challenge for Washington's Indo-Pacific strategy has been the apparent divergence between the letter and spirit of the strategy, on the one hand, and President Trump's statements and actions on the other hand. But even in these cases, allies and partners to date have been quite forgiving because they seem to be willing to distinguish between the two. Following the president's trip to the G-20 hosted by Japan in late June 2019, for example, a senior Japanese foreign affairs official noted "we should not react to a tweet by the president each time…if it's their official position, we need to deal with it, but the president says various things" (Barnes 2019).

Moreover, allies and partners, at least so far, seem to have prevented the numerous trade wars against many of them to negatively impact enhancements in security cooperation with Washington. For instance, during heightened US–India trade friction in late spring 2019, New Delhi responded to US import tariffs by circumscribing its retaliation to raising export tariffs on 28 different US products (Iyengar 2019). Yet, as if operating in a completely parallel universe, US–India bilateral defense and security exchanges have improved significantly. After their first-ever "2 + 2 dialogue" in September 2018, held between US secretaries of state and defense as well as their Indian counterparts, New Delhi and Washington inked military information-sharing agreement and operationalized a military logistics agreement (Pubby 2018; Peri 2018). In October 2019, Indian Prime Minister Narendra Modi visited Trump in Houston, Texas for a "Howdy Modi" event to strengthen ties between the two nations (Ratcliffe 2019). Modi repaid the favor in February 2020 by hosting the US president for a "Namaste Trump" event (Ellis-Petersen 2020). Meanwhile, Trump's trade pressure on another key Indo-Pacific partner, Vietnam, has also not resulted in any appreciable degradation of security ties. In fact, quite the opposite has been the trend, with Washington in March sending the *USS Theodore Roosevelt* to Da Nang for a port visit—the second visit by an American aircraft carrier in three years (Olson 2020). Similarly, past trade pressure on US allies Japan and South Korea has not harmed security cooperation.

Even the US decision to withdraw from the Trans-Pacific Partnership (TPP) in 2017, which left several key allies and partners in the lurch, has not appreciably impacted their security relationships with Washington. The Indo-Pacific strategy has probably benefited from the decision by former TPP members, namely, Japan, Australia, Vietnam, Malaysia, and Singapore, to pick up the pieces of TPP and establish their own trade bloc, known as the Comprehensive Progressive Trans-Pacific Partnership (CPTPP). To be sure, President Trump has occasionally weighed in and complicated select security aspects of the Indo-Pacific strategy as well. For example, while on his way to the G-20 in Tokyo, Trump in June 2019 argued the US–Japan alliance was imbalanced and that he might have to reconsider the terms of the alliance (Reuters 2019b). Meanwhile, President Trump's decision to unilaterally suspend large US–South Korea military exercises meant to deter North Korea in 2018 resulted in regional consternation, particularly among US allies, but among partners as well (Cooper 2018). The Trump administration's tough negotiating stance on the future costs of maintaining the US–South Korea alliance, known as the Special Measures Agreement, has further strained Seoul's patience (Reuters 2020). And President Trump's response to Filipino President Rodrigo Duterte's decision to send notice of intent to terminate the Visiting Forces Agreement—a key agreement enabling easy US military access into and within the Philippines in the event of a contingency against China—was "I don't really mind if they would like to do that, it will save a lot of money" (Holland and Brunnstrom 2020). Thus, it is certainly difficult for allies and partners to consistently trust US security commitments to the region. According to a recent annual survey of Southeast Asian views on many issues, including rising US–China competition, close to half (47%) had little or no confidence in Washington as a strategic partner or provider of regional security (Mun et al. 2020).

But implementation of the security side of the strategy is not all bad. Indeed, the Trump administration has done important work in several key areas and continues to push hard in many others. Notably, Washington has significantly boosted US–Taiwan defense ties, reiterated US security alliance commitments under the Mutual Defense Treaty to the Philippines in the South China Sea, bolstered US–India ties as discussed above, and for the first time ever established a dedicated director at the National Security Council for Pacific Island issues (Chung 2018; Ranada 2019; Dziedzic and Graue 2019). On the latter point, President Trump was the first sitting president ever to invite all three leaders from the Freely Associated States (Marshall Islands, Micronesia, and Palau) to the White House to underscore the unique international agreements they maintain with the United States to ensure military access to the Second Island Chain, and Secretary of State Pompeo became the first sitting secretary to visit Micronesia in a clear bid to counter Chinese influence (Grossman and Chase 2019). In other words, the "Pacific" part of the Indo-Pacific strategy is also getting its rightful spotlight, and not just the "Indo," or India and Indian Ocean, part.

Moreover, the United States during President Trump's Asia visit in November 2017 quietly resurrected the Quadrilateral Security Dialogue, or "Quad," which ten years prior had been an informal group comprised of Australia, India, Japan, and the United States for dealing with the rise of China. Since 2017, the Quad has met twice a year (though no meetings in person in 2020) and has emphasized maintaining the rules-based international order. In spite of not holding any joint military exercises, as it did in 2007 with Singapore, the United States probably believes the Quad has served the basic purpose of signaling unity of resolve among democracies and like-minded partners to counter China's growing assertiveness in the Indo-Pacific region (Grossman 2019). In 2019, the Quad was also elevated to the ministerial level, underscoring its growing importance as a multilateral venue of Indo-Pacific cooperation (Panda 2019). An interesting new development in the Quad is the creation of a Quad Plus mechanism. In addition to the normal Quad participants, the Plus version added New Zealand, South Korea, and Vietnam with the purpose of sharing lessons learned on the coronavirus pandemic and coordinating responses (Grossman 2020). The bottom line is that Quad serves as a useful complement to the US Indo-Pacific strategy's focus on maintaining a rules-based order by coordinating with like-minded, i.e., democratic, major powers in the region.

To complicate China's expansive sovereignty claims in the East and South China Seas, the United States under the Trump administration has stepped up multinational exercises and conducted more FONOPs on average than was the case under Obama (Reuters 2019a; Ng 2019; DoD Annual Freedom of Navigation Report, Undated; Koh 2020). Indeed, in May 2020, the United States conducted two close-in FONOPs in the South China Sea over two consecutive days (Long 2020). Additionally, starting in March and ongoing the United States sent several naval vessels to challenge Chinese geological survey ship *Haiyang Dizhi 8* along with Chinese coast guard escorts' harassment of the Malaysian ship *West Capella*'s drilling operations in disputed waters. Australia participated in some of these activities as well, demonstrating not only cooperation between allies, but also instilling greater confidence in allies and partners in United States staying power throughout the Indo-Pacific (Mahadzir and Werner 2020).

On the economic front, the US Indo-Pacific strategy has struggled to get its footing, not least because of President Trump's trade wars with allies and partners. However, the strategy emphasizes the importance of the BUILD Act (Better Utilization of Investments Leading to Development Act) passed in 2018 to counter China's Belt & Road Initiative (BRI). Additionally, the Department of State's implementation update to the Indo-Pacific strategy highlighted a new initiative, called the "Blue Dot Network," seeks to offer consultative and evaluative services to recipient countries of Chinese infrastructure projects to determine whether they meet internationally accepted standards. Neither of these initiatives appear to have matured significantly since the publication of the Indo-Pacific strategy report, and Asian interlocutors often complain that the strategy is too focused on the security domain to the exclusion of economic interactions.

The Indo-Pacific strategy has also probably fallen short in the most important subregion for competition with China: Southeast Asia. Polling over the last three years has consistently shown that most Southeast Asians—who are believed to be the heart of the "Indo-Pacific"—have a dimming view of America's role in the region vis-à-vis China (Mun et al. 2020). This is due to China's rising economic and military power, while the United States focuses on its "America First" policy. A concrete example of America First in action was when the Trump administration decided in November 2019 to send National Security Adviser Robert O'Brien to the East Asia Summit and ASEAN Regional Forum. It had been customary for the United States to send the president, vice president, or at least a cabinet-level secretary to these important multilateral fora. By not doing so, the United States incurred a significant reputational cost (Voice of America 2019b). And unfortunately, Trump's attempt to fix the problem by hosting the ASEAN leaders for a summit in Las Vegas in March 2020 was postponed because of the pandemic (Behrmann

2020). Despite these missed opportunities for engagement, when examining American interactions with the Indo-Pacific more closely, it becomes evident that the Trump administration interacts with the region about the same as the Obama administration if viewed strictly from the perspective of numbers of visits (Langan-Marmur and Saunders 2020). Of course, Southeast Asian impressions of the United States are more important than this indicator of engagement.

The Trump administration's Indo-Pacific strategy has certainly faced many challenges. However, the strategy on the whole has proven thus far successful, probably because US allies and partners have nowhere better to turn in order to balance China's growing military and economic power. In this vein, it is useful to revisit the then-Secretary of Defense Bob Gates' statement in 2010 after *Wikileaks* had put intelligence sources at risk and exposed secret American critiques of friends (Department of Defense 2010). With concerns swirling over whether the United States could be relied upon to keep secrets in the future, Gates calmly observed:

> The fact is, governments deal with the United States because it's in their interest, not because they like us, not because they trust us, and not because they believe we can keep secrets. Many governments—some governments deal with us because they fear us, some because they respect us, most because they need us. We are still essentially, as has been said before, the indispensable nation.

Indo-Pacific countries similarly need Washington and are likely to look past US missteps so long as it supports their national security strategies. This is not to say that Washington has a never-ending blank check, because it almost certainly does not, but the United States is yet to reach the real tipping point in the Indo-Pacific strategy in which partners decide they can no longer ignore the inconsistencies raised here, and to compartmentalize the negative effects. That day may eventually arrive, however, if Washington demonstrates that it can no longer lead in the region due to displacement by China, its own shortcomings, or a combination of both.

How to Strengthen the US Indo-Pacific Strategy for the Future

Keeping the Indo-Pacific "free and open" to preserve the rules-based international order established after World War II in the face of a rising

China is consistent with decades of US policy. It also works well with US allies and partners who seek this same core objective. However, as the aforementioned analysis further suggests, implementation of the US Indo-Pacific strategy has been lacking due to seemingly conflicting approaches between President Trump and his strategists at the Department of Defense and Department of State. For the strategy to be more successful in the future, the White House will have to bridge that gap. But it must not go too far. In the new coronavirus environment, President Trump has taken an increasingly tough stance against China, even suggesting in May that he might "cut off the whole relationship" (Chiacu and Brunnstrom 2020). Such extreme actions in retaliation for Beijing's behavior in the early days of the coronavirus outbreak—and there are many others under consideration—would certainly be counterproductive, not only because the United States and China are inextricably intertwined economically and have nuclear weapons, but also because American allies and partners will feel increasingly uncomfortable getting caught up in great power competition. Generally, they do not want to publicly "choose" between the United States and China. Preservation of a rules-based order is important, but preserving peace and stability in the Indo-Pacific is even more important. Going forward, then, the US Indo-Pacific strategy should seek the proper calibration of competition with China on the one hand, while paying close attention to ally and partner preferences on the other hand. Washington will also have to demonstrate its staying power in the region by fully funding the Indo-Pacific strategy. Simply saying, as Acting Secretary of Defense Patrick Shanahan did in 2019, that "China, China, China" is the Pentagon's main objective without the requisite funding only undermines the strategy. INDOPACOM's recent request to Congress to better resource an Indo-Pacific Deterrence Initiative (IPDI) is a good start. INDOPACOM is seeking approximately $20 billion to deter China, in an effort that will mirror the European Deterrence Initiative (EDI) designed to deter Russia (Bowman and Hardie 2020; Mehta 2020).

In the absence of the TPP as the pillar of US economic engagement in the Indo-Pacific, the United States will likely have to forge bilateral free trade agreements with allies and partners or attempt to join the new CPTPP. Without a strong economic component to the Indo-Pacific strategy, particularly to counter China's BRI in the form of BUILD or Blue Dot Network, Asian governments are prone to criticize the United States for focusing too much on military solutions to the growing China threat. Indeed, FONOPs are not a strategy unto themselves (Cooper and Poling 2019). Washington, however, has engaged in some diversification of its role in the region. For example, the United States has played a role in the Lower Mekong Initiative to deal with the negative consequences of Chinese dam construction along the Mekong, such as erosion, drought, and higher saline content in the water. Another promising way of diversifying the US role is through the Quad. As discussed above, Quad Plus coordinated coronavirus relief efforts. China has been attempting to garner influence through its own efforts, making this a worthwhile competitive effort. Finally, constant US diplomatic engagement in key bilateral and multilateral fora is essential to building trust with allies and partners in the Indo-Pacific. Although the number of engagements during the Trump administration has been roughly the same as under President Obama, missed opportunities damage Washington's standing in the region. This was certainly the case with the lack of senior-level US attendance in November 2019 at the East Asia Summit and ASEAN Regional Summit. In the future, the United States will have to demonstrate that it is indeed prioritizing diplomacy in what it says is the priority theater. Showing up in Asia is more than half the battle.

Conclusion

As US–China competition continues to unfold, the durability and sustainability of Washington's Indo-Pacific strategy will continue to be tested. There are many challenges, such as the coronavirus pandemic, trade frictions, and sovereignty disputes, that will make it imperative for the Trump administration or the next administration to remain focused on the Indo-Pacific region. This analysis has demonstrated that in spite of several self-inflicted wounds, Washington generally offers an attractive vision for the region. Over the long-term, so long as the United States can avoid major missteps, its allies and partners are likely to be at least quietly supportive if not actively cooperative, as we saw with the Quad. If this trend persists, then it will become imperative for China to find ways of peacefully integrating into the rules-based international order or risk heightened conflict. When it comes to the South China Sea in particular, the United States thus far has done a fair job of corralling like-minded countries to ensure the region remains "free and open." Although Washington in concert with allies and partners has certainly not reversed Beijing's growing military advantages in the region, the United States nowadays appears to have more skin in the game. That said, Trump's tendency to undermine his own strategy through trade wars and questioning of alliances could eventually convince allies and partners to turn away from the United States and work on building their own bilateral and trilateral ties. This author contributed to a RAND volume in 2019 on precisely this topic (Harold et al. 2019), and the United States has actually encouraged the development of these intra-regional connections to complement relations with Washington. But if maritime counterclaimants seek to most effectively hedge against China's growing military power in the South China Sea, then it will be difficult for them to ignore the usefulness of cooperation with the United States, given the considerable diplomatic, economic, and security benefits Washington can provide allies and partners. This is an enduring advantage for the United States, even if the Indo-Pacific Strategy is not implemented well or is abandoned altogether in the future.

References

Abe, Shinzo 2007, "Confluence of the Two Seas," Speech at the Parliament of the Republic of India," Ministry of Foreign Affairs of Japan, August 22, https://www.mofa.go.jp/region/asia-paci/pmv0708/speech-2.html.

Abe, Shinzo 2012, "Asia's Democratic Security Diamond," *Project Syndicate*, December 27, 2012, https://www.project-syndicate.org/onpoint/a-strategic-alliance-for-japan-and-india-by-shinzo-abe?barrier=accesspaylog.

Abe, Shinzo 2016, "Address by Prime Minister Shinzo Abe at the Opening Session of the Sixth Tokyo International Conference on African Development (TICAD VI)," Ministry of Foreign Affairs of Japan, August 27, 2016, https://www.mofa.go.jp/afr/af2/page4e_000496.html.

Aso, Taro 2007, "On the 'Arc of Freedom and Prosperity,'" Ministry of Foreign Affairs of Japan, March 12, https://www.mofa.go.jp/policy/pillar/address0703.html.

Australian Department of Defence 2013, *Defence White Paper 2013*, Australian Government, https://www.defence.gov.au/whitepaper/2013/docs/WP_2013_web.pdf.

Australian Department of Defence 2016, *Defence White Paper 2016*, Australian Government, https://www.defence.gov.au/WhitePaper/Docs/2016-Defence-White-Paper.pdf.

Australian Department of Foreign Affairs and Trade 2019, "The Indo-Pacific: Australia's Perspective," Australian Government, April 29, https://www.dfat.gov.au/news/speeches/Pages/the-indo-pacific-australias-perspective.

Bagchi, Indrani 2020, "Raisina Dialogue: 'Indo-Pacific' a Global Common, Says Foreign Secy Vijay Gokhale," *Times of India*, January 17, https://timesofindia.indiatimes.com/india/raisina-dialogue-indo-pacific-a-global-common-says-foreign-secy-vijay-gokhale/articleshow/73337528.cms.

Barnes, Tom 2019, "'Various Remarks About Almost Everything:' Japan Says Trump Tweets Are Irrelevant to Actual U.S. Policy," *Independent*, July 4, https://www.independent.co.uk/news/world/americas/us-politics/trump-twitter-japan-us-foreign-policy-shinzo-abe-military-a8988211.html.

Behrmann, Savannah 2020, "U.S. Postpones ASEAN Summit with Southeast Asia Leaders Amid Coronavirus Fears," *USA Today*, February 28, https://www.usatoday.com/story/news/politics/2020/02/28/us-cancels-asean-summit-with-asia-leaders-amid-coronavirus-fears/4909766002/.

Bowman, Bradley and John Hardie 2020, "Aligning America's Ends and Means in the Indo-Pacific," *Defense News*, April 22,:https://www.defensenews.com/opinion/commentary/2020/04/22/aligning-americas-ends-and-means-in-the-indo-pacific/.

Carafano, James Jay 2019, "America's Next 5 Moves in the Indo-Pacific Region," Heritage Foundation, April 9, https://www.heritage.org/asia/commentary/americas-next-5-moves-the-indo-pacific-region.

Chan, Minnie and Catherine Wong 2019, "Singapore Prime Minister Urges China and US Not to Pressure Small Nations to Take Sides During Shangri La Dialogue," *South China Morning Post*, June 1, https://www.scmp.com/news/china/diplomacy/article/3012690/singapore-prime-minister-urges-china-and-us-not-pressure-small.

Chiacu, Doina and David Brunnstrom 2020, "Trump Says Doesn't Want to Talk to Xi, Could Even Cut China Ties," *Reuters*, May 14, https://www.reuters.com/article/us-health-coronavirus-usa-china/trump-says-he-doesnt-want-to-talk-to-xi-right-now-could-even-cut-china-ties-idUSKBN22Q2BD.

Chung, Lawrence 2018, "U.S., Taiwan Military Ties Closer Than Ever as Donald Trump Challenges Beijing," *South China Morning Post*, October 29, https://www.scmp.com/news/china/diplomacy/article/2170449/us-taiwan-military-ties-closer-ever-donald-trump-challenges.

Clinton, Hillary 2011, "America's Pacific Century," *Foreign Policy*, October 11, https://foreignpolicy.com/2011/10/11/americas-pacific-century/.

Cooper, Helene 2018, "Pentagon Again Suspends Large-Scale Military Exercises with South Korea," *New York Times*, March 1, https://www.nytimes.com/2019/03/01/world/asia/us-military-exercises-south-korea.html.

Cooper, Zack and Gregory Poling 2019, "America's Freedom of Navigation Operations Are Lost at Sea," *Foreign Policy*, January 8, https://foreignpolicy.com/2019/01/08/americas-freedom-of-navigation-operations-are-lost-at-sea/.

Department of Defense 2010, "DoD News Briefing with Secretary Gates and Adm. Mullen from the Pentagon," Office of the Assistant Secretary Public Affairs, November 30, 2010, https://fas.org/sgp/news/2010/11/dod113 010.html.

Department of Defense 2018, *Summary of the 2018 National Defense Strategy of the United States of America: Sharpening the American Military's Competitive Edge*, January, https://dod.defense.gov/Portals/1/Documents/pubs/2018-National-Defense-Strategy-Summary.pdf.

Department of Defense 2019, "Indo-Pacific Strategy Report: Preparedness, Partnerships, and Promoting a Networked Region," June 1, https://media.defense.gov/2019/Jul/01/2002152311/-1/-1/1/DEPARTMENT-OF-DEFENSE-INDO-PACIFIC-STRATEGY-REPORT-2019.PDF.

Department of Defense, "DoD Annual Freedom of Navigation (FON) Reports," https://policy.defense.gov/OUSDP-Offices/FON/.

Department of State 2019, *A Free and Open Indo-Pacific: Advancing a Shared Vision*, November 4, https://www.state.gov/wp-content/uploads/2019/11/Free-and-Open-Indo-Pacific-4Nov2019.pdf.

Dziedzic, Stephen and Catherine Graue 2019, "Donald Trump's Top Security Advisers Visit the Pacific, Signifying Growing U.S. Focus in the Region," *Australian Broadcasting Corporation News*, March 10, 2019, https://www.abc.net.au/news/2019-03-11/two-of-donald-trumps-top-security-advisers-visit-pacific/10887678.

Ellis-Petersen, Hannah 2020, "'Namaste Trump:' India Welcomes U.S. President at Modi Rally," *Guardian*, February 24, https://www.theguardian.com/world/2020/feb/24/namaste-donald-trump-india-welcomes-us-president-narendra-modi-rally.

Ford, Lindsey 2020, "The Trump Administration and the 'Free and Open Indo-Pacific,'" The Brooking Institution, May, https://www.brookings.edu/wp-content/uploads/2020/05/fp_20200505_free_open_indo_pacific.pdf.

Grossman, Derek 2019, "Quad Supports Goal to Preserve Rules-Based Order," *Australian Strategic Policy Institute*, February 9, https://www.aspistrategist.org.au/quad-supports-us-goal-to-preserve-rules-based-order/.

Grossman, Derek 2020, "Don't Get Excited, 'Quad Plus' Meetings Won't Cover China," *The Diplomat*, April 9, https://thediplomat.com/2020/04/dont-get-too-excited-quad-plus-meetings-wont-cover-china/.

Grossman, Derek and Michael Chase 2019, "Maintaining the U.S. Edge and in the Freely Associated States," *East Asia Forum*, September 2, https://www.eastasiaforum.org/2019/09/02/maintaining-the-us-edge-in-the-freely-associated-states/.

Harris Jr., Harry B. 2016, "Let's Be Ambitious Together," Raisina Dialogue Remarks, March 2, https://www.pacom.mil/Media/Speeches-Testimony/Article/683842/raisina-dialogue-remarks-lets-be-ambitious-together/.

Harold, Scott W., Derek Grossman, Brian Harding, Jeffrey W. Hornung, Gregory Poling, Jeffrey Smith, Meagan L. Smith, *The Thickening Web of Asian Security Cooperation: Deepening Defense Ties Among U.S. Allies and Partners in the Indo-Pacific*, RAND, Santa Monica: CA, 2019, RR-3125-MCF, https://www.rand.org/pubs/research_reports/RR3125.html.

Holland, Steve and David Brunnstrom 2020, "Trump Says He Does Not Mind If Philippines Cuts Military Pact with U.S.," *Reuters*, February 12, https://www.reuters.com/article/us-philippines-usa-defense-trump/trump-says-he-does-not-mind-if-philippines-cuts-military-pact-with-us-idUSKBN2062TL.

Hosoya, Yuichi, "FOIP 2.0: The Evolution of Japan's Free and Open Indo-Pacific Strategy," *Asia-Pacific Security Review*, Volume 26, Issue 1, pp. 18–28, https://www.tandfonline.com/doi/full/10.1080/13439006.2019.1622868?src=recsys.

Indian Ministry of External Affairs 2018, "India-Vietnam Joint Statement During State Visit of the President of Vietnam to India," Indian Government, March 3, https://www.mea.gov.in/bilateral-documents.htm?dtl/29535/IndiaVietnam+Joint+Statement+during+State+visit+of+President+of+Vietnam+to+India+March+03+2018.

Indian Ministry of External Affairs 2019, "External Affairs Minister's Remarks During Press Interaction with Secretary of State of the United States of America," Indian Government, June 26, https://mea.gov.in/Speeches-Statements.htm?dtl/31471/External_Affairs_Ministers_remarks_during_Press_Interaction_with_Secretary_of_State_of_the_United_States_of_America.

Iyengar, Rishi 2019, "India is Hitting the United States with More Tariffs," *CNN*, June 17, 2019, https://www.cnn.com/2019/06/15/economy/india-tariffs-us-trump/index.html.

Japanese Ministry of Foreign Affairs 2017, "Priority Policy for Development Cooperation, FY 2017," International Cooperation Bureau, April, https://www.mofa.go.jp/files/000259285.pdf.

Kadir, Rizal Abdul 2019, "'Mahathir Doctrine' Keeps South China Sea Peaceful," *New Straits Times*, May 5, https://www.nst.com.my/opinion/columnists/2019/05/485931/mahathir-doctrine-keeps-south-china-sea-peaceful.

Khurana, Gurpreet S. 2007, "Security of Sea Lines: Prospects for India-Japan Cooperation," Manohar Parrikar Institute for Defence Studies and Analysis, January, Volume 31, Issue 1, https://idsa.in/strategicanalysis/SecurityofSeaLinesProspectsforIndiaJapanCooperation_gskhurana_0107.

Khurana, Gurpreet S. 2017, "Trump's New Cold War Alliance in Asia is Dangerous," *Washington Post*, November 14, https://www.washingtonpost.com/news/theworldpost/wp/2017/11/14/trump-asia-trip/.

Koh, Collin, Twitter (@collinSLKoh), https://twitter.com/CollinSLKoh/status/1222347764278816769.

Langan-Marmur, Jonah and Phillip C. Saunders 2020, "Absent Without Leaving? Gauging U.S. Commitment to the Indo-Pacific," *The Diplomat*, May 6, https://thediplomat.com/2020/05/absent-without-leave-gauging-us-commitment-to-the-indo-pacific/.

Liptak, Kevin 2017, "Trump, Abe Friendship Remains On Par," *CNN*, November 4, https://www.cnn.com/2017/11/04/politics/president-donald-trump-shinzo-abe-golf-tokyo/index.html.

Long, Drake 2020, "Two FONOPS in Two Days: U.S. Navy Moves Through the South China Sea," *Radio Free Asia*, April 29, https://www.rfa.org/english/news/china/usa-southchinasea-04292020150319.html.

Mahadzir, Dzirhan and Ben Werner 2020, "U.S. Navy Maintains Operations in Western Pacific as Other Navies Slow Down," *USNI News*, May 11, https://news.usni.org/2020/05/11/u-s-navy-maintains-operations-in-western-pacific-as-other-navies-slow-down.

Medcalf, Rory 2007, "Australian Relations with India," Incoming Government Brief: West Asia, *The Interpreter*, Lowy Institute, December 21, https://archive.lowyinstitute.org/the-interpreter/australia-relations-india.

Medcalf, Rory 2013, "The Indo-Pacific: What's in a Name?," *The American Interest*, October 10, https://www.the-american-interest.com/2013/10/10/the-indo-pacific-whats-in-a-name/.

Mehta, Aaron 2020, "Inside the U.S. Indo-Pacific Command's $20 Billion Wish List to Deter China—and Why Congress May Approve It," *Defense News*, April 2, https://www.defensenews.com/global/asia-pacific/2020/04/02/inside-us-indo-pacific-commands-20-billion-wish-list-to-deter-china-and-why-congress-may-approve-it/.

Mun, Tang Siew, Hoang Thi Ha, Anuthida Saelaow Qian, Glenn Ong, and Pham Thi Phuong Thao 2020, "The State of Southeast Asia: 2020 Survey Report," ASEAN Studies Centre, ISEAS-Yusof Ishak Institute, https://www.iseas.edu.sg/images/pdf/TheStateofSEASurveyReport_2020.pdf.

Ng, Teddy 2019, "U.S. Steps Up Freedom of Navigation Patrols in South China Sea to Counter Beijing's Ambitions," *South China Morning Post*, February 16, https://www.scmp.com/news/china/diplomacy/article/2186461/us-steps-freedom-navigation-patrols-south-china-sea-counter.

Olson, Wyatt 2020, "USS Theodore Roosevelt Arrives in Vietnam, Becoming Second U.S. Carrier to Visit Since the 1970s," *Stars and Stripes*, March 4, https://www.stripes.com/news/pacific/uss-theodore-roosevelt-arrives-in-vietnam-becoming-second-us-carrier-to-visit-since-the-1970s-1.621313.

Panda, Ankit 2019, "U.S., India, Australia, Japan 'Quad' Holds Senior Officials Meeting in Bangkok," *The Diplomat*, November 5, https://thediplomat.com/2019/11/us-india-australia-japan-quad-holds-senior-officials-meeting-in-bangkok/.

Peri, Dinakar 2018, "LEMOA Fully Operational Now," *The Hindu*, September 8, https://www.thehindu.com/news/national/lemoa-already-fully-operational/article24904359.ece.

Pubby, Manu 2018, "India, U.S. Ink Comcasa Deal at 2 + 2 Dialogue," *The Economic Times*, September 7, https://economictimes.indiatimes.com/news/defence/comcasa-india-to-get-access-to-real-time-encrypted-information-from-us/articleshow/65710975.cms?from=mdr.

Ranada, Pia 2019, "Philippines Gets Timely Assurance from Oldest Ally," *Rappler*, 21 March, https://www.rappler.com/newsbreak/in-depth/224729-mike-pompeo-visit-philippines-gets-timely-assurance-from-oldest-ally.

Ratcliffe, Rebecca 2019, "Howdy Modi: Indian PM Appears with Trump at Texas Rally," *Guardian*, June 23, https://www.theguardian.com/world/2019/sep/23/modi-defends-removing-kashmirs-autonomy-at-trump-rally.

Republic of China (Taiwan) Ministry of Foreign Affairs 2018, "MOFA Minister Advances Taiwan's Front-Line Indo-Pacific Role," ROC Government, August 31, https://nspp.mofa.gov.tw/nsppe/news.php?post=140801&unit=370.

Reuters 2019a, "U.S., Japan, South Korea, Australia Hold First Naval Drills in Western Pacific," May 22, https://www.reuters.com/article/us-usa-japan-australia-southkorea/u-s-japan-south-korea-australia-hold-first-naval-drills-in-western-pacific-idUSKCN1ST0MA.

Reuters 2019b, Reuer, Linda and Daniel Leussink "Trump Renews Criticism of Japan-U.S. Alliance Before G-20 Summit," June 26, https://www.reuters.com/article/us-g20-summit-trump-japan/trump-renews-criticism-of-japan-us-alliance-before-g20-summit-idUSKCN1TS057.

Reuters 2020, Stewart, Phil and Idrees Ali, "Exclusive: Inside Trump's Standoff with South Korea Over Defense Costs," April 10, https://www.reuters.com/article/us-usa-southkorea-trump-defense-exclusiv/exclusive-inside-trumps-standoff-with-south-korea-over-defense-costs-idUSKCN21S1W7.

Samaan, Jean-Loup 2019, "Confronting the Flaws in America's Indo-Pacific Strategy," *War on the Rocks*, February 11, https://warontherocks.com/2019/02/confronting-the-flaws-in-americas-indo-pacific-strategy/.

Vicedo, Christian 2018, "The Philippines Stays Free and Open in its Position on the Indo-Pacific," *East Asia Forum*, August 2, 2018, https://www.eastasiaforum.org/2018/08/02/the-philippines-stays-free-and-open-in-its-position-on-the-indo-pacific/.

Voice of America 2019a, Xu, Ning, "U.S. Official Tells ASEAN Leaders to Choose Between U.S., and China," June 22, https://www.voanews.com/east-asia/us-official-tells-asean-leaders-choose-between-china-us.

Voice of America 2019b, "Most ASEAN Leaders No-Shows in Meeting with Trump's Proxy," *Associated Press* republished November 4, https://www.voanews.com/east-asia-pacific/most-asean-leaders-no-shows-meeting-trumps-proxy.

Weatherbee, Donald E 2019, "Indonesia, ASEAN, and the Indo-Pacific Cooperation Concept," Institute for Southeast Asian Studies (ISEAS), June 7, 2019, Issue 2019, Number 47, https://www.iseas.edu.sg/images/pdf/ISEAS_Perspective_2019_47.pdf.

White House 2017a, "President Donald J. Trump's Summit Meeting with Prime Minister Shinzo Abe of Japan," U.S. Government, Statements and Releases, November 6, 2017, https://www.whitehouse.gov/briefings-statements/president-donald-j-trumps-summit-meeting-prime-minister-shinzo-abe-japan/.

White House 2017b, "Remarks by President Trump at APEC CEO Summit, Da Nang, Vietnam," Remarks, U.S. Government, November 10, 2017, https://www.whitehouse.gov/briefings-statements/remarks-president-trump-apec-ceo-summit-da-nang-vietnam/.

White House 2017c, *National Security Strategy of the United States of America*, U.S. Government, December 2017, https://www.whitehouse.gov/wp-content/uploads/2017/12/NSS-Final-12-18-2017-0905.pdf.

White House 2019, "Remarks by President Trump and President Moon of the Republic of Korea in Joint Press Conference," U.S. Government, June 30, 2019, https://www.whitehouse.gov/briefings-statements/remarks-president-trump-president-moon-republic-korea-joint-press-conference/.

CHAPTER 13

India and the Indo-Pacific

Udai Bhanu Singh

INTRODUCTION

India's vision for the Indo-Pacific is that of a free, open, transparent, rules-based, peaceful, prosperous, and inclusive region, governed by international law, in particular, the United Nations Convention on the Law of the Sea (UNCLOS), including freedom of navigation and overflight. India views it as one interconnected, interdependent natural region that extends from the shores of Africa to the shores of America. India's interest in the emerging security and cooperative dynamics of the Indo-Pacific became evident with the upgrading of its Look East Policy to its Act East Policy in November 2014 which extended India's vision beyond ASEAN. By virtue of geographical location, the Indo-Pacific is the crossroads of the world's maritime traffic. Over half of the world's commercial shipping passes through these waterways. India views the seas and oceans as "critical enablers of our prosperity." The Indo-Pacific signifies the increasing human dependence on the maritime domain. The term has an implied reference in it to the Indian Ocean, not India alone but India with its central position in the region, its large economy, and a strong Navy. But

U. B. Singh (✉)
Manohar Parrikar Institute for Defence Studies and Analyses, New Delhi, India

© The Author(s), under exclusive license to Springer Nature Switzerland AG 2021
L. Buszynski and D. T. Hai (eds.), *Maritime Issues and Regional Order in the Indo-Pacific*, Palgrave Studies in Maritime Politics and Security, https://doi.org/10.1007/978-3-030-68038-1_13

this growing human interface with the maritime domain has created new strategic uncertainties including unresolved territorial disputes, contest for natural resources, the rise of terrorism, non-traditional threats like piracy, transnational crime, etc. The maritime challenge of the Indo-Pacific affects India directly, as the bulk of its trade is via maritime routes and thus requires freedom of navigation and the security of its sea lines of communication. India is committed to helping shape the regional security architecture and is working with like-minded countries to explore policy convergences and complementarities through its program for Security and Growth for All in the Region (SAGAR). China's military and economic rise accompanied by the rise of Chinese nationalism has also been a factor in shaping India's Outlook on the Indo-Pacific. India decided to resist President Xi's ambitious Belt and Road Initiative (BRI) that attracts attention in the Indo-Pacific landscape. India and China have long-standing differences over an unresolved border conflict, and differences over China–Pakistan nexus and sovereignty conflict over the China–Pakistan Economic Corridor (CPEC).

THE INDO-PACIFIC AS A MENTAL MAP

The notion of Indo-Pacific has gained increasing currency. In recognizing the Indian and Pacific Oceans as a single geostrategic and geo-economic space, India made a conscious choice to accept the Indo-Pacific as a natural region that informs its priorities and influences its decisions. Far from being an externally imposed idea, it is part of India's independent foreign policy and one shaped by its geography. It signifies a major shift in the global power axis from the west (Atlantic Ocean) to the east (Indian Ocean). Major political upheavals and the emergence of new power centers and economic dynamos in the region have led to the emergence of the new concept of the Indo-Pacific. It does not replace the earlier term "Asia-Pacific," or the term "Indo-Pacific Asia," but subsumes it (Mahapatra 2019). The Indo-Pacific is inhabited by half the world's population, is marked by large and modernizing militaries, with the top three global economies alongside emerging ones, half a dozen nuclear powers, and its waters carry 60% of global maritime trade, including critical energy supplies. The Indo-Pacific is a product of the increasing connectedness of the Indian Ocean and the Pacific Ocean. Some fundamental differences remain in terms of geopolitics, security, economic, and social development which distinguish the Indian Ocean Region from the Western Pacific. The geographical scope of the Indo-Pacific region has often varied from country to country (Singh 2019). From India's perspective it encompasses a vast area which extends from the east coast of Africa to the west coast of the United States. On the other hand, the area of operation of the US Indo-Pacific Command extends from the west coast of India (Indian Ocean) to the west coast of the United States (Pacific Ocean) (Haruko 2020). While there are clear opportunities to be harnessed from this emerging strategic space, there are equally a number of potential security hazards lurking as seen in the conflicts simmering in the South China Sea and the East China Sea.

India has great stakes in the long-term stability in the Indo-Pacific and has come to accept the idea of the Indo-Pacific after considerable debate and some early hesitation. Even as conflicts and disputes have intensified and economic interdependence increased, the de-hyphenated term "the Indo-Pacific" still lacked clarity. There was an apprehension that India would be drawn into the United States' strategic calculations. Prior to a change of government in 2014, India was debating whether it should continue with a policy of issue-based alignment, bandwagon with China, align with the United States, or aim for a strategically autonomous policy. There was a fear of Sino-US tensions complicating matters for India. Second, constrained by limited resources (and a restricted defense budget), there were concerns that it should not spread itself thin over a large area. Third, India needed to assess if it was internally prepared for external engagements which would have economic implications for regional value chains. So Indian think tanks like the Indian Council of World Affairs (ICWA) engaged academia on the subject, and academic journals carried the debate[1] (Yadav 2014). A freshly renamed Centre for Indo-Pacific Studies (CIPS) emerged in New Delhi's Jawaharlal Nehru University in 2013.[2] India's Ministry of External Affairs created a new Indo-Pacific division covering the Indian Ocean, ASEAN, East Asia, and the South Pacific (Jaishankar 2019). The United States had prodded New Delhi to play a leading role in the region, projecting India as the "net

---

[1] ICWA organized a seminar on "Indo-Pacific Region: Political and Strategic Prospects" in March 2013.

[2] The JNU website reads: "The Centre for Indo-Pacific Studies (CIPS) is a new Centre created in 2013 keeping in view the profound shifts that are taking place around India and India's rapidly rising stakes in the Indian Ocean and East Asia. Equally, it is also a reflection of today's geopolitical realities."

security provider" in the Indo-Pacific.[3] But when Prime Minister Modi and President Obama in January 2015 issued the Joint Strategic Vision for the Asia-Pacific and Indian Ocean Region, the term "Asia-Pacific" was retained instead of the "Indo-Pacific" which could be attributed possibly to a residual resistance to embracing the new terminology (Singh 2016a). However, as it turned out, the emerging view was that India's economic, diplomatic, security interests are tied up in the Indo-Pacific. According to this view, the earlier term "Asia-Pacific" did not serve India's interest as the term excluded India as did the Asia-Pacific Economic Cooperation (APEC) forum which did not consider it necessary to admit India as a member. China (and even Russia) harbor suspicions about the notion of the Indo-Pacific viewing it as a geostrategic move by its adversaries against it, even though (at least from India's perspective) the "Indo-Pacific" is not an exclusive club which shuts the door on others.

Maritime Connectivity and Security

With a coastline of 7,500 kilometers, more than 1,380 islands, and more than two million square kilometers of Exclusive Economic Zone, India occupies a pivotal position in the Indo-Pacific. The Indian and Pacific oceans together represent a maritime space of significant consequence for trade and commerce as the bulk of India's trade flows via maritime routes. Freedom of navigation and the security of sea lines of communication assume significance as any adventurism would disrupt the process of economic growth and development not only for India but for the broader region. India has undertaken connectivity projects both on its eastern and western flanks. Prime Minister Modi introduced the concept of SAGAR (Security and Growth for All in the Region) in Mauritius in 2015 (De 2020). Maritime cooperation is an important part of India's security and economic policy to ensure a rules-based order in the Indo-Pacific. In the east, the two main projects are the Trilateral Highway (India–Myanmar–Thailand) and the Kaladan Multimodal Transit Transport Project (KMTTP) connecting Mizoram with Sittwe port in Myanmar. In West Asia, there is the Duqm port in Oman and the Chabahar port in Iran, and in Africa, there is the Beira port in Mozambique.

---

[3] It is quite another matter that at present, India would opt for being a "preferred strategic partner" rather than a "net security provider."

Even though India is not a party to any of the disputes in the South China Sea, it has a significant stake in the stability of the area. India has undertaken to adhere to the rights and obligations mentioned in the UN Charter, and abides by the UNCLOS and the ASEAN's 1976 Treaty of Amity and Cooperation in Southeast Asia (TAC). The 12 July 2016 Arbitral Award on the South China Sea held out the prospect of a positive transformation of the regional security environment. As Leszek Buszynski points out, the ruling removed hurdles in the way of establishing a South China Sea maritime regime: "The Tribunal decided that China's claim had no legal basis…Second, it declared that there are no islands that can generate maritime zones within the meaning of Article 121 of the UNCLOS which removed the problem of overlapping claims to EEZs" (Buszynski 2019). From India's perspective, a verdict that re-establishes trust in international law and norms on maritime issues was the best outcome that India could hope for. India's Minister of State for External Affairs, V.K. Singh reiterated India's well-known position that it supports the ruling by the Tribunal (constituted under Annex VII to the UNCLOS) in the arbitration instituted by Philippines against China. He said:

> India supports freedom of navigation and over flight, and unimpeded commerce, based on the principles of international law, as reflected notably in the UNCLOS. India believes that States should resolve disputes through peaceful means without threat or use of force and exercise self-restraint in the conduct of activities that could complicate or escalate disputes affecting peace and stability. As a State Party to the UNCLOS, India urges all parties to show utmost respect for the UNCLOS, which establishes the international legal order of the seas and oceans. (Rajya Sabha 2017)

India leads by example: To resolve a maritime dispute between India and Bangladesh, in July 2014 the Permanent Court of Arbitration (PCA) awarded Bangladesh 19,467 square kilometers of sea area in the Bay of Bengal, and New Delhi readily accepted the decision even though the verdict went against it. India was a founding member of the Indian Ocean Rim Association (IORA). It also founded the Indian Ocean Naval Symposium (IONS) in 2009, with 35 members providing a forum to discuss issues that have a bearing on maritime security in the Indian Ocean region. India has been admitted to the Indian Ocean Commission (IOC) as an Observer in March 2020. This is important given

India's plans to expand in the Western Indian Ocean (WIO) (Mohan 2020). The Indian Navy has stepped up its activities in regional waters to address challenges in the maritime domain. It released its maritime security strategy "Ensuring Secure Seas: Indian Maritime Security Strategy" at the Naval Commanders' Conference in October 2015, which replaced and updated the 2007 strategy. Moreover, the Indian Navy adopted a proactive approach to maritime security when it organized the 2016 International Fleet Review (its second ever) and the Milan ("confluence") exercises in the Bay of Bengal (held since 1995). The multilateral exercise Milan 2020 was scheduled for 18–20 March 2020 at Visakhapatnam but it had to be postponed due to COVID-19 restrictions. The Navies of nearly 30 countries (including Australia, South Korea, Singapore, Malaysia, and Indonesia) were expected to participate—though not China. The last Milan exercises were held in March 2018. India also conducts the (bilateral) Malabar naval exercise with the United States which Japan has joined on a regular basis since 2015. India also conducts bilateral naval exercise AUSINDEX with Australia. India has proactively sought to promote maritime security through ASEAN-led regional forums. At the 14th East Asia Summit (EAS), in November 2019 in Bangkok, India mooted the idea of the "Indo-Pacific Oceans Initiative" which calls for establishing a free, open, and cooperative platform to respond to a range of maritime challenges such as maritime security; managing the maritime environment; disaster risk mitigation; sustainable use of marine resources, and illegal, unreported, and unregulated (IUU) fishing; capacity building; and maritime trade and transport (India, Ministry of External Affairs 2019a). It was followed by the Fourth EAS Conference on Maritime Security Cooperation in Chennai, India, on 6–7 February 2020.

Modi's Understanding of the Indo-Pacific

Prime Minister Modi spelt out India's perspective of the Indo-Pacific in his Keynote Address at the Shangri-La Dialogue in June 2018. He advocated inclusivity and spoke of the Indo-Pacific region in which "Southeast Asia is at its centre, and ASEAN has been and will be central to its future. That is the vision that will always guide India, as we seek to cooperate for an architecture for peace and security in this region." He added that

The Indo-Pacific is a natural region. It is also home to a vast array of global opportunities and challenges. I am increasingly convinced with each passing day that the destinies of those of us who live in the region are linked. Today, we are being called to rise above divisions and competition to work together. Inclusiveness, openness and ASEAN centrality and unity, therefore, lie at the heart of the new Indo-Pacific. India does not see the Indo-Pacific Region as a strategy or as a club of limited members. Nor as a grouping that seeks to dominate. And by no means do we consider it as directed against any country. A geographical definition, as such, cannot be. India's vision for the Indo-Pacific Region is, therefore, a positive one. And, it has many elements… It stands for a free, open, inclusive region, which embraces us all in a common pursuit of progress and prosperity. It includes all nations in this geography as also others beyond who have a stake in it… We should all have equal access as a right under international law to the use of common spaces on sea and in the air that would require freedom of navigation, unimpeded commerce and peaceful settlement of disputes in accordance with international law. (India, Ministry of External Affairs 2018a)

PARTNERS IN INDIA'S INDO-PACIFIC POLICY

India's Indo-Pacific policy is a work in progress and has several elements. As India's External Affairs Minister indicated, the Indo-Pacific, "is a reality, it is a naval reality, it is a political reality, a trade reality, an economic reality. Why is it a reality? Because Indo-Pacific means we cannot deal with the Indian Ocean and the Pacific Ocean as two separate arenas and silo them" (India, Ministry of External Affairs 2020a). The Act East Policy (AEP) unveiled in 2014 (an upgraded version of the Look East Policy that originated in the early 1990s) expanded New Delhi's vision to include the region denoted by the emerging concept of the Indo-Pacific. The AEP includes within its ambit a wider geographical expanse, extending up to the Pacific island countries. While prioritizing its "Neighbourhood First" policy and the Act East Policy, New Delhi now seeks to reach out to the larger Indo-Pacific to achieve its larger strategic objectives. India reposes faith in the centrality of ASEAN, and this was best illustrated by the ASEAN–India Commemorative Summit, held in New Delhi on January 25, 2018 themed "Shared Values, Common

Destiny"; it was attended by the ten ASEAN Heads of State or Government.[4] It issued the Delhi Declaration (January 2018) which reaffirmed ASEAN centrality and the ASEAN–India "commitment to work closely together on common regional and international security issues of mutual concern and ensure an open, transparent, inclusive, and rules-based architecture through existing ASEAN-led frameworks and mechanisms such as the Post Ministerial Conference + 1 (PMC + 1) with India, ASEAN Regional Forum (ARF), East Asia Summit (EAS), the ASEAN Defence Ministers' Meeting Plus (ADMM-Plus), and ASEAN Senior Officials' Meeting on Transnational Crimes (SOMTC) + India Consultations." The East Asia Summit (EAS) as a leaders-led forum providing a region-wide platform for negotiating and articulating policy decisions has emerged as an important feature in the regional security architecture.[5] The ADMM-Plus, comprising the same set of members, not only discusses security issues but also takes practical steps to promote military cooperation and engages in confidence-building activities. It is attended by the defense ministers (or their representatives) of the member countries and the ASEAN secretary general (Singh 2016b).

As pointed out by Amitav Acharya, ASEAN is increasingly challenged by China's approach to regionalism wherein "China has shifted from the pursuit of an ASEAN-centric regionalism in the 1990s … to one with multiple and parallel tracks." China's One Belt, One Road (OBOR) is "essentially a system of bilateral cooperation" which is a hugely ambitious, "economic version of the US hub-and-spoke alliance system" (Acharya 2017). In as much as some ASEAN member countries have joined the Beijing-led Belt and Road Initiative (BRI), ASEAN centrality has been weakened. When China created the Asian Infrastructure Investment Bank (AIIB) all the ASEAN Members joined. The Master Plan on ASEAN Connectivity 2025 requires an annual investment of $110 billion for infrastructure development and that perhaps explains the importance of AIIB. After Sri Lanka's experience with Hambantota port, ASEAN states

---

[4] The Commemorative Summit issued the 36 paragraph Delhi Declaration. It captures India's commitment to work closely with ASEAN to uphold respect for international law, primacy of United Nations Convention on the Laws of the Seas (UNCLOS), freedom of navigation and overflights in the region, peaceful resolution of disputes, and an early conclusion of the Code of Conduct (CoC) in the South China Sea.

[5] EAS members include the ten ASEAN countries and their eight dialogue partners (Australia, China, India, Japan, New Zealand, Russia, South Korea, and the United States).

are showing cautious optimism towards the BRI.[6] Sri Lankan President Gotabhaya Rajapaksa expressed some concerns against the previous government's Hambantota port lease agreement with China. Sri Lanka leased the port to a Chinese company for 99 years in exchange for $1.2 billion that the government needed to cover balance of payment (BOP) problems (Moramudali 2020). Tomotaka Shoji notes that China's Infrastructure aid is not without encumbrances for ASEAN. "The question of how to balance security issues, most notably South China Sea disputes, and economic cooperation has been a challenge for ASEAN for many years" (Shoji 2018). The states of the region have some unresolved territorial disputes besides those in the South China Sea which makes the situation increasingly volatile. There is a growing recognition that these disputes need to be managed through some mechanism even if more substantive policy commitments are not feasible.

India announced its full support for the ASEAN Outlook on the Indo-Pacific (AOIP) which was adopted by ASEAN at the 34th ASEAN Summit in Bangkok in June 2019. Indonesia had first initiated the process of drafting the document in August 2018 at the 51st ASEAN Foreign Ministers Meeting. At the outset, the document pointed out that it was not intended to create new mechanisms or to replace existing ones, but to strengthen ASEAN's community building process and ASEAN-led mechanisms to better face challenges like conflict in the South China Sea. The enunciation of the "Act East Policy" also meant that India now has a dedicated mission to ASEAN (in Jakarta) and the ASEAN-India Centre (in New Delhi). The India–ASEAN relationship is however confronted with many challenges. ASEAN-led forums like ADMM+ are yet to reach their full potential, and much the same can be said of the Bay of Bengal Initiative for Multi-Sectoral Technical and Economic Cooperation (BIMSTEC) which brings together seven South Asian and Southeast Asian countries together, and the Mekong-Ganga Cooperation (MGC) forum which culturally and economically binds two river-based civilizations of India and mainland Southeast Asia. The ASEAN–India

---

[6] In a survey conducted among respondents from ASEAN countries (except Singapore) with BRI projects or negotiating them, when asked what were the lessons from past BRI projects like Hambantota port in Sri Lanka and East Coast Rail Link (ECRL) in Malaysia, an overwhelming majority (70%) opined their government should negotiate cautiously to avoid getting into debt with China. See Tang Siew Mun et al. (2019) State of Southeast Asia: 2019 Survey Report, ASEAN Studies Centre at ISEAS-Yusof Ishak Institute, Singapore.

Free Trade Agreement (AIFTA) intends to raise current trade to $200 billion by 2022. In keeping with its strategic priorities, which are not limited to ASEAN, Africa, Australia, New Zealand, and the Pacific islands, India's External Affairs Minister S. Jaishankar asserted that India's Indo-Pacific approach will also include the Gulf, the Arabian Sea states, and India's African partners. He said: "India's approach to this concept led us to recognize that both geographical extremities of the Indo-Pacific and everything in between should ideally have their own indigenously evolved approach to the Indo-Pacific" (India, Ministry of External Affairs 2019a). Engagement with the immediate and extended neighborhood (preceding COVID-19) was marked by high-level visits to countries both to its east and west.[7] This facilitated a better understanding and coordinated approach during the pandemic itself. India's area of interest covers a large expanse of land and water which no country can handle single-handedly, and it needs the support of other stakeholders who have strategic and economic interests in the region.

Vietnam

Vietnam is a key pillar of India's Act East Policy as it is strategically placed and is in close proximity to important trade routes transiting the South China Sea. The burgeoning India–Vietnam strategic partnership is an expression of their shared apprehension of an aggressive China (Pant 2018). Chinese assertiveness in the South China Sea against Vietnam has necessitated the development of a strong reliable navy. Regular Joint exercises with the Indian Navy and visits by friendly navies then become an expression of a close relationship. India and Vietnam upgraded their relations to the level of a Comprehensive Strategic Partnership in 2016 which entails a commitment to policy coordination at bilateral and multilateral levels. It implies a coordinated approach through the many forums of institutionalized interaction under the auspices of the Ministry of External affairs or under the Ministry of Defence like the Annual Security Dialogue at Defence Secretary Level. It also entails a practical commitment in terms of the supply of necessary military hardware and training, and increasing the number of all-level delegation exchanges, especially among young military officials, as well as promoting deputy

---

[7] For instance in the east to Myanmar, Vietnam, Singapore, Japan, Australia, and Fiji.

ministerial-level defense policy dialogue, and enhancing collaboration in training. Vietnam's "Omnidirectional diplomacy" and India's quest for "strategic autonomy" has resulted in stronger bonding as the two countries seek out strategic partnerships with the United States and other Indo-Pacific countries (including Japan and Australia). Defense cooperation between the two countries serves as one of the most important factors for maintaining regional and international peace and stability. The challenges facing Indian, Vietnamese, and Japanese policy makers are similar, although not identical, and make a triangular partnership both possible and desirable. The year 2020 was the 25th year of Vietnam's admittance into ASEAN, when it also assumed the Chairmanship of ASEAN. An opportunity exists for India and Vietnam to work together in the United Nations, given that Vietnam will be a non-permanent member of the UN Security Council over 2020–2021 and India over 2021–2022. While Vietnam faces an aggressive China in the South China Sea, India does so on land across a long unsettled border. Besides, Vietnam has the experience of having successfully fought a war with China on land. Vietnam's priorities will have implications for the larger Indo-Pacific region (and ASEAN) as seen in its 2019 Defence White Paper, that was released on 25 November 2019. The White Paper introduces the 4 "Nos.": no military alliances, no alignment with a second country against a third, and no foreign military base on its territory, and no threat or use of force. In decoding the nuanced White Paper there are some "Yeses" which leave opportunities for cooperation with partners. It includes "security and defense mechanisms in the Indo-Pacific region." This is one rare occasion when the term "Indo-Pacific" has been used by the Vietnamese. As Derek Grossman and Christopher Sharman point out, the only other time the word "Indo-Pacific" was mentioned by a Vietnamese leader was "during former President Tran Dai Quang's March 2018 visit to India" (Grossman and Sharman 2019).

Indonesia

Owing to their respective geostrategic locations, India and Indonesia share common concerns in the Indo-Pacific region, which have only been buttressed by over 70 years of diplomatic relations. During Prime Minister Narendra Modi's visit to Indonesia (29–30 May 2018), the bilateral relationship was upgraded from a strategic partnership (2005), to a New Comprehensive Strategic Partnership. India and Indonesia issued the "Shared Vision of India–Indonesia Maritime Cooperation in the Indo-Pacific" in which the two sides agreed to take "necessary steps to enhance connectivity (institutional, physical, digital, and people to people) between Andaman and Nicobar Islands of India and Provinces in the Sumatera Islands of Indonesia to promote trade, tourism, and people-to-people contacts; facilitate B to B linkages between the Chamber of Commerce of Andaman and the ones of the Provinces in Sumatera, including Aceh" (India, Ministry of External Affairs 2018b). More importantly, India and Indonesia agreed on a joint plan of action to develop and manage Sabang Port, located close to the Malacca Strait. There is immense potential for creating synergies between India's Act East Policy, Prime Minister Modi's vision of "SAGAR" (Security and Growth for All in the Region), and President Joko Widodo's (Jokowi) Global Maritime Fulcrum Policy. The Indonesian President declared the Global Maritime Fulcrum (GMF) or what has been termed Jokowi's "maritime axis doctrine" at the Ninth East Asia Summit in Naypyidaw, Myanmar, on 13 November 2014 in which he presented the five pillars of the concept. Despite the fact that there are many commonalities in the maritime concerns of the two countries, Indonesia's approach differs from India's in that it has welcomed BRI projects.

Indonesia's geographical location means that it is "gatekeeper of the two oceans" and commands the major sea-lanes such as the Straits of Malacca, the Sunda Strait, the Lombok Strait, and the Ombai-We-tar Strait off Timor Island. It may be recalled that when President Jokowi visited India in 2016, Maritime cooperation was an important focus of the discussions as a separate Joint Statement on Maritime cooperation was issued on 12 December 2016 in which it was mentioned that the two had similar perceptions of the regional and global maritime environment. The two countries have been Chairs of the Indian Ocean Rim Association (IORA) and played active roles in building a peaceful, stable, and prosperous Indian Ocean region. The GMF idea was a good one if Indonesia could implement it but according to Evan Laksmana, it lost force during Jokowi's second term in office. Indonesia's attention was overtaken by domestic issues and it spent diplomatic effort in getting ASEAN to pass what has been termed a largely "flawed" Outlook on the Indo-Pacific (Saha et al. 2020). Indonesia's Foreign Minister Retno Marsudi, at the Delhi Dialogue XI in December 2019, said that the promotion of maritime cooperation between ASEAN and India was a necessity and not an option.

The Strategic Component of India's Indo-Pacific

The Quadrilateral Security Dialogue (the Quad) involving India with the United States, Japan, and Australia re-emerged after a long hiatus as Quad 2.0 in November 2017.[8] The Quad was upgraded to the Ministerial level when the foreign ministers of India (S. Jaishankar), Japan (Toshimitsu Motegi), Australia (Marise Payne), and the United States (Mike Pompeo) met on the sidelines of the UN General Assembly in September 2019 (The Wire 2019). The Quad is evolving in response to the changed geopolitics in the Indo-Pacific, notably the rise of China and its aggressive moves as manifested in its ambitious Belt and Road Initiative. China's assertiveness was evident in its actions in the South China Sea, East China Sea, the Doklam stand-off (2017), the recent Galwan valley (2020) stand-off with India, in addition to the Sino-US trade war. India has engaged with the other quad member countries through official level consultations since 2017 on regional and global issues of common interest and focused on cooperation in areas such as connectivity, sustainable development, counter-terrorism, non-proliferation, and maritime and cyber security, with a view to promoting peace, stability, and prosperity in an increasingly interconnected Indo-Pacific region (Rajya Sabha 2019).

President Trump paid a state visit to India on 24–25 February 2020 just before the COVID-19 pandemic struck. According to the June 2019 Indo-Pacific Strategy Report (IPSR), issued by the US Department of Defence:

> The United States and India share a common outlook on the Indo-Pacific. Both countries recognize the importance of the Indo-Pacific to global trade and commerce and acknowledge that developments in this region will shape the larger trajectory of the rules-based order. India, through its "Act East" policy, continues to make significant security, economic and development investments to secure the vision of a free and open Indo-Pacific region.....The United States and India maintain a broad-based strategic

---

[8] The Quad was formed in December 2004 in the aftermath of the earthquake and tsunami when the navies of four nations—the United States, Australia, Japan, and India—joined in the humanitarian assistance and disaster relief operation. This was followed by naval exercises, organized by the four countries plus Singapore in the Bay of Bengal, but because of Chinese diplomatic protests, Prime Minister Kevin Rudd pulled Australia out of the exercise and the Quad became inactive over the next ten years; it was revived when the leaders of the four democracies met on the sidelines of the ASEAN–India meeting in Manila in 2017.

partnership, underpinned by shared interests, democratic values, and strong people-to-people ties. (U.S. Department of Defence 2019)

India became a "Major Defence Partner" of the United States in June 2016. The two countries were brought closer with the signing of the Logistics Exchange Memorandum of Agreement (LEMOA), 2016, by the then Indian Defence Minister Manohar Parrikar and US Defence Secretary Ashton Carter, which gave the militaries of both countries access to each other's facilities for supplies and repairs (George 2016). The Communications Compatibility and Security Agreement (COMCASA) signed at the inaugural US–India 2 + 2 Ministerial Dialogue in September 2018 took this partnership a notch further (Business Standard 2018). This reaffirmed the sentiment expressed earlier in the December 2017 National Security Strategy issued by the White House which said: "We welcome India's emergence as a leading global power and stronger strategic and defense partner. We will seek to increase quadrilateral cooperation with Japan, Australia and India." Although the Trump Administration walked away from the Trans-Pacific Partnership, it readily supported the Free and Open Indo-Pacific policy of Japan's Prime Minister Abe.

The close understanding between Prime Minister Modi and Shinzo Abe has helped India and Japan align their policy towards the Indo-Pacific. Shinzo Abe's "Confluence of the Two Seas" lecture in the Indian Parliament in August 2007 presaged Japan's Free and Open Pacific (FOIP) of 2016 (Horimoto 2020). The momentum in relations with Japan has continued and has been facilitated by the Asia Africa Growth Corridor (AAGC) of 2017. Abe's visit to India was postponed (as well as the Tokyo 2020 Olympics) because of the COVID-19 pandemic. Indian Prime Minister Modi and his Australian counterpart Scott Morrison met in the first-ever bilateral virtual summit on 4 June 2020 (Chinoy 2020) when they concluded a landmark Mutual Logistics Support Agreement (MLSA) which allows the militaries of the two sides to use each other's bases for repair and replenishment of supplies besides increasing defense cooperation.[9] Other agreements covered cyber and cyber-enabled critical technology, mining and strategic minerals, defense science and technology, vocational education, public administration and governance

---

[9] India and Japan are also finalizing negotiations of an Acquisition and Cross-Servicing Agreement (ACSA) the process began in October 2018.

reforms, and water resources management. Terrorism and maritime issues in the Indo-Pacific were also discussed during the summit, and a Joint Statement on a Comprehensive Strategic Partnership and a Joint Declaration on a Shared Vision for Maritime Cooperation in the Indo-Pacific were announced (India, Ministry of External Affairs 2020b). Australia has systematically discussed the Indo-Pacific in its defense white papers over the years. Although Australia is part of the US alliance system, it is conscious of the decline of US power and has close economic ties with China. However, in April 2020, an Australian frigate HMAS Parramatta joined three US warships (USS America, USS Bunker Hill, and USS Barry) in the South China Sea near an area where a Chinese vessel was suspected to be exploring for oil in the waters claimed by Malaysia (which was in the part of Malaysia's claimed EEZ).

As exploratory moves to expand the Quad mechanism are made, a nascent "Quad Plus" has already begun to emerge. Although the contours of this arrangement are yet very fluid, it might suit India which is finding the aggressive posturing by China in the region irksome (Saha 2018; Lohman et al. 2015). A teleconferencing meeting to discuss ways to counter COVID-19, initiated by the United States, and in which India's Foreign Secretary Harsh Vardhan Shringla participated, was held on 20 March 2020 (India, Ministry of External Affairs 2020b). Other participants in the so-called "quad-plus" meeting included senior officials from the United States, Australia, and Japan who were joined by their counterparts from three countries—the Republic of Korea, Vietnam, and New Zealand. They agreed to continue meeting on a weekly basis to discuss matters such as vaccine development, stranded citizens, mitigating the impact on the global economy, etc.

THE ECONOMIC COMPONENT OF INDIA'S INDO-PACIFIC

India has to leverage the Indo-Pacific environment to promote its economic growth. India's industrialization was achieved without collaboration with other countries, and facilitated by diplomacy. In the 1990s economic reform and the Look East policy advanced on parallel tracks, but the pace in India–ASEAN economic ties was not kept up. India joined the Regional Comprehensive Economic Partnership (RCEP) negotiations in 2012 but announced its decision to withdraw in November 2019. India's trade deficit had been rising vis-à-vis the RCEP countries, not as an outcome of competitive advantage but because of non-tariff barriers erected against India and denial of market access. The large influx of goods from China had resulted in a mounting deficit, and growing opposition from business and agricultural interests. The possibility of India rejoining the RCEP would hinge on whether Indian concerns get adequately addressed. India's withdrawal was viewed by Japan as a setback to its own Indo-Pacific policy which had not yet recovered from the US decision to opt out of the TPP. "Without India, Japan's influence in the RCEP would be significantly reduced." But, according to S Jaishankar, this should not be construed as a retreat from India's Act East policy which is rooted in history "and spans so many domains that this one decision does not really undermine the basics. Even in trade, India already has FTAs with 12 out of the 15 RCEP partners. Nor is there really a connection with our Indo-Pacific approach, as that goes well beyond the RCEP membership" (India, Ministry of External Affairs 2019b). As a maritime nation, occupying a central position in the Indian Ocean, India seeks to encourage a blue (or ocean) economy with the twin objectives of growth and sustainability and one aligned with India's sustainable development goal-14 (SDG-14). This includes fisheries and aquaculture, renewable ocean energy, seaports and shipping, offshore hydrocarbons and seabed minerals, marine biotechnology, research and development, and tourism. India's SAGAR policy, combined with its plans for infrastructure connectivity through Southeast Asia and Southwest Asia, and port development under the Sagarmala project provide momentum to its Indo-Pacific policy.

CONCLUSION—THE WAY FORWARD

The twin crises of COVID-19 and the Galwan valley clash in Ladakh (June 2020) provide both an opportunity and a challenge to India to reframe its Indo-Pacific policy, and perhaps to reset its China policy. China's assertive action on India's borders which led to 20 Indian soldiers being martyred, breached 45 years of a relatively peaceful border. It is expected that India's relations with China at the bilateral level will likely be transformed.[10] Given the turbulent border, New Delhi is

---

[10] Diplomatically, India could revisit its one China policy and leverage Chinese sensitivities on Tibet, Xinjiang, Hong Kong, and Taiwan. Economically, India could initiate the process of economic decoupling with China (although that would entail a willingness to bear pain).

likely to consider China an unreliable partner in any multilateral initiative in the foreseeable future. Besides joining the Asian Infrastructure Investment Bank (AIIB), India has engaged China in multilateral institutions/forums like the Shanghai Cooperation Organization (SCO); Brazil, Russia, India, China, and South Africa (BRICS); and Bangladesh, China, India, Myanmar (BCIM). India's aim was to cooperate with Beijing on a case-by-case basis, with the aim of reforming Bretton Woods institutions and to secure better representation therein. Nevertheless, at a time when the policy of engagement with China has run aground, it might be difficult to envisage continuing business as usual with Beijing. In public perception the Chinese assertive behavior in Galwan is a betrayal. While the Chinese Navy has undergone massive modernization, its naval vessels (both ships and submarines) have been making regular forays into the Indian Ocean. India has been upgrading its coastal and SLOC security in response and a chain of static radar sensors has been positioned on the coastline and an Information Management and Analysis Centre (IMAC) set up (Rai 2014). In addition, India's navy assists some Indian Ocean states (Seychelles and Mauritius) in EEZ surveillance.

Given the long Sino-Indian border and the immense power differential, New Delhi may choose not to take on China on its own. The Indian Navy has an edge over the Chinese navy in the Indian Ocean but the military option is less likely to be exercised given the economic downturn and India's development imperative. Instead, it is more likely that India would seek to balance China by joining forces with like-minded countries. Already countries with common concerns about China are beginning to come together globally and regionally. India is already engaged in a 2 + 2 dialogue (either at ministerial or official level) with the United States, Japan, and Australia. It is similarly engaged in a trilateral format (India–US–Japan; India–Japan–Australia; India–Australia–Indonesia; and Russia–India–China (RIC)).[11] India has upgraded its mil–mil relationship in the Indo-Pacific by participating in military exercises[12] for improving interoperability and maritime domain awareness.[13] Australia and India

---

[11] Some are already questioning the viability of RIC, and predict its early demise.

[12] For instance, Cope India 2019 (CI19) the India–US joint air exercise, and Pitch Black air exercises in Australia.

[13] India and Singapore Defence Ministers signed the India–Singapore Bilateral Agreement for Navy Cooperation to deepen maritime cooperation. It provides for joint exercises and temporary deployments from each other's naval facilities and mutual logistics support.

have already enhanced their defense cooperation with Australian Navy participating in Exercise Malabar in November 2020, along with the other two (Japan and the United States). Having already signed logistic support agreements with countries such as the United States, France, Australia, South Korea, and Singapore, India finally concluded the Acquisition and Cross-Servicing Agreement (ACSA) with Japan in September 2020.

The Indo-Pacific is a strategic conundrum which requires delicate and sensitive handling to avoid possible miscalculation. In the emerging multipolar world, the role of incipient coalitions like Quad 2.0 to balance China's assertive behavior will be important. The Quad has the advantage of flexibility of form so that it can "be ratcheted up in response to negative behavior by China, or dialled down if Beijing behaves better" (Graham 2018). This requires close understanding between the leadership of the four member countries. Any extension of its membership beyond the four (Quad Plus) has the advantage of bringing in the weight of other important stakeholders into the balance, but has the attendant danger of diluting its effectiveness. The Indo-Pacific is witnessing a new churning, and a realistic appraisal indicates that new challenges beckon India and the Indo-Pacific. Many of the Indo-Pacific countries had been hedging their bets prior to the pandemic because of dependence on China for trade and an ambivalent stance of the United States. The very conditions which signal the need for a complete break from the past also indicate the need for caution because of growing economic and political uncertainty. On the economic front, states are resorting to protectionism and India's one weakness has been that it was not part of the Asian supply chains. India has reposed confidence in ASEAN centrality while partnering with the wider Indo-Pacific. It aspires for a free, open, secure, and prosperous Indo-Pacific but the success of this policy hinges on the ability of the regional countries to align their national interests and threat perceptions. The Indo-Pacific of the future will be shaped by the extent to which India and other regional stakeholders rally together to build a consensus.

India, Singapore sign deal to boost cooperation in maritime security, 30 November 2017, Live Mint https://www.livemint.com/.

REFERENCES

Acharya, A. (2017), "The Myth of ASEAN Centrality?" *Contemporary Southeast Asia*, 39 (2): 273–279.

Business Standard (2018), "India-US sign COMCASA: What Is It and How Does It Help Indian Defence?" 6 September, https://www.business-sta ndard.com/article/economy-policy/india-us-sign-comcasa-what-s-what-and-how-it-helps-indian-defence-118090600988_1.html.

Buszynski, L. (2019), "The South China Sea: an arena for great power strategic rivalry," In: T.T. Thuy, J.B. Welfield and L.T. Trang (eds) *Building a Normative Order in the South China Sea: Evolving Disputes, Expanding Options*. Cheltenham and Northampton: Edward Elgar Publishing, pp. 68–91.

Chinoy, S.R. (2020), "Time to Leverage the Strategic Potential of Andaman & Nicobar Islands," MP-IDSA website, 26 June, https://idsa.in/policybrief/str ategic-potential-andaman-nicobar-sujanchinoy-260620.

De, P. (2020), *Act East to Act Indo-Pacific: India's Expanding Neighbourhood*, New Delhi: Knowledge World.

George, V.K. (2016), "India, US Sign Military Logistics Pact," *The Hindu*, 30 August, https://www.thehindu.com/news/international/India-US-sign-military-logistics-pact/article14598282.ece.

Graham, E. (2018), "The Quad Deserves Its Second Chance," in E. Graham, C. Pan, I. Hall et al. The Centre of Gravity series.

Grossman, D. and Sharman, C. (2019), "Message to Great Powers," 31 December, 2019, https://warontherocks.com/2019/12/how-to-read-vie tnams-latest-defense-white-paper-a-message-to-great-powers/.

Haruko, W. (2020), "The Indo-Pacific" Concept: Geographical Adjustments and Their Implications," RSIS Working Paper No. 326, 16 March, https://www. rsis.edu.sg/wp-content/uploads/2020/03/WP326.pdf.

Horimoto, T. (2020), "Modi Diplomacy" and the Future of Japan-India Relations," *Nippon.com* 18 May, https://www.nippon.com/en/in-depth/a06 701/.

India, Ministry of External Affairs (2018a), "Prime Minister's Keynote Address at Shangri-La Dialogue, 1 June," http://www.mea.gov.in/outoging-visit-detail.htm?29943/Prime+Ministers+Keynote+Address+at+Shangri+La+Dia logue+June+01+2018.

India, Ministry of External Affairs (2018b), "Shared Vision of India-Indonesia Maritime Cooperation in the Indo–Pacific," 30 May, 2018, https://mea.gov. in/bilateral-documents.htm?dtl/29933/Shared_Vision_of_IndiaIndonesia_ Maritime_Cooperation_in_the_IndoPacific.

India, Ministry of External Affairs (2019a), "Valedictory Address by External Affairs Minister, GOI at 11th Delhi Dialogue," December 14, https://mea. gov.in/Speeches-Statements.htm?dtl/32212/Valedictory_Address_by_Exte rnal_Affairs_Minister_at_11th_Delhi_Dialogue_December_14_201.

India, Ministry of External Affairs (2019b), "External Affairs Minister's Speech at the 4th Ramnath Goenka Lecture, 2019," 14 November, 2019, https://www.mea.gov.in/Speeches-Statements.htm?dtl/32038/External_Affairs_Ministers_speech_at_the_4th_Ramnath_Goenka_Lecture_2019.

India, Ministry of External Affairs (2020a), "External Affairs Minister's Interview to India Today," 8 March, 2020, https://mea.gov.in/interviews.htm?dtl/32488/external+affairs+ministers+interview+to+india+today accessed 8 April 2020.

India, Ministry of External Affairs (2020b), "List of the Documents Announced/Signed During India–Australia Virtual Summit 4 June 2020," https://mea.gov.in/bilateral-documents.htm?dtl/32728/list+of+the+documents+announcedsigned+during+india++australia+virtual+summit.

India, Rajya Sabha (2017), "Question No. 808, Trade through South China Sea," 9 February, https://www.mea.gov.in/rajya-sabha.htm?dtl/28041/question+no808+trade+through+south+china+sea.

India, Rajya Sabha (2019), Question No. 2411, Features of Quadrilateral Security Dialogue, 3 January, https://mea.gov.in/rajya-sabha.htm?dtl/30869/question+no2411+features+of+quadrilateral+security+dialogue.

Jaishankar, D. (2019), "Five Myths About India and the Indo-Pacific," China India Brief#141, 12 July, Lee Kuan Yew School of Public Policy, Singapore.

Laksmana, E. (2019). "Indonesia as "Global Maritime Fulcrum": A Post Mortem Analysis," *Asian Maritime Transparency Initiative (AMTI)*, 8 November, https://amti.csis.org/indonesia-as-global-maritime-fulcrum-a-post-mortem-analysis/.

Lohman, et al. (2015), "The Quad Plus: Towards a Shared Strategic Vision for the Indo-Pacific," Wisdom Tree, New Delhi.

Mahapatra, C. (2019), "Introduction: Emerging Trends in Indo-Pacific: Shifting Paradigms & New Power Coalitions," in: C. Mahapatra (ed) *Rise of the Indo-Pacific: Perspectives, Dimensions and Challenges*. New Delhi: ICSSR- Pentagon Press.

Mohan, G. (2020), "India Admitted as Fifth Observer to Indian Ocean Commission," India Today, 7 March, https://www.indiatoday.in/india/story/india-admitted-as-fifth-observer-to-indian-ocean-commission.

Moramudali, U. (2020), "The Hambantota Port Deal: Myths and Realities," *The Diplomat*, 1 January 1, 2020, https://thediplomat.com/2020/01/the-hambantota-port-deal-myths-and-realities.

Mun, T.S., et al. (2019), State of Southeast Asia: 2019, Survey Report, ASEAN Studies Centre at Institute of Southeast Asian Studies ISEAS, Singapore.

Pant, H.V. (2018), "India and Vietnam: A 'Strategic Partnership' in the Making," Policy Brief, March, https://www.rsis.edu.sg/wp-content/uploads/2018/04/PB180409_-India-and-Vietnam.pdf.

Rai, R. (2014), "IMAC: Indian Navy's Eyes and Ears Hitech Data Fusion Centre Inaugurated," *India Strategic*, December 2014, https://www.indiastrategic.in/topstories3616_Indian_Navy_setting_up_Coastal_Eyes_and_Ears.htm, accessed 2 June 2020.

Saha, P. (2018), "The Quad in the Indo-Pacific: Why ASEAN Remains Cautious," *ORF Issue Brief* 12. 26 February, https://www.orfonline.org/research/asean-quad.

Saha, P., Bland, B. and Laksmana, E.A. (2020), "Anchoring the Indo-Pacific: The Case for Deeper Australia-India-Indonesia Trilateral Cooperation," ORF, The Lowy Institute and CSIS Policy Report, January.

Shoji, T. (2018), "'Belt and Road' vs 'Free and Open Indo-Pacific': Competition Over Regional Order and ASEAN," *The National Institute for Defense Studies* (Japan), NIDS Commentary No. 881 November 2018.

Singh, S. (2016a), "Strategic Scenario in the Indo-Pacific Region: An Indian Perspective," in: G.S. Khurana and A.G. Singh (eds) *India and China: Constructing a Peaceful Order in the Indo-Pacific*. New Delhi: National Maritime Foundation, pp. 10–20.

Singh, S. (2019), "The Indo-Pacific and India-US Strategic Convergence: An Assessment," *Asia Policy*, 14 (1): 77–94.

Singh, U.B. (2016b), "The Significance of the ADMM-Plus: A Perspective from India," *Asia Policy*, 22 (7): 96–101.

U.S. Department of Defense (2019), Indo-Pacific Strategy Report: Preparedness, Partnerships and Promoting a Networked Region.

The Wire (2019), "'Quad' Gets an Upgrade as Foreign Ministers of India, Japan, Australia, US Meet," 27 September, https://thewire.in/diplomacy/quad-gets-an-upgrade-as-foreign-ministers-of-india-japan-australia-us-meet.

Yadav, R.S (2014), "'Indo-Pacific': Likely to be Peripheral for India," *Indian Foreign Affairs Journal*, 9 (2): 125–130.

CHAPTER 14

Indonesia and the Indo-Pacific: Cooperation, Interests, and Strategies

Senia Febrica

INTRODUCTION: INDONESIA IN THE INDO-PACIFIC

In recent years, the concept of Indo-Pacific has been advanced by many states in the Asia-Pacific, including Indonesia. This concept involves an extension of Indonesia's foreign policy focus, which primarily centers on Southeast Asia, to include countries in the Indian and the Pacific Oceans. This raises the crucial question of what does the Indo-Pacific mean to Indonesia? Almost half of the world's trading goods and oil supply pass through key Indonesian straits including the Straits of Malacca and Singapore, the Strait of Sunda, and the Strait of Lombok (Carana 2004: 14). As the largest archipelagic state in the world, Indonesia comprising 17,480 islands, with a maritime territory measuring close to 6 million square kilometers, is located between the two key shipping routes of the Pacific and Indian Ocean, and between two continents, Asia and Australia (Indonesian Ministry of Defence 2008: 145). It also sits at the crossroads of busy maritime traffic between Europe and the Far East, between Australia and

---

S. Febrica (✉)
University of Strathclyde, Glasgow, Scotland, UK

© The Author(s), under exclusive license to Springer Nature Switzerland AG 2021
L. Buszynski and D. T. Hai (eds.), *Maritime Issues and Regional Order in the Indo-Pacific*, Palgrave Studies in Maritime Politics and Security, https://doi.org/10.1007/978-3-030-68038-1_14

Asia, and between the Persian Gulf and Japan (Coutrier 1988: 186). There are three major sea-lanes in Southeast Asia which connect the Indian and Pacific Oceans and overlap with Indonesia's maritime jurisdiction (Ho 2007: 205). These are the archipelagic sea-lanes I, II, and III (see Map. 14.1). Archipelagic sea-lane I facilitates navigation from the Indian Ocean through the Sunda Strait to Natuna Sea and eventually reaches the South China Sea (Djalal 2009: 63). Archipelagic sea-lane II assists the flow of maritime transport from the Indian Ocean through the Lombok Strait to the Makassar Strait and then finally to the Sulawesi Sea and the Pacific Ocean and Philippine waterway (Djalal 2009: 63). Finally, sea-lane III links the Timor Sea and Arafuru Sea to the Pacific Ocean through the Sawu Sea, the Banda Sea, the Seram Sea, and the Moluccas Sea (Djalal 2009: 63).

The region's major sea-lanes are centered on the key straits of Malacca and Singapore, and Lombok (Ho 2007: 205). Of these three straits, the Straits of Malacca and Singapore are the most important trading routes. Most of Middle East oil exports to Asia and commerce between Asia and Europe pass through this 610-mile-long strait (U.S. Department of the Homeland Security 20 September 2005; Coutrier 1988: 186). At least 600 ships navigate through the Straits of Malacca and

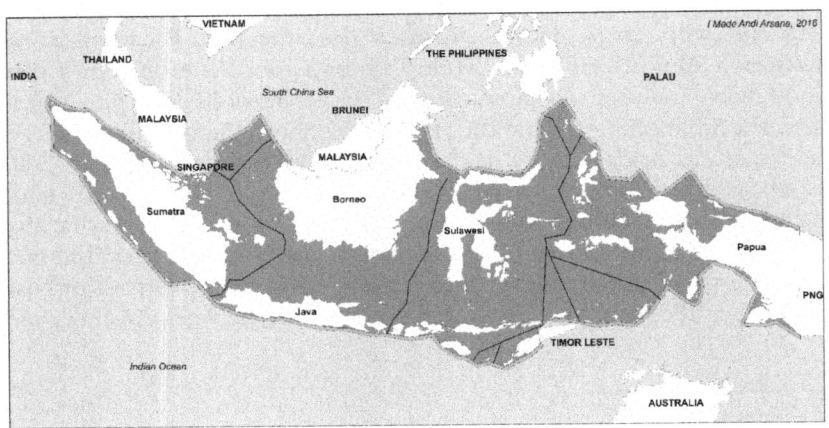

Map. 14.1 Map of Indonesia (*Source* This map was produced by Dr. I Made Andi Arsana, Department of Geodetic Engineering, Faculty of Engineering Universitas Gadjah Mada)

Singapore every day (Indonesian Ministry of Foreign Affairs 2006: 14). This includes 72% of super-tankers plying between the Indian and Pacific Oceans making these straits the busiest sea-lane of communication globally (U.S. Energy Information Administration, 22 August 2012). Most of the oil for Asia-Pacific countries, including around 80% of Japan's and China's imported oil originating from the Persian Gulf transits through the Straits of Malacca and Singapore (U.S. Energy Information Administration, 22 August 2012). This is because this sea-lane is the shortest sea route between the Middle East and Asia (U.S. Energy Information Administration, 2012). Currently, 45% of the world's annual merchant fleet tonnage passes through the Straits of Malacca and Singapore, the Sunda Strait, and the Lombok Strait (Carana 2004: 14; U.S. Department of Homeland Security, 20 September 2005). The total value of goods transported via these waters reaches US$1.3 trillion annually (Bakorkamla 2010: 34). Indonesian waters also serve as an important sea-lane for the oil trade. Half of the world's oil navigates through Indonesian waterways (Carana 2004: 14; U.S. Department of Homeland Security, 20 September 2005).

THE GLOBAL MARITIME FULCRUM

Indonesia's Global Maritime Fulcrum vision seeks to place Indonesia as a maritime power in the Indian and Pacific Oceans, and it has shaped its idea of the Indo-Pacific cooperation. The Global Maritime Fulcrum aims to transform Indonesia into a maritime power in the Indian and Pacific Oceans. It intends to strengthen the country's maritime culture, marine resource management, infrastructure development, maritime diplomacy, and defense. It is designed to "maximize all the potential that Indonesia has" as a country to play an active role in shaping geopolitical and economic change in the Indo-Pacific (Indonesian Ministry of Communication and Informatics, 25 February 2019). Under President Joko Widodo (Jokowi) Indonesia is keen to improve the country's strategic geographic position between the two oceans. Efforts to exploit this strategic position is reflected in Jokowi's Global Maritime Fulcrum vision. Since the resignation of Soeharto, Indonesia has been led by five Presidents: Habibie, Abdurrahman Wahid, Megawati, Yudhoyono, and most recently, Jokowi. Of these five, Jokowi is the only president who announced a commitment to make maritime security concerns a national priority soon after he took office on 20 October 2014. After winning the 2014 elections he articulated his purpose to transform Indonesia to be "the Global Maritime Fulcrum, a locus of great civilization in the future" (Tempo, 22 July 2014). On 13 November 2015 at the East Asia Summit in Naypyidaw, Myanmar, Jokowi announced his administration's plan to transform Indonesia to be the maritime fulcrum in the Indo-Pacific. This means turning Indonesia's potential as the largest archipelagic country in the world into a maritime power to be reckoned with in the Indian and Pacific oceans (Indonesian Ministry of Communication and Informatics 2020). From a security point of view, the Global Maritime Fulcrum is underscored by the need to improve the country's maritime security and secure maritime interests against threats posed by boundary disputes, illegal fishing, and marine pollution (Indonesian Presidential Office 2015). From an economic perspective it is designed to improve connections between the developed western part of the country with the underdeveloped eastern part by developing ports, shipyards, and shipping lines so the price of goods between the two regions in Indonesia do not differ as much (Febrica and Sudarman 2018: 103; Dahuri 2015: 125).

The Global Maritime Fulcrum plan is built upon five pillars (Indonesian Presidential Office, 13 November 2015). First is the development of Indonesia's maritime culture. Second is a commitment to safeguard and manage marine resources, especially fishery resources. Third is a pledge to improve Indonesia's maritime infrastructure and connectivity by developing seaports, shipping industry, and maritime tourism. Fourth is the encouragement of maritime cooperation between Indonesia and other countries by using diplomacy. Fifth is the development of Indonesia's maritime defense capacity. The need to develop maritime defense is underscored by the country's vast maritime areas (5.8 million square kilometers) and the lack of equipment that has made Indonesia vulnerable to various maritime security concerns including, Illegal, Unreported, and Unregulated (IUU) fishing, maritime terrorism, and armed robbery against ships. Out of these maritime security concerns, IUU fishing sits at the top of national security priorities list. IUU fishing is a broad term that encapsulates a diverse range of fishing activities. It can include fishing activities conducted by national or foreign vessels without permission, activities which have not been reported or have been misreported, and activities that contravene the conservation and management measures set by relevant authorities.

During President Jokowi's second term, the words "Global Maritime Fulcrum" did not feature much in senior officials' key speeches or important government documents. Jokowi's inauguration speech in October 2019 and the Foreign Minister Retno Marsudi's address on Indonesian foreign policy priorities for 2019–2024, for example, hardly mentioned the word maritime. There is widespread disappointment among analysts that Indonesia's efforts to realize the Global Maritime Fulcrum have dwindled (see Laksmana, 8 November 2019). The Jokowi administration's lack of reference to Global Maritime Fulcrum vision could be understood in two ways. First, the lack of reference to it is a way for the Indonesian government to implement the country's free and active foreign policy doctrine, particularly in the context of the South China Sea dispute. As an Indonesian foreign policy analyst, Suzie Sudarman, suggested the free and active [doctrine] provides Indonesia with leeway from pressure exercised by the major powers.[1] During Jokowi's first presidential term, China's growing assertiveness in the South China Sea had caused major friction with Indonesian authorities primarily over IUU fishing. This led to the renaming of the Indonesian EEZ adjacent to the South China Sea as the North Natuna Sea to assert Indonesian sovereign rights. During the same time, the United States has been active in carrying out its maritime "transit" operation, placing US naval vessels in areas China considered as its sovereign territory in the South China Sea (CNN, 27 October 2015). By not articulating the Global Maritime Fulcrum vision explicitly in key speeches and documents, the Indonesian government could avoid the impression that Indonesia is alienating China and favoring the United States.

Second, the Jokowi administration's lack of reference to the Global Maritime Fulcrum vision should be seen as Indonesia's way to maintain a delicate balance between protecting its sovereign rights and the need for Chinese infrastructure investment. Indonesia has consistently highlighted the importance of protecting its sovereignty and its sovereign rights over the Natuna islands and the North Natuna Sea that are located close to the South China Sea. For instance, following the incursion of China coast guard and fishing vessels in the North Natuna Sea in January 2020, President Jokowi stressed that "there is no compromise in maintaining Indonesian sovereignty" (CNN, 4 January 2020b). Since the

---

[1] Phone interview with the Director of the American Studies Center, the Universitas Indonesia, Suzie Sudarman, May 6, 2020, Jakarta.

initial stage of the Jokowi administration, however, China has also played an essential role in the development of Indonesia's maritime infrastructure, one of the key pillars of Indonesia's Global Maritime Fulcrum vision. With regard to maritime infrastructure development between 2015 and 2019, Indonesia has estimated that the country would need Indonesian Rupiah (IDR) 5,519.4 trillion to build 172 new seaports, 65 pier crossings, and other infrastructure including airports, railways, road, highway, power plants, and industrial and special economy complexes outside of Java (Indonesian Investment Coordinating Board 2015: 11). However, the government budget can only meet 40.14% of the targeted expenses, therefore, leaving a significant gap of IDR 3,303.8 trillion. China's Asian Infrastructure Investment Bank is expected to fund the development of 24 seaports, 15 airports, 1,000 kilometers of road, 8,700 kilometers of railway networks, and power plants with a 35,000-megawatt capacity in Indonesia (Jakarta Post, 2 May 2015). By not making too many political references to the Global Maritime Fulcrum vision Indonesia seeks to sustain a balance between protecting its sovereignty and securing its economic interests. The term Global Maritime Fulcrum may not have been often mentioned during Jokowi's second presidential term, but in practice the government has continued to embed the Global Maritime Fulcrum plan in various government ministerial programs. In the second term, the Indonesian government has continued to focus on maritime infrastructure development and counter-IUU fishing efforts. With regard to maritime connectivity development Jokowi placed "addressing obstacles to sea-highways" on his agenda within the first ten days after his inauguration in 2019 (Dzakwan, 4 November 2019).

Indonesia's Indo-Pacific Concept: Cooperation, Interests, and Strategies

The concept of the Indo-Pacific region has been regarded as an expanded theater of US–China rivalry as Washington's promotion of the Indo-Pacific strategy clashes with China's One Belt and One Road Initiative (see Weatherbee 2019: 1). However, the Indo-Pacific idea has gained momentum beyond US and China rivalry as middle power states in the region including Australia, Japan, India, and Indonesia all have come up with their own conceptions. Japan has its Free and Open Indo-Pacific concept as has Australia, and India has introduced its SAGAR (Security and Growth for All in the Region) vision of the region (Nagy, 12

December 2019; Giridharadas, 23 January 2020). Indonesia, the largest country in Southeast Asia, has also developed and advanced its own concept of the Indo-Pacific cooperation which builds on the country's Global Maritime Fulcrum vision. The Indo-Pacific cooperation has been promoted by Indonesia to defuse tensions caused by strategic rivalry between countries. Supporting the notion of a pluralistic, free, and open Indo-Pacific, including the United States, Japan, Australia, India, and China, enhances the credibility of Indonesia's vision to be a "Global Maritime Fulcrum" in the Indo-Pacific region.

The use of the term Indo-Pacific in Indonesia's official foreign policy discourse began in 2013 as the country's foreign minister at that time, Marty Natalegawa, acknowledged in his keynote speech at the Conference on Indonesia in Washington that "the term 'Indo-Pacific' has become increasingly common in the lexicon of geopolitics" (Natalegawa, 20 May 2013; Scott 2019: 199). Prior to this, Indonesia had mainly used the term Asia-Pacific. The adoption of the Indo-Pacific term shows the widening of Indonesia's geostrategic canvas from the Asia-Pacific to the Indo-Pacific, a symbolic move that is in line with President Joko Widodo's goal to make Indonesia a Global Maritime Fulcrum (Anwar 2020: 111). In practice, however, Indonesia still uses the term Asia-Pacific alongside Indo-Pacific in its official foreign policy communication (Indonesian Ministry of Foreign Affairs, 3 May 2020). Indonesia's former Foreign Minister, Natalegawa, explained that the term Indo-Pacific geographically refers to "an important triangle spanning two oceans, the Pacific and Indian Oceans" (Natalegawa, 20 May 2013). For Indonesia, "the largest archipelagic state in the world, amid its archipelagic waters, are found some of the most strategic sea-lanes in the world: connecting the Indian and Pacific Oceans. Serving as highways for the movement of global trade, as well as of people and the associated ideas and cultural expressions they bring forth" (Natalegawa, 20 May 2013).

Given Indonesia's strategic geographical position, Natalegawa highlighted that the future course of the Indo-Pacific region is in Indonesia's profound interest (Natalegawa, 20 May 2013). Recognizing the challenges in the Indo-Pacific including the "sharpening of distrust and its attendant cycle of tensions" in the Korean peninsula, the unresolved maritime disputes in the South China Sea, and major power rivalry in the region, Natalegawa proposed an Indo-Pacific wide treaty of friendship and cooperation (Natalegawa, 20 May 2013). Natalegawa claimed that this treaty would be "a commitment by states in the region to build confidence, to solve disputes by peaceful means, and to promote a concept of security that is all encompassing; underscoring that security is a common good" (Natalegawa, 20 May 2013). At the domestic level the Indonesian Ministry of Foreign Affairs was leading the deliberation process involving government officials, academics, and representatives of local governments to come up with a grand concept of Indonesia's perspective on the ASEAN Outlook on the Indo-Pacific (Priatna, 21 March 2019). The ASEAN Outlook on the Indo-Pacific is intended to provide guidance for cooperation in the region, promote peace and closer economic cooperation, enhance ASEAN's community-building process through the existing ASEAN-led mechanisms such as the EAS, and implement priority areas of cooperation such as maritime cooperation, connectivity, and the Sustainable Development Goals (SDGs) (ASEAN 2019).

Three Key Features

There are three key features that inform Indonesia's Indo-Pacific cooperation concept. First, it put the emphasis on the centrality of ASEAN as the driver of cooperation. Given this, Indonesia has played a leading role in drafting the ASEAN Outlook on the Indo-Pacific document that was accepted by all member states of this regional organization in June 2019 (Anwar 2020). In terms of ASEAN's central role in Indonesia's Indo-Pacific cooperation, Retno Marsudi, in her 2019 annual press statement reiterated the centrality of ASEAN in driving the cooperation. To quote Marsudi:

> Indonesia's maritime diplomacy continues its work to advance the regional architecture in the two oceans, the Pacific Ocean and the Indian Ocean. For Indonesia, the two oceans, the Indian and Pacific, is a Single Geo-Strategic Theatre. We need to maintain the stability, security, and prosperity in the Indian Ocean and the Pacific Ocean. We must ensure that the Indian and Pacific Oceans does not become an arena for competition of natural resources, territorial conflicts and maritime supremacy. In this context, Indonesia is developing an "Indo-Pacific" cooperation concept…Indonesia, alongside other ASEAN member countries, invites all partners to continue developing the "Indo-Pacific" cooperation concept. For Indonesia, ASEAN must be proactive in addressing strategic developments and changes in the region. ASEAN must always be the driver for progress in the region. (Indonesian Minister for Foreign Affairs 2019)

Second, Indonesia's Indo-Pacific cooperation maintains the principle of inclusivity to avoid alienating any major powers in the region, particularly China, from participating in the cooperation venture. The inclusivity principle has been advanced in bilateral and regional forums. The term inclusivity was, for instance, incorporated into the joint statement of the Indonesia–Australia foreign and defense ministers meeting in April 2018. To quote the statement: "Ministers emphasised...shared interest in an Indo-Pacific region that is open, transparent, inclusive, rules-based, prosperous and resilient, in which the rights of all states are respected" (Australian Department of Defence, 16 March 2018). The Shared Vision of India–Indonesia Maritime Cooperation in the Indo-Pacific issued on 30 May 2018 also reiterated "the importance of achieving ...[an] inclusive Indo-Pacific region, where sovereignty and territorial integrity, international law, in particular UNCLOS, freedom of navigation...are respected" (India Ministry of External Affairs, 30 May 2018). Japan's Prime Minister Shinzo Abe at the 14th East Asia Summit in Bangkok on 4 November 2019 also declared his support for the ASEAN Outlook.

Third, the Indo-Pacific cooperation concept focuses on non-traditional maritime security concerns. The Director-General of ASEAN Cooperation at the Indonesian Foreign Ministry, Jose Antonio Morato Tavares stresses a "soft approach" (Antara, 16 November 2018). In a speech to the East Asia Summit in 2018, Jokowi claimed that the focus of the Indo-Pacific cooperation rested on cooperation to eliminate maritime crimes, improve connectivity to boost economic growth, and create sustainable development (Antara, 16 November 2018; Scott 2019: 204). There is an expectation that cooperation in non-controversial areas can evolve into an interlocking network of a regional system. This expectation is drawn from the Southeast Asian experience where bilateral border security arrangements have developed into "an overlapping and interlocking network" of a regional security system (Acharya 1992: 10; 1995: 191).

Non-traditional maritime security issues embrace cooperation over maritime infrastructure development and efforts to deal with maritime crime. This is in line with Indonesia's Global Maritime Fulcrum vision that has focused on improving maritime connectivity and efforts dealing with maritime transnational crimes such as IUU fishing at domestic level. As Retno Marsudi pointed out in January 2015 cooperation to tackle IUU fishing is one of Indonesia's foreign policy priorities (Indonesian Cabinet Secretariat, 8 January 2015). This focus was affirmed by the Indonesian Representative to the United Nations Economic and Social

Commission for Asia and the Pacific (ESCAP) 71st session in May 2015 as he explained that "Indonesia continues to strengthen the development of its maritime sector and calls all parties in the Asia Pacific region to combat IUU fishing" (Indonesian Embassy in Bangkok 2015). During the session, Indonesia proposed a resolution to invite countries to fight IUU fishing. It became the first UNESCAP resolution that called for interstate cooperation to deal with IUU fishing (Indonesian Embassy in Bangkok 2015). The Indo-Pacific countries including the coastal states of the South China Sea, the Bay of Bengal, and the Pacific Islands experience disputes over maritime boundaries alongside IUU fishing. In these areas, due to a deep-seated lack of trust, any states' enforcement efforts to address maritime security threats such as IUU fishing are viewed suspiciously by others and tend to be resisted. Consequently, years of poor security enforcement have led to rampant illegal fishing activities in the South China Sea, the Bay of Bengal, and the Pacific Islands (Febrica 2016; Ghosh and Lobo, 31 January 2017). In the South China Sea region alone, mainly as a consequence of IUU fishing practices in the past three decades, fish stocks have declined by a third and in the past ten years coral reefs have decreased by 16% (Astuti 2017: 3). In the Pacific Islands region, the value of the IUU catch was between USD 707 million and USD 1,557 million—more than 12% of the USD 5 billion that was paid to fishermen for their tuna catches in the region (Pew, 2 May 2016). The value of the IUU catch represents a substantial economic loss for fishing nations with scarce resources and jobs in this region (Pew, 2 May 2016). In the Bay of Bengal, in 2015, Sri Lankan authorities seized 70 of these trawlers and arrested 450 fishermen (Ghosh and Lobo, 31 January 2017). On the other side of the border, Indian authorities have also arrested many Sri Lankan tuna fishermen (Ghosh and Lobo, 31 January 2017).

Indonesia and Maritime Connectivity

During Jokowi's second term, Indonesia's Global Maritime Fulcrum vision was projected to the ASEAN Outlook in the Indo-Pacific that was adopted by member states in June 2019. Maritime connectivity and counter-IUU fishing are the areas of cooperation identified in the ASEAN Outlook on the Indo-Pacific document. To demonstrate its leadership, Indonesia planned to host the first ASEAN Indo-Pacific Infrastructure and Connectivity Forum in 2020. In terms of IUU fishing, an official from the Indonesian Ministry of Foreign Affairs explained that efforts to improve maritime diplomacy in dealing with IUU fishing have continued to be an essential part of the ministry's objective during Jokowi's second term. He further claimed that in dealing with this problem in the South China Sea, for example, Indonesia is committed to accelerate boundary settlement negotiations with Vietnam. Retno Marsudi, in her Annual Press Statement on 8 January 2020, confirmed this point as she noted that "with regards to the sovereignty and national identity diplomacy, Indonesia is trying to intensify both land and maritime negotiations, including with Vietnam on an Exclusive Economic Zone (EEZ) border" (Indonesian Ministry of Foreign Affairs, 8 January 2020).

In 2019 there were couple of maritime incidents between the Indonesian Navy and the Vietnam Fisheries Resources Surveillance (VFRS) agency. In February 2019 the Indonesian Maritime Affairs and Fishery Minister, Susi Pudjiastuti, requested "that Vietnam's government explain about and apologise" for the action of the VFRS agency vessel that was allegedly disrupting the Indonesian Navy's efforts to seize four Vietnam-flagged vessels for illegally fishing in Indonesian waters (Jakarta Post, 27 February 2019). In April 2019 two Vietnamese coast guard ships rammed an Indonesian navy ship after it intercepted an allegedly illegal Vietnamese fishing boat in Indonesian waters in the South China Sea (ABC, 29 April 2019). Despite the stand-offs that took place between Indonesia and China over illegal fishing in December 2019 and January 2020, Indonesia will not negotiate a boundary settlement with China. As part of Indonesia's official position, when it comes to maritime boundaries in the South China Sea it only considers Malaysia and Vietnam as neighboring countries that it has to deal with (Arsana, 8 August 2011). Indonesia's focus on the need to address IUU fishing is also reflected in the identification of cooperation for the sustainable management of marine resources as one of the maritime cooperation areas that need to be enhanced in the ASEAN Outlook on the Indo-Pacific.

Indo-Pacific Cooperation in Regional Forums

Indonesia has advocated the Indo-Pacific cooperation in various bilateral and regional forums. Indonesia began to promote the Indo-Pacific cooperation at various ASEAN meetings throughout 2018 including the ASEAN Heads of Government Summit in April 2018, the ASEAN Foreign Ministers' Meeting in August 2018, the ASEAN Senior Official Retreat Meeting in Jakarta in September 2018, and the ASEAN Summit in November 2018 (Scott 2019: 203). Outside of ASEAN, Indonesia presented this cooperation concept at the East Asia Summit which provides a platform for Indonesia to communicate this Indo-Pacific cooperation concept to non-ASEAN countries including the United States, Japan, India, and China. Indonesia began to present the cooperation concept at the East Asia Summit Foreign Minister's meeting in August 2018 (Scott 2019: 203). The Indo-Pacific cooperation was the central focus of President Jokowi's speech at the 13th East Asia Summit in Singapore in November 2018. The Chairman's statement from this summit noted that "cooperation in the Indo-Pacific region should embrace key principles such as ASEAN Centrality, openness, transparency, inclusivity, and a rules-based approach, in order to enhance mutual trust, respect, and benefit" (ASEAN, 15 November 2018). The rules-based approach here points to adherence to international law particularly the rules and principles embodied in the 1982 United Nations Convention on the Law of the Sea.

At present, Indonesia's draft concept for the Indo-Pacific cooperation has not been formally accepted or adopted by the participating countries involved at the EAS (see Scott 2019: 203–204). The Chairman's statement of the 14th EAS, held in Bangkok in November 2019, merely "noted the adoption of the ASEAN Outlook on the Indo-Pacific, based on the principles of …ASEAN centrality, openness,…inclusivity….and respect for international law and ASEAN's intention to use the Outlook as a guide for ASEAN's engagement in the Asia-Pacific and Indian Ocean regions" (ASEAN, 4 November 2019). The statement then continued to welcome "further discussions on working with ASEAN to promote engagement and international cooperation in the areas identified in the Outlook and of common interest" (ASEAN, 4 November 2019). The 15th EAS that will be convened by Vietnam in 2020 is expected to play a defining role to determine whether or not the participating countries will endorse the ASEAN common Outlook on the Indo-Pacific. According to a senior official from the Ministry of Foreign Affairs, Indonesia has engaged Vietnam to play a more active role in advocating the ASEAN Outlook on Indo-Pacific.[2] The expectation is that Vietnam can use its role as the chairman of ASEAN to speak on behalf of the member states

---

[2] Discussion with an Indonesian senior official (Hanoi, November 5, 2019).

regarding the Indo-Pacific cooperation with ASEAN Outlook at international forums including the EAS.[3] Indonesia understands that this circumstance will present both opportunities and challenges for Vietnam and ASEAN.[4] On one hand, the development of the ASEAN Outlook on the Indo-Pacific cooperation will provide Vietnam with opportunities to advocate a cooperative agreement that can help both Vietnam and ASEAN member countries to protect their maritime rights and interests. On the other hand, it will also present challenges for Vietnam in finding a practical cooperation initiative that can be agreed by all the participating countries of EAS.

Indonesia—The United States, Japan, and India

The Indo-Pacific concept put forward by Indonesia and ASEAN on the Indo-Pacific cooperation is different from the "free and open" Indo-Pacific proposed by the United States, Australia, Japan, and India (Leong, 6 March 2020). Indonesia's concept of the Indo-Pacific focuses on ASEAN centrality in driving the cooperation forward and the notion of inclusivity. The United States, Australia, Japan, and India concepts of "free and open" Indo-Pacific emphasize freedom from coercion by other countries, unfettered access to the seas, and cooperation among democratic countries on the basis of freedom, market economies, and open investment (Ayres, 20 November 2018). Prime Minister Shinzo Abe, at the opening session of the sixth Tokyo International Conference on African Development in Kenya in August 2016, introduced Japan's vision of Indo-Pacific for the first time claiming that "Japan bears the responsibility of fostering the confluence of the Pacific and Indian Oceans and of Asia and Africa into a place that values freedom, the rule of law, and the market economy, free from force or coercion, and making it prosperous" (Japan Ministry of Foreign Affairs, 27 August 2016). Japan showed strong support for the ASEAN Indo-Pacific cooperation stating that it was epoch-making demonstrating its unity and centrality and declared that Japan would cooperate with ASEAN towards materializing the AOIP, by achieving synergies with its own "Free and Open Indo-Pacific." (Japan Ministry of Foreign Affairs, 4 November 2019).

---

[3] Discussion with an Indonesian senior official (Hanoi, November 5, 2019).

[4] Discussion with an Indonesian senior official (Hanoi, November 5, 2019).

Prime Minister Narendra Modi's keynote address at the annual Shangri-La Dialogue on 1 June 2018 claimed that India's own engagement of the Indo-Pacific region will be marked by the promotion of "a democratic and rules-based international order, in which all nations, small and large, thrive as equal and sovereign" and cooperation "with others to keep our seas, space and airways free and open" (Indian Ministry of External Affairs, 1 June 2018). The core themes of Australia's Indo-Pacific vision as outlined by the Secretary of the Department of Foreign Affairs and Trade, Frances Adamson, also include peaceful resolution of disputes "in accordance with international law and without the threat or use of force or coercion, open markets...", economic integration that "is inclusive of and open to all the region's economies" and "rights of freedom of navigation and overflight that are upheld..." (Australian Department of Foreign Affairs and Trade, 29 April 2019). In 2019 the US Secretary of State, Mike Pompeo, highlighted the "free and open" nature of the Indo-Pacific as he called upon US allies and partners to assume a shared responsibility to uphold the rules and values underpinning the US vision. That includes "free, fair, and reciprocal trade, open investment environments, good governance, and freedom of the seas" (US Department of State, 4 November 2019a).

The increasingly close cooperation between the four democracies of the United States, Australia, Japan, and India "for consultations on collective efforts to advance a free, open, and inclusive Indo-Pacific" stimulated Indonesia's concern regarding the possibility of the four powers alienating China and side-lining ASEAN in the development of the Indo-Pacific cooperation (US Department of State, 4 November 2019b). Since 2017, the United States, Australia, Japan, and India have regularly met to consult on how the four countries could cooperate in the areas of security, infrastructure development, and disaster management (Ayres, 20 November 2018). Over 2017 to 2018, senior officials at the assistant secretary level from the four countries attended three US–Australia–India–Japan Consultations (Ayres, 20 November 2018). In September 2019 the four countries conducted their first ministerial-level meeting of the Quadrilateral dialogue (US Department of State, 4 November 2019a). The growing collaboration between the United States, Australia, India, and Japan to advance a "free and open" Indo-Pacific informed Indonesia's decision to promote its own concept of the Indo-Pacific cooperation (see Priatna, 21 March 2019).

Indonesia and China

The notion of a free, open, and inclusive Indo-Pacific points to the need to draw all countries in the region into the Indo-Pacific regional process including China. By including China in the Indo-Pacific regional process, Indonesia seeks opportunities to encourage transparency in China (see Ba 2003: 629). As part of its policy line, Indonesia has carefully crafted its Indo-Pacific cooperation concept to remain inclusive and therefore, to avoid any move to exclude China. However, China's behavior in the South China Sea, a key shipping route and fishing ground in the region, is a major challenge for the Indo-Pacific. China's behavior there has directly stimulated Indonesia's growing resistance. In a number of incidents, China's increasing coordination and physical support between its maritime agencies and fishermen in the South China Sea has led to friction with Southeast Asian countries, including Indonesian maritime authorities (Pitlo, 2013). From 2007 to 2015, the Indonesian maritime agencies arrested 31 China-flagged vessels (Indonesian Ministry of Marine and Fishery Affairs, 2015). In 2010, a Chinese naval vessel confronted an Indonesian patrol boat and demanded the release of a Chinese trawler that had fished illegally in Natuna waters. This incident was widely reported by the media. An Indonesian official claimed that at least three such incidents between Indonesia's maritime authorities and its Chinese counterparts took place in 2010 alone. In 2013, armed Chinese vessels compelled an Indonesian maritime and fisheries ministry patrol boat to release Chinese fishermen apprehended in Natuna waters (Reuters, 26 August 2014). Similar incidents that led to naval stand-offs in the Natuna waters also took place in 2016. Most recent, a sustained spate of illegal fishing by Chinese fishing vessels under the protection of China's Coast Guard from December 2019 until January 2020 led Indonesia to make a firm stance against China (CNN, 4 January 2020a). Responding to what Indonesia viewed as China's violation of Indonesia's sovereign rights in January 2020, Retno L. Marsudi, claimed that "Indonesia will never recognise nine dash lines, unilateral claims made by China that do not have legal reasons recognised by international law, especially UNCLOS 1982" (CNN, 4 January 2020b). Indonesia has put in place a range of policies to assert itself against China. These policies resulted in the scuttling of 71 foreign vessels including some Chinese flagged vessels to commemorate Indonesia's 71 years of independence in August 2016, and the renaming of the northernmost part of its EEZ in the South

China Sea as the North Natuna Sea in July 2017 (Kompas, 1 August 2016; Reuters, 14 July 2017). In January 2020 Indonesia invited Japan to invest in the construction of the Integrated Maritime and Fisheries Centre, and the development of fishermen capacity building and tourism in the Natuna islands (Kompas, 10 January 2020). In January 2020, the Indonesian Coordinating Ministry for Maritime Affairs, Luhut Pandjaitan, also announced Indonesia's plan to purchase an ocean-going vessel of 138–140 meters length to strengthen the Indonesian Maritime Security Board patrol operation in the North Natuna Sea, to equip the Indonesian coast guard, and to develop a naval base and a coast guard unit base in the Natuna islands (CNN, 4 January 2020c).

Indonesia and the Pacific and Indian Oceans

Under Jokowi's leadership the government has shown renewed interest in the Pacific region and the Indian Ocean. The vision to strengthen the Indonesian position in the Indo-Pacific featured in Jokowi's election manifestos of 2014 and 2019. His re-election manifesto published in 2018 noted the need to "enhance Indonesia's position as an archipelagic country situated between two oceans and continents through maritime diplomacy in Indian Ocean Rim Association (IORA) and Indo-Pacific" (Widodo and Amin 2018: 27). Indonesia's regional activism in the Pacific is proved by its participation in and leadership of a number of initiatives including the Coral Triangle Initiative, the Melanesian Spearheaded Group, the Southwest Pacific Dialogue, the Pacific Island Forum, and the Pacific Island Development Forum (Scott 2019: 196). Indonesia's leadership could be seen in the establishment of the Southwest Pacific Dialogue that was first held in Yogyakarta, Indonesia, in October 2002. It is an annual dialogue forum for Australia, the Philippines, Indonesia, Papua New Guinea, New Zealand, and East Timor to exchange views and discuss important issues in the region. Despite the issue of Indonesia's control over Papua, which was seen as an issue by members of the Melanesian Spearheaded Group, Indonesia has maintained observer status in this group since 2011. Indonesia has also obtained dialogue status with the Pacific Island Forum in 2001 and observer status with the Pacific Island Development Forum in 2013 (Scott 2019: 197).

In the Indian Ocean, the IORA has been named as an essential priority for the Indonesian government. Indonesia took the leadership position of

IORA in 2016. During its leadership term, Indonesia has made significant contributions in the development of the Jakarta Concord, gaining approval for it at the IORA Council of Ministers in 2016, and organizing the first IORA Summit held in Jakarta in 2017. The Concord is an agreement between 22 member states of IORA to promote regional cooperation for a peaceful, stable, and prosperous Indian Ocean. Some of the areas of cooperation covered by the agreement include maritime safety and security, trade and investment, fisheries management, and disaster risk management. At a bilateral level, President Jokowi visited a number of countries in the Indian Ocean region including India and Iran in the first half of his first presidential term (Chacko and Willis 2018: 140). Improved cooperation between Indonesia and the Indian Ocean region does not necessarily achieve the economic goals that Indonesia has sought. There was no major breakthrough in terms of deeper economic relations or investment between Indonesia and countries in the region (Chacko and Willis 2018: 140). For instance, Indonesia's plan to export more crude palm oil to India has been hampered by India's import duties to protect its farmers (Chacko and Willis 2018). However, Indonesia's active role in approaching bilateral and regional cooperation in the Indian Ocean region should be viewed as its outreach strategy to provide a measure of credibility of Indonesia's Global Maritime Fulcrum vision (Chacko and Willis 2018; Weatherbee 2019).

Engagement with coastal states of the Indian Ocean provided Indonesia with opportunities to strengthen maritime security cooperation with major powers in the region such as India and achieve consensus to promote a "truly free, open, and inclusive" Indo-Pacific (Kaura 2018: 2). At the same time when Indonesia and India were declaring their agreement over the concept of free, open, and inclusive Indo-Pacific in May 2018, the leaders of the two countries agreed to step up defense and maritime cooperation. The two countries plan to develop a strategic Indonesian naval port and an economic zone at Sabang. The Sabang port has strategic importance because it is located close to the Strait of Malacca (Reuters, 30 May 2018). A week prior to the Indonesian and Indian heads of states meeting, Indonesia's Coordinating Minister for Maritime Affairs, Luhut Pandjaitan, pointed out that the existing port at Sabang, which is 40 meters (131 ft) deep, could be developed to accommodate both commercial vessels and submarines (Reuters, 30 May 2018). This could be regarded as evidence of Indonesia's growing resistance to China.

Conclusion

This chapter has shown that Indonesia's Indo-Pacific cooperation was derived from its Global Maritime Fulcrum vision and has been promoted by the Jokowi administration to improve maritime connectivity, to address problems posed by IUU fishing, and to ensure the peaceful settlement of disputes. By actively advocating the Indo-Pacific cooperation at various bilateral and regional forums, Indonesia aims to enhance the credibility of Indonesia's Global Maritime Fulcrum vision at the domestic and international levels. Indonesia's Indo-Pacific concept places ASEAN in the "driving seat" of the Indo-Pacific cooperation, to prevent the regional organization from being sidelined by rivalry between the United States and China while ensuring that every country, including China, is included. An analysis of both the Indonesian and the ASEAN Indo-Pacific cooperation concept shows a focus on advocating cooperation over non-controversial areas such as maritime crimes and connectivity. There is the expectation that cooperation in non-controversial areas can overtime evolve into an interlocking network of a regional system and therefore, lessen tensions in controversial areas such as security. The Indo-Pacific cooperation will continue to be important in Indonesia's foreign policy agenda in the years to come given its centrality in the Presidential Office and the Indonesian Foreign Ministry policy discourse. Despite portraying the Indian and Pacific Oceans as a single geostrategic theatre, the concept of the Indo-Pacific cooperation put forward by Indonesia is not overtly shaped by security features and the three key features that sit at the core are not security-related. They include the centrality of ASEAN in advancing cooperation; the emphasis on inclusivity to avoid excluding any major powers in the region; and cooperation over non-traditional maritime security issues such as maritime crimes and IUU fishing.

References

ABC News, "Indonesia and Vietnam Vessels Collide in South China Sea, 12 Detained," 29 April 2019. https://www.abc.net.au/news/2019-04-30/indonesia-and-vietnam-ships-collide-in-south-china-sea/11056752.

Acharya, Amitav. (1992). "Regional Military-Security Cooperation in the Third World: A Conceptual Analysis of the Relevance and Limitations of ASEAN (Association of Southeast Asian Nations)," *Journal of Peace Research* 29, pp. 7–21.

Acharya, Amitav. (1995). "A Regional Security Community in Southeast Asia?" *Journal of Strategic Studies* 18:3, pp. 175–200.
Antara, "ASEAN Expected to Adopt Indo-Pacific Concept in 2019," 16 November 2018. https://en.antaranews.com/news/120565/asean-expected-to-adopt-indo-pacific-concept-in-2019.
Anwar, Dewi Fortuna. (2020). "Indonesia and the ASEAN Outlook on the Indo-Pacific," *International Affairs* 96:1, pp. 111–129.
Arsana, Andi, "Is China A Neighbour to Indonesia," *The Jakarta Post*, 8 August 2011.
ASEAN, "Chairman's Statement of the 13th East Asia Summit, Singapore," 15 November 2018. https://asean.org/storage/2018/11/East_Asia_Summit_Chairman_Statement_Final.pdf.
ASEAN, "Chairman's Statement of the 14th East Asia Summit, Bangkok/Non Thaburi," 4 November 2019. https://asean.org/storage/2019/11/FINAL-Chairman-Statement-14th-EAS_CLEAN.pdf.
Astuti, Rini. (2017). "Protecting Our Sea—Marine Environmental Governance in the South China Sea." NTS Commentary. https://www.rsis.edu.sg/wp-content/uploads/2017/06/CO17112.pdf.
Australian Department of Defence, "Joint Statement on the Fifth Indonesia-Australia Foreign and Defence Ministers 2 + 2 Meeting," 16 March 2018. https://www.minister.defence.gov.au/minister/marise-payne/statements/joint-statement-fifth-indonesia-australia-foreign-and-defence.
Australian Department of Foreign Affairs and Trade, "The Indo-Pacific: Australia's Perspective," 29 April 2019. https://www.dfat.gov.au/news/speeches/Pages/the-indo-pacific-australias-perspective.
Ayres, Alyssa, "The Quad and the Free and Open Indo-Pacific," 20 November 2018, Council on Foreign Relations. https://www.cfr.org/blog/quad-and-free-and-open-indo-pacific. Accessed 8 May 2020.
Ba, Alice D. (2003). "China and ASEAN: Re-navigating Relations for a 21st Century Asia," *Asian Survey* 43: 4, pp. 622–647.
Bakorkamla. (2010). *Buku Putih Bakorkamla 2009*. Jakarta: Pustaka Cakra.
Carana. (2004). *Impact of Transport and Logistics on Indonesia's Trade Competitiveness*. http://www.carana.com/images/PDF_car/Indonesia%20Transport%20and%20Logistics%20Report.pdf. Accessed 20 January 2011.
Chacko, Priya and Willis, David. (2018). "Pivoting to Indo-Pacific? The Limits of Indian and Indonesian Integration." *East Asia* 35:2, pp. 133–148.
CNN, "U.S. Warship Sails Close to Chinese Artificial Island in South China Sea," 27 October 2015. http://edition.cnn.com/2015/10/26/politics/south-china-sea-islands-u-s-destroyer/.
CNN Indonesia, "China Ngotot Punya Hak dan Kedaulatan di Laut Natuna," 4 January 2020a. https://www.cnnindonesia.com/internasional/20200103194528-113-462273/china-ngotot-punya-hak-dan-kedaulatan-di-laut-natuna.

CNN Indonesia, "Jokowi soal Kapal China di Natuna: Tak Ada Kompromi," 4 January 2020b. https://www.cnnindonesia.com/nasional/20200104125555-20-462354/jokowi-soal-kapal-china-di-natuna-tak-ada-kompromi.

CNN Indonesia, "Demi Natuna, Luhut Sebut RI Bakal Beli Kapal Penjaga," 4 January 2020c. https://www.cnnindonesia.com/ekonomi/20200103203701-92-462293/demi-natuna-luhut-sebut-ri-bakal-beli-kapal-penjaga.

Coutrier, P.L. (1988). "Living on an Oil Highway." *Ambio* 17:3, pp. 186–188.

Dahuri, Rokhmin (2015), Menuju Indonesia Sebagai Poros Maritim Dunia, Bogor: Roda Bahari.

Djalal, Hasjim. (2009). "Indonesia's Archipelagic Sea Lanes," in *Indonesia Beyond the Water's Edge*. Singapore: Institute of Southeast Asian Studies.

Dzakwan, Muhammad Habib Abiyan, "Is This the Twilight of Indonesia's Global Maritime Fulcrum?" *The Diplomat*, 4 November 2019. https://thediplomat.com/2019/11/is-this-the-twilight-of-indonesias-global-maritime-fulcrum/.

Febrica, Senia. (2016). "Indonesia's Diplomatic and Security Responses," in *South China Sea Lawfare*. Taipei: South China Sea Think Tank and Taiwan Center for Security Studies, pp. 101–110.

Febrica, Senia and Sudarman, Suzie. (2018). "Analysing Indonesian Media and Government Representation of China." *British Journal of Chinese Studies* 8:2, pp. 89–119.

Ghosh, Amitav and Lobo, Aaron Savio, "Bay of Bengal: Depleted Fish Stocks and Huge Dead Zone Signal," *The Guardian*, 31 January 2017.

Giridharadas, Akshobh, "India's Role in the Great-Power Struggle Over the Indo-Pacific Region," *The National Interest*, 23 January 2020. https://nationalinterest.org/feature/indias-role-great-power-struggle-over-indo-pacific-region-116556.

Ho, Joshua. (2007). "Securing the Seas as a Medium of Transportation in Southeast Asia," in *The Security of Sea Lanes of Communication in the Indian Ocean Region*. Kuala Lumpur: Maritime Institute of Malaysia.

Indian Ministry of External Affairs, "Shared Vision of India-Indonesia Maritime Cooperation in the Indo-Pacific," 30 May 2018. https://www.mea.gov.in/bilateral-documents.htm?dtl/29933/Shared_Vision_of_IndiaIndonesia_Maritime_Cooperation_in_the_IndoPacific.

Indian Ministry of External Affairs, "Prime Minister's Keynote Address at Shangri La Dialogue," 1 June 2018. https://mea.gov.in/Speeches-Statements.htm?dtl/29943/Prime+Ministers+Keynote+Address+at+Shangri+La+Dialogue+June+01+2018.

Indonesian Cabinet Secretariat, "Inilah Prioritas Politik Luar Negeri Indonesia 5 Tahun Ke Depan," 8 January 2015. https://setkab.go.id/inilah-prioritas-politik-luar-negeri-indonesia-5-tahun-ke-depan/.

Indonesian Embassy in Bangkok, "Indonesia berhasil bawa resolusi maritime dan mengajak perangi IUU fishing untuk Asia-Pasifik," 2015. https://ex.

kemlu.go.id/bangkok/Buku/finalsiaranPers-MaritimdanIUUFishing_asof28 may.doc.

Indonesian Investment Coordinating Board. (2015). *Rencana Strategis Badan Koordinasi Penanaman Modal Tahun 2014–2019*. https://www.bkpm.go.id/images/uploads/ppid/file_upload/Rencana_Strategis_%28RENSTRA%29_BKPM_TA_2015_-_2019.pdf.

Indonesian Ministry of Communication and Informatics, "Kebijakan Nasional: Indonesia Poros Maritim Dunia," 25 February 2019. https://www.indonesia.go.id/narasi/indonesia-dalam-angka/ekonomi/indonesia-poros-maritim-dunia.

Indonesian Ministry of Communication and Informatics, "Menuju Poros Maritim Dunia," 2020. https://www.kominfo.go.id/content/detail/8231/menuju-poros-maritim-dunia/0/kerja_nyata.

Indonesian Ministry of Defence. (2008). *Defence White Paper*. Jakarta: Ministry of Defence.

Indonesian Ministry of Foreign Affairs. (2006). *Pertemuan Kelompok Ahli Membahas Aspek Strategis Diplomasi Kelautan Dalam Mendukung Pembangunan Nasional*. Jakarta: Indonesian MFA.

Indonesian Ministry of Foreign Affairs, "Search Result for Asia Pacific Keywords [Hasil Pencarian Kata Kunci Asia Pasifik]," 3 May 2020. https://kemlu.go.id/portal/id/search/asia%20pasifik.

Indonesian Minister of Foreign Affairs, "2019 Annual Press Statement of the Minister for Foreign Affairs of the Republic of Indonesia," 9 January 2019. https://www.en.indonesia.nl/gallery/download/send/5-speeches/14-2019-annual-press-statement-of-retno-lp-marsudi-minister-for-foreign-affairs.

Indonesian Ministry of Foreign Affairs, "Indonesian Foreign Minister Annual Press Statement 2020," 8 January 2020. https://kemlu.go.id/hanoi/en/news/4123/indonesian-foreign-minister-annual-press-statement-2020.

Indonesian Ministry of Marine and Fishery Affairs, "Rekapitulasi Kapal Hasil Tangkapan Kapal Pengawas Berdasarkan Kebangsaan Kapal," 19 March 2015. Jakarta: Indonesian Ministry of Marine and Fishery Affairs.

Indonesian Presidential Office. (2015). "Indonesia Sebagai Poros Maritim Dunia," 13 November 2015. www.presidenri.go.id/maritim/indonesia-sebagai-poros-maritim-dunia.html.

Intrafish, "Illegal Fishing in Bay of Bengal Threatens Resources," 7 March 2019. https://www.intrafish.com/news/516550/illegal-fishing-in-bay-of-bengal-threatens-resources.

Jakarta Post, "RI Should Seeks Better Realization in AIIB Projects," 2 May 2015.

Jakarta Post, "Indonesia Clams Vietnam for Disrupting Arrests," 27 February 2019. https://www.thejakartapost.com/seasia/2019/02/27/ri-slams-vietnam-for-disrupting-arrests.html.

Japan Ministry of Foreign Affairs, "The 14th East Asia Summit," 4 November 2019. https://www.mofa.go.jp/a_o/rp/page3e_001123.html.

Japan Ministry of Foreign Affairs, 27 August 2016. https://www.mofa.go.jp/afr/af2/page4e_000496.html.

Kaura, Vinay. (2018). "India-Indonesia Relations and Indo-Pacific Security." *Asia Pacific Bulletin* No. 437, pp. 1–2. https://www.eastwestcenter.org/publications/india-indonesia-relations-and-indo-pacific-security.

Kompas, "17 Agustus Nanti, Menteri Susi Siap Tenggelamkan 71 Kapal," 1 August 2016. https://money.kompas.com/read/2016/08/01/132454526/17.agustus.nanti.menteri.susi.siap.tenggelamkan.71.kapal.

Kompas, "Jokowi Gandeng Jepang Investasi di Kepulauan Natuna," 10 January 2020. https://www.kompas.tv/article/62433/jokowi-gandeng-jepang-investasi-di-kepulauan-natuna.

Laksmana, Evan, "Indonesia as "Global Maritime Fulcrum": A Post-Mortem Analysis," 8 November 2019. https://amti.csis.org/indonesia-as-global-maritime-fulcrum-a-post-mortem-analysis/.

Leong, Karl Lee Chee, "What to Expect from Indonesia's Indo-Pacific Push in 2020?" 6 March 2020. https://thediplomat.com/2020/03/what-to-expect-from-indonesias-indo-pacific-push-in-2020/.

Nagy, Stephen R., "Shifting into the Era of the Indo-Pacific," 12 December 2019. https://www.japantimes.co.jp/opinion/2019/12/12/commentary/japan-commentary/shifting-era-indo-pacific/#.Xq8UGahKjIV.

Natalegawa, Marty in *The Jakarta Post*, "An Indonesian Perspective on the Indo-Pacific," 20 May 2013. https://www.thejakartapost.com/news/2013/05/20/an-indonesian-perspective-indo-pacific.html.

Pew, "Illegal Fishing Costs Pacific Islands Millions Annually in Lost Tuna Revenue: New Reports Highlight Expensive Threat to Regions' Fisheries," 2 May 2016. https://www.pewtrusts.org/en/research-andanalysis/articles/2016/05/02/illegal-fishing-costs-pacific-islands-millions-annually-in-lost-tuna-revenue. Accessed 6 February 2021.

Pitlo (2013), "Fishing Wars: Competition for South China Sea's Fishery Resources," July 10. http://isnblog.ethz.ch/security/fishing-wars-competition-for-south-china-seas-fishery-resources.

Priatna, P.L.E [Diplomat at the Indonesian Ministry of Foreign Affairs], "Diplomasi Indonesia Merangkul Indo-Pasifik," 21 March 2019. https://news.detik.com/kolom/d-/diplomasi-indonesia-merangkul-indo-pasifik.

Reuters, "Asserting sovereignty, Indonesia Renames Part of South China Sea," 14 July 2017. https://www.reuters.com/article/us-indonesia-politics-map/asserting-sovereignty-indonesia-renames-part-of-south-china-sea-idUSKBN19Z0YQ.

Reuters, "Remote, Gas- Rich Islands on Indonesia's South China Sea Frontline," 26 August 2014. www.reuters.com/article/2014/08/26/us-southchinase

aindonesia-natuna-insigh-idUSKBN0GP1WA20140826#LPgJh1iqOzEe0gyz.97.

Reuters, "Indonesia, India to Develop Strategic Indian Ocean Port," 30 May 2018. https://www.reuters.com/article/indonesia-india/indonesia-india-to-develop-strategic-indian-ocean-port-idUSL3N1T11XL.

Scott, David. (2019). "Indonesia Grapples with the Indo-Pacific: Outreach, Strategic Discourse, and Diplomacy." *Journal of Current Southeast Asian Affairs* 38:2, pp. 194–217.

Tempo, "Ini Isi Pidato Kemenangan Jokowi-JK," 22 July 2014. https://pemilu.tempo.co/read/595082/ini-isi-pidato-kemenangan-jokowi-jk.

United States Department of the Homeland Security, "The National Strategy for Maritime Security," 20 September 2005. http://georgewbush-whitehouse.archives.gov/homeland/maritime-security.html.

United States Department of State, "A Free and Open Indo-Pacific: Advancing A Shared Vision," 4 November 2019a. https://www.state.gov/wp-content/uploads/2019/11/Free-and-Open-Indo-Pacific-4Nov2019.pdf.

United States Department of State, "U.S.-Australia-India-Japan Consultations ("The Quad")," 4 November 2019b. https://www.state.gov/u-s-australia-india-japan-consultations-the-quad-2/.

United States Energy Information Administration, "World Oil Transit Chokepoints: Malacca," 22 August 2012, http://www.eia.doe.gov/cabs/world_oil_transit_chokepoints/malacca.html.

Weatherbee, Donald E. (2019). "Indonesia, ASEAN, and the Indo-Pacific Cooperation Concept." ISEAS Perspective No. 47: pp. 1–9. https://www.iseas.edu.sg/images/pdf/ISEAS_Perspective_2019_47.pdf.

Widodo, Joko and Amin, Ma'ruf. (2018). "Menuruskan Jalan Perubahan untuk Indonesia Maju: Berdaulat, Mandiri, dan Berkepribadian Berlandaskan Gotong Royong: Visi Misi Ir. H. Joko Widodo dan Prof. Dr. K.H. Ma'ruf Amin." https://www5.jetro.go.jp/newsletter/jkt/2018/VISI%20MISI%20FINAL%2022%20SEPT%202018.pdf.

CHAPTER 15

ASEAN and Its Indo-Pacific Outlook

To Anh Tuan and Do Thanh Hai

INTRODUCTION

In June 2019, the Association of the Southeast Asian Nations (ASEAN) endorsed the ASEAN Outlook on the Indo-Pacific (AOIP) at its 34th Summit held in Bangkok, Thailand. This development was seen as important for a couple of reasons. First, it was ASEAN's long-awaited response to the emerging concept of the Indo-Pacific which has been adopted by the major powers. Second, the Outlook represents ASEAN's hard-won consensus on the adoption of Indo-Pacific concept despite the fact that it could irritate China. Indonesia took the initiative to push the grouping to discuss the concept since 2018 (Tham 2018). After one year, ASEAN managed to come up with the AOIP, which was an expression of ASEAN's collective position over the new geopolitics which has been played out in the region. It remained a question of how ASEAN could reach a consensus on the Outlook in view of its diverse interests and opinions. Over the last decade, ASEAN faced difficulties in forging a consensus on issues related to the great powers, especially in the maritime

T. A. Tuan · D. T. Hai (✉)
Diplomatic Academy of Vietnam, Hanoi, Vietnam
e-mail: haidt@dav.edu.vn

© The Author(s), under exclusive license to Springer Nature Switzerland AG 2021
L. Buszynski and D. T. Hai (eds.), *Maritime Issues and Regional Order in the Indo-Pacific*, Palgrave Studies in Maritime Politics and Security, https://doi.org/10.1007/978-3-030-68038-1_15

domain. In July 2012, for the first time in the group's history, ASEAN Foreign Ministers failed to reach a consensus on a joint communiqué after their annual meeting due to differing views on whether the Scarborough stand-off should be mentioned. This chapter tracks the emergence of the AOIP to explore the interests and motivations behind ASEAN efforts and deciphers the key message that ASEAN wanted to convey in the Outlook, and who should be the main audience. To this end, the chapter will answer three interrelated questions. What were ASEAN's interests in working out an Indo-Pacific vision? What were the points of contention and how could ASEAN as a grouping come up with a common position over them? What are the key points of the AOIP, and how have they reflected ASEAN's understanding of regional changes? It is equally important to analyze ASEAN's internal dynamics in the context of increased tensions among the major powers. It is argued that ASEAN was collectively concerned about its relevance in the context of rising geopolitical competition and about the possibility of being pressed into taking sides in US–China rivalry.

ASEAN Centrality

Since the end of the Cold War, ASEAN's focus has shifted from maintaining its existence to asserting its role in the regional affairs. When the conflict in Cambodia was settled, ASEAN became a pacifying force by extending membership to the Indochinese states and initiating a range of mechanisms to address regional issues. Regional observers also recognized ASEAN as "the glue that binds key actors together, either through direct membership or via regional structures such as the ASEAN + 1, ASEAN + 3, ASEAN Regional Forum (ARF), ASEAN Defence Ministers Meeting Plus (ADMM+), East Asia Summit (EAS) and Asia Pacific Economic Cooperation (APEC)" (quoted in Tan 2012). With the exception of the APEC, all these multilateral mechanisms put ASEAN at the center and adopted ASEAN rules and norms as their mode of operation. ASEAN asserted its central role in these regional structure by codifying the concept of "centrality." ASEAN officials use various terms to express centrality such as "leader," "driver's seat," "architect," or "institutional hub" of the regional processes and institutions as the core of Asia-Pacific regional architecture. ASEAN's 2008 Charter asserted the objective "to maintain the centrality and proactive role of ASEAN as the primary driving force in its relations and cooperation with its external partners in a regional architecture that is open, transparent and inclusive" (ASEAN 2008, p. 5). As Acharya put it, ASEAN centrality is not defined by a physical center, or locus of power, but two elements, acceptance and norms-setting. First, it places ASEAN at the core of the regional institutional structure, which served ASEAN's strategic interests "by ensuring the relevance of ASEAN in the post-Cold War world" (Acharya 2017, p. 273). They may distrust each other, but the major powers in the region, namely, China, the United States, Japan, and India, find and embrace ASEAN-led platforms as convenient places for communicating their strategic interests.

Second, ASEAN centrality is associated with the extension of ASEAN's core norms based on open regionalism and inclusivity. ASEAN promoted the "ASEAN way" including the sacred principles of sovereignty and non-intervention, informal exchanges, consensus decision-making, and incrementalism. It also sought inclusivity, which means the involvement of all major powers in the ASEAN-led processes for the sake of confidence-building and preventive diplomacy. As a result, key platforms such as the ARF, the EAS, and the ADMM+ were designed "to involve various partners in multilateral negotiations, providing a venue for compromise" (Mueller 2019, p. 190). ASEAN draws its regional legitimacy from its ability to act as key provider of inclusive arrangements while other actors are unable to do so. For almost three decades, ASEAN harbored the sense of being the legitimate leader of East Asian institutional building. Though little progress was made in resolving substantive disagreements, Southeast Asian elites viewed ASEAN as the center of the web of Plus One dialogues (with China, Japan, South Korea, Australia, India, New Zealand, and the United States) and the all major powers in the ARF and the EAS as evidence for ASEAN's central role. Katsumata argues that ASEAN has actively constructed a social environment and defines itself as the legitimate leader of East Asian community building (Katsumaya 2014, p. 248). This also explains why ASEAN gave the cold shoulder to Australian Prime Minister Kevin Rudd's proposal for Asia-Pacific Community in 2008 and ex-Japanese Prime Minister Yukio Hatoyama's East Asian Community in 2009 which had the potential of sidelining the existing ASEAN processes (Satu 2016; Dobell 2008).

Anxieties About a Polarized Region

Since early 2010, ASEAN faced new geopolitical headwinds which challenged its notion of centrality. The first and prominent challenge was the rise of China and increased tensions across maritime Southeast Asia. Much to some Southeast Asian countries' displeasure, China's rise was not peaceful as expected since it attempted to use its overwhelming military, political, and economic power to change the status quo in the East and South China Seas. Naturally, ASEAN was seen as the first and most appropriate venue to discuss the issue, and the South China Sea became a frequent topic for discussions in the annual ASEAN Foreign Ministers' meetings and its meetings with dialogue partners. The situation did not improve and worsened. The Philippines became frustrated with the lack of ASEAN support and in January 2013 decided to bring the issue to the Arbitral Tribunal of the law of the Sea. Since late 2013, China built up military facilities on 7 artificial islands it had constructed in the Spratlys, which enabled it to project power further south.

ASEAN proved itself incapable of dealing with the South China Sea issue, and rifts among ASEAN members surfaced and widened. While it can forge a consensus on general principles, ASEAN seemed unable to speak with one voice or mention China by name. Any strong push in ASEAN would result in a breakdown, as was the case of the ASEAN Ministerial Meeting (AMM) in Phnom Penh in July 2012 when it failed to produce a joint statement. Some ASEAN members were drawn closer to China as Beijing in 2013 launched its flagship One Belt, One Road, later changed to the Belt and Road Initiative (BRI). As one of the leading infrastructural development programs in the region, BRI operated in bilateral formats and did not overlap with the Master Plan for ASEAN Connectivity (MPAC). As a result, ASEAN credibility was crippled by its inability to maintain unity and to stabilize the maritime domain at its doorstep.

Partially as the result of this challenge, ASEAN saw regional politics spilling out of its purview. Frustrated with limited outcomes from ASEAN processes, external powers formulated strategies to counter China's expansionism, which gave significance to the concept of the Indo Pacific. In 2016, Japanese Prime Minister Abe announced the Free and Open Indo-Pacific (FOIP) strategy, which was aimed at securing a free and open maritime order. Australia also mentioned the concept of the Indo-Pacific in its defense and foreign policy white papers in 2016 and

2017, respectively; they called for respecting the existing rules and norms and the promotion of inclusive economic integration. However, the concept of the Indo-Pacific only gained regional traction as the United States adopted the Free and Open Indo-Pacific Strategy (FOIPS) under the Trump administration. Later, India and France also adopted this concept. Notably, all Indo-Pacific visions recognized ASEAN's centrality and pledged to further its core principles.

Despite positive overtones from Tokyo, New Delhi, Canberra, and Washington, the rise of the Indo-Pacific caused anxieties in the Southeast Asian capitals. There existed a fear that the inclusion of the Indian Ocean and the accentuated role of India would draw the center of gravity out of ASEAN. Former Malaysian Prime Minister Mahathir Mohamad commented that the concept of the region should not keep enlarging so that it would become like the United Nations (Tyler 2019). The ASEAN concern is about the diluting effect of the Indo-Pacific upon ASEAN. Pongsudhirak opined that the shift from the Asia-Pacific to the Indo-Pacific entails a shift from the economy to security and whether as an articulated strategy, or a vision, or just a prevalent geopolitical mindset, it underpinned the response to China's assertiveness and its BRI scheme. Accordingly, the US Indo-Pacific strategy (IPS) was short of a viable trade and investment component (Pongsudhirak 2019).

Tung and Mai, echoing some voices in Vietnam, raised three concerns. First, though expressed inclusive and non-confrontational language, the US FOIPS and China's BRI were naturally exclusive, forcing other countries to take sides. Second, they both recognized that the importance of ASEAN, FOIPS, and BRI might weaken ASEAN's cohesion and its central role. Such ad hoc arrangements are seen as a threat to the existing multilateral mechanisms such as the ARF, EAS, or ADMM+. Third, increased competition between the United States and China would prompt new dynamics and alignments across the region, which would overshadow ASEAN's activities (Tung and Mai 2019). There was the concern that the emergence of Indo-Pacific strategies with the formation and the revitalization of the Quadrilateral Security Dialogue, or the Quad in short (the strategic forum involving the United States, Japan, Australia, and India), would sideline ASEAN-led mechanisms, its centrality and unity (Chong 2018). In many ways, the term Indo-Pacific is often associated with increased power rivalry between the United States and China. These concerns about rising US–China geopolitical competition and its implications on ASEAN as a group and were noted across the region (Vermone 2019; Kausikan 2019).

ASEAN AND COMPETING INDO-PACIFIC VISIONS

It is noted that the United States, Australia, India, Japan, and France proposed their own Indo-Pacific visions. Those visions are similar in that they stress the importance of the Indo-Pacific in economic activity, connectivity, environment, and biodiversity. They all aim to build peace, stability, and prosperity for the Indo-Pacific by promoting the rules-based order, open markets, dialogue, cooperation, and peaceful settlement of disputes. However, they vary in terms of the scope of the Indo-Pacific as India, Japan, and France included East Africa in their understanding of the concept while the United States and Australia exclude the western area of the Indian Ocean. Australia focuses on investment, economic relations, and defense relations (Australian Government 2017, p. 38). India promotes economic and defense relations (Government of India—Ministry of External Affairs 2018). Japan emphasizes political cooperation, trade, infrastructure for connectivity, and contributions to peace and security through capacity-building, humanitarian assistance, and disaster relief (The Government of Japan 2019). France also wants to build ties with the region in defense economic relations, sciences, culture, language, and education (Directorate for Asia and Oceania 2018).

These Indo-Pacific visions have different views of the role of China. The US FOIPS does not rule out cooperation with China, but emphasizes that China must support the rules-based international order (Department of Defense 2019). Other countries stress the rule of law and freedom of navigation (except France which mentioned freedom of movement) in general terms, avoiding any specific reference to China. Japan values its relationship with China and its Free and Open Indo-Pacific Strategy is ambiguous about the role of China (Abe 2018). India, Australia, and France somewhat share the same belief that China's rise will affect the power balance of the Indo-Pacific. They want to engage constructively with both China and other powers in the Indo-Pacific (Government of India—Ministry of External Affairs 2018; Directorate for Asia and Oceania 2018; Australian Government 2017).

The different Indo-Pacific initiatives and China's BRI place opposing pressures on ASEAN. The United States has been the most active in encouraging ASEAN to align with its FOIPS strategy. It invested heavily in ASEAN, making it the largest recipient of US investment with a cumulative total of US$271 billion in 2018, more than the combination of US FDI in China and Japan. It helped ASEAN to counter threats from transnational crimes, cyber security, environmental security, and maritime security. The United States has been the most active in maintaining freedom of navigation and other lawful uses of the South China Sea and more vocal in urging all claimants including China to "resolve disputes peacefully, without coercion, and in accordance with international law" (Department of State 2019, p. 21). In its various statements, the United States supports ASEAN's efforts to maintain its centrality and encourages ASEAN to promote "a strong, rules-based architecture" for the Indo-Pacific region (Department of State 2019, p. 7).

Despite all this, the United States has not won the trust of ASEAN countries. The main reason is because ASEAN countries still see discrepancies between the United States' words and deeds. The United States promised a strong commitment to the region but President Donald Trump never attended an East Asia Summit (EAS). The United States said it was helping other countries; but it keeps asking regional allies to share the burden of military spending. The United States advocates a rules-based order; but its unilateral actions in the Middle East are difficult to justify, particularly in countries where Muslim people are majorities. The United States' insistence on not taking sides in the sovereignty disputes in the South China Sea makes some ASEAN claimants wary that it implicitly turns a blind eye to China's bullying of weaker countries. Japan, India, Australia, and France also put a premium on their relations with ASEAN in their Indo-Pacific plans. France aims to strengthen bilateral relations with ASEAN countries and the position of the European Union in the region. This would mean elevating the EU–ASEAN relationship to a strategic partnership, bringing the EU into the EAS, and negotiating trade and investment agreements (Directorate for Asia and Oceania 2018). Australia promotes its Indo-Pacific vision by strengthening bilateral relations with ASEAN members and supports "an increasingly prosperous, outwardly-focused, stable and resilient Southeast Asia" (Australian Government 2017, p. 55). In 2018, an ASEAN–Australia Special Summit was held to advance the two sides' shared interests and to strengthen their ties. Japan worked to strengthen relations with ASEAN by promoting "infrastructure development, trade and investment, and enhance business environment and human development, strengthening connectivity in ASEAN region" (The Government of Japan 2019, p. 1). In 2018, India outlined its Indo-Pacific vision and one year later, it proposed a more concrete plan, called the "Indo-Pacific Oceans Initiative," to strengthen the region's maritime security and promote trade, investment, freedom of navigation, overflight, sustainable development, and marine environment (Chaudhury 2019).

Japan, India, Australia, and France attracted some attention to their Indo-Pacific designs from ASEAN and in the 33rd ASEAN Summit, ASEAN leaders admitted that they had discussed initiatives proposed by external partners, including "concepts and strategies on the Indo-Pacific" (ASEAN 2018b). However, these visions have fallen short for ASEAN as these major powers committed only limited resources to them. India and France proposed their Indo-Pacific visions late in 2018 with little follow-up and India's "Indian-Pacific Oceans Initiative" proposed in 2019 has been paralyzed by the outbreak of the COVID-19 pandemic. In the meantime, ASEAN's centrality could be diluted if the center of gravity moves westward from the Pacific to the Indian Ocean. ASEAN and ASEAN-related meetings would be reluctant to discuss Indian Ocean issues which were previously covered by the Indian Ocean Rim Association (IORA) or the Bay of Bengal Initiative for Multi-Sectoral Technical and Economic Cooperation (BIMSTEC). ASEAN-led mechanisms, such as the EAS and ARF, may need to expand their membership to include the Indian-Ocean countries.

Meanwhile, ASEAN countries also have to deal with both pressures and incentives from China, which opposes these Indo-Pacific concepts (Chongkittavorn 2019). Beijing saw the US FOIPS as a "containment strategy" and did not want ASEAN to support it (Cheng 2018). China has increased relations with ASEAN in various areas including policy planning, security cooperation, trade and trade facilitation, infrastructure building, and people-to-people exchanges (ASEAN 2019b). In particular, China has tried to explore cooperation with ASEAN over the blue economy or the exploitation and preservation of the marine environment (although it has not been defined). It seeks to connect its BRI with the Master Plan on ASEAN Connectivity (MPAC) 2025 and the ASEAN Smart Cities Network (ASCN), which are ASEAN's spearheading efforts towards smart and sustainable urban development in the global context of rapid urbanization and environmental degradation. Though BRI projects face increasing resistance across the region because of their loan conditions, low quality, environmental problems, and conflicts with local people, they are seen as necessary as no alternative sources of funding are available for their infrastructural needs

However, the new situation also offers opportunities for ASEAN. Firstly, as Southeast Asia is situated at the heart of the Indo-Pacific continuum, all Indo-Pacific visions call for strengthening economic relations with ASEAN, highlighting its market of 600 million as an important economic powerhouse. Secondly, ASEAN is the most promising candidate to serve as the foundation of the Indo-Pacific region's political architecture. ASEAN has a well-established structure and ASEAN-led mechanisms such as the EAS and ARF include all the major powers in the Indo-Pacific. Other regional mechanisms, such as the IORA or BIMSTEC, do not. Thirdly, ASEAN has a rule-making role to play in the region. Absent from the COC negotiating table, the US and western powers have to rely on ASEAN to prevent developments which would threaten their interests in the South China Sea. On the other hand, China would find it hard to limit the US influence without the support of ASEAN. All these challenges and opportunities have prompted ASEAN to respond to the new strategic visions of the major powers and to assert its raison d'être.

ASEAN AND THE NEGOTIATION OF THE INDO-PACIFIC OUTLOOK

The Leading Role of Indonesia

Indonesia has a great interest in urging ASEAN to cope with the evolving regional architecture as it is the only country in Southeast Asia that geographically lies between the Indian Ocean and the Pacific. As it is the world's largest archipelagic country, Indonesia shows great interest in the management of the maritime domains to protect its national interests. The most recent example is the Global Maritime Fulcrum (GMF) proposed by President Joko Widodo (or Jokowi) in 2014, which was intended to strengthen Indonesia's maritime culture, maintain and manage sea resources and its maritime connectivity, its maritime diplomacy, and maritime defense power (Witular 2014). As Indonesia grows economically, it has become more enthusiastic as a middle power in promoting multilateral cooperation, rather than rivalry, in the Indo-Pacific region. Since the inception of ASEAN, Indonesia has played an important role in defining the Association's directions. Indonesia has been active in promoting ASEAN's cooperation, mediating intraregional conflicts and managing ASEAN's relations with external partners (Anwar 2020, p. 123).

Before the Indo-Pacific became a buzzword in 2017, Indonesia already proposed its own Indo-Pacific vision. In 2013, Foreign Minister Marty

Natalegawa envisioned "An Indonesian Perspective on the Indo-Pacific," which raised three challenges for the future, such as overcoming the trust deficit, resolving territorial claims, and managing the impact of climate change. He advocated "an Indo-Pacific wide treaty of friendship and cooperation," which emphasized confidence-building, the peaceful settlements of territorial disputes, and the common good (Natalegawa 2013). In ASEAN meetings, Indonesia promoted the idea of an Indo-Pacific treaty which was based on ASEAN's Treaty of Amity and Cooperation (TAC). The Chairman's Statement from ASEAN's 24th Summit in May 2014 and the Joint Communique of 47th ASEAN Ministerial Meeting in August clearly stated that ASEAN countries welcomed Indonesia's initiative and looked forward to further details. However, after coming to power and for the first few years in his presidency, President Joko Widodo tended towards a unilateral approach in foreign affairs and downplayed the role of ASEAN. In late 2017, Jakarta had second thoughts on ASEAN and became active again with its proposal for ASEAN's Indo-Pacific vision. Indonesia's Foreign Minister Retno Marsudi had a different approach than Marty Natalegawa. Marty's initiative for a regional treaty faced resistance from some countries; they wanted to know the detailed content of the treaty before they could accept it. To circumvent Marty's problem, Retno avoided the treaty proposal and adopted the Indo-Pacific Cooperation Concept.

Forging Consensus

Retno's ideas were first revealed to the public in her talk at a Jakarta based Centre for Strategic and International Studies (CSIS) in May 2018. Then she said that relations in the Indo-Pacific could be "open, transparent and inclusive, promoting the habit of dialogue, promoting cooperation and friendship, and upholding international law" and close connections between the Indian Ocean and the Pacific. She emphasized ASEAN's centrality and unity. Accordingly, ASEAN would have three main roles: enabling an environment for cooperation, addressing transnational security challenges, and creating a center of economic growth (Tham 2018). In August 2018, Indonesia officially tabled an 8-page draft of an Indo-Pacific Cooperation Concept for ASEAN. Retno introduced the idea to the Ministerial Meeting of the East Asia Summit also in August 2018. The content of the 8-page document presented to ASEAN in August 2018 was drawn from Retno's speech to the CSIS earlier. In addition, it proposed that cooperation in the Indo-Pacific would be carried out through the strengthened role of ASEAN-led mechanisms especially the East Asia Summit and connections with non-ASEAN mechanisms in the Indo-Pacific region. Indonesia's proposed areas of cooperation included maritime cooperation, infrastructure and connectivity, and sustainable development (Anwar 2020, p. 126). During 2018 and early 2019, Indonesia lobbied ASEAN countries to support this Cooperation Concept (Tham 2018; Weatherbee 2019).

Initially, ASEAN had reservations in regard to Indonesia's proposal. The Chairman's Statement of the 32nd ASEAN Summit held in Singapore in April 2018 had only one sentence referring to Indonesia's initiative which said ASEAN "looked forward to further discussion on recent initiatives, including the Indo-Pacific concept" (ASEAN 2018a). The Chairman's Statement of the 33rd ASEAN Summit, held in Singapore in November 2018, adopted a similar attitude when it noted that ASEAN leaders "discussed the initiative to develop ASEAN's collective cooperation in the Indo-Pacific region" (ASEAN 2018b). ASEAN's reluctance to accept the Indo-Pacific Cooperation Concept was for several reasons. First, it was feared that the term Indo-Pacific might have political connotations of an inclination towards the United States. Although a number of countries had used this term, some thought that China might show its displeasure if ASEAN embarked on a discourse of this term. Second, ASEAN's centrality might be undermined as the Indonesian proposal focuses on the EAS. Third, Indonesia's proposal did not mention economic cooperation, which is one of ASEAN's three pillars. And fourth, as a concept, the proposal appeared to have few follow-up or implementation mechanisms.

However, ASEAN countries later saw the proposal as a good way for the group to position itself in the region's changing political landscape. They share the need to strive for a region of peace, dialogue, and confidence-building while ASEAN maintains its centrality and unity in the evolving regional architecture. ASEAN started embracing Indonesia's draft and the negotiations proceeded rapidly and it drafted its Indo-Pacific document in a way unrelated to the US FOIPS. To this end, ASEAN changed the document's title to Outlook (instead of Concept) to show its vision for the future. ASEAN highlighted the objectives of the Outlook which were to facilitate the dynamic growth of the Indo-Pacific and emphasized the principles of cooperation. Apart from Indonesia's proposed principles, the ASEAN Outlook also underlined the importance of the Treaty of Amity and Cooperation in Southeast Asia (TAC), which bans the threat or use of force to settle disputes, and advocates "strategic trust and win-win cooperation in the region" (ASEAN 2019a). The negotiations proceeded slowly at the beginning. A few months before assuming the Chairmanship, Thailand encouraged Indonesia to flesh out ASEAN's future paths for peace and development sustainability. When ASEAN Foreign Ministers met informally in January 2019, Indonesia circulated a new draft and ASEAN senior officials were quick to improve it. Initially, Indonesia focused on maritime cooperation as the main form of Indo-Pacific cooperation, but ASEAN discussions widened the areas of cooperation. Thailand highlighted connectivity and sustainability and also strengthened the Outlook by adding the 3M principles—mutual respect, mutual trust, and mutual benefit. Brunei included economic cooperation and wanted to emphasize the maintenance of an open and fair economic system. Singapore incorporated in the Outlook its preferred agenda of the ASEAN Smart Cities Network and the Open Skies policy (Chongkittavorn 2019).

However, ASEAN also went over some bumps along the road of the negotiations. A week before the 34th ASEAN Summit in June 2019, Singapore still refused to sign the Outlook. Jakarta was frustrated as Singapore's intention was unclear. There were rumors that Singapore had its own concept of the Indo-Pacific and wanted to tilt ASEAN's Indo-Pacific vision towards the United States (Yuniar 2019). However, Singapore wanted to add freedom of navigation and overflight to the principles of the Outlook. Furthermore, Malaysia, Cambodia, and the Philippines also wanted to make some adjustments to deal with these issues before the ASEAN Summit. Singapore's call for a Senior Official Meeting (SOM), to assist the work of the Foreign Ministers, was a logical step (Mun 2019). As a compromise, freedom of navigation and overflight was included in the section on maritime cooperation (ASEAN 2019a). The ASEAN Outlook on the Indo-Pacific (AOIP) was adopted at the 34th ASEAN Summit held in Thailand in June 2019, making it one of the fastest-negotiated documents in ASEAN (Chongkittavorn 2019).

Although the AOIP has the term Indo-Pacific in its title, it is not another version of the US FOIPS. It was born "consistent with decades of ASEAN's role in developing and shaping regional architectures in Southeast Asia and beyond" (ASEAN 2019a). It is based on principles that ASEAN has held dear for a long time, including ASEAN's centrality, openness, transparency, a rules-based framework, mutual respect, mutual trust, and respect for international law. The AOIP holds to the Treaty of Amity and Cooperation in Southeast Asia (TAC). "Freedom" as mentioned in the AOIP is placed in the context of "the maintenance of peace, freedom, and prosperity" and the principle of respect for sovereignty and non-interference in the next paragraph. Therefore, "freedom" in the AOIP implies interstate relations and is different from "freedom" in the US FOIPS, which has both international and domestic implications (Hoang 2019). The AOIP is an effort by ASEAN to maintain its centrality in the evolving political landscape. By adopting the AOIP, ASEAN has revealed its attitude towards and its position on major power rivalry. ASEAN expresses its view that the Indian and the Pacific oceans should be areas of dialogue and cooperation, and not rivalry. However, the AOIP has some weaknesses as it is just a vision. It is not legally binding, particularly on non-ASEAN countries, it does not have a defined structure nor financial resources for its implementation.

The Meaning of AOIP in Maritime Security

Maritime issues make up an important part of the AOIP. The Outlook affirms that one of its key elements is "the importance of the maritime domain and perspective in the evolving regional architecture." The UN Convention on the Law of the Sea (UNCLOS) is a foundation of maritime cooperation, which the Outlook mentions twice in the sections on principles and areas of maritime cooperation. The Outlook also mentions four areas of cooperation, namely, maritime cooperation, connectivity, UN Sustainable Development 2030, and economic and other possible areas of cooperation. To promote maritime cooperation, the Outlook identifies existing and emerging maritime challenges including geopolitics, unresolved maritime disputes, unsustainable exploitation of maritime resources, and maritime pollution. It notes areas of maritime cooperation that can be further enhanced. The Outlook categorizes four groups of maritime cooperation areas, including conflict settlement and safety at sea, marine resources and coastal community, protection of marine environment, and scientific marine research and cooperation.

The AOIP is the first document adopted by ASEAN leaders which has a separate section on maritime cooperation, to which it has made a significant contribution. First, it emphasized the importance of the maritime domain, and maritime cooperation was placed first before connectivity and others. Second, ASEAN makes clear that it aims to move towards maritime cooperation but not confrontation or rivalry. ASEAN affirms that the way to manage and solve maritime issues is through a "more focused, peaceful, and comprehensive way." Third, the Outlook reveals a comprehensive approach to maritime cooperation when it states that the Indo-Pacific region is not "contiguous territorial spaces" but "a closely integrated and interconnected region." This implies that the Indo-Pacific is tied together in a borderless-maritime space. Maritime threats come not only from military and paramilitary actors, but also from other maritime activities like illegal fishing or environmental destruction. Areas of maritime cooperation include not only dispute settlement, but also cooperation on economic activities, environmental protection, scientific research, and development. Fourth, ASEAN emphasizes principles for dispute settlements and cooperation, and stresses the importance of the UNCLOS by mentioning it twice in the sections of both principles and areas of cooperation. This position will be an important foundation for ASEAN to consolidate its unity in the negotiation of the Code of Conduct (COC) for the South China Sea and the settlement of disputes. And fifth, the AOIP stresses the role of ASEAN-led mechanisms, though it does not intend to create new mechanisms, but relies on ASEAN-led structures including the East Asia Summit (EAS), ASEAN Regional Forum (ARF), ASEAN Defence Ministerial Meeting Plus (ADMM+), the Expanded ASEAN Maritime Forum (EAMF), and others.

Conclusion

In a snapshot, the creation of the AOIP is an indication that ASEAN has adapted and responded to the new strategic landscape. From an organization which mainly attempted to promote relations among the members, ASEAN expanded its membership and wielded more influence over regional politics in a relatively favorable security environment in the post-Cold War period. ASEAN played a central role in creating a range of regional mechanisms that attracted the participation of the major powers. However, ASEAN's credibility as the core of regional security structures was challenged when China became more assertive in the South China Sea, the East China Sea, and the Indian Ocean. China's heavy-handed approach in the maritime domain and the expansion of its economic footprint across the region has divided ASEAN into different camps. ASEAN has been also put between a rock and a hard place as the major powers have prompted new alignments under the new geopolitical construct of Indo-Pacific to cope with the rise of China. Increasingly, ASEAN has been compelled to articulate its own visions vis-à-vis new strategic trends for the purpose of showing cohesiveness and avoiding taking sides while retaining some degree of relevance in new political environment. Indonesia's activism played a central role in forging a consensus on the Outlook, which speaks less about geopolitics but reaffirms ASEAN's key principles and its institutional platforms for inclusive cooperation. The AOIP serves as a symbolic manifestation of the group's aspirations rather than a concrete pathway to achieve specific outcomes. For ASEAN, the process is sometimes more important than the outcome.

REFERENCES

Abe, S. (2018) Address by Prime Minister Abe at the Seventy-Third Session of the United Nations General Assembly. Available at: https://www.mofa.go.jp/fp/unp_a/page3e_000926.html.

Acharya, A. (2017) The Myth of ASEAN Centrality? *Contemporary Southeast Asia*, 39(2), 273–279.

Anwar, D.F. (2020) Indonesia and the ASEAN Outlook on the Indo-Pacific. *International Affairs*, 96(1), 111–129.

ASEAN (2008) The ASEAN Charter, ASEAN Secretariat.

ASEAN (2018a) Chairman's Statement of the 32nd ASEAN Summit.

ASEAN (2018b) Chairman's Statement of the 33rd ASEAN Summit.

ASEAN (2019a) ASEAN Outlook on the Indo-Pacific. Available at: https://asean.org/storage/2019/06/ASEAN-Outlook-on-the-Indo-Pacific_FINAL_22062019.pdf.

ASEAN (2019b) Chairman's Statement of the 22nd ASEAN-China Summit.

Australian Government (2017) 2017 Foreign Policy White Paper.

Chaudhury, D. (2019) India's Indo-Pacific Ocean's Initiative Aims Maritime Security Pillar for Inclusive Region. *The Economic Times*, 21 November 2019 [online]. Available at: https://economictimes.indiatimes.com/news/defence/indias-indo-pacific-oceans-initiative-aims-maritime-security-pillar-for-inclusive-region/articleshow/72153070.cms.

Cheng, D. (2018), What China Thinks of the Indo-Pacific Strategy. *The Diplomat*, 27 April 2018. Available at: https://thediplomat.com/2018/05/what-china-thinks-of-the-indo-pacific-strategy/.

Chongkittavorn, K. (2019) ASEAN Sets Sail with Its Indo-Pacific Vision. VERA Files, 22 September [online]. Available at: https://verafiles.org/articles/asean-sets-sail-its-indo-pacific-vision.

Department of Defense (2019) Indo-Pacific Strategy Report: Preparedness, Partnerships, and Promoting a Networked Region.

Department of State (2019) A Free and Open Indo-Pacific: Advancing a Shared Vision.

Directorate for Asia and Oceania (2018) French Strategy in the Indo-Pacific 'For an Inclusive Indo-Pacific'.

Dobell, G. (2008), Asia Pacific Community: An Idea, an Envoy and ASEAN. The Interpreter, 15 October 2008. Available at: https://archive.lowyinstitute.org/the-interpreter/asia-pacific-community-idea-envoy-and-asean.

Government of India—Ministry of External Affairs (2018) Prime Minister's Keynote Address at Shangri La Dialogue. Available at: https://www.mea.gov.in/Speeches-Statements.htm?dtl/29943/Prime+Ministers+Keynote+Address+at+Shangri+La+Dialogue+June+01+2018.

Hoang, T.H. (2019) ASEAN Outlook on the Indo-Pacific: Old Wine in New Bottle? *ISEAS: Perspective*, 51(2019).

Katsumaya, H. (2014), What Explains ASEAN's Leadership in East Asian Community Building? *Pacific Review*, 87(2), 247–264.

Kausikan, B. (2019) *ASEAN and US-China Competition* (Ron Huisken, Ed.). CSCAP Regional Security Outlook 2019, 37–40.

Mueller, L. M. (2019). ASEAN Centrality Under Threat—The Cases of RCEP and Connectivity. *Journal of Contemporary East Asia Studies*, 8(2), 177–198.

Mun, T.S. (2019) Asean Found Its Voice with the Indo-Pacific Concept. Now It Has to Use It or Risk Losing Out. *South China Morning Post*, 24 June [online]. Available at: https://www.scmp.com/week-asia/geopolitics/article/3015809/asean-found-its-voice-indo-pacific-concept-now-it-has-use-it.

Natalegawa, M. (2013)An Indonesian Perspective on the Indo-Pacific. *The Jakarta Post*, 20 May [online]. Available at: https://www.thejakartapost.com/news/2013/05/20/an-indonesian-perspective-indo-pacific.html.

Natalegawa, R.M.M. (2017) The Expansion of Asean and the Changing Dynamics of Southeast Asia. *Contemporary Southeast Asia*, 39(2), 232–238.

Pongsudhirak, T. (2019). Is the Indo-Pacific Eclipsing Asia-Pacific? *Bangkok Post*, 2 August 2019. Available at: https://www.bangkokpost.com/opinion/opinion/1722875/is-the-indo-pacific-eclipsing-asia-pacific-.

Satu, L. (2016). Why ASEAN Is Here to Stay and What That Means for the US. *The Diplomat*, 30 August 2018. Available at: https://thediplomat.com/2016/08/why-asean-is-here-to-stay/.

Tan, S. (2012). *CSCAP Regional Security Outlook 2013* (pp. 26–29, Rep.) (Ball D., Milner A., Sukma R., and Wanandi Y., Eds.). Council for Security Cooperation in the Asia Pacific, 26–29.

Tham, J. (2018) What's in Indonesia's Indo-Pacific Cooperation Concept? *The Diplomat*, 16 May 2018. Available at: https://thediplomat.com/2018/05/whats-in-indonesias-indo-pacific-cooperation-concept/.

The Goverment of Japan (2019) Towards Free and Open Indo-Pacific. Available at: https://www.mofa.go.jp/files/000407643.pdf.

Tung, N.V and Mai, N.T.Q. (2019) *Vietnamese Perspectives on the Current Strategic Landscape* (Ron Huisken, Ed.). CSCAP Regional Security Outlook 2019, 30–33.

Tyler, M. C. (2019) The Indo-Pacific is the New Asia. *The Interpreter*, 28 June 2019. Available at: https://www.lowyinstitute.org/the-interpreter/indopacific-new-asia.

Vermone, P. (2019) *U.S-China Competition and ASEAN: A View from Jakarta* (Ron Huisken, Ed.). CSCAP Regional Security Outlook 2019, 24–26.

Weatherbee, D.E. (2019) Indonesia, ASEAN, and the Indo-Pacific Cooperation Concept. *ISEAS: Perspective*, 47(2019).

Witular, R.A. (2014) Presenting Maritime Doctrine. *The Jakarta Post*, 14 November.

Yuniar, R.W. (2019) Indonesia Reveals Frustration with Singapore over Delay in Asean Adopting President Joko Widodo's Indo-Pacific Concept. *South China Morning Post*, 16 June [online]. Available at: https://www.scmp.com/news/asia/southeast-asia/article/3014651/vision-impaired-singapore-deliberately-delaying-indonesian.

Conclusion: Geographical Connectedness and Conceptual Discrepancy

The concept of Indo-Pacific has gained greater prominence gradually over the old construct, the Asia-Pacific. Interestingly, the term Asia-Pacific emerged in the 1980s and has been, by and large, associated with trade liberalization and regionalism. The term Indo-Pacific is defined more in security terms, and with a stronger focus on maritime order. Escalating tensions around the territorial and maritime disputes in the East and South China Sea, mostly prompted by Chinese increased assertiveness, have been the key drivers. Since 2009, overlapping claims and contradicting positions have not been confined to diplomatic forums and social media but also evolved into serious stands-off and incidents at sea. The likelihood of armed conflict has increased significantly as naval vessels from different claimants are engaged in shadowing or confronting each other. Concerns about changing rules in the maritime space underpin new strategic thinking under the Indo-Pacific nomenclature. Simmering tensions in the East China and South China Seas featured significantly in the rise of Indo-Pacific concept. New strategic dynamisms have been played out in the maritime domain neighboring the Asia continent. In the mid-2000s, the key question for academic and politicians in the Asia-Pacific was whether China would rise peacefully. It was feared that a China occupied in amassing significant military and economic power would resort to force to change the status quo over the disputed territories in its peripheries. As it unfolded overtime, this fear became reality.

© The Editor(s) (if applicable) and The Author(s), under exclusive license to Springer Nature Switzerland AG 2021
L. Buszynski and D. T. Hai (eds.), *Maritime Issues and Regional Order in the Indo-Pacific*, Palgrave Studies in Maritime Politics and Security, https://doi.org/10.1007/978-3-030-68038-1

However, large-scale armed conflicts have not occurred; China has, one way or another, incrementally sought domination over strategic waterways. It has tried to achieve it less by confronting the US directly, than by leveraging its smaller neighbors to accept Chinese claims and rules. Against this backdrop, the emerging Indo-Pacific visions have been, by and large, a region-wide response to China's rise and its attempts to impose new rules in the region. The causes for new regional dynamisms have been analyzed in the book's chapters. The motion for change was perhaps put in place since the mid-2000s.

Based on recent developments, Greg Poling has noted that the South China Sea is moving to a "new phase of coercion" in which China has confidently raised the risks of operating in the South China Sea to unacceptable levels for other claimants, whether engaging in surveying and exploiting hydrocarbon reserves or fishing. The infrastructure and facilities erected on the Spratly reefs and shoals have enabled China's coast guard to bolster its surveillance capacity and have increased its operational range and resilience. Cases in point are Chinese coastguard's interference with Vietnam and Malaysia's energy development in their Exclusive Economic Zones in 2019 and 2020, respectively, showing that Beijing does not tolerate new drillings, even in the existing concessions. The Chinese maritime militia, which is the force in the shadow of the commercial entities, also engages in acts of intimidation when needed. In doing so, it forces Southeast Asian claimants into a stark choice: accept China-proposed joint exploitation of resources in their own Exclusive Economic Zones or face coercive actions. Beijing has blunted international criticisms by increased bilateral engagement with the Philippines, and renewed talks with ASEAN on the code of conduct in the South China Sea. In doing so, China has gained ground vis-à-vis other claimants and also other great powers.

Yoji Koda observed that China aims to dominate the sea area within the first island chain in the Western Pacific, which includes the South China Sea, through deliberate pursuit of its anti-access and area denial (A2AD) strategy. This intention is revealed by China's massive build-up of anti-ship ballistic missiles, hypersonic anti-ship/land-attack missiles, submarine forces, offensive sea-bed mines, together with anti-satellite, cyber-attack capabilities to keep the United States out of local areas including the Western Pacific, the South China Sea, and eastern part of the Indian Ocean. The PLA-N also harbors blue water navy ambitions and develops large surface combatants, including aircraft carriers, and logistical support capabilities to operate in distant regions. Thanks to this build-up, Koda argues that China has overwhelming power over any single neighbor in its near seas and even has vis-à-vis the United States in its near seas. That has provided a greater incentive for the United States, Japan, and other regional actors to address such imbalances by developing capabilities to neutralize China's militarized artificial islands in the South China Sea. Those capabilities include networked maritime domain awareness across the island chain, and controls over the checkpoints that link East Asian Seas to the outer spaces in the Indian and Pacific Oceans.

However, concerns about East Asian maritime security are not limited to the strategic imbalance. Both Martin Sebastian and Greg Poling in their chapters pointed to China's gray zone operations at sea and its subtle maneuvers in the diplomatic sphere to weaken the existing maritime order. Sebastian argues that Beijing uses the unlawful nine-dash line claim to seek both strategic domination and control of maritime resource development in the South China Sea. China's "cunning tactic" is to use "white hulls," or law enforcement vessels, as a foreign policy tool. Backed by the militia and the navy and equipped with big and sturdy ships, this force has been at the frontline to push China's claim and harass vessels from other countries, subduing other contestants with some level of violence but without smoking guns. As Sebastian argues, it is just matter of time that the pattern of China's behavior in the South China Sea would spread into the Indian and Pacific Oceans.

Despite different interpretations of China's intentions, its assertiveness has not only created a "new normal" in the maritime domain, but also somehow changed regional politics. Marites Vitug focuses on the specific case of the Philippines and argues that Beijing's coercive tactics temporarily put Manila down the road of appeasement. Once a close ally of the United States, the Philippines under President Rodrigo Duterte has avoided raising the award of the South China Sea Arbitral Tribunal of 12 July 2016 and has engaged China bilaterally. Duterte had the hope that he could reap the benefits from economic relations with China, particularly the Belt and Road Initiative. It is also quite important to note that external powers are also aware of China's strategic intentions but are short on concrete action to challenge China directly. As Nicola Casarini argued, European powers were aware of China's challenges to the maritime rules-based order, even being alarmed by the fast pace of China's maritime expansion. However, their interventions did not go beyond normative approaches and the occasional show of presence in the South China Sea.

More interestingly, Carl Thayer's thorough analysis of five case studies, including the 45th ASEAN Ministerial Meeting (July 2012), the Third ADMM Plus Meeting (November 2015), the Special China–ASEAN Foreign Ministers Meeting (June 2016), the Mid-Term Meeting of the Non-Aligned Movement (April 2018), and the 32nd ASEAN Summit (April 2018), revealed that the existing ASEAN-led multilateral arrangements failed to moderate China's assertive behavior in the South China Sea disputes and mitigate power rivalry. The main reason is that these mechanisms rest on consensus-based decision-making, which often makes it very difficult for a group of small- and medium-sized countries to forge a strong common position and develop effective enforcement mechanisms to punish non-compliance. China's assertive interferences have divided ASEAN and crippled other multilateral forums when it comes to contentious issues. These case studies are indicative of the relatively inconsequential effect of multilateralism in dealing with the strategic interests of great powers.

New geopolitics in the maritime domain has resulted in rising distrust and tensions among the claimants and the major powers. The most affected has been the marine environment and ecosystems which are a common natural heritage. Nguyen Chu Hoi argues that the territorial and maritime disputes and deteriorating security environment prevent countries from cooperating to protect the marine ecology and environment. For example, China's land reclamation in the Spratlys had devastating effects on fish stock and marine ecosystems, which gave affected the lives of millions of people in the surrounding coastal communities. Destructive fishing practices are also a critical threat to the ecosystem generally and some marine species are on the brink of extinction. Therefore, urgent actions are needed to address these non-traditional security challenges, which could include the promotion of multi-stakeholder regional-wide cooperation on the basis of international law.

A similar pattern of behavior was also seen in the East China Sea, which has rattled the status quo there. As presented, this area hosts a range of disputes over the ownership of Senkaku/Diaoyu Islands, the legal status of offshore islands and their role in maritime boundary delimitation, and the maritime boundary in the undelimited area. According to Yann-huei Song, despite some signs of improvement in bilateral relations between Japan and China, their disputes have deteriorated because of China's unilateral actions over 2015–2019. Japan voiced concerns about and criticisms of China's unilateralism, particularly the increased presence of the latter's coast guard in the waters off the Senkaku Islands, its hydrocarbon drilling activities in the area Japan claimed as the median line, the operation of Chinese research vessels in the EEZ off *Okinotorishima*, and the creation of an Air Defense Identification Zone (ADIZ) in the area. Tomotaka Shoji argues that Beijing also intensified naval and aerial activism over the Senkaku area, putting the Japanese Self-Defense Force on high alert and prompting Tokyo to look beyond. From the Japanese point of view, the situations in South China Sea and East China Sea are closely connected with each other, and also linked to the peace and stability of Indo-Pacific region. In other words, it is not just about the security of the critical energy supply routes going through the South China and East China Seas, but more about the overall regional order based on existing rules. Of course, that view is not always shared by Chinese scholars. A case in point is Cao Qun's argument that China's establishment of the ADIZ in the East China Sea did not deviate from the practices of the United States and other countries.

History shows that control of the oceans is the pathway to hegemony. The ancient Roman empire (27 BC–476 AD) rose to preponderance because of its mastery of the Mediterranean Sea, which was a vital trade link between Europe, the Middle East, and North Africa. The British Empire of the eighteenth and nineteenth centuries dominated a vast swathe of territories across the globe because its great navy enabled it to control the Atlantic and Indian Oceans. After the Second World War, the United States became the greatest power on earth as it was able to dominate both Atlantic and Pacific Oceans. As the seas cover three-quarter of the world surface, and serve as main arteries for trade, their control is matter of necessity for any state which aspires to join the ranks of the global powers. For that reason, China's acquisition of massive naval power and its attempts to dominate its near seas have attracted significant strategic attention. The idea of the Indo-Pacific, which is the maritime continuum linking Africa, the Middle East to East Asia and beyond, emerged in the mid-2000s. However, it did not take hold in regional strategic thinking until the mid-2010s when China's assertiveness became a "new normal" across the East Asian maritime domain. As the traditional actor in the region, Japan was among the most enthusiastic advocate of "the confluence of the two oceans." According to Toshiya Takahashi, Japan's initiative for a Free and Open Indo-Pacific puts a premium on upholding norms such as freedom of navigation, the rule of law, free trade, and cooperative maritime security. Not intending to prepare for a military confrontation with China, Japan seeks to use these norms to constrain it and enhance the regional countries' maritime capabilities and bolster their autonomy as a way to resist its coercion. To this end, Tokyo also employed multilateral dialogue, joint exercises, and support for capability-building in countries on the front line vis-à-vis Chinese expansion. From the Japanese point of view, the Indo-Pacific works as a framework for cooperation on the basis of norms, so it is not necessary to exclude China. China can join such cooperation as long as it accepts those norms.

The US Indo-Pacific vision as articulated by Trump in Vietnam in November 2017 and subsequently in various strategic documents, the National Security Strategy and the National Defense Strategy built upon the premise that China is a "revisionist power," a "rival," an "adversary," and a "competitor". As pointed out by Derek Grossman in his chapter, the main thrust of US strategy is to preserve the existing order through the idea of a "Free and Open Indo-Pacific," upon the basis of the principles of respect for each other's sovereignty and independence, peaceful resolution of disputes, free, fair and reciprocal trade, adherence to international rules and norms, including freedom of navigation and overflight. All these norms underpin the perceived rules-based order and stand in contrast to China's coercive and dominating behavior. To this end, Washington has worked to consolidate its military power, to deepen ties with allies and partners to meet the challenges from China, to step up FONOPs and other activities in the South China Sea and nearby areas. Grossman argues that the main challenge to the United States in implementing its Indo-Pacific strategy is the gap between the rhetoric and actions and the transactional mindset of the Trump administration, which has caused confusion and anger among its key allies and partners. Despite this the US idea of the Indo-Pacific is a work in progress, not yet a fixed and cohesive strategy.

India's Indo-Pacific vision reflects its ideal of a free, open, transparent, rules-based, peaceful, prosperous, and inclusive region and stresses the importance of international law as the main means of regulating relations among nations. Udai Bhanu Singh argues that India views the Indo-Pacific not merely as a geopolitical construct but as a naturally interconnected, interdependent region that extends from the shores of Africa to the shores of America. As such, the region is the crossroads of the world's maritime traffic. India views the seas and oceans as "critical enablers of our prosperity." However, India has two concerns. First is the long-term stability in the Indo-Pacific in the context of simmering tensions in the South China and East China Seas. Therefore, the issue of UNCLOS, including freedom of navigation and overflight, is of particular concern. Second, India is concerned about China's increasing influence through its Belt and Road Initiative, which is adversely affecting the former's relations with regional countries like Pakistan, Myanmar, and Indonesia. To address these concerns, India has moved beyond the ASEAN-centric Act East Policy to work with Indo-Pacific partners through bilateral and multilateral mechanisms, particularly Security and Growth for All in the Region (SAGAR) and the Quadrilateral Security Dialogue (the Quad) to achieve a free, open, transparent, and rules-based region.

Indonesia's shift from the Asia-Pacific to the Indo-Pacific reflects Jakarta's broadened geopolitical vision and its perceived role in the region. Senia Febrica explains that the Indonesian concept of the Indo-Pacific puts the emphasis on cooperation rather than competition and features three components: (i) ASEAN centrality as the driver of cooperation; (ii) inclusiveness; (iii) cooperation with a focus on non-traditional maritime security concerns. The adoption of the concept was driven by the fear of being increased great power rivalry and the desire to put Indonesia at the center of the Indo-Pacific through its Global Maritime Fulcrum initiative. Though worried about China's repeated intrusions into the Natuna Islands' waters, Jakarta did not attempt to exclude Beijing from regional cooperation as Jokowi's government has some hope for infrastructural investments from China. Therefore, it is expected that ASEAN-led inclusive cooperation on non-traditional maritime issues would create security networks which would then help reduce tensions.

Driven by Indonesia's active role, ASEAN started discussing the Indo-Pacific when the concept was adopted by the US President Donald Trump and became a point of convergence among those major powers which were frustrated by China's sustained assertiveness. As a grouping, ASEAN was interested in the concept for two reasons. First was the fear that ASEAN's centrality would be adversely affected. The rise of the Quad raised the concern that some major regional security issues would be discussed outside of the ASEAN forums. Second, given the fact that there had existed many Indo-Pacific definitions and visions, ASEAN wanted to reclaim the narrative and enhance its role in shaping the strategic discourse about regional order. As a result, ASEAN's Outlook on the Indo-Pacific (AOIP) is not about geopolitical alignments so much as the re-assertion of its self-perceived centrality and the primacy of its derivative institutions, such as the East Asian Forum (EAS), the ASEAN Regional Forum (ARF), and the ASEAN Defence Ministers Meeting Plus (ADMM+). It calls for inclusive cooperation on non-traditional security issues. In other words, the AOIP fits into ASEAN's tradition of open regionalism and consensus building.

It should be noted that the common theme among these five Indo-Pacific visions is the reference to international norms and a rules-based order. In addition, they all stressed the importance of infrastructural development and increased connectivity across separate geographical areas. Concerns about China's maritime assertiveness and its sustained efforts to disrupt the current order figure significantly in these visions. UNCLOS, including freedom of navigation and overflight, was highlighted in these texts. It is safe to say that almost all Indo-Pacific visions are intended to prevent China from establishing its hegemony in the region. However, these visions reflect different approaches as to how to meet the China challenge, and what kind of regional order should emerge in the future. On the one hand, the Indo-Pacific is a political term with value-oriented geopolitical designs. Though denying any intention of excluding China, the United States and Japan adopted an adversarial approach based on the idea of "free" and "open" as a way to highlight China's deceptive and coercive behavior. Such a definition naturally and implicitly excludes China from any type of cooperation where the United States and Japan take the lead. Sitting in the middle, India has attempted to hedge while engaging China and expanding partnerships with other countries to balance against China's increased influence. In spite of their unease with China's expansive maritime claims and intimidating actions, Indonesia and ASEAN have been reluctant to embrace value-based concepts and have worked to de-securitize the concept by stressing ASEAN as a key platform to drive inclusive cooperation on non-traditional security challenges. To be specific, India and ASEAN have advocated cooperation with China as a way to moderate its behavior while the United States under the Trump administration aims to contain it. It should be noted that Japan, India, and ASEAN show strong support for multilateralism, while the United States put the emphasis on bilateralism. All in all, the Indo-Pacific is less about natural geographic linkage but it is a political and strategic concept with a variety of preferences. While the concern about the rules-based order and international norms is common to all, the concept varies in terms of geographical scope, interests, doctrines, and capabilities. The rise of Indo-Pacific reflects a shift in both material and ideological worlds, marking the end of strategic stability and the dawn of a new political contest.

The first half of 2020 witnessed the outbreak of the COVID-19 pandemic across the globe and corrosions in China's relations with a range of countries. Chinese diplomats and envoys emerged undiplomatically, adopting unusually harsh language to hit back the criticisms by the United States, Australia, Canada, France, and Sweden. The *Global Times*, an English subsidiary of the *Xinhuanet*, the mouthpiece of the Communist Party, was given the greenlight to threaten and insult government officials and elected politicians in these countries. Interestingly, Chinese diplomats mimicked a retired Chinese commando in a heroic fiction movie "Wolf Warrior 2" to fight against a band of heavily equipped Western mercenaries to save Chinese and African refugees. It is clear that China wanted to shift the narrative to defend its "innocence" and promote the Chinese model in disease control. As a common threat to mankind, the pandemic could be a driver for solidarity and for collective efforts. However, this time the pandemic has been clearly driving a wedge between China and other major powers, accusations about the origin, of the virus, and blamed one another for mishandling its spread. The existing multilateral mechanisms such as the World Health Organization, the United Nations Security Council, G-7 or G-20 almost failed to mobilize concerted actions. At the same time, China has been criticized for exploiting the COVID-19 pandemic to pursue its long-standing foreign policy objectives, expanding in the South China Sea and East China Sea, seeking greater control over Hong Kong and over the Taiwan Strait, as well as changing the status quo in the Himalayas in its favor. These events may have occurred in different localities, but they all involved Chinese assertive actions.

It seems that Beijing has not been afraid of the possibility of a broad-based realignment under the Indo-Pacific banner. By picking fights in Himalayas, in the East China Sea, and in the South China Sea, China has antagonized most of its key neighbors and has engaged in multiple fronts at the same time. While China's moves may seem strategically irrational, China's neighbors, from India to Vietnam, from Indonesia to Japan, have not been willing to join a US-led alliance to confront China directly. India, Vietnam, and Indonesia are also reluctant to drop their non-aligned posture. Chinese strategists may think that the Indo-Pacific project is doomed to fail as neighboring countries would be constrained from taking sides with the United States against China because it is willing to go to great lengths to punish defiant acts. By keeping existing territorial and maritime disputes unresolved, China uses them as bargaining chips to keep its neighbors within its orbit and prove that the distant US power, though the world's greatest, has limits. That may be so in the short term. However, in the longer term, Beijing might not realize that tactical gains breed deep-seated distrust and frustration, which would lay the ground for stronger and concerted action against it at the regional level. If this trend continues, the Indo-Pacific construct will eventually lead to geopolitical convergence. Rule by fear is not as enduring as the rule of law.

Index

A
Abe, Shinzo, xiii, xv, 120, 127–129, 159, 160, 165, 171–175, 177, 180–182, 188–191, 224, 241, 245, 260, 262
Aquino, Benigno III, 53, 55, 66, 67
ASEAN Code of Conduct (COC), 1, 44, 48, 72, 75, 81, 82, 85, 106, 111, 127, 270, 276
ASEAN Declaration on the Conduct of Parties in the South China Sea (DOC), 75, 81, 94, 96
ASEAN Indo Pacific Outlook, xvi
ASEAN regional Forum (ARF), viii, xvi, xvii, 72, 105, 106, 109, 112, 199, 218, 258, 259, 261, 264, 265, 270, 282
ASEAN Treaty of Amity and Cooperation (TAC), viii, 215, 266, 269
Aso, Taro, 172, 188
Association of Southeast Asian Nations (ASEAN)
Cambodia, xii, 66, 72, 73, 79, 106, 258, 268
centrality, xvi, xvii, 217, 218, 228, 240, 244, 245, 250, 258, 259, 261, 263, 264, 266–268, 281
China, viii, xii, 39, 44, 65, 75, 76, 78, 79, 82, 83, 88, 97, 98, 105
Philippines, x–xii, 44, 52, 65–67, 73, 79, 97, 106, 124, 260, 268, 276
See also South China Sea (SCS)
Australia, xiii, xiv, 2, 13, 27, 30, 31, 33, 34, 62, 64, 82, 110, 114, 130, 144, 165, 167, 173–175, 178–180, 188–190, 195, 197–199, 216, 218, 220, 221, 223–225, 227, 228, 233, 238, 239, 241, 245, 246, 248, 259–264, 283
Indonesia, 189, 216, 227, 234, 238, 239, 246, 248
Indo Pacific, xiii, 225, 238

© The Editor(s) (if applicable) and The Author(s), under exclusive license to Springer Nature Switzerland AG 2021
L. Buszynski and D. T. Hai (eds.), *Maritime Issues and Regional Order in the Indo-Pacific*, Palgrave Studies in Maritime Politics and Security, https://doi.org/10.1007/978-3-030-68038-1

B

Balakrishnan, Vivian, 76
Bashi Strait, 30, 34
Brunei, 22, 39, 46, 47, 63–65, 79, 96, 110, 268

C

Cambodia. *See* Association of Southeast Asian Nations (ASEAN)
Carpio, Antonio, 56, 63, 64
China
  Air Defense Identification Zone (ADIZ), xiii, 122, 135–138, 142, 143, 145, 146, 279
  Anti-Access and Area Denial (A2AD), xi, 18, 19, 22, 27, 31, 33–35
  Central Military Commission (CMC), 17, 40, 42
  Communist Party, viii, 17, 53
  Diaoyu/Senkaku Islands, 157
  East China Sea (ECS), 28, 29, 31, 36, 124, 158, 175, 180, 283
  Exclusive Economic Zone (EEZ), 12, 45, 55, 59, 63–65, 72, 94, 155, 237, 247, 276
  gray zone operations, xi, xii
  Hainan Island, 23, 24, 91
  island building, 3
  Japan, xiii, 20, 21, 26, 29, 31, 33, 36, 62, 103, 104, 108, 110, 120, 121, 124–126, 130, 149, 158–160, 166, 171–182, 198, 218, 239, 244, 259, 262, 278, 280
  maritime militia, xii, 1, 7, 12, 42, 44, 48
  nine-dash line, 247
  People's Armed Police (PAP), xi, 42
  People's Liberation Army (PLA), 18, 20, 21, 23–25, 33, 109
  People's Liberation Army Air force (PLA-AF), 21, 29
  People's Liberation Army-Navy (PLA-N), 20, 27, 29, 31, 276
  Sanya base, 29
  Woody Island, 3, 22, 24, 35
  See also Association of Southeast Asian Nations (ASEAN); Philippines; South China Sea (SCS)
China Coast Guard (CCG), 1–12, 60, 82, 121, 237
Clinton, Hillary, 105, 190
Coronavirus disease (COVID), 159, 160

D

Declaration of the Conduct of Parties in the South China Sea (DOC). *See* Association of Southeast Asian Nations (ASEAN)
Del Rosario, Albert, 53, 64, 72, 74
Duterte, Rodrigo, xi, xii, 1, 9, 51, 52, 56–60, 62, 63, 66, 67, 80, 128, 130, 197, 277

E

East Asia Summit (EAS), xvi, 72, 127, 199, 202, 216, 218, 222, 236, 240, 241, 244, 245, 258, 259, 261, 263–267, 270, 282
East China Sea (ECS), viii, xii, xviii, 18, 20, 28, 29, 31, 35, 36, 42, 114, 119–122, 124, 126, 127, 130, 135–139, 146, 149–151, 153–161, 171, 175, 178–180, 213, 223, 270, 278, 279, 281, 283
European Union (EU), 62, 67, 82, 103–109, 111–115, 263

INDEX   287

F
France, 33, 62, 64, 104, 107, 108, 111–115, 180, 188, 246, 261–264, 283
Fukuda, Takeo, xvi, 166, 168–171

H
Harris, Harry, 190
Hatoyama, Yukio, 259
Hor Namhong, 73, 74
Hu Jintao, viii

I
India
    Association of Southeast Asian Nations (ASEAN), ix, xiii, xiv, 130, 165, 178, 211, 217–219, 221–223, 225, 259, 263, 264, 282
    Australia, xiv, 31, 33, 64, 165, 173, 174, 178–180, 188–190, 198, 216, 218, 223, 224, 227, 238, 246, 259, 261–264
    China, ix, xiv, 33, 47, 174, 179, 181, 188, 192, 198, 212, 214, 218, 221, 225–227, 239, 244, 259, 262, 263, 281–283
    China border clash (Galwan Valley), 223, 226
    Indian Ocean, ix, xiv, xvii, 191, 198, 211, 213, 215, 217, 226, 227, 249, 261
    Indonesia, xiv, 112, 189, 216, 219, 221, 222, 227, 238, 241, 245, 249, 281, 283
    Indo Pacific, xiv, xvii, 212, 213
    Look East/Act East Policy (AEP), xiv, 211, 217, 219, 220, 222, 225, 226, 281
    Vietnam, xiv, 35, 47, 167, 181, 196, 220, 221, 283

Indonesia
    Australia, 189, 216, 227, 241, 245, 248
    China, 21, 33, 64, 65, 196, 227, 237, 238, 243, 247, 249, 267, 281–283
    Exclusive Economic Zone (EEZ), 46, 63–65, 237, 243, 247
    Global Maritime Fulcrum (GMF), xvi, 222, 235–239, 242, 249, 250
    India, 35, 112, 189, 222, 227, 238, 239, 241, 244–246, 249, 281–283
    Indo Pacific, xiv, xvi, 238
    Lombok Strait, 29, 30, 222, 235
    Makassar Strait, 234
    Natuna Islands, 46, 65, 237, 248, 281
    Pacific and Indian Ocean, 222, 233, 239, 240, 248, 249, 265
    South China Sea (SCS), xiv, 19, 20, 22, 28, 33, 45, 46, 64, 65, 72, 79, 80, 219, 237, 243, 248, 283
    Sunda Strait, 29, 30, 222, 234, 235
    Vietnam, 21, 35, 45, 64–66, 73, 77, 79, 80, 109, 112, 196, 243, 244, 283
Iwaya, Takeshi, 121

J
Japan
    Article 9, 167, 172, 181, 182
    Association of Southeast Asian Nations (ASEAN), ix, xiii, xvii, 1, 108, 125, 127–130, 165, 171, 218, 225, 244, 245, 259, 262, 263, 282
    Australia, xiv, 2, 13, 31, 33, 64, 130, 144, 167, 173, 174, 178–180, 188, 190, 195, 197,

198, 216, 218, 220, 221, 223, 224, 227, 233, 238, 239, 245, 246, 259, 261–264

China, x–xvi, 20, 21, 26, 29, 31, 33, 36, 62, 103, 104, 108, 110, 120, 121, 124–126, 130, 149, 158–160, 166, 171–182, 198, 218, 239, 244, 259, 262, 278, 280

constitution, 25, 167

Exclusive Economic Zone (EEZ), xii, 13, 108, 111, 150, 154, 155, 158, 159

geopolitical interests, x, 165–167, 169, 181

India, ix, xiii, xiv, xvii, 31, 33, 35, 104, 112, 130, 167, 168, 171, 173, 174, 177–179, 181, 188, 191, 192, 198, 216, 218, 221, 223, 224, 226, 227, 238, 244–246, 259, 262–264, 282, 283

Indo Pacific strategy, xii, xv

Indo Pacific Vision, xv, xvi

navy Japan Maritime Self-Defense Force (JMSDF), 26, 177

Philippines, 2, 21, 35, 39, 62, 64, 110, 111, 124, 127, 129, 130, 144, 167, 170, 171, 176, 180

San Francisco conference/Peace Treaty, 167, 168

Self-Defense Force (JSDF), 25, 26, 29, 31, 35, 36, 122, 123, 129, 167, 170–172, 176, 177, 182

Senkaku/Diaoyu islands, xii, xiii, 180, 278

South China Sea (SCS), viii, x, xii, xvi, 21–24, 29, 33–36, 64, 82, 103, 104, 108, 111, 119, 120, 124–127, 130, 149, 171, 176–178, 180, 188, 248, 277

United States (US), ix–xi, xiv, xv, 2, 13, 20, 22, 24–26, 28, 29, 31, 33–36, 62, 64, 82, 111, 114, 123, 127, 128, 130, 168, 170, 177, 178, 216, 223, 226–228, 238, 239, 245, 246, 259, 261, 277, 282

Vientiane Vision, xiii, 125, 130

Vietnam, 2, 35, 47, 82, 112, 127, 128, 167, 169, 171, 176, 181, 196, 220, 221, 283

Western Pacific, ix, xi, xiv, 26, 169–171, 176, 182, 276

Joko Widodo (Jokowi), 222, 235, 239, 248, 265, 266

K

Kishi, Nousuke, 166, 168, 170, 171, 174

Kono, Taro, 127, 160, 175, 176

Korea
North, viii, 13, 104, 137, 191, 192, 197
South, 62, 108, 137, 142, 144, 178, 195, 197, 198, 216, 218, 228, 259

L

Locsin, Teodoro, 59

M

Mackinder, Halford, 172, 173

Mahathir, Mohamad, 261

Malacca Strait, 19, 29, 30, 35, 114, 222, 233–235, 249

Malaysia, x, xi, 4, 6, 7, 9, 11, 12, 19, 21, 22, 39, 46, 47, 63–66, 73, 75–77, 79, 80, 83, 96, 109, 110, 188, 196, 197, 216, 219, 225, 243, 261, 268

Marty Natalegawa, xvi, 72, 239, 240, 266
Mekong sub-region, 120
Modi, Narendra, xiv, 196, 214, 216, 221, 222, 224, 246

N

Nakasone, Yasuhiro, 166, 169–171
Nehru, Jawaharlal, 168, 213
New Zealand, 167, 178, 188, 198, 218, 220, 225, 248, 259

O

Obama, Barack, x, 57, 109, 190, 195, 198, 200, 202, 214

P

Pakistan, ix, xiv, 168, 212, 281
Permanent Court of Arbitration. *See* United Nations Convention Law of the Sea (UNCLOS)
Philippines. *See* South China Sea (SCS)
    Arbitral Tribunal, x, xii, 52, 79, 82, 111, 260
    China, x–xii, 1, 3, 9, 11, 13, 19, 21, 22, 24, 29, 34, 39, 44, 47, 51–62, 65–67, 73, 93, 97, 110, 124, 180, 197, 260
    Department of Foreign Affairs (DFA), 52, 53, 58–60, 196
    Exclusive Economic Zone (EEZ), xi, 11, 55, 56, 66
    United States (US), 2, 13, 24, 30, 34, 35, 62, 63, 67, 129, 130, 144, 268, 277
    Visiting Forces Agreement (VFA), 63, 197
    See also Association of Southeast Asian Nations (ASEAN)

Pompeo, Mike, 198, 223, 246

Q

Quad plus, 198, 202, 225, 228
Quadrilateralism (Quadrilateral Security Dialogue), xiv–xvi, xviii, 35, 173, 179, 188, 198, 223, 261, 281

R

Retno Marsudi, xvi, 222, 237, 240, 241, 243, 247, 266
Rudd, Kevin, 173, 223, 259
Russia, Rosneft, 6, 11, 82

S

Senkaku/Diaoyu islands. *See* Japan
Shangri-La Dialogue, xiv
Singapore, xiv, 22, 35, 62, 65, 76–81, 109, 111, 113, 114, 121, 167, 188, 196–198, 216, 219, 220, 223, 227, 228, 233–235, 244, 267, 268
South China Sea arbitration. *See* United Nations Convention Law of the Sea (UNCLOS)
South China Sea (SCS)
    Association of Southeast Asian Nations (ASEAN), viii, ix, xi–xiii, 39, 43, 44, 65, 67, 73, 75, 76, 78, 79, 81, 83, 97, 103, 106, 108, 111, 125–127, 130, 215, 219, 242, 260, 262, 263, 265, 270, 276, 278
    environment, 23, 94, 99, 103, 115, 270
    Fiery Cross reef, 3, 113
    Gem Ver incident, 12
    Luconia Shoals, 4–6
    Macclesfield Bank, 110, 113

Mischief Reef, 3, 22, 67
natural resources, 97
Paracel Islands, xi, 3, 113
Pratas Reefs, 34, 88, 110, 113
Reed Bank, 45, 47, 55
Scarborough Shoal, xi, 3, 4, 8, 55, 56, 72, 74, 113
Second Thomas Shoal, 4
Spratly Islands, x, 1, 8, 22, 24, 94
Subi Reef, 3, 4, 22, 113
Thitu Island (Pag Asa), 9, 10
Vanguard Bank, 6, 11, 47, 83
Woody Island, 3, 22–24, 35
Southeast Asia, viii, xvi, 13, 77, 78, 84, 166–171, 173, 181, 215, 216, 226, 233, 234, 239, 264, 265, 268, 269
Suga, Yoshihide, 158
Sunda Strait, 19, 29, 30, 222, 233–235
Suzuki, Zenko, 166, 170

T

Taiwan, 20–22, 29, 34, 42, 91, 96, 104, 109, 110, 114, 137, 144, 168, 170, 195–197, 226, 283
Tanaka, Kakuei, 169
Thailand, xii, 21, 22, 35, 45, 46, 79, 97, 109, 168, 214, 257, 268
Treaty of Amity and Cooperation (TAC), 268, 269
Trump, Donald, xv, 187, 189–192, 195–203, 223, 224, 261, 263, 280–282

U

United Kingdom (UK), 33, 64, 104, 107, 108, 113–115
United Nations (UN), 59, 62, 64, 95, 153, 155–157, 167, 221, 261, 269
United Nations (UN) Charter, 150, 153, 215
United Nations Convention Law of the Sea (UNCLOS), Arbitral Tribunal, 52, 54, 79, 94, 107, 111
United Nations General Assembly, 64, 82, 223
United Nations Secretary General, 172, 174
United States (US)
  Air Defense Identification Zone (ADIZ), 137, 141, 143, 144, 146, 279
  Association of Southeast Asian Nations (ASEAN), xvii, 1, 62, 67, 106, 108, 115, 127, 130, 218, 245, 246, 258, 259, 261–265, 267, 268, 281, 282
  Australia, xiv, 2, 27, 31, 82, 110, 130, 165, 173–175, 179, 180, 190, 216, 218, 223, 225, 227, 228, 245, 246, 260, 262, 283
  China, viii–xi, xiv, xv, xvii, 2, 13, 17–22, 24, 26–28, 31, 33, 34, 47, 62, 63, 67, 75, 106, 108, 113, 115, 165, 173, 213, 218, 225, 227, 238, 259, 261, 263, 277, 282, 284
  Department of Defense (DoD), 140, 141, 143, 191, 193, 194, 200, 262
  Department of State, xv, 82, 191, 194, 246, 263
  Indo Pacific, ix, x, xiii–xv, 225, 238, 246
  Japan, ix–xi, xiv, xv, 2, 13, 20, 22, 24–26, 28, 29, 31, 33–36, 62, 64, 82, 111, 114, 123, 127, 128, 130, 168, 170, 177, 178, 216, 223, 226–228, 238, 239, 245, 246, 259, 261, 277, 282

Philippines, 2, 13, 19, 34, 35, 62, 63, 67, 129, 130, 144, 268, 277

V

Vietnam. *See* South China Sea (SCS)
 Haiyang Dizhi 8 incident, 6, 7, 10, 11, 47, 108
 Indonesia, 21, 35, 45, 64–66, 73, 77, 79, 80, 109, 112, 196, 243, 244, 283
 Japan, 2, 35, 47, 82, 112, 127, 128, 167, 169, 171, 176, 181, 196, 221, 283

W

Wang Yi, 76
Wei Fenghe, 121
Wen Jiabao, viii

X

Xi Jinping, viii–x, 7, 17, 57, 58, 110, 120, 121

Y

Yachi, Shotaro, 172–175, 182
Yano, Sakutaro, 169, 174, 181
Yasay, Perfecto, 52, 58